Organizations

Rational, Natural, and Open Systems

W. RICHARD SCOTT

Stanford University

Prentice-Hall, Inc., *Englewood Cliffs, New Jersey 07632*

Library of Congress Cataloging in Publication Data

SCOTT, W RICHARD.
  Organizations: rational, natural, and open systems.

  Bibliography: p.
  Includes index.
  1. Organization.   I. Title.
HM131.S385   302.3   80-24640
ISBN 0-13-641977-1

© 1981 by Prentice Hall, Inc., Englewood Cliffs, N.J. 07632

Printed in the United States of America

10   9   8   7   6   5

Editorial/production supervision
  and interior design by Joan L. Lee
Manufacturing buyer: John Hall

PRENTICE-HALL INTERNATIONAL, INC., *London*
PRENTICE-HALL OF AUSTRALIA PTY. LIMITED, *Sydney*
PRENTICE-HALL OF CANADA, LTD., *Toronto*
PRENTICE-HALL OF INDIA PRIVATE LIMITED, *New Delhi*
PRENTICE-HALL OF JAPAN, INC., *Tokyo*
PRENTICE-HALL OF SOUTHEAST ASIA PTE. LTD., *Singapore*
WHITEHALL BOOKS LIMITED, *Wellington, New Zealand*

The author wishes to thank the copyright owners for permission to reprint in the text the following figures, tables and quotations:

Fig. 1–1. From Harold J. Leavitt, Applied organizational change in industry: structural, technological and humanistic approaches, in J. G. March (ed.), *Handbook of Organizations,* p. 1145. Copyright © 1965 by Rand McNally College Publishing Company, Chicago, Illinois. Reprinted by permission.

Figs. 5–1 and 5–2. Adapted from Robert L. Swinth, *Organizational Systems for Management,* pp. 18 & 23. Grid, Inc., Columbus, Ohio, 1974. Reprinted by permission.

Fig. 7–1. Adapted from Oliver E. Williamson, *Markets and Hierarchies: Analysis and Antitrust Implications,* p. 40. New York, The Free Press, Copyright © 1975 by The Free Press; A Division of Macmillan Publishing Co., Inc. Reprinted by permission.

Fig. 10–1. From George A. Steiner and William G. Ryan, *Industrial Project Management,* p. 10. New York, The Trustees of Columbia University of the City of New York, 1968. Reprinted by permission.

Fig. 11–1. Reprinted from Alfred D. Chandler, Jr., *Strategy and Structure,* p. 10. by permission of The MIT Press, Cambridge, Massachusetts. Copyright © 1962 by Massachusetts Institute of Technology.

for
Jennifer, Elliot, and Sydney

Contents –
An Overview

Part Four

Organizations and Society, 291

Contents

Part Three

ENVIRONMENTS,
STRATEGIES,
AND
STRUCTURES

chapter 7

Creating Organizations, 135

chapter 12

Goals, Power, and Authority,   260

Part Four

ORGANIZATIONS AND SOCIETY

Preface

This book attempts to provide a coherent introduction to the sociological study of organizations. This is no mean or simple task. The area has developed rapidly during the past three decades: it is the scene of much effort and activity, and, probably as a consequence, of much controversy and confusion. Conceptual schemas, typologies, and theories are generated with accelerating frequency but seem often not to be evaluated or sorted out but simply added to a growing pile. And empirical studies abound: case studies of single situations, comparative studies of many similar or diverse units, and, increasingly, longitudinal or panel studies of organizations viewed over time. The result, however, has not often been an addition to our knowledge but simply an augmentation of our information. When a field of study is growing rapidly, we would expect to see increasing signs of differentiation and fragmentation. These are quite evident in the area of organizational studies. The past decade has produced a disparate set of specialized approaches: organizations viewed as coalitions, as quasi-markets, as political-economies, and as elements in ecological populations. And it has produced a collection of larger and more eclectic textbooks that mirror the diversity and incoherence of a too-rapidly-expanding domain. The number of approaches, studies, books, and journals increases, but we do not seem to realize a commensurate gain in our understanding.

I have attempted to acknowledge this complexity and diversity not simply by reflecting it but by condensing and refining it so that its major underlying dimensions are exposed. My approach to injecting some order into the present scene is to make use of three general theoretical perspectives: one that views organizations as rational systems; a second that views them as natural systems; and a third that approaches them as open systems. More than one perspective is employed because I believe that no single existing perspective is adequate to comprehend the important features of organizations. Only three perspectives are used because I believe that most—I would not claim all—of the models and approaches currently in use may be viewed as variants of one of these general types. The perspectives are not novel: they have been identified by previous students of organizations. But none of my predecessors has developed them as fully or pressed them as far as I attempt to do. Each of the perspectives suggests differing answers to fundamental questions concerning organizations; more important, each suggests different questions.

The three perspectives are employed to summarize and integrate previous contributions to our understanding of organizations. However, they are not simply of historical interest: they continue to shape the work and define the issues confronting contemporary investigators. The perspectives are introduced as though they were pure types, but much of the analysis in the latter half of the volume is based on the use of varied and changing combinations of types. Since the perspectives are based on different and often conflicting assumptions, they can be juxtaposed and joined in varying combinations, but never fully integrated. Nevertheless, in both forms—pure and mixed types— they carry forward much of the theoretical work contained in this volume.

In addition to a heavy emphasis on rational, natural, and open systems perspectives, my approach to the study of organizations is shaped by the assumption that it is not possible to separate the analysis of internal organizational arrangements from their external settings and relations. Most theorists now pay lip service to the open systems perspective, which stresses the critical importance of organization-environment connections, but few pursue the implications of these relations for the organization's internal structures and processes. I attempt to do so.

I noted at the outset that this book is devoted to the development of a *sociological* approach to the analysis of organizations. My intent is not to endorse a narrowly parochial perspective. One of the most attractive facets of the contemporary scene is the increasingly multidisciplinary character of research on organizations. Organizations are one of the primary phenomena around which researchers from the social science disciplines and scholars and practitioners from the professional schools, as well as thoughtful participants in "real-world" settings, gather to exchange complaints and suggestions, insights and explanations. While attempting to incorporate inputs from neighboring disciplines, my approach remains primarily sociological. It is my belief that sociology is in the best position both to integrate and to transcend the more specialized contributions stemming from alternative points of view. Only sociologists have attempted to deal with the full range of organizational types —ancient and modern, public and private, large and small—and only sociologists have concerned themselves with how the specialized structures and distinct variables come together to comprise a functioning whole. Moreover, only sociologists regularly ponder the nature of that wholeness: what we mean by organizations, what their essential features are, and how they differ from alternative social arrangements.

Many persons have contributed to my own development as a sociologist and student of organizations, and the writing of a book such as this provides a welcome occasion for expressing my indebtedness and appreciation. At the University of Kansas, Marston M. McCluggage introduced me to sociology in such a manner as to enlist my loyalties for the duration, and Charles K. Warriner provided me with my first systematic exposure to the study of organizations and gave me my first taste of field research in an organizational setting. At the University of Chicago, I was fortunate to work closely with two superb sociologists: Otis Dudley Duncan and Peter M. Blau. From Dudley, I learned many things but especially that some problems are better approached from a structural or an ecological perspective than from a social psychological point of view. To Peter, I owe more than I can say. He not only converted me to the study of organizations but launched my career by inviting me to collaborate with him in a comparative research project resulting in the publication of *Formal Organizations,* an early treatise in a newly emerging field of study. From all of these men, I learned not only how sociologists work and think but also what professional colleagiality is all about.

At Stanford University, where I have worked for twenty years, I have had the good fortune to be associated with many productive and amiable colleagues —both fellow faculty members and graduate students. In the former category, I cannot name all those from whom I have learned but must not fail to acknowledge the contribution to my education of Joseph Berger, Bernard P. Cohen, Elizabeth G. Cohen, Terrence E. Deal, Sanford M. Dornbusch, Michael T. Hannan, Harold J. Leavitt, James G. March, Joanne Martin, John W. Meyer, William G. Ouchi, Jeffrey Pfeffer, Joan Talbert, Edmund H. Volkart, Eugene J. Webb, and Morris Zelditch, Jr. Student colleagues and collaborators have also been too numerous to allow a full accounting, but I especially acknowledge the assistance and challenge received from Robert E. Bies, Joan R. Bloom, Bruce C. Bushing, Glen R. Carroll, Donald E. Comstock, Margaret R. Davis, Jacques Delacroix, Mary L. Fennell, Ann Barry Flood, David V. Gibson, Michael S. Knapp, James D. Laing, Mary Ann McGuire, Anne S. Miner, William Joseph Reeves, Brian Rowan, Claudia Kay Schoonhoven, John H. Simpson, Lee L. Sproull, and John M. Wattendorf.

The opportunity for collaborative research on organizations at Stanford has been strengthened and extended by the existence of a multidisciplinary research training program on Organizations supported by a National Research Service Institutional Award under the auspices of the National Institute of Mental Health. As director of this program since 1972, I have gained much from these associations that bridge the artificial but too often impenetrable barriers formed by school and departmental distinctions. The depth and breadth of the organizations research community built at Stanford is, I believe, remarkable and has been a major source of continuing intellectual stimulation over the years. The debts I owe my colleagues for my own continuing postgraduate education are substantial and are only hinted at in my frequent references to their work in the following pages.

A number of individuals contributed directly and importantly to the appearance of this volume. I received helpful comments and suggestions from William T. Clute, George A. Miller, and Jeffrey Pfeffer, each of whom read one or more versions of the developing manuscript. Edward H. Stanford, sociology editor at Prentice-Hall, took an early interest in the project and encouraged me to see it through. Joan Lee and her associates in the West Coast offices of Prentice-Hall provided expert editorial and technical assistance. Valerie J. Dews and Hazel Rand typed and retyped the changing manuscript with care and unfailing good humor. Meanwhile, my secretary Mai Thi Lam performed heroically in managing the office while I hid out to write and rewrite.

Finally, it goes without saying that an activity of this sort places a considerable strain on the home team. My wife Joy, team captain, managed the perturbations with consummate skill and a light, loving touch. This book is dedicated to our children, Jennifer, Elliot, and Sydney, who made what was for them the supreme sacrifice—turning down the volume on the stereo set because "daddy is writing."

Part One

AN INTRODUCTION TO ORGANIZATIONS

Organizations play a leading role in our modern world. Their presence affects —some would insist that the proper term is *infects*—virtually every sector of contemporary social life. Peter Drucker thus observes: "Young people today will have to learn organizations the way their forefathers learned farming." Chapter 1 endeavors to amplify and justify this advice by examining both the practical and theoretical benefits to be gained from a better understanding of organizations.

Part 1 pursues the two major themes of *commonality* and *diversity.* Organizations share certain features, which serve to differentiate organizations from other social forms. Students of this field believe that we can understand much about a specific organization from knowing about other organizations. Understanding how a factory functions can illuminate the workings of a hospital; and knowledge of a governmental bureau can help us understand how a football team operates.

Diversity appears in two guises. First, the theoretical perspectives applied to organizations vary greatly, and they focus on different facets of these systems. These perspectives appear in chapter 1 as competing definitions of organizations; Part 2 examines them in detail. Second, organizations themselves exhibit a wide variety of forms and carry on many functions, and no serious inquiry into their nature can be blind to this type of diversity. Rather than attempting the impossible task of depicting it directly, we review in chapter 2 a number of organizational typologies. Employing typologies as our vehicle of reconnaissance permits us to survey the varied organizational terrain; it also allows us to confront some of the leading variables researchers have proposed to account for organizational form and function. These variables will help us and haunt us throughout the remainder of our work.

As a bonus, we use our review of typologies in an inductive manner to help us derive some principles by which "good"—that is, instructive—typologies can be created. And we ponder the sobering question of why, with so much effort expended and so many proposed systems of classification, typologies have not been as helpful in the study of organizations as in some other fields of inquiry.

chapter 1

The Subject
is
Organizations

*The recurrent problem in sociology is to
conceive of corporate organization, and to
study it, in ways that do not anthropomorphize
it and do not reduce it to the behavior of
individuals or of human aggregates.*

GUY E. SWANSON (1976)

The philosopher Alfred North Whitehead has
suggested that, properly organized, education should proceed through three
stages. In the first stage, that of "romance," the student's interest is aroused:
he or she is brought face to face with the phenomenon in all its power and
mystery. If the subject is mechanical engineering, for example, the student
could be taken to see a steam locomotive or a steel mill in operation. In the
second stage, labeled "discipline," the student acquires the concepts and methods required to analyze the subject and its component parts and processes. And
in the third stage, that of "fruition," the methods and concepts are applied to
the subject so that its structure and functioning may be understood and,
perhaps, improved (Whitehead, 1929).

Our topic here is organizations. We do not need to plan a field trip for
students to observe this phenomenon in action: organizations are all around
us. Because of their ubiquity, however, they fade into the background, and we
need to be reminded of their impact. This chapter begins with a discussion of
the practical and the theoretical importance of organizations: we attempt to
arouse your interest so that an intellectual courtship can begin. We also begin
the task of developing concepts for analyzing organizations; this work will
continue throughout the volume. We do not intend to postpone the phase of

fruition until the final chapters but will attempt early and often to demonstrate how the use of the concepts and methods can improve our understanding of the structure and functioning of organizations and, in some cases, contribute to their betterment.

The Importance
of Understanding Organizations

There is no need to belabor the assertion that ours is an organizational society—that organizations are a prominent, if not the dominant, characteristic of modern societies. Organizations were present in older civilizations— Chinese, Greek, Indian—but only in modern industrialized societies do we find large numbers of organizations engaged in performing many highly diverse tasks. To the ancient organizational assignments of soldiering, public administration, and tax collection have been added such varied tasks as discovery (research organizations), child and adult socialization (schools and universities), resocialization (mental hospitals and prisons), production and distribution of goods (industrial firms, wholesale and retail establishments), provision of services (organizations dispensing assistance ranging from laundry and shoe repair to medical care and investment counseling), protection of personal and financial security (police department, insurance firms, banking and trust companies), preservation of culture (museums, art galleries, universities, libraries), communication (radio and television studios, telephone companies, the post office), and recreation (bowling alleys, pool halls, national park service, professional football teams). Even such a partial listing testifies to the truth of Parsons's statement that "the development of organizations is the principal mechanism by which, in a highly differentiated society, it is possible to 'get things done,' to achieve goals beyond the reach of the individual" (1960: 41).

The prevalence of organizations in every arena of social life is one indicator of their importance. Another rather different index of their significance is the increasing frequency with which organizations are singled out as the source of many of the ills besetting contemporary society. Thus, writing in 1956, C. Wright Mills pointed with alarm to the emergence of a "power elite" comprised of members occupying the top positions in three overlapping organizational hierarchies: the state bureaucracy, the military, and the larger corporations. At about the same time, Ralf Dahrendorf (1959 tr.) in Germany was engaged in revising and updating Marxist doctrine by insisting that the basis of the class structure was no longer the ownership of the means of production but occupancy of positions that allowed the wielding of organizational authority. Such views, which remain controversial, focus on the effects of organizations on societal stratification systems, taking account of the changing bases of power and prestige occasioned by the growth in number and size of organizations.

A related criticism concerns the seemingly inexorable growth in public-sector organizations. The two great German sociologists, Max Weber (1947 tr.) and Robert Michels (1949 tr.), were among the first to insist that the central political issue for all modern societies was no longer what type of economic structure prevailed—whether capitalist, socialist, or communist—but the increasing dominance of the public bureaucracy over the ostensible political leaders.

Other criticisms point to the negative consequences of the growth of organizations in virtually *every* area of social existence. Borrowing from and enlarging on a theme pervading the thought of Weber, these critics decry the rationalization of modern life—in Weber's phrase, the "disenchantment of the world" (1946 tr.: 51). The essence of this view is graphically captured by Norman Mailer: "Civilization extracts its thousand fees from the best nights of man, but none so cruel as the replacement of the good fairy by the expert, the demon by the rational crisis, and the witch by the neurotic female" (1968: 83). Organizations are viewed as the primary vehicle by which, systematically, the areas of our lives are rationalized—planned, articulated, scientized, made more efficient and orderly, and managed by "experts." (See, for example, Mannheim, 1950 tr.; Ellul, 1964 tr.; Goodman, 1968; and Galbraith, 1967). The dark side of such progress is depicted by Roszak, who defines the technocracy as "that social form in which an industrial society reaches the peak of its organizational integration." He writes, "Under the technocracy we become the most scientific of societies; yet, like Kafka's K., men throughout the 'developed world' become more and more the bewildered dependents of inaccessible castles wherein inscrutable technicians conjure with their fate" (1969: 5, 13).

Still other critics have called attention to how organizational structure affects the personalities and psyches of its participants. Alienation, overconformity, and stunting of normal personality development are among the consequences attributed, not to such special cases as prisons and concentration camps, but to everyday garden variety organizations (see Argyris, 1957; Maslow, 1954; Whyte, 1956).

We attempt to evaluate such criticisms of organizations at appropriate points throughout this volume. Here we simply note that these negative views towards organizations provide further testimony to their importance in the modern world.

In addition to their being mechanisms for accomplishing a great variety of objectives and, perhaps as a necessary consequence, the source of many of our current difficulties, organizations have yet another important effect on our collective lives. This effect is more subtle and less widely recognized. but it may be quite profound in its implications. It is, perhaps, best introduced by an analogy:

"The medium is the message." This twentieth-century aphorism was coined by Marshall McLuhan (1964) to focus attention on the characteristics of the mass media themselves—print, radio, movies, television—in contrast to the content transmitted by these media. McLuhan defines media very broadly as "any extension of ourselves," and elaborating his thesis, he notes: "The message of any medium is the change in scale or pace or pattern that it introduces into human affairs" (1964: 23, 24).

McLuhan's thesis appears to be more clearly applicable to our subject—organizations—than to any specific media of communication. First, like media, organizations represent extensions of ourselves. Organizations can achieve goals that are quite beyond the reach of any individual—from building skyscrapers and dams to putting a man on the moon. But to focus on what organizations *do* may conceal from us the more basic and far-reaching effects that occur because organizations are the *mechanisms*—the media—by which those goals are pursued. A few examples may suggest some of these unanticipated organizational effects:

- In his crucial decision on how to react to the installation of Russian missiles in Cuba, President Kennedy had to select from among a naval blockade, a "surgical" air strike, and a massive land invasion, not because these were the only conceivable responses, but because these were the principal organizational routines that had been worked out by the Pentagon (see Allison, 1971).
- Although we seek "health" when we visit the clinic or the hospital, what we get is "medical care." Clients are encouraged to view these outputs as synonymous although there may be no relation between them. In some cases, the relation can even be negative: more care can result in poorer health (see Illich, 1976).
- Products manufactured by organizations reflect the manufacturing process. They often reflect the need to subdivide work and to simplify tasks, and the manufacturing pressures toward standardization of parts and personnel (Veblen, 1904). Customization—in the genuine sense, not in the Detroit sense—becomes prohibitively expensive. Metal replaces wood and plastic replaces metal in many products to satisfy organizational, not consumer, needs.

To suggest that our organizational tools shape the products and services they produce would appear to be a relatively sweeping and unsettling generalization on which we might be content to rest our case. However, our arguments concerning the importance of organizations are not quite finished: we give the screw one final turn.

We will fail to perceive the importance of organizations for our own lives if we view them merely as tools for achieving goals. Organizations must also be viewed as actors in their own right, as "corporate persons," to use Coleman's phrase (1974). They can take actions, utilize resources, enter into contracts, and own property. Coleman describes how these rights have gradually developed since the Middle Ages to the point where now it is accurate to speak of two kinds of persons—"natural" persons (like you and me) and corporate or "juristic" persons (like the Red Cross and General Motors). The social structure of the modern society can no longer be described accurately as consisting only of relations among natural persons: our understanding must be stretched to include as well those relations between natural and corporate persons, and between corporate and corporate persons. In short, we must come to "the recognition that the society has changed over the past few centuries in the very structural elements of which it is composed" (Coleman, 1974: 13).

A different kind of rationale for justifying the study of organizations as a basic social science pursuit is suggested by the following statement of Homans: "The fact is that the organization of the large formal enterprises, governmental or private, in modern society is modeled on, is a rationalization of, tendencies that exist in all human groups" (1950:186–87). To say that organizations exhibit "tendencies that exist in all human groups" is to suggest that organizations provide the setting for a wide variety of basic social processes, such as socialization, communication, ranking, the formation of norms, the exercise of power, and goal setting and attainment. If these generic social processes operate in organizations, then we can add as much to our knowledge of the principles that govern their behavior by studying organizations as by studying any other specific type of social system. But Homans asserts something more.

To say that we can perceive in organizations "a rationalization of tendencies that exist in all human groups" suggests that organizations are characterized by somewhat distinctive structural arrangements that affect the operation of the processes occurring within them. For example, social control processes occur within all social groups, but there are some forms or mechanisms of control—for instance, a hierarchical authority structure—that are best studied in organizations, since it is within these systems that they appear in their most highly developed form.[1] The processes of interest can occur at various levels of analysis, as will be discussed in the following section. Also, decidedly, one of the important tasks is to spell out clearly what is meant by "distinctive structural arrangements." We will begin this task in the present chapter but will find it sufficiently challenging that we will need to keep the problem before us throughout this volume.

At this point, however, we assert our belief that the study of organizations

---

[1]This general argument has been elaborated elsewhere (Scott, 1970). The basic premise is that a set of generic social processes—such as socialization, integration, status, power, adaptation— may be identified in all social structures. However, each of these processes operates differently depending on the structural context in which it is acting; so that, for example, the process of integration is effected in a small group differently than in an organization, and both differ from the same process occurring within a community, and so on.

can contribute to basic sociological knowledge by increasing our understanding of how generic social processes operate within distinctive social structures.

Organizations as an Area of Study

EMERGENCE OF THE AREA

The study of organizations is both a specialized field of inquiry within the discipline of sociology as well as an increasingly recognized focus of multidisciplinary research and training. It is impossible to determine with precision the moment of its appearance, but it is safe to conclude that until the late 1940s, organizations did not exist as a distinct field of sociological inquiry. Precursors may be identified, but each lacked some critical feature. Thus, there was some empirical research on organizations by, for example, criminologists who studied prisons (for example, Clemmer, 1940), political analysts who examined party structures (for example, Gosnell, 1937), and industrial sociologists who studied factories and labor unions (for example, Whyte, 1946); but these investigators rarely attempted to generalize beyond the specific organizational form they were studying. The subject was prisons or parties or factories or unions—not organizations. Similarly, in the neighboring disciplines, political scientists were examining the functioning of legislative bodies or public agencies, and economists were developing their theory of the firm, but they were not attempting to generalize beyond these specific forms.

Industrial psychologists did pursue such general problems as low morale, fatigue, and turnover within several types of organizational settings, but they did not attempt to determine systematically how the varying characteristics of different organizational contexts influenced these worker reactions. And while, from early in this century, administrative and management theorists such as Fayol (1949 tr.) and Gulick and Urwick (1937) did concentrate on the development of general principles concerning administrative arrangements, their approach was more often prescriptive than empirical. That is, they were interested in determining what "should be" in the interests of maximizing efficiency and effectiveness rather than in examining and explaining organizational arrangements as they existed.

Within sociology, the emergence of the field of organizations may be roughly dated from the translation into English of Weber's (1946 tr., 1947 tr.) and, to a lesser extent, Michel's (1949 tr.) analyses of bureaucracy. Shortly after these classic statements became accessible to American sociologists, Robert K. Merton and his students at Columbia University attempted to outline the boundaries of this new field of inquiry by compiling theoretical and empirical materials dealing with various aspects of organizations (Merton et al., 1952). Equally important, a series of path-breaking and influential case studies of diverse types of organizations was launched under Merton's influence, including an examination of the Tennessee Valley Authority (Selznick, 1949), a gypsum mine and factory (Gouldner, 1954), a government employment and a regulatory agency (Blau, 1955), and a union (Lipset, Trow, and Coleman, 1956). For the first time, sociologists were engaged in the development and empirical testing of generalizations dealing with the structure and functioning of organizations viewed as organizations.

In a similar fashion, analysts working in other social science traditions focused increasingly on general organizational issues. During the period after World War II, students of industrial psychology, public administration, social anthropology, and institutional economics began to pay less attention to divergent backgrounds and more to common interests. Intellectual ancestors, such as Machiavelli, St. Simon, Weber, and Frederick Winslow Taylor were uncovered, and more recent academic forebears, such as Elton Mayo (1945) and Chester Barnard (1938; 1948), were rediscovered and reprinted. After about a decade of empirical research and theory development, three textbook-treatises—March and Simon (1958), Likert (1961), and Blau and Scott (1962)—provided needed integration and heightened interest in the field. Also, a new journal, *Administrative Science Quarterly,* founded in 1956, emphasized the interdisciplinary character of the field.

COMMON AND DIVERGENT INTERESTS

What features do all organizations exhibit in common? What are the general organizational issues analysts began to perceive among the great diversity of specific goals and structural arrangements? Most analysts conceived of organizations as social structures created by individuals to support the collaborative pursuit of specified goals. Given this conception, all organizations confront a number of common problems. All must define (and redefine) their objectives; all must induce participants to contribute services; all must control and coordinate these contributions; resources must be garnered from the environment and products or services dispensed; participants must be selected, trained, and replaced; and some sort of working accommodation with the neighbors must be achieved.

In addition to these common operational requirements, some analysts also emphasized that all organizations are beset by a common curse. A high proportion of the resources utilized by any organization is expended in maintaining the organization itself rather than in achieving the specified goals. Although organizations are viewed as means to accomplish ends, the means themselves absorb much energy, and in the extreme (but perhaps not rare) case, become ends in themselves.

There is convergence of interest around these common features, but there also remain important bases for specialization among the various disciplines. Political scientists continue to focus on political parties and state administrative structures, economists on business firms, sociologists on voluntary associations and on agencies engaged in social welfare and social control functions, and anthropologists on comparative administration in primitive, colonial, and developing societies. Disciplinary differences remain even when a single type of organization is selected for study: specialists tend to look not only at different objects, but also at different aspects of the same object. Thus, the political scientist will be likely to emphasize power processes and decision making within the organization; the economist will examine the acquisition and allocation of scarce resources within the organization and will attend to such issues as productivity and efficiency; the sociologist will concentrate on status orderings and on the effect of norms and sentiments on behavior; the psychologist will be interested in variations in perception, learning, and motivation among participants; and the anthropologist will call attention to the effects of diverse cultural values on the functioning of the system and its members. The study of organizations embraces all these interests, and students of organizations work to develop conceptual frameworks within which each of these topics and their interrelations may be examined. And, increasingly, organizational analysts attempt to specify what is distinctive about power, or status, or motivation because that process is carried on within the context of organizations.

LEVELS OF ANALYSIS

While organizations furnish a common locus of research for many social scientists, all investigators are by no means interested in finding answers to the same questions. Even apart from the variety of conceptual schemes that guide inquiry and the differences in methodological tools, investigators differ with respect to the level of analysis at which they choose to work (see Blau, 1957). For present purposes, the level of analysis is determined by the nature of the dependent variable, that is, by whether the phenomenon to be explained is (1) the behavior or attributes of individual participants within organizations, (2) the functioning or characteristics of some aspect or segment of organizational structure, or (3) the characteristics or actions of the organization viewed as a collective entity. We will briefly discuss each of these levels.

Some investigators are interested in explaining individual behavior within the context of organizations. At this level, organizational characteristics are viewed as context or "environment," and the investigator attempts to explore their impact on social psychological variables as reflected in the attitudes or behavior of individuals. Such a perspective is labeled *social psychological* and is exemplified by the work of March and Simon (1958) and Porter, Lawler, and Hackman (1975).

At the second level, the major concern is to explain the structural features and social processes that characterize organizations and their subdivisions. The investigator working at this level may focus on the various subunits that comprise the organization (for example, work groups, departments, authority ranks) or may examine various analytical components (for example, specialization, communication, hierarchy), attempting in both cases to account for their characteristics and to explore their interrelations. This level of analysis is labeled the *structural,* and examples of its use are found in the works of Udy (1959*b*) and Blau and Schoenherr (1971).

At the third level of analysis, the focus is on the organization as a collective actor functioning in a larger system of relations. Within this approach, the analyst may choose either to examine the relation between a specific organization or class of organizations and the environment (for example, Selznick, 1949; Pugh et al., 1969*a*), or may wish to examine the relations that develop among a number of organizations viewed as an interdependent system (for example, Aiken and Hage, 1968; Warren, 1967). This level of analysis is labeled *ecological.*

Admittedly, distinguishing among these three levels of analysis is somewhat arbitrary and ambiguous. Many levels of analytical complexity can be identified as one moves from organizational-individual to societal-organizational relations.[2] Nevertheless, if only to remind us of the complexity of the subject matter and the variety of aims and interests with which analysts approach it, the three types can prove useful as a rough gauge for distinguishing among broad categories of studies.

Of course, the level of analysis at which we choose to examine organizational behavior also affects somewhat the types of data gathered and how they are treated. We cannot provide in this volume a detailed discussion of research methods used in the study of organizations,[3] but one set of methodological distinctions is of particular significance in discussing levels of analysis. Lazarsfeld and his colleagues (Lazarsfeld, 1959; Lazarsfeld and Menzel, 1961) have developed a typology of measures that usefully illustrates ways in which information gathered at one level may be employed in analyses at a different level. They begin by distinguishing between two generalized units: "members" and "collectives"—units at different levels in the sense that members are defined as constituent parts of collectives. The subjects of interest may vary: for example, for one type of analysis, the members may be persons and the

[2]For example, recent developments at the ecological level suggest that it is useful to distinguish between the type of analysis that focuses on (a) a single organization and its specific environment, often termed the "organization set"; (b) populations of organizations, that is, aggregates of organizations of the same type such as restaurants or universities; and (c) communities of organizations, referring to the interdependencies existing between all organizations located in a common area. (See Hannan and Freeman, 1977) These distinctions are discussed in chapter 8.

[3]Overviews of research methods and strategies for studying organizations are provided by Cohen and Cyert (1965), Cook and Campbell (1976), Scott (1965*a*), Stone (1978), and Weick (1965).

collectives, departments; for another, the members may be departments and the collectives, organizations.

Members may be characterized by a number of different types of properties:

1. *Absolute*—properties based solely on information concerning the member, for example, the age or sex of an individual

2. *Relational*—properties obtained from information about relationships among the members, for example, sociometric (preference) choices given or received by an individual

3. *Comparative*—properties based on information obtained from comparing the member's value on some property with the distribution of values on that property over the collective, for example, the relative seniority of an individual worker

4. *Contextual*—properties based on information about the collective to which the member belongs, for example, an individual being characterized as an employee of a large versus a small department (Lazarsfeld and Menzel, 1961: 431–33)

Note that the fourth measure differs from the first three in that it is based on information gathered at a different level: a property of a collective is used to characterize its members. In reverse fashion, information based on members can be combined and used to characterize a collective. The first two of the following three measures of *collectives* are of this type:

1. *Analytical*—properties based on a summary measure of some property of each member of the collective, for example, the average age of the members of a department

2. *Structural*—properties based on a summary measure of the relationships among members, for example a measure of cohesion based on the relative number of sociometric choices directed by members to others within the collective as compared to those directed outside

3. *Global*—properties of collectives not based on information concerning individual members or their relationships, for example, the assets of a company (Lazarsfeld and Menzel, 1961: 426–29)

Perhaps it is obvious that these measures were spawned in the effort by survey analysts to find ways to utilize survey data obtained from individual respondents to characterize structural features of groups (see Kendall and Lazarsfeld, 1950). These innovations, and their codification in the typology proposed by Lazarsfeld and Menzel, were instrumental in shifting the attention of analysts from the social psychological characteristics of participants to the structural properties of collectives such as organizations. They ushered in a wave of studies that examined the impact of the properties of organizations (collectives) on individual (member) behavior (for example, Lazarsfeld and Thielens, 1958; Lipset, Trow, and Coleman, 1956; Blau, 1960), and they paved the way for later work that focused on the interrelations of structural features within organizations (collectives).

Early research on organizations was conducted almost exclusively at the social psychological level. The structural level of analysis became prominent in the early 1960s and continues to be heavily utilized by sociologists. The ecological level was the last to develop, emerging in the late 1960s, and continues to acquire adherents.

The Elements of Organizations

Organizations are highly varied and often highly complex, so it may be helpful to begin with a simplifying model allowing us to focus on basic characteristics. The proposed model shown in figure 1–1 is adapted from Leavitt (1965).[4] Let us briefly consider each element.

SOCIAL STRUCTURE

Social structure refers to the patterned or regularized aspects of relationships existing among participants in an organization. The social structure of any human grouping can be analytically separated into two components. As Kingsley Davis suggests:

[4]Leavitt identifies the four "internal" elements but does not include the environment as a separate factor. As will be obvious from our discussion, we regard the environment as an indispensable ingredient in any organizational model.

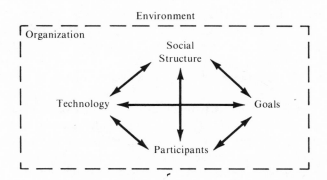

Figure 1–1

... always in human society there is what may be called a double reality—on the one hand a normative system embodying what *ought* to be, and on the other a factual order embodying what is. In the nature of the case these two orders cannot be completely identical, nor can they be completely disparate. (Davis, 1949: 52)

We shall refer to Davis's first component as the *normative structure;* this component includes values, norms, and role expectations. Briefly, *values* are the criteria employed in selecting the goals of behavior; *norms* are the generalized rules governing behavior that specify, in particular, appropriate means for pursuing goals; and *roles* are expectations for or evaluative standards employed in assessing the behavior of occupants of specific social positions. A social position is simply a location in a system of social relationships. (For a basic formulation of positions and roles, see Gross, Mason, and McEachern, 1958.) In any social grouping, values, norms, and roles are not randomly arranged, but are organized so as to constitute a relatively coherent and consistent set of beliefs and prescriptions governing the behavior of participants. It is for this reason that we speak of a normative *structure.*

The second component, which Davis refers to as "a factual order," we will call the *behavioral structure.* This component focuses on actual behavior rather than on prescriptions for behavior. Homans's (1950: 33–40) well-known classification of social behavior into activities, interactions, and sentiments suggests the types of elements that comprise the behavioral structure. Because our concern is with the analysis of behavioral *structure,* rather than simply behavior, we focus on those activities, interactions, and sentiments that exhibit some degree of regularity—recurrent behavior of a given individual or similarities in the behavior of a class of individuals. Such actions, exhibiting some consistency and constancy in their general characteristics, are themselves arranged into larger patterns or networks of behavior. For example, we may observe in a group over a period of time which individuals attempt to influence others and with what degree of success, and in this way obtain a description of the power structure within that group. Or by observing the patterning of sentiments among group members—who is attracted to or rejected by whom—we can describe the sociometric structure of the group. Both the power structure and the sociometric structure are specific instances of behavioral structures.

As the passage from Davis reminds us, the normative structure and the behavioral structure of a social group are neither independent nor identical, but are, to varying degrees, interrelated. The normative structure imposes an important set of constraints on the behavioral structure, shaping and channeling behavior and helping to account for much of the regularity and patterning that exist. On the other hand, much behavior departs from the normative structure and is an important source of additions to and changes in that structure. Behavior shapes norms just as norms shape behavior. Groups vary in the extent to which their normative and their behavioral structures are closely aligned. In some situations precept corresponds closely to practice: this appears to be the case in many utopian communities or communes—at least in their early stages of development (see Kanter, 1972). In other situations a sizable gulf appears between professed beliefs and behavior. Reports suggest that Victorian England might represent an instance of this situation with respect to sexual morality versus practice. In any case, the normative and the behavioral structures are always in a state of dynamic tension—each existing and changing somewhat independently of the other at the same time each exerts continuing force on the other.

All social groups—or *collectivities,* to use the more general term—are characterized by a normative structure applicable to the participants and by a behavioral structure linking participants in a common network or pattern of activities, interactions, and sentiments. These two interrelated structures together comprise the *social structure* of a collectivity. (For a more extended discussion of normative, behavioral, and social structures, see Scott, 1970: 102–10.)

Organizational participants are likely to emphasize the amount of confusion, the indeterminacy, and the unpredictability of the actions of their coworkers, in part because such matters draw their attention and require their energies. However, to focus on the social structure of organizations is to emphasize the impressive amount of order exhibited by the behavior of participants in organizations. Every day hundreds or thousands of persons perform millions of individual acts; yet the outcome is not bedlam, not total confusion or chaos, but a reasonable approximation of order. This phenomenon deserves our attention.

Emphasizing the importance of the social structure of organizations does not commit us to the view that relations among participants are all sweetness and light: social structure does not connote social harmony. Conflict is always possible and usually present among participants in any social structure. An emphasis on social structure should enable us to see that much of whatever conflict is present in the organization is patterned in the sense that it is built into the structure of relations between individuals and groups and is not due to innately aggressive individual participants. Not only tensions and stresses, but also deviance and change can often be attributed to structural factors.

The social structure of an organization varies in the extent to which it is formalized. A *formal* social structure is one in which the social positions and the relationships among them have been explicitly specified and are defined independently of the personal characteristics of the participants occupying these positions. By contrast, in an *informal* social structure, it is impossible to distinguish between the characteristics of the positions and the characteristics of the participants. In an informal structure, when specific participants leave or enter the system, their roles and relationships develop and change as a function of their personal characteristics and the interactions that occur.

PARTICIPANTS

Organizational participants are those individuals who, in return for a variety of inducements, make contributions to the organization (Barnard, 1938; Simon, 1957). All individuals participate in more than one organization, and the extent and intensiveness of their involvement may vary greatly; the decision as to who is to be regarded as a participant is thus often a difficult one and may legitimately vary depending on the issue at hand. For example, a single individual may simultaneously be an employee of an industrial firm, a member of a union, a church member, a member of a fraternal lodge, a "member" of a political party, a citizen of the state, a client in a group medical practice, a stockholder in one or more companies, and a customer in numerous retail and service organizations. Analysts disagree, as we shall see, on the extent to which organizations do and should incorporate facets of participants. How much of the personality and personal characteristics of individual participants is relevant to the functioning of the organization also varies from one type of organization and role to another—consider the situation of a novice in a religious order versus that of an occasional customer in a supermarket.

Participants also vary greatly in the level of skills or expertise they bring to the organization. Structural arrangements within organizations must be designed to accommodate these differences in skill level, which are almost always accompanied by differences in power and in demands for autonomy. These issues are most dramatically raised when professionals are employed by organizations.

GOALS

The concept of organizational goals is among the most important—and most controversial—concepts to be confronted in the study of organizations. Some analysts insist that goals are indispensable to the understanding of organizations; others question whether goals perform any function other than to justify past actions. Then, too, behavioralists are fond of pointing out: Only individuals have goals—collectivities, such as organizations, do not. We will not attempt to tackle these prickly issues here but promise not to duck them indefinitely.

For most analysts, goals constitute a central point of reference in the analysis of organizations. Goals are tentatively defined as *conceptions of desired ends*—conditions that participants attempt to effect through their performance of task activities.

Since goals figure prominently in some definitions of organizations, we will consider them further in the following section, and we will discuss the major issues and problems bearing on their analysis in chapter 12.

TECHNOLOGY

To focus on the technology of an organization is to view the organization as a place where some type of work is done, as a location where energy is applied to the transformation of materials, as a mechanism for transforming inputs into outputs. The connotations of the term *technology* are narrow and hard, but we will insist that every organization does work and possesses a technology for doing that work. Some organizations process material inputs and fabricate new equipment and hardware. Others "process" people, their products consisting of more knowledgeable individuals, in the case of effective school systems, or healthier individuals, in the case of effective medical clinics. Still others process primarily symbolic materials such as information or music. Technologies consist in part of machines and mechanical equipment but are also comprised of the technical knowledge and skills of participants.

All organizations possess technologies, but organizations vary in the extent to which these techniques are understood, or routinized, or efficacious in producing the desired outcomes. Some of the most interesting theoretical and empirical work in recent years has focused on the interrelation between the characteristics of technology and the structural features of organizations. This work is described and evaluated in chapter 10.

ENVIRONMENT

Every organization exists in a specific physical, technological, cultural, and social environment to which it must adapt. No organization is self-sufficient: all depend for survival on the types of relations they establish with the larger systems of which they are a part. Early analysts of organizations, as we will see, tended to overlook or underestimate the importance of organization-environmental linkages, but recent work places great emphasis on these connections. And, indeed, the number and variety of these connections are impressive. Let us briefly reconsider each of the four organizational components in this light.

Very few organizations assume full responsibility for the socialization and training of their participants. Employees come to the organization with heavy cultural and social baggage obtained from interactions in other social contexts. With very few exceptions—such as inmates in "total institutions" (Goffman, 1961)—participants are involved in more than one organization at any given time. These outside interests and commitments inevitably constrain the behavior of participants in any given organization and, in some instances, completely determine it. To regard participants as completely contained by the organization is to misperceive one of the fundamental characteristics of organizations: namely, that they are systems built on the *partial involvement* of their members.

Similarly, few organizations create their own technologies; rather, they import them from the environment in the form of mechanical equipment, packaged programs and sets of instructions, and trained workers. Any specific organization must also adapt to the larger occupational structure in the selection and deployment of workers within the organization. Moreover, the environment is the source of the inputs to be processed by the organization, just as it is the "sink" to which all outputs are delivered—as products to be sold, clients restored to function, or waste materials to be eliminated.

Parsons (1960) has called attention to the important relation between an organization's goals and the larger societal environment. What is termed a goal or objective by a specific organization is, from the point of view of the larger society, its specialized function. An organization may thus expect societal support for its activities to reflect the relative value society places on those functions: if health represents a strong positive value for a society, for example, then those organizations that supply health care may expect to receive a disproportional share of resources in support of their work.

Lastly, the social structure of the organization will reflect important features borrowed from or impressed upon it by the environment. Structural forms, no less than technologies, are rarely invented and are usually borrowed from the environment. Part 3 of this volume, especially chapters 10 and 11, explores the thesis that environmental complexity tends to be incorporated within and reflected by the structural features of organizations.

Each of these organizational elements—social structure, participants, goals, technology, environment—represents an important component of all organizations. Indeed, each element has been regarded as of surpassing importance by one or more analysts of organizations. These views are illustrated in chapter 2 where Leavitt's diamond is used as the basis for classifying a number of organizational typologies, each of which focuses attention on a specific element.

However, the chief value of Leavitt's model is as a graphic reminder that no one element is so dominant as to be safely considered in isolation from the others. Organizations are, first and foremost, *systems* of elements, each of which affects and is affected by the others. Goals are not *the* key to understanding the nature and functioning of organizations, no more than are the participants, the technology, or the social structure. And no organization can be understood in isolation from the larger environment. We will miss the essence of organization if we insist on focusing on any single feature to the exclusion of all others.

Defining the Concept of Organization

Consistent with the objectives of this volume, not one but three definitions of organizations will be presented. These definitions pave the way for our description and evaluation in part 2 of three major perspectives employed in the analysis of organizations. Thus, we leave to later chapters the considerable task of spelling out the implications of these differing definitions. We give special attention here to the first definition—actually, several related definitions will be discussed—both because it has tended until recently to dominate the field and because it has served to establish organizations as a distinctive field of study. This definition is most consistent with a *rational system* perspective on organization. Two other definitions—one associated with the *natural system* perspective and the other with the *open systems* perspective—will be briefly described here and will be examined more fully in later chapters.

RATIONAL SYSTEM DEFINITIONS

Since a primary function of a definition is to help us to distinguish one phenomenon from another, most definitions of organizations emphasize the distinctive features of organizations—those that help to distinguish them from related social forms. Many analysts have attempted to formulate such definitions, and their views appear similar, as illustrated by the following four influential definitions:

According to Barnard,

> Formal organization is that kind of cooperation among men that is conscious, deliberate, purposeful. (Barnard, 1938: 4)

According to March and Simon,

> Organizations are assemblages of interacting human beings and they are the largest assemblages in our society that have anything resembling a central coordinative system. . . . The high specificity of structure and coordination within organizations—as contrasted with the diffuse and variable relations *among* organizations and among unorganized individuals—marks off the individual organization as a sociological unit comparable in significance to the individual organism in biology. (March and Simon, 1958: 4)

According to Blau and Scott,

> Since the distinctive characteristic of these organizations is that they have been formally established for the explicit purpose of achieving certain goals, the term "formal organizations" is used to designate them. (Blau and Scott, 1962: 5)[5]

And, according to Etzioni,

> Organizations are social units (or human groupings) deliberately constructed and reconstructed to seek specific goals. (Etzioni, 1964: 3)

All of these definitions point to the existence of two structural features that distinguish organizations from other types of collectivities.

1. Organizations are collectivities oriented to the pursuit of relatively specific goals. They are "purposeful" in the sense that the activities and interactions of participants are centrally coordinated to achieve specified goals. Goals are *specific* to the extent that they are explicit, clearly defined, and provide unambiguous criteria for selecting among alternative activities.

2. Organizations are collectivities that exhibit a relatively high degree of formalization. The cooperation among participants is "conscious" and "deliberate"; the structure of relations is made explicit and can be "deliberately constructed and reconstructed." As previously defined, a structure is *formalized* to the extent that the rules governing behavior are precisely and explicitly formulated and to the extent that roles and role relations are prescribed independently of the personal attributes of individuals occupying positions in the structure.

It is the combination of relatively high goal specificity and relatively high formalization that distinguishes organizations from other types of collectivities. Note that both goal specificity and formalization are viewed as variables —organizations may be characterized by higher or lower levels of each. Nevertheless, as a structural type, organizations are expected to exhibit higher levels of formalization and goal specificity than other types of collectivities such as primary groups, families, communities, and social movements. In general— there certainly are exceptions—families and kinship structures tend to rank high on formalization but low on goal specificity (Litwak, 1968; Litwak and

---

[5]This definition, which I developed with Blau a good many years ago, now strikes me as somewhat misleading. Emphasis is placed on the conditions present at the founding of the organization: on whether the unit was "formally established for the explicit purpose of achieving certain goals." The wording suggests that factors associated with the founding of the unit—in particular, the intent of the founders—are of critical importance. Such historical considerations seem much less important to me now than the current state of the system, that is, the extent of goal specificity and of formalization.

Meyer, 1966); social movements tend to exhibit low levels of formalization combined with higher levels of goal specificity, although the specificity of goals varies greatly from movement to movement and from time to time (Gusfield 1968); and communities are characterized by low levels of both goal specificity and formalization (Hillery, 1968: 145–152; and Moe, 1959).

We arrive then, at the first definition: *an organization is a collectivity oriented to the pursuit of relatively specific goals and exhibiting a relatively highly formalized social structure*. Note that this definition focuses attention not only on the distinctive characteristics of organizations but also on their normative structure. It is compatible with the rational system perspective.

A NATURAL SYSTEM DEFINITION

Gouldner (1959) reminds us that the distinguishing features of a phenomenon are not its only characteristics and, indeed, may not be the most important ones. Although organizations often—not always—espouse specific goals, the behavior of participants is frequently not guided by them, nor can they be safely used to predict organizational actions. Similarly, formal role definitions and written rules may have been developed, but they generally provide few if any restrictions on the behavior of members. Thus, if the behavioral structure is attended to, rather than the normative structure, the first definition of organizations can be quite misleading.

It is of interest to note that although many conventional organizations, such as public schools and government mental health services, have felt the need to develop explicit goal statements and formalized job titles and procedures, other organizations have decided to do away with such superfluous decorations and camouflage. Such appears to be the case with a set of organizational forms labeled "collectivist" organizations (Rothschild-Whitt, 1979). These organizations include many recently developed innovative forms, particularly in the service sector—for example, free medical clinics, alternative schools, rape counseling centers, and legal collectives—as well as some earlier forms such as food and producer cooperatives. Some of these organizations clearly are pursuing relatively broad and diffuse objectives, such as societal reform or developing more open and authentic relations among their participants. Others have defined relatively specific objectives. However, virtually all of them eschew formalization as a structural characteristic. Rothschild-Whitt's (1979) survey of the structural features of these forms suggests that many go to great lengths to eliminate or reduce formalization. They deny the authority of office, seek to minimize the promulgation of rules and procedures, attempt to eliminate status gradations among participants, and do away with role differentiation and specialization of function. Great stress is laid on equality in decision making; and individual differences in interests and preferences among members are deemed of great importance. The personal qualities of members do matter! Thus, if the first definition of organization is used, organizations such as these are excluded.[6]

A natural system conception of organizations is not entirely based on what organizations are not, although this is an important ingredient in the perspective. Positive attention is devoted to examining the way in which organizations —like all collectivities—attend to the needs or requirements of their own system. Organizations are viewed as organic systems imbued with a strong drive to survive, to maintain themselves as a system. The development of informal structures is regarded as an important means to this end. These structures grow out of the natural abilities and interests of participants and enable the collectivity to benefit from the human resources of its membership.

Hence, a second definition of organizations, useful for viewing them as natural systems, is proposed: *an organization is a collectivity whose participants are little affected by the formal structure or official goals but who share a common interest in the survival of the system and who engage in collective activities, informally structured, to secure this end.*

AN OPEN SYSTEMS DEFINITION

The previous definitions tend to view the organization as a closed system, separate from its environment and comprised of a set of stable and easily identified participants. However, organizations are not closed systems, sealed off from their environments, but are open to and dependent on flows of personnel and resources from outside their own system. Also, if an organization is to survive, it must induce participants to contribute resources, energy, and time to it. Individuals have different interests and value various inducements: they join and leave the organization depending on the bargains they can strike —the relative advantage to be had from staying or going. Thus, rather than viewing the organization as a coherent system of relations oriented to the pursuit of specific goals, it may be more accurate to view it as an opportunistic collection of divergent interest groups temporarily banded together.

We arrive, then, at a third definition, useful for viewing organizations as open systems: *an organization is a coalition of shifting interest groups that*

---

[6]We would argue, however, that although these forms are excluded by the rational system definition, they are also illuminated by it. Collectivist forms do not simply exhibit relatively low levels of formalization; they are characterized by active hostility to formalization. They are self-consciously and energetically anti-formal in practice and, more importantly, in their ideologies and normative systems. Indeed, much of the interest and energy they generate among their participants can be directly attributed to the ideological battle they wage against the more conventional formalized and hierarchical models. They are organized in opposition to the prevailing model of organizations—a model so widely shared that its *negation* can serve as a potent basis of organization.

develop goals by negotiation; the structure of the coalition, its activities, and its outcomes are strongly influenced by environmental factors.

It is no doubt unsettling to be confronted so early with three such diverse views of organizations. But better to know the worst at the outset! The definitions are quite different in that they not only encompass somewhat divergent types of collectivities but also emphasize different facets of a given organization. But this is precisely why they are useful. It is essential to remember that definitions are neither true nor false but are only more or less helpful in calling attention to certain aspects of the phenomenon under study. With the help of these definitions, and the more general perspectives with which they are associated, we expect to see and learn more about organizations than would be possible were we to employ a single point of view. As we proceed, we will call attention to the stimulating vistas and profound depths charted by each of the conceptions. Each has its own charms (as well as its own blemishes), and each carries its own truth (as well as its own biases).

A NOTE ON BUREAUCRACY

The term *bureaucracy* will come up again and again throughout this volume, and so we would do well to confront this concept head-on at an early stage. The term is a problem because, although frequently used by students of organizations, it is defined in many ways. The term also carries with it a great deal of emotional freight. For many the terms *bureaucracy* and *bureaucrat* are epithets—accusations connoting rule-encumbered inefficiency and mindless overconformity. Indeed, such views are probably those most commonly held by individuals in this society. By contrast, the foremost student of bureaucracy, Max Weber, used the term to refer to that form of administrative organization which, in his view, was capable of attaining the highest level of efficiency! (Weber, 1949 tr.: 339). Some organizational theorists use the term bureaucracy as a general synonym for organization; others reserve the term to refer to public organizations or to the administrative units of the nation state; and still others, most notably, Weber, use the term to designate a particular type of administrative structure. All of this can be very confusing, not only to beginning students, but to all of us who attempt to study organizations. While we cannot dispel all of the confusion, we will try to be clear about the way in which we propose to use the concept, and we can suggest how our own usage relates to some of the other definitions.

Our definition of bureaucracy is indebted to the work of Bendix, who writes: "Seen historically, bureaucratization may be interpreted as the increasing subdivision of the functions which the owner-managers of the early enterprises had performed personally in the course of their daily routine" (1956: 211–12). Such functions include supervision, personnel selection and management, accounting and financial management, record keeping, job design, and long-range planning. In this sense, bureaucracy refers to the middle layer of the organization: the head of the organization—whether president, dictator, owner, or leader—is excluded, as are the lower levels, for example, the production workers. A useful way of thinking about a bureaucracy is that it consists of those positions (or activities) whose function is to maintain the organization itself as a going concern. In short, *bureaucracy* may be defined as the existence of a specialized administrative staff.

Like formalization and goal specificity, bureaucracy should be viewed as a variable: organizations vary in terms of how much of their personnel resources are devoted to administrative, as opposed to production, activities. Bendix, following Melman (1951), has proposed that for industrial organizations a crude but serviceable index of the degree of bureaucratization is the ratio of administrative (salaried) to production (wage) employees. Data compiled by Bendix (1956: 214) from several sources show that for a number of western countries the ratio of administrative to production workers in industry has steadily increased from under 10 percent in 1900 to over 20 percent by 1950. The causes of increased bureaucratization will be discussed in part 3 of this volume.

Although the precise identification of bureaucratic positions or activities may often pose problems to the investigator, the conceptual distinction suggested by Bendix seems clear in the case of industrial or commercial organizations. Unfortunately, this is not the case for public organizations. Consider the Internal Revenue Service or the State Department of our federal government. In the case of these units, the entire organization is devoted to administrative activities! We believe that our conception of bureaucracy can encompass these situations, but only if we are clear about the level of analysis at which we approach such systems.

If we choose the ecological level and focus on the State Department as an organization within a larger system of organizations, as a specialized administrative arm of the executive office of the president, then it is consistent with our definition to view the entire department as a bureaucracy. These "bureaus" and their associated officials may appropriately be seen as working to maintain our nation. On the other hand, if we choose the structural level of analysis, concentrating attention on the internal structures and processes of the State Department, then we will observe that there is within this bureau a specialized administrative staff that assists the Secretary of State in the administration of the department. Each bureau has its own internal bureaucracy: a group of officials who do not directly carry out the work of the agency but supervise, regulate, and support those who do (see Blau and Scott, 1962: 7–8).

Weber's conception differs from our own. As noted, he defines bureaucracy as a special type of administrative structure. He employs the term to designate the type of administrative structure that developed in association with a rational-legal mode of authority relation. The distinctive characteristics of these structures include a clear differentiation of responsibilities among officials, the arrangement of offices in a hierarchical pattern, the use of technical criteria of recruitment, and impersonal norms governing the relations among officials. Weber argued that these bureaucratic structures—present in both private and public organizations—were gradually replacing administrative systems based on traditional authority relations. His conception of these structures and the processes leading to their ascendancy will be discussed in more detail in chapters 2 and 3. It is introduced here merely to distinguish it from our own definition of bureaucracy.

It is of interest to note that from all three points of view described, the level of bureaucratization is increasing. If we define bureaucratization at the structural level as an increase in the proportion of resources devoted to administrative as compared to production activities, then, as we have seen, bureaucracy is increasing. If we define bureaucratization at the ecological level as an increase in the size of the administrative machinery of the nation state, then in virtually all contemporary societies, bureaucracy is increasing. It is in this sense that Jacoby (1973 tr.) writes of *The Bureaucratization of the World.* And if we adopt Weber's definition and view bureaucracy as a special type of administrative structure, then he is clearly correct that in most modernizing societies over the past century, bureaucracies have been replacing more traditional administrative forms. It is with reference to Weber's definition of bureaucracy that some analysts such as Bennis (Bennis and Slater, 1968) assert that the most advanced organizations are currently moving toward the development of "postbureaucratic" forms. These developments will be described and evaluated in chapter 10.

Finally, although we will not ourselves employ the term bureaucracy as a perjorative label for stagnant, incompetent administration, we will want to consider the causes of administrative pathology and, in particular, to struggle to understand how it is that arrangements created and adopted to ensure efficient and responsive administrative performance sometimes—indeed, all too often—result in the exact opposite.

Summary

Organizations are important objects of study and concern for many reasons. They are vital mechanisms for pursuing collective goals in modern societies. They are not neutral tools because they affect what they produce; and they function as collective actors that independently possess certain rights and powers. Both as mechanisms and as actors, organizations are alleged to be the source of some of contemporary society's most serious problems. Organizations encompass generic social processes but carry them out by means of distinctive structural arrangements.

Although an interest in organizational forms and processes may be traced far back in history, a distinctive field of sociological inquiry focusing on the creation and empirical testing of generalized knowledge concerning organizations did not develop until after 1950. This development was linked with and greatly stimulated by the translation into English of Max Weber's historical and comparative studies of administrative organizations, conducted during the first two decades of this century. The field of organizational studies is becoming increasingly interdisciplinary. Among the bases on which studies vary is the level at which analysis is carried out: some research occurs at the social psychological level emphasizing the interaction of individuals and groups within organizations and the impact of organizational characteristics on these processes; other studies are conducted at the structural level and attempt to account for variations in the patterned features of organizations; and still other research is focused at the ecological level, viewing the organization as an actor or subunit in a more comprehensive system of relationships.

Three contrasting definitions of organizations are presented. Each is associated with one of three perspectives on organizations to be elaborated in part 2: the rational system, the natural system, and the open systems perspectives. The first definition views organizations as highly formalized collectivities oriented to the pursuit of specific goals. The second definition views organizations as collectivities seeking to survive. And the third definition views organizations as coalitions of interest groups highly influenced by their environments. Each of these definitions is viewed as opening up a useful, if partial, view of organizations.

chapter 2

Varieties
of Organizations

> *Organization science, and especially the
> application of its findings to the problems of
> organizations and managers, is not likely to
> emerge with viable laws and principles until
> substantial progress is made toward an
> acceptable taxonomy and classification of
> organizations.*

> BILL MCKELVEY (1975)

One organization is like all other organizations: thus, in chapter 1 we reviewed general definitions of organizations, specified elements all organizations hold in common, and attempted to identify those features that distinguish organizations from other types of collectivities. This chapter provides a variation on the original theme: One organization is like *some* other organizations.[1] It is vital for students of organizations to realize the variety of the phenomena with which we deal. There is an all-too-common tendency for analysts of one type of organization to presume that the arrangements and processes that characterize it are applicable to many or most other types of organizations. There is, in short, a tendency to overgeneralize findings applicable in one setting to others. Organizational typologies help to mitigate this impulse. By reminding us of the variety of organizations that did, do, and will exist, and by stressing some of the important differences among them, those who construct typologies have performed an important service for us all.

Let us supply an overview, a rationale, and some guidelines for approaching this chapter. We begin with a brief review of a number of well-known—and

---

[1]This language is borrowed from Robert Wilson (1954) who, in his analysis of the characteristics of operating rooms in hospitals noted that: "Every operating room is: (a) like *all* other operating rooms; (b) like *some* other operating rooms; (c) like *no* other operating rooms."

some not so well-known—typologies which analysts have devised to catalog the diversity of organizations. These typologies are themselves classified according to the major organizational element identified as the basis for the proposed distinctions. We will see that one or more analysts have focused attention on each of the elements of organizations identified in chapter 1 as a primary basis for distinguishing among organizations. In this first section, we quickly survey a number of different bases for classifying organizations. Our intent is to emphasize the diversity of organizational forms—and the variety of bases for distinguishing among them—not to assess the merits or deficiencies of each proposed schema.

In describing the diversity of organizations, we use the medium of typologies because these classification systems, if they are good ones, focus attention on one or a few features of organizations that are asserted to be of primary importance. Hence, in reviewing typologies, we begin to identify specific dimensions or variables that are viewed as significant by one or another analyst in accounting for the differences among organizations. We confess that many such variables are all too quickly introduced, and anticipate that some readers may experience confusion due to overloading. Not to worry. Our rapid survey merely previews many of the concepts and distinctions which are dealt with at greater length—and in a more critical fashion—in later chapters.

Midway in the chapter, the emphasis shifts from content to method as we seek to determine what rules govern the construction of good—analytically useful—typologies. Several principles are derived and are illustrated by a more detailed examination of two widely-used typologies. We also compare theoretically driven with empirically derived typologies.

It is important to take note of the limitations and potential dangers associated with the use of typologies. Numerous contemporary analysts have concluded that their problems outweigh their benefits, but a new generation of researchers is convinced that the construction of more adequate typologies is the key to a better understanding of organizations.

Survey of Organization Typologies

Typologies abound in the study of organizations. Without going out of our way at all, we will encounter a large number of typologies throughout this volume. Typologies are numerous in part because organizations tend to be complex and to exhibit a large number of features, any of which can become the basis for distinguishing among them. Some typologies focus attention on organizational goals, others on their structural features or technologies. Indeed, we can without undue strain describe examples which are based on each of the elements of organizations identified in chapter 1. Table 2–1 displays the

Table 2-1. Organization Typologies Classified by Organizational Element

ORGANIZATIONAL ELEMENT	TYPOLOGY	KEY VARIABLE
Goals	a. Standard Industrial Classification	Industrial divisions (functional categories)
	b. Parsons's AGIL schema	Societal function
	c. Blau-Scott's *cui bono*	Prime beneficiary
Social Structure		
Normative Structure	a. Weber's authority types	Belief systems legitimating power structure
	b. Gouldner's typology of rules	Identity of groups supporting rules
	c. M. Marx's typology of bureaucracies	Criteria of appointment in bureaucracies
Behavioral Structure	d. Etzioni's compliance types	Principal types of sanctions
	e. Duverger's types of political parties	Basic components of party structure
	f. Pugh's empirical typology of structure	Major structural factors
Technology	a. Woodward's categories of industrial technology	Technical complexity
	b. Perrow's types of technology	Technical uncertainty
	c. Thompson's types of technology	Variability of inputs and outputs
Participants	a. Lefton-Rosengren's client dimensions	Time-space relation of clients to organization
	b. Etzioni's compliance types	Involvement of lower level participants
Environment	a. Market types	Extent of market concentration
	b. K. Marx's political/ economic systems	Class group in whose interest state functions
	c. Warren's typology of organizational fields	Inclusiveness of decision making structures
	d. McKelvey's evolutionary schema	Dominant environmental/technical system

major typologies to be reviewed, classified by the organizational element that they emphasize. We provide a brief overview of these typologies in order both to illustrate the diversity of organizations and to preview some of the important dimensions or variables which have been identified as important in accounting for these differences.

TYPOLOGIES EMPHASIZING GOALS

Many social scientists, but especially economists and demographers, make use of a valuable typology developed over many years by the United States government for classifying all goods and services produced in this country. The Standard Industrial Classification (SIC) system was devised to classify an "establishment" according to its primary product (Office of Management and Budget, 1972). An establishment is defined as "an economic unit, generally at a single physical location where business is conducted or where services or industrial operations are performed." (p. 10) The SIC is organized in a hierarchical fashion beginning with ten broad functional divisions (for example, manufacture, wholesale and retail trade, public administration) that are assigned a one-digit number from 0 to 9. These divisions are each subdivided into industry groups, which are identified by adding a second digit. These industry groups are, in turn, subdivided into individual industries, with the addition of a third digit to the classification. Finally, industries are subdivided into specific products or services that could be carried on at the level of a single establishment. A fourth digit identifies these specific products. Some illustrations will help to make the classification system clear.

3	Manufacturing
37	Transportation equipment
376	Guided missile and space vehicles and parts
3761	Guided missile and space vehicles
7	Services
78	Motion pictures
783	Theaters
7833	Drive-in motion picture theaters

As the examples suggest, all manufacturing activities are assigned a number beginning with 3, and all services are assigned a number beginning with 7; all transportation equipment is designated by the number 37, and so on. This type of nested series has a simplicity and practicality that make it a very useful vehicle for gathering and systematically storing information. Depending on the level of analysis desired, information can be aggregated to the industry group or divisional level, or disaggregated to the industry or establishment level.

A large amount of data is regularly gathered in the United States based on the SIC codes. Since establishments represent separate locations, such as individual factories and stores, and thus are not necessarily the same as firms, these data are not appropriate for all organizational analyses. On the other hand, the establishment level may be the best level at which to test certain ideas concerning organizational behavior. Like all classifications, the SIC codes are sometimes arbitrary and fit the empirical situation poorly. Each establishment is to be classified according to its *primary* activity. However, when two or more distinct economic activities are being carried on at a single location, such activities are to be treated as separate establishments (Office of Management and Budget, 1972: 646). While the SIC does not resolve all the problems associated with classifying organizations based on their products and services, in comparison with most classification systems, it is highly developed, is accompanied by clear rules for its application, and has a long enough history and a wide enough use to be an invaluable resource for organizational analysts. Although there are some important restrictions, it merits greater use.[2]

Parsons (1960) proposes a typology based primarily on organizational goals classified in terms of the "social function" they perform for the larger society. As a basis for classifying these societal functions, Parsons employs his well-known schema for the analysis of any social system, identified by the acronymn AGIL (see Parsons, Bales, and Shils, 1953).[3] The model posits that all social systems, if they are to persist, must satisfy four basic functions:

Adaptation—the problem of acquiring sufficient resources

Goal attainment—the problem of setting and implementing goals

Integration—the problem of maintaining solidarity or coordination among the subunits of the system

Latency—the problem of creating, preserving, and transmitting the system's distinctive culture and values

Viewing an entire society as a social system, Parsons (1960: 44–56) argues that it is possible and useful to classify organizations in terms of the primary societal functions to which they contribute, as shown in table 2–2.

Parsons argues that his typology may be used to predict differences in the internal structure and operation of organizations. Further, as briefly noted in chapter 1, he suggests the interesting hypothesis that organizations of each

---

[2]The census data gathered on individual establishments and firms are not available to researchers for reasons of confidentiality. The data are made public only at more highly aggregated levels. However, officials of the Census Bureau have expressed willingness to consider conducting some analyses at the establishment or firm level under contract by their own employees. (See Kallek, 1975) These data may become an important resource for organizational research in the future.

[3]Parson's approach to analyzing social systems is further discussed and critically evaluated in chapter 4.

Table 2-2. Parsons's Typology Based on Societal Functions

SOCIETAL FUNCTION	ORGANIZATIONAL TYPE	EXAMPLES
Adaption	Organizations oriented to economic production	Business firms
Goal attainment	Organizations oriented to political goals	Government agencies Other organizations that allocate power, such as banks.
Integration	Integrative organizations	Courts and the legal profession Political parties Social control agencies
Latency	Pattern-maintenance organizations	Cultural organizations, such as museums Educational organizations Religious organizations

type will receive societal support, in the form of resources and legitimacy, according to the importance placed on each function by the members of that society. For example, in the U.S. our values are such that we might expect primary support to be given to those organizations engaged in economic production; however, in India, the ordering of values might place greater importance on religious bodies and other organizations serving to maintain their distinctive cultural patterns (see Parsons, 1953:106).

A third typology emphasizing goals which I developed in association with Peter Blau (Blau and Scott, 1962) is described in the second section of this chapter.

TYPOLOGIES EMPHASIZING SOCIAL STRUCTURE

Normative Structure   The following three typologies emphasize the importance of some feature of the normative structure of organizations. By far the best known of all organizational typologies is that proposed by Max Weber.

In his justly famous typology, Weber distinguishes among three types of authority:

Traditional authority—resting on an established belief in the sanctity of immemorial traditions and the legitimacy of those exercising authority under them

Rational-legal authority—resting on a belief in the 'legality' of patterns of normative rules and the right of those elevated to authority under such rules to issue commands

Charismatic authority—resting on devotion to the specific and exceptional sanctity, heroism or exemplary character of an individual person, and of the
normative patterns or order revealed or ordained by him. (Weber, 1947
tr.:328)

Clearly, the basis for the typology is differences in beliefs by which legitimacy is attributed to an authority relation. Associated with each authority
type is a distinctive administrative structure. Traditional authority gives rise
to the particularistic and diffuse structures exemplified by patrimonialism and
its various manifestations, including gerontocracy, patriarchalism, and feudal-
ism. (Patrimonial authority systems are defined and illustrated in chapter 3,
where Weber's theory of bureaucracy is more fully described.) Rational-legal
authority provides the basis for the more specific and universalistic structures
of which the clearest example is the "rational" bureaucracy. And charismatic
authority is associated with the "strictly personal" relations linking an impressive leader with his devoted coterie of followers.

In Weber's view, only traditional and rational-legal authority relations are
sufficiently stable to provide the basis for the formation of permanent administrative structures. And, during recent centuries, particularly in Western societies, traditional structures are viewed as gradually giving way to rational-level
structures due to their "purely technical superiority over any other form of
organization" (Weber, 1946 tr.: 214). However, neither the traditional nor the
rational-legal structures are well adapted to the satisfaction of extraordinary
needs or are capable of quick transformations to keep pace with rapidly
changing times. Hence, in crisis situations, neither legally empowered officials
nor the leader whose authority is based on the sanctity of tradition can provide
effective leadership; rather, under such circumstances, people look to individuals perceived as possessing extraordinary gifts of spirit and mind, and these
remarkable individuals vie for support for themselves and the programs they
espouse. Such charismatic leadership develops in crisis situations, but approxi-
mates its pure type only at the time of its origin. The successful charismatic
movement is one that can achieve some permanency and stability, and this can
occur only by moving in the direction of establishing "new" traditional structures, if this is not a contradiction in terms, or new rational-legal structures.
In Weber's terms, charisma, if successful, becomes routinized: the circle of
adherents is expanded to include less committed participants; systematic
sources of support are sought to replace voluntary and heartfelt, but irregular,
contributions; personal ties between leader and disciples are replaced by more
impersonal arrangements as the membership expands; and rules of succession
are developed in recognition of the truth that no one lives forever—not even
a "superman" (Weber, 1947 tr.: 358–73).

Weber's vision is of the slow but inexorable replacement of traditional with
rational-legal structures, punctuated by radical reorganizations inspired by
saints and demagogues; these innovations in turn are caught up in the fabric

of reinterpreted traditions and spawn new rules and regulations. This prescient vision was pre-Lenin and Hitler, pre-Roosevelt and Gandhi, pre-Mao and Castro. Seldom in the history of ideas has a theoretical formulation forecast with such accuracy, at least in general outline, the future.

Weber's typology is of interest not only because it underlies his conception of basic changes occurring in administrative systems; the distinction between traditional and rational-legal systems is also the basis for his influential "ideal-type" conception of the characteristics of rational bureaucratic systems. However, these concerns are better postponed and discussed as a part of the rational system model of organizations (see chapter 3).

Much more briefly, two other typologies emphasize normative aspects of the social structure. One was developed by the sociologist Alvin Gouldner and the other by the political scientist Morstein Marx.

Based on different sets of rules observed in his case study of a gypsum mine and factory, Gouldner (1954) proposes a general typology of organizations. The typology rests on an identification of which groups promulgate and enforce rules within an organization. Three types are identified:

Mock bureaucracy—rules are imposed on the organization by some outside agency and are not supported by either the managers or the rank-and-file participants

Representative bureaucracy—rules are developed and enforced within an organization by both managers and other participants

Punishment-centered bureaucracy—rules are unilaterally defined and enforced either by managers or by other participants

The typology can be applied to classes of rules within a single organization or may be generalized to classify various organizations according to which class of rules predominates. Gouldner (1954: 181–228) develops a number of implications that follow from this typology, including what types of explanation are given for deviant behaviors and what effects nonconformity has on the status of participants.

Morstein Marx (1957: 54–72) distinguishes four types of bureaucracy:

Guardian bureaucracy—composed of public officials who are the personification of, the custodians of, the approved ideology and its devoted instruments; for example, the ancient Chinese bureaucracy

Caste bureaucracy—arises from the class connections of those in the controlling positions; for example, German civil service under Bismarck

Patronage bureaucracy—appointment based on political criteria; office viewed as a reward for political service and loyalty; for example, Jacksonian spoils system

Merit bureaucracy—appointment governed by objective standards, specifically by the principle of admission on the basis of prescribed qualifications; for example, civil service system in U.S.

Marx's typology rests primarily on criteria by which public officials are appointed. While he does not attempt to develop specific predictions about the correlates or consequences of the typology, he does examine the associated cultural and social context by describing specific historical cases of each type.

Behavioral Structure   Several well-known typologies focus attention on the behavioral structure. An example is provided by Duverger's (1963) influential typology of political parties. He distinguishes among four types in terms of their "basic elements"—the component units of the party organization:

The Caucus—a small group of members whose strength depends not on quantity but on quality, such as their notability or expertise; for example, major U.S. political parties

The Branch—a mass-based organization whose strength depends on the size of its membership and the effectiveness of its hierarchical structures that coordinate the activities of the various branches; for example, European socialist parties

The Cell—small collections of individuals who are organized on the basis of work place, designed for action at the work place, not for participation in a political election; for example, the Russian Communist party

The Militia—a kind of private army whose members are enrolled along military lines, wear uniforms, and are ready to meet the enemy with weapons in physical combat; for example, Germany's Nazi party

Duverger argues that these basic elements are associated with a large number of other differences including the class bases of membership, ideology, extent of articulation and centralization, discipline, type of leadership, enthusiasm of members, range of activity (whether limited to political activity), and duration of activity (whether seasonal or year-round). (See also Wildavsky, 1959.)

Other examples of typologies which stress behavioral structural elements in organizations are those proposed by Etzioni (1961), which focuses on the types of sanctions which underlie compliance, and by Pugh and associates (Pugh, Hickson, and Hinings, 1969), which focuses on a set of empirically derived structural factors. Both of these typologies are described in the next section of this chapter.

TYPOLOGIES EMPHASIZING TECHNOLOGY

A large number of typologies have been proposed that emphasize the nature of the technology or the type of work being carried on by the organization. In her pioneering work on industrial organizations, Woodward (1965: 40) develops a typology emphasizing chronological development and technical complexity: "the production of unit articles to customers' individual requirements being the oldest and simplest form of manufacture, and the continuous-flow production of dimensional products, the most advanced and most complicated."[4] Three general types of production systems are identified, and in studying a sample of 92 firms in South Essex, England, a number of subtypes were also distinguished and ordered in terms of their technical complexity:

Unit and Small-Batch Production

Production of units to customers' requirements

Production of prototypes

Fabrication of large equipment in stages

Production of small batches to customer's orders

Large-Batch and Mass Production

Production of large batches

Production of large batches on assembly lines

Mass production

Process Production

Intermittent production of chemicals in multipurpose plant

Continuous-flow production of liquids, gases, and crystalline substances

Twelve of the 92 firms could not be placed in any of the above categories and are classified into a residual category of "combined systems" (Woodward, 1965: 39).

Woodward examines the relation between these distinctions based on the technical complexity of production systems and a number of other structural features of industrial organizations. In general, she reports consistent patterns relating technical complexity to such features as length of chain of command, span of control of the chief executive and the first-line supervisors, relative size of administrative structure, and flexibility of management systems (Woodward, 1965: 51–67). If her early work tends to foster an image of technological determinism in which the technical requirements of the production process impose specific structural features on the organization, her later analyses soften this imperative and recognize the influence of other factors shaping organizational structure (see Woodward, 1970). However, her work did call the attention of other organizational analysts to the importance of technical factors, and many were quick to follow her lead.

Perrow (1967; 1970) built on Woodward's work by making more explicit

[4]"Dimensional products" are those produced by process industries, such as petroleum and chemicals, that are measured by width, capacity, or volume. They are distinguished from "integral products" produced by manufacturing industries, such as machine tools and mechanical devices, which can be counted (see Woodward, 1965: 38).

the dimensions or variables distinguishing among technical work systems and by expanding the scope of the concepts so that they could be used in the study of nonindustrial, people-processing organizations. He identifies two dimensions: (1) the number of exceptional cases encountered in the work, or (for nonindustrial cases) the extent to which the material is perceived as nonuniform and variable; and (2) when exceptions occur, the extent to which the "search" or problem-solving processes are conducted in a logical and analytical manner, or (for nonindustrial cases) the extent to which the variability of material is well understood. A cross-classification of the two dimensions yields the typology shown in table 2–3.

Perrow predicts these types will vary in terms of such factors as where discretion is located, how power is distributed, how much interdependence is present among the work groups, and how coordination is effected. These and related arguments are pursued and evaluated in chapters 10 and 11.

A somewhat similar typology emphasizing technological features has also been developed by Thompson (1967). He distinguishes among three types:

Long-linked technology—involves serial interdependence in the sense that act C can be performed only after act B, which in turn can be performed only after act A, and so on; for example, production assembly-line manufacturing

Mediating technology—requires operating in standardized ways with many diverse clients; for example, the telephone company, the post office

Intensive technology—calls on a variety of techniques in order to achieve changes; selection of techniques is determined by feedback from the object itself; for example, an electronics laboratory developing and testing a new product

Table 2–3.   Perrow's Typology Based on Technology

DIMENSIONS	INDUSTRIAL EXAMPLES	NONINDUSTRIAL EXAMPLES
Few exceptions and analyzable searches	Routine manufacturing— for example, tonnage steel mills	Custodial institutions— for example, vocational training
Few exceptions and unanalyzable searches	Craft industries— for example, glass	Socializing institutions— for example, schools
Many exceptions and analyzable searches	Engineering firms— for example, heavy machinery	Programmed learning schools
Many exceptions and unanalyzable searches	Nonroutine manufacturing—for example, aerospace	Therapeutic institutions—for example, elite psychiatric hospitals

Although these are clearly interesting and different technical systems, Thompson fails to make explicit the systematic basis on which the typology rests. It appears to us that, implicitly, the typology emphasizes the extent to which the inputs and the outputs of the process are either variable or uniform, as follows:

	INPUTS	OUTPUTS
Long-linked technology	Uniform	Uniform
Mediating technology	Variable	Uniform
Intensive technology	Variable	Variable

While these distinctions may not capture all of the meaning carried by the types, they help to make clearer some of the considerations that affect the typology. As we will emphasize in the next section of this chapter, the more explicit and clearly defined the dimensions on which the typology rests, the more useful it is for guiding organizational analyses.

TYPOLOGIES EMPHASIZING PARTICIPANTS

Several typologies focus attention on some aspect of participants' characteristics as the basis for classifying organizations. For example, Lefton and Rosengren (1966) identify two dimensions along which client groups vary as a basis for developing a typology of service organizations. They note that there is a "longitudinal" dimension in the relation between an organization and its clients pertaining to whether the relation is projected over a relatively short or long span of time, and there is a "lateral" dimension pertaining to whether the organization's interest in the client is relatively narrowly or broadly defined. Since these dimensions are relatively independent, they can be cross-classified, yielding four types of organization-client relationships, as displayed in table 2–4.

Table 2–4. Lefton and Rosengren's Typology Based on Client Dimensions

CLIENT DIMENSIONS		EXAMPLES OF SERVICE ORGANIZATIONS
Lateral	*Longitudinal*	
narrow	short	Acute care general hospital
narrow	long	TB hospital; rehabilitation department; public health department
wide	short	Short-term therapeutic psychiatric hospital
wide	long	Long-term therapeutic psychiatric hospital; resident liberal arts college

Lefton and Rosengren argue that numerous features of organization-client relations vary according to these dimensions including the extent to which effort is made to invest the client in the ideology of the institution, the types of conflicts that occur among staff in obtaining consensus regarding client needs, and the extent to which informal or formal means are used to facilitate collaboration between clients and staff (Lefton and Rosengren, 1966: 806–9).

We have categorized the Blau-Scott typology as emphasizing organizational goals, but it could as appropriately be viewed as a typology focused on participants since organizational goals are described in terms of the interests of varying participant groups. Similarly, one of Etzioni's two dimensions focuses on participants' orientation to the power structure. Both the Blau-Scott and the Etzioni typologies are described later in this chapter.

TYPOLOGIES EMPHASIZING ENVIRONMENTS

Finally, and briefly, several typologies focusing attention on the environment are described. The first is among the most widely employed typologies in the study of organizations. It was developed by economists to classify markets in terms of their degree of concentration. The more concentrated the market, the smaller the number of firms accounting for most of the sales in that arena. Market concentration is, obviously, a continuum varying from high to low. Although analysts use quantitative indices of extent of concentration —for example, the proportion of sales accounted for by the largest four organizations—they have also found it useful to categorize markets into typologies of the following sort (see, for example, Bach, 1977):

Pure competition—many sellers of an identical product

Monopolistic competition—a substantial number of sellers of closely substitutable products

Oligopoly—a few sellers of closely substitutable products

Pure monopoly—one seller of a product without close substitutes

As is clear from the specific types identified, the focus of this typology is neither the market nor the firm, but the relation between them. The typology has been widely employed as a basis for developing predictions about the behavior of firms in a variety of areas including pricing decisions, advertising behavior, growth patterns, and efficiency in the allocation of resources.

Political scientists have developed a number of typologies to characterize the political structure or the political/economic structure of the nation state. Such a wide variety of schemas are in use that we can only select one or two quite arbitrarily for illustrative purposes. Of course, Karl Marx's typology is still widely employed, the major distinctions—between feudal, bourgeois, and proletarian systems—resting on the identity of the economic class in whose interests the state operates (see Marx, 1964 tr.; see also Bendix and Lipset, 1966). Apter (1958: 221–24), who defines government as "a concrete group" possessing "defined responsibilities for the maintenance of the system of which it is a part" and " a practical monopoly of coercive powers," distinguishes among nation states on the basis of their degree of representativeness, as follows: dictatorial, oligarchical, indirectly representational, and directly representational. He argues that these types can be shown to vary in the performance of basic governmental activities—for example, the structure of decision making and of coercion—and their sensitivity to the society's stratification system. Apter's typology can be used either as a classification of the state apparatus viewed as itself a formal organization, or as a classification of the state apparatus viewed as an important environmental element for other organizations within the same society. Although specific predictions have not been made relating type of state to the characteristics of organizations which evolve in the society, we will see in later chapters that the state is an increasingly important component of the environment for all organizations in modern societies.

Warren (1967) proposes a typology based on the relations that link a set of organizations together in a larger network or "field." The typology is designed to distinguish "between the ways in which organizational units interact in the decision-making process as these are influenced by their relationships to an inclusive decision-making structure" (Warren, 1967: 404). The types of inter-organizational fields identified are:

Unitary context—decision making as to policy and program takes place at the top of the structure where final authority rests; for example, a planning department within a municipal government

Federative context—member units have individual goals but also participate in a structure to set more inclusive goals; these corporate decisions must be ratified by member units; for example, member agencies within a council of social agencies

Coalitional context—each member unit has its own decision-making apparatus and set of goals but collaborates informally and on an ad hoc basis when some of its goals are similar to those of other member units; for example, group of independent agencies collaborating to obtain federal grant

Social-choice context—no formal or informal inclusive structure within which the units make their decisions; all decisions made at the level of the individual units; for example, diverse organizations that happen to reside in the same community

Warren predicts that organizations participating in these contexts will vary in terms of their relation to an inclusive goal, locus of authority, structural provision for a division of labor, commitment to a leadership subsystem, and degree of collectivity orientation.

A final example focusing on the environment of organizations is provided by McKelvey's typology based on evolutionary forms of organizations. This typology is described in the final section of this chapter. We turn now to consider four typologies in greater detail in order to formulate rules for constructing typologies.

Constructing Typologies

Two Conceptually Based Typologies

Two typologies developed by sociologists have been widely employed in the study of organizations: the first developed by Blau and me (Blau and Scott, 1962: 42–58), and the second by Etzioni (1961; rev. 1975). We will present more complete descriptions of these two typologies to provide detailed examples of the sorts of typologies that have been developed and the uses to which they are put, and to elicit some principles for constructing typologies.

The Blau-Scott typology rests on a single criterion: *cui bono*—who benefits? Four categories of participants are distinguished in relation to any formal organization: (1) the members or rank-and-file participants; (2) the owners or managers; (3) the clients or, more generally, the "public-in-contact"; and (4) the "public-at-large," that is, members of the society in which the organization operates. Although all of these groups may be expected to benefit from the functioning of the organization—otherwise they would be unlikely to contribute to it—one of the categories will be regarded as the prime beneficiary. Depending on which category is so defined, four general types of organizations are identified, as shown in table 2–5.

Blau and I assert that distinctive problems or issues are associated with each type. Thus, the crucial problem in mutual-benefit associations is that of maintaining internal democratic processes—providing for participation and control by the membership; the central problem for business concerns is that of maximizing operating efficiency in a competitive situation; the problems associated with the conflict between professional service to clients and administrative procedures are characteristic of service organizations; and the crucial problem posed by commonweal organizations is the development and maintenance of democratic mechanisms whereby they can be externally controlled by the public (Blau and Scott, 1962: 43). Further, we argue that the significance of the *cui bono* criterion is underscored by the fundamental changes and conflicts resulting when one class of participants is supplanted by another as prime beneficiary. For example, oligarchical tendencies—increasing concentration of power in the hands of a minority—in democratic political parties and unions are decried because they replace rank-and-file members as prime beneficiaries and instead serve the interests of managers or bosses (see Michels, 1949tr.;

Table 2–5. Blau and Scott's Typology Based on Prime Beneficiary

PRIME BENEFICIARY	ORGANIZATIONAL TYPE	CONCRETE EXAMPLES
Rank-and-file members	Mutual benefit associations	Political parties, unions, fraternal associations, clubs, professional associations, religious sects
Owners and managers	Business concerns	Industrial firms, wholesale and retail stores, banks, for-profit service agencies
Public-in-contact (clients)	Service organizations	Social work agencies, hospitals, schools, mental health clinics
Public-at-large	Commonweal organizations	State bureaus, military establishment, police and fire departments, research firms, custodial prisons

Lipset, Trow, and Coleman, 1956). Similarly, some mental hospitals assume a therapeutic orientation in order to focus primarily on the interests of their clients, operating as a service organization, while others assume a custodial orientation in order to serve primarily the interests of the public-at-large by keeping costs down and protecting their safety (see Belknap, 1956; Greenblatt, Levinson, and Williams, 1957; Street, Vinter, and Perrow, 1966). To move from one orientation to the other requires quite fundamental changes in structure and operation and is expected to elicit much resistance and conflict.

We will describe the typology proposed by Etzioni before commenting on the strengths and weaknesses of the Blau-Scott typology. Etzioni's (1961, rev. 1975) typology is based on a cross-classification of two dimensions: (1) what type of power is used to make participants comply and (2) what type of involvement participants exhibit toward the organization. The first dimension, power, is measured in terms of the types of sanctions used to enforce compliance. Three types are identified: (1) coercive power, which rests on the application or the threat of physical sanctions such as inflicting pain, confinement, or death; (2) remunerative power, based on control over material resources such as monetary payments, commodities, or services; and (3) normative power, which rests on the manipulation of symbolic rewards such as esteem, prestige, and acceptance. The second dimension, involvement, refers to the intensity and direction of the participants' orientation to the organization. Three types of involvement are identified: (1) alienative involvement, referring to an intense and negative attitude toward the organization; (2) calculative involvement, referring to either a positive or negative orientation of low intensity; and (3) moral involvement, designating a positive orientation of high intensity.

A cross-classification of the power and the involvement dimensions produces nine logically possible types of compliance, as illustrated in table 2–6. Etzioni asserts that while instances of each of the nine possible types can be found, the three diagonal cases—numbered 1, 5, and 9 in table 2–6—are found more frequently than are the other six types. Indeed, labeling these types as "congruent," Etzioni (1961: 12–14) argues that "organizations tend to shift their compliance structures from incongruent to congruent types," and that congruent types tend not to shift in the direction of incongruity. The organizational type produced by the combination of coercive power and alienation involvement is labeled a *coercive* organization; remunerative power combined with calculative involvement produces a *utilitarian* organization; and the combination of normative power and moral involvement produces a *normative* organization. Coercive organizations are exemplified by prisons, custodial mental hospitals, and concentration camps; utilitarian organizations include most blue- and white-collar industries and peacetime military organizations; normative organizations encompass many voluntary associations, professionally staffed hospitals and mental health agencies, and religious organizations. Etzioni recognizes that an organization may be characterized by more than one type of compliance but insists that it is usually possible to identify its dominant mode of compliance structure. In addition, he notes that in all organizations, the higher the level of participants, the more likely that normative compliance predominates; hence, the typology is to be applied by emphasizing the compliance modes that characterize lower level participants in organizations.[5]

Etzioni develops a large number of predictions based on the predominant

[5]To determine what types of lower level participants are to be considered within the boundaries of the organization, Etzioni argues that lower level participants should score high on at least one of the following dimensions: level of intensity, degree of subordination to organizational power, and level of performance obligations (see Etzioni, 1961: 17–20). Using these criteria, lower level participants such as students, inmates, soldiers, workers, and patients would be included within the boundary of their respective types of organizations, but customers and more casual client groups would be excluded.

Table 2–6.   Etzioni's Typology Based on Compliance

KINDS OF POWER	KINDS OF INVOLVEMENT		
	Alienative	Calculative	Moral
Coercive	1 (Coercive)	2	3
Remunerative	4	5 (Utilitarian)	6
Normative	7	8	9 (Normative)

compliance type of an organization. He expects compliance to relate to nature of goals served, kinds of organizational elites, modes of personnel recruitment, extent of peer cohesion, and the distribution of charisma throughout the organization. This typology together with its associated predictions has generated a sizable body of empirical work that Etzioni has reviewed and summarized in the second edition of his work (Etzioni, rev. 1975).

Strengths and weaknesses of the Blau-Scott and the Etzioni typologies can be used as a basis for generating some principles for constructing typologies. One principle of obvious importance is to

(1) Select a dimension or set of dimensions that will help to account for important aspects of organizational structures or functions.

Stated in this bald manner, the principle seems obvious. However, as we noted at the beginning of this chapter, there are many possible properties or dimensions along which organizations vary, and the burden of proof must be placed on the analyst to demonstrate that the proposed distinctions are worthy of attention. To be employed as the basis for a typology, the dimension should be shown to have an impact on—or be highly correlated with—other important aspects of the organization. Hall, Haas, and Johnson (1967a) take this principle quite literally. They conducted a test of the explanatory power of the Blau-Scott and the Etzioni typologies by gathering information on the structural properties of 75 varied organizations. Classifying all of the organizations according to the criteria provided by the two typologies, Hall and his colleagues assessed the degree to which each typology was associated with such variables as degree of complexity, formalization, goal specificity, types of activities, degree of interdependency among organizational units, emphasis placed on status and power, type of external relations, and measures of organizational change. The study results were rather disappointing: although each typology was associated with some differences among organizations in their structural characteristics, many important features of organizations revealed little or no association with either typology. (Hall, Haas, and Johnson, 1967 a: 137) This mode of testing a typology appears to us inappropriate. To show that a particular typology does not correlate strongly with a variety of general structural features is not of consequence unless the typology was constructed to generate such explanations.[6] Neither Blau-Scott nor Etzioni make such claims for their handiwork. Rather, both are rather explicit about what sets of issues, problems, or structural features may be expected to be responsive to —or to co-vary with—their categories. In particular, Etzioni has been very explicit about the expected correlates of his typology.

Perhaps the most important message of the first principle for constructing typologies is that the classification scheme should be "forward-looking": a

[6]For other criticisms of this study, see Weldon (1972).

good typology is not the end point for an analysis, but the starting point, and a critical test of a typology is the clarity and the interest of the predictions it generates.

A second principle to follow in constructing typologies is to

(2) Define clearly the dimension or dimensions around which the typology is to be constructed and specify how they are to be operationalized.

The Blau-Scott typology does not rate well on this criterion. Burns (1967), among others, has appropriately criticized our typology for assuming that it is easily possible to isolate an explicit, stable, and coherent group whose interests are given primacy by the organization. Although we illustrate how various organizations might be classified, we fail to spell out a set of rules for applying the typology to complex and multifaceted real-world organizations. Those who have attempted such applications (for example, Hall, Haas, and Johnson, 1967a) have complained that there exist many mixed or ambiguous types that resist easy classification. Moreover, the focus of the typology seems to shift back and forth between the questions, "Who does benefit?" and "Who should benefit?" both in the normative and expectational sense. Thus, both conceptual and measurement problems hamper the applicability of this typology. The Etzioni typology appears to fare somewhat better with respect to this principle. His two underlying dimensions are defined with reasonable clarity, and both have been operationalized in numerous studies. Although the problem of mixed types remains, the general clarity and operationality of the Etzioni appears satisfactory in comparison with other typologies formulated at a similar level of abstraction.

A third principle to follow in constructing typologies is that

(3) When two or more dimensions are utilized to create the property-space for the typology, the dimensions should be independent in a statistical sense.

The problem to which this principle is addressed is exemplified by Etzioni's typology. Etzioni argues that his schema rests on two dimensions, power and involvement. Conceptually, these dimensions appear to be independent, power being defined in terms of the predominant mode of sanctions employed, and involvement in terms of the intensity and direction of the lower participants' activities in the organization. The dimensions, however, are highly correlated empirically, largely because there is a clear reciprocal association between them: the particular sanctions employed create specific types of involvement, and at the same time, a given type of involvement necessitates the use of a specific type of sanctions. For example, coercive power generates alienation; and the control of alienated participants tends to require the use of coercive power. Thus, when empirically applied, the two dimensions tend to collapse into one. Once we know the dominant type of sanction employed little additional explanatory power is added by information on involvement. Hence, the nine logically possible categories shrink to three usable cells.[7]

Typologies can be more sound theoretically and more useful empirically if our three principles are adopted as guidelines. Even if followed, however, other, more general problems afflict even the best of these efforts. We will consider these problems after we briefly describe and comment on two empirically generated typologies.

Two Empirically Based Typologies

To illustrate a different approach to the construction of typologies, two additional efforts will be briefly described. The first was derived by the same team, Haas, Hall, and Johnson (1966), that conducted the empirical evaluation of the Blau-Scott and Etzioni typologies (see also Hall, 1972). Indeed, the same data set containing structural measures for 75 organizations used for that evaluation was employed in deriving the new typology. Data on 99 variables were assembled from each of these organizations and a statistical program used to group organizations according to the characteristics they held in common. The results were disappointing. According to the researchers themselves, although nine classes of organizations were created, many involved "seemingly strange combinations of organizations." In a number of cases "quite trivial" characteristics became the basis on which organizations were differentiated. In short, the effort did not result in a set of usable or even interpretable classes.

The second effort to be described was carried out by Pugh and his colleagues at the University of Aston (Pugh, Hickson, and Hinings, 1969). This team of researchers—the so-called Aston group—collected data on a large number of organizations in the Birmingham area in order to examine the interrelation of structural characteristics. (Some of the results of this work are discussed in chapter 11.) In the course of their work, the Aston group developed 64 scales to measure five structural variables regarded as primary: role specialization, standardization, formalization, centralization, and configuration (shape) of structure (see Pugh et al., 1963; and Pugh et al., 1968). Factor analytic techniques were used to determine the presence of underlying structural dimensions by examining the patterns of interrelations among the various scales and arranging them so that those showing the highest degree of convergence were combined together and appropriately relabeled. Four dimensions (underlying factors) were identified in this manner; and the first three of these were used in the construction of the typology. Data from 52 diverse work organizations were employed in this analysis.

---

[7]The Lefton-Rosengren typology provides a positive example of the third principle. As defined and measured, the lateral and longitudinal dimensions of clients served appear to be sufficiently independent to make their joint use helpful in differentiating among service organizations (see Lefton and Rosengren, 1966).

The three dimensions used in the typology are: (1) a dimension labeled *structuring of activities* that emphasizes role specialization, standardization, and formalization; (2) *concentration of authority*, a dimension emphasizing centralization; and (3) *line control of workflow*, a dimension that assesses the degree to which control over work is exercised by line personnel rather than impersonal procedures such as rules. Employing the three dimensions as a property-space for the typology provides a good spread of organizations since, consistent with the third principle for constructing typologies discussed in the previous section, the factors are (by design) not highly correlated with each other. Although a large number of logical possibilities are generated by this type of three-dimensional space (see diagram in Pugh, Hickson, and Hinings, 1969: 123), four major types with three subtypes are identified and labeled, as shown in table 2–7.

As the terminology employed to label the major types implies, the Aston group argues that their cross-sectional study may represent organizations caught at differing stages in a developmental process. They argue that as size increases, so does the structuring of activities. Second, as technology develops, work becomes increasingly subject to impersonal controls. By contrast, concentration of authority does not appear to represent a developmental sequence, but "a difference in kind"—and is primarily determined by whether an organization is or is not under the control of some external body (for example, a retail store in a chain, or a public service organization under the control of the central government).

Table 2–7　　Pugh, Hickson and Hining's Typology
Based on Empirically Derived Factors

ORGANIZATIONAL TYPES	DIMENSIONS (FACTORS)		
	Structuring of Activities	*Concentration of Authority*	*Impersonal Control of Workflow*
Full bureaucracy	High	High	High
Nascent full bureaucracy	Low	High	High
Workflow bureaucracy	High	Low	High
Nascent workflow bureaucracy	Medium	Low	High
Preworkflow bureaucracy	Low	Low	High
Personnel bureaucracy	Low	High	Low
Implicitly structured organizations	Low	Low	Low

Such empirically based typologies are relatively recent innovations and, to this point, have inspired few imitators. However, McKelvey has argued that they are the wave of the future. Proclaiming that the deductive typologies, such as Blau-Scott and Etzioni, "are useless for empirical research," McKelvey (1975: 523–24) insists that the inductive typologies, represented by the efforts of Hall, Haas, and Johnson and the Aston group, constitute "major turning points in the development of organization science." These efforts receive high praise not for what they accomplished but for what they set out to do. McKelvey argues that future typological efforts will be much more productive if researchers give more attention to ensuring that the original population of organizations surveyed is broadly representative of all organizations, that no stratification variables are employed in selecting the sample so that all types of organizations have an equal chance to be included, that the broadest possible group of organizational characteristics be included, and so on. In short, any constraints imposed on the selection of organizations or on the selection of concepts will influence the results and may bias the conclusions drawn from them. It is hard to quarrel with McKelvey's prescriptions for improving the quality of the organizational samples drawn. On the other hand, we are not in accord with his conclusion that inductive or empirically based typologies are likely to produce significant knowledge, at least in the foreseeable future. In our view, organizations are too complex and multifaceted, and too loose in their structural interconnections, to yield readily to a purely empiricist strategy. We will expand on these concerns in the final section of this chapter.

Problems with Typologies

Typologies appear to offer the promise of moving us toward more complex multivariant analyses of organizations. Replacing the simple assumption that all organizations are alike, typologies support the view that organizations vary in important ways—ways that influence their internal structure and functioning. Typologies assert, in effect, that processes and relationships may differ because they occur within differing contexts. This argument can be more easily understood if it is diagrammed:

ORGANIZATIONAL TYPE

A	B
$x\text{---}y$	$x\text{---}y$

The diagram suggests that the relation between variable x and variable y may differ depending on whether the process occurs within a Type A or a Type B organization. For example, the relation between cohesiveness of workers (x) and productivity (y) may vary depending on whether the relations are being observed in a coercive (Type A) or in a normative (Type B) organization. This formulation represents a useful advance by emphasizing that the relation between these variables may be influenced by "the conditions under which" the variables are observed.

However, most typologies do not make clear the nature of the causal processes that are presumed to operate. The relation between x and y could itself take various forms and be influenced by type of organization in a number of ways, which can be diagrammed as follows:

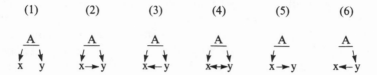

Diagrams 1 through 6 remind us that a number of different arguments are concealed within the assertion that organizational type influences relationships. Diagram 1 suggests that the organizational context has a direct influence on both variables x and y, but there may not be a direct relation between these variables. Diagrams 2 through 4 suggest that the organizational context influences both x and y, but that the direction of the association between these two variables can be one way in either direction or be reciprocal. Diagrams 5 and 6 suggest that the organizational context may directly affect only one of the two variables, which in turn influences the other. Thus, although typologies do move us closer to a multivariate mode of analysis, they seldom specify *how* the organizational context is thought to affect the relationships of interest. But let us not be overcritical of typologies. Since analysts not using typologies often fail to specify precisely the nature of their causal arguments, typologies share in this problem but do not hold a monopoly.

A second, related danger is more clearly associated specifically with the use of typologies. Even when the analyst spells out the nature of the causal arguments linking organizational type to associated variables, errors may result because the typology emphasizes the wrong contextual variable. In terms of the illustration we are using, it may be that compliance type—whether the organization's power structure is predominantly coercive or normative—does not directly influence either worker cohesiveness or productivity. Rather, the power structure may affect some intervening variable, z, for example, the mode of leadership exercised, and it is this factor that directly affects worker cohesiveness or productivity or both. (One version of this situation appears in diagram 7.)

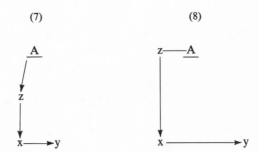

Worse, it may be that the true relation is between mode of leadership and worker cohesiveness, and because leadership mode is associated with type of power, we mistakenly attribute the effect to power (see diagram 8). In this case, the relation between type of power and worker cohesiveness is spurious—the relation would disappear if we took into account the effect of leadership style.

Unfortunately, typologies are *very* likely to create situations of this sort because they tend to select for criterion variables those dimensions that are known to be associated with many other variables. Indeed, as indicated by our first principle for constructing typologies, investigators are expected to select variables that can "clearly be shown to have an impact on—be highly correlated with—other important aspects of the organization." The more successful the analyst is in fulfilling this criterion, the more difficulty we will have in attempting to distinguish among the effects of the multiple, highly correlated, variables. Rather than supporting multivariant causal analysis, the creation of typologies tends to hamper efforts to develop and test causal arguments.

SPECIAL PROBLEMS IN CONSTRUCTING TYPOLOGIES OF ORGANIZATIONS

While some insight into our subject area has been gained through the use of typologies, on balance we would have to conclude that the typologies developed by organizational researchers up to the present are not nearly as impressive or as predictive as those developed in other scientific fields, such as chemistry or biology. The explanation for this difference may well lie partly in the intelligence and creativity of the investigators recruited into these fields; but we think it more likely that it is caused by the nature of the subject matter. We believe that one major factor frustrating attempts to classify organizations is that organizations are *open systems*—more open than the systems studied by chemists and biologists. The more open a system, as will be discussed in chapter 5, the harder it is to distinguish between the system and its environment, the looser the connections among structural elements, and the more autonomous the behavior of the elements—individuals, groups, departments—comprising the system. These characteristics imply, in turn, that knowledge of the state of one element—any element—will provide less predictive power concerning the characteristics or behavior of other elements than would be the case in a less open, more tightly coupled, system.

What to do? Many investigators have given up, turning away from the construction of typologies to employ multivariant techniques that allow the stimultaneous examination of several variables but assume that any and all combinations of them may occur. A new generation of researchers, however, is busy attempting to breathe new life into the typological enterprise. The most interesting new work is that stimulated by the emergence of the natural selection or population ecology approach, recently revitalized and applied to organizations by Hannan and Freeman (1977) and by Aldrich (1979). This approach is described in more detail in later chapters (see chapters 5 and 9), but in brief, it attempts to explain the diversity of organizational forms by suggesting that environments differentially select organizations for survival on the basis of the fit between organizational structure and environmental requirements. The emergence of this approach has important implications for typologies because "a proper application of the natural selection model requires a system of classification and categorization of organizational forms analogous to species in biology" (Aldrich and Pfeffer, 1976: 82). That is, if the population ecologists are going to test arguments to the effect that environments determine what forms will be viable in certain environments, then they must develop a clear basis for distinguishing among organizational forms (species). Hannan and Freeman (1977: 935) note that biologic species are defined in terms of genetic structure; and they propose that the appropriate analogue for organizations may be the "blueprint for organizational action, for transforming inputs into outputs." In a related discussion, McKelvey (1978: 1431) argues that a possible species concept for organizations lies in their core technology, including (a) "the technologies organizations use in the unit operations of their primary workplaces"; and (b) "the management technologies directly associated with the management of the primary workplace."

McKelvey has begun the development of such a typology, and a portion of his schema is reproduced here in table 2–8 (selected portion of table 2 in McKelvey, 1978: 1434).

His approach to the construction of typologies is notable in several respects. First, it combines elements and dictinctions from previous typologies: the discerning reader will note echoes of the work of Etzioni, Woodward, Perrow and Thompson. McKelvey argues that such deductive approaches—which he apparently has come to believe have some utility—can be combined with empiricist efforts to collect as many measures as possible on representative samples of organizations. Second, the typology is based on an evolutionary approach that both emphasizes the origins of different organizational forms and presumes that there is a general movement to "higher order" forms. Third, and most important for present purposes, the approach acknowledges the open

Table 2–8. McKelvey's Typology Based on Evolutionary Forms

TIME PERIOD	ERA	DOMINANT ENVIRONMENTAL FEATURE	TECHNICAL INNOVATION	ORGANIZATIONAL FORM
1940–1970	R&D Product-oriented organization	Technical change Product innovation and diversity	Organic form Grid and matrix forms	Organics Matrices
1900–1940	Assembly line	Workplace interdependencies	Sequential coordination	Sequentials
1700–1900	Steam engine	Large workplaces, many operations	Workplace coordination	Factories
1500–1700	Textile revolution	Combining many family units into cottage industry	Coordination of many units not under same roof	Textiles
2100–1750 B.C.	Pre-Babylonian dynasties	Dynastic weaknesses	Mediating interdependency; utilitarian legitimacy	Commercials
2900–2100 B.C.	Earliest dynasties in Mesopotamia	Threat of intercity warfare	Mediating interdependency; coercive legitimacy	Palaces

system character of organizations by constructing types that take into account the interrelations of organizations with their environments. Environmental diversity is seen as the source of organizational variety, and the typology is constructed to make this nexus clear.

Population ecologists, and more generally, open systems theorists, are also attempting to recognize that organizations are loosely coupled systems. Loose coupling of organizational elements refers to absence of tight and rigid connections among the several components of organizations and assumes that many of these elements are capable of autonomous action. (See Weick, 1976) Again, we will examine this aspect of organizations in more detail in later chapters (see chapters 5 and 11), restricting attention here to its impact on the construction of typologies. There are no easy solutions to the problems posed by loose coupling, but one strong implication is apparent: analysts must be very careful and self-conscious in determining the boundaries of the "organization" to be examined. In some cases the relevant boundaries of the study unit may coincide with only a subunit of the organization as officially defined, in other cases the appropriate study unit may encompass several such organizations. Further, during their lifetimes, organizations may change their characteristics in such a fundamental manner that they must be regarded as having shifted from one structural type to another. Their flexibility in this respect far exceeds that of biological organisms. The question of organizational boundaries—the issue of deciding what constitutes the appropriate unit of analysis—is receiving more attention from organizational researchers (see Aldrich, 1979; Freeman, 1978; Warriner, 1979).

If we are to determine how organizations differ from one another in their forms and functions, it is first necessary to understand what we mean by the concept *organization* including how we are to bound these systems. Current efforts to build better typologies thus confront us with some as yet unresolved fundamental issues.

Summary

Organizational researchers have generated a great many typologies of organizations, and there is no end in sight. Efforts to construct typologies may be subdivided into theoretical or deductive, and empiricist or inductive approaches. In the former, analysts attempt to select some organizational dimension or dimensions regarded as significant on theoretical grounds; organizations varying by this criterion are expected to reveal other significant differences in form or function. Among the most popular bases for typing organizations are authority and power differences, distinctions among goals, and varying modes of technology. Empiricist approaches make no a priori assumptions about significant variables. Instead, large amounts of data are collected from samples of organizations, and analysis seeks to determine whether there are highly intercorrelated clusters of variables. To the present time, neither deductive nor inductive efforts have produced highly convincing results.

Three rules intended to improve the development of deductive typologies are proposed: (1) select a dimension or set of dimensions that will help to account for important aspects of organizational structures or functions; (2) define clearly the dimensions around which the typology is to be constructured and specify how they are to be operationalized; and (3) when two or more dimensions are utilized to create the property-space for the typology, the dimensions should be independent in a statistical sense. Although these rules may seem quite straightforward, they are often violated.

Typologies are frequently praised as promoting multivariant analyses of organizations, but they can act to obscure causal connections. The very strength of a good typology—the clustering together of several significant organizational features—becomes a hindrance to the testing of specific causal arguments concerning variables.

Organizational typologies are relatively weak and nonpredictive (in comparison with, for example, biological schema) because by their nature social organizations are open systems—highly permeated by and interdependent with their environments and comprised of loosely linked and semiautonomous component systems. Some of the most recent efforts by organization theorists attempt to take these special characteristics into account by building typologies that recognize the environment-organization nexus and by constructing models of organizations that allow for possible separation of basic components and for changes over time in their fundamental forms and functions.

Part Two

THREE
PERSPECTIVES
ON
ORGANIZATIONS

In the course of this century, three more or less distinct perspectives have been employed in the study of organizational structure. The term *perspective* is used advisedly since we will be dealing in each case not with a single, unified model of organizational structure but rather with a number of varying approaches that bear a strong family resemblance. Thus, our concern will be with three types of approaches or three schools of thought, the notion of perspective serving as a conceptual umbrella under which we may gather the related views. To add further to the complexity, the three perspectives are partially conflicting, partially overlapping, and partially complementary to one another.

An understanding of these perspectives is valuable for several reasons. It is very difficult to comprehend or to fully utilize the large literature on organizations without knowledge of the differing perspectives underlying this work. Why does one analyst concentrate on one type of problem while another completely ignores it? Why do some investigators emphasize historical materials while others deal exclusively with contemporary data? These are the sorts of questions we can begin to answer by examining the perspectives employed. Also, we should expect to receive help not only in making sense out of past studies, but in examining the current efforts of organizational analysts. For although these perspectives emerged at different times, later perspectives have not succeeded in supplanting earlier ones: the three perspectives continue to coexist and to claim their share of advocates.

Although we devote some effort to describing the history of each perspective, the perspectives are not primarily of historical interest. They are analytical models intended to guide—and to interpret—empirical research. They have changed over time as one school has replaced another within each of the traditions, but to a surprising extent, the general outlines of the three perspectives have remained reasonably clear.

It is true, as we shall see, that various investigators have attempted to combine the perspectives to create a unified approach to the study of organizational structure. While such efforts are praiseworthy, they have not to this date been completely successful; indeed, perhaps they never will be. Let us be clear on this point. We would not defend the sanctity of any particular perspective or set of perspectives for the study of organizations. However, given the complexity of the phenomenon involved, it may be appropriate to continue to use several competing perspectives to guide our analysis. Just as there is a conflict and a consensus model for analyzing the integration of societies—and we learn something (different) by employing each—so relevant aspects of organization structure that are ignored or obscured by one perspective may be illuminated by another. The three perspectives to be considered are:

1. The *rational system* perspective (including the classical, the traditional, the scientific management, and the Weberian approaches)
2. The *natural system* perspective (including the human relations and the institutional approaches)
3. The *open systems* perspective (including the general systems, systems design, and environmental approaches)

The perspectives will be considered in the order of their emergence. For each perspective we first discuss the basic model that forms its core. Then we consider three or four representative theorists or schools within each tradition. Each chapter evaluates and compares the perspectives as well.

Chapter 6 examines several attempts to combine the three perspectives. Each is instructive, and we learn that many of the most important recent theoretical developments can be viewed as new combinations of the basic perspectives. We employ the insights associated with each of the three perspectives and their combinations in part 3 as we attempt to account for the emergence of organizations, their structural characteristics, and their adaptation to the environment.

chapter 3

Organizations
as
Rational Systems

A well-designed machine is an instance of total organization, that is, a series of interrelated means contrived to achieve a single end. The machine consists always of particular parts that have no meaning and no function separate from the organized entity to which they contribute. A machine consists of a coherent bringing together of all parts toward the highest possible efficiency of the functioning whole, or interrelationships marshalled wholly toward a given result. In the ideal machine, there can be no extraneous part, no extraneous movement; all is set, part for part, motion for motion, toward the functioning of the whole. The machine is, then, a perfect instance of total rationalization of a field of action and of total organization. This is perhaps even more quickly evident in that larger machine, the assembly line.

JOHN WILLIAM WARD (1964)

From the rational system perspective, organizations are instruments designed to attain specified goals. How blunt or fine an instrument they are depends on many factors that are summarized by the concept of *rationality* of structure. The term *rationality* in this context is used in the narrow sense of "technical" or "functional" rationality (Mannheim, 1950tr.: 53) and refers to the extent to which a series of actions is organized in such a way as to lead to predetermined goals with maximum efficiency. Thus, rationality refers not to the selection of goals but to their implementation. Indeed, it is perfectly possible to pursue irrational or foolish goals by rational means. Captain Ahab in Melville's classic *Moby Dick* chases the white whale across the seven seas musing: "all my means are sane, my motive and my object mad." Nazi Germany provides a more terrible, nonfiction example. Adolf Hitler's insane objective of eradicating Europe's Jewish population was efficiently pursued by hosts of functionaries who, like Adolph Eichmann, took the goal as given and worked faithfully to rationally bring it about. (Arendt, 1963) It is essential to keep in mind the restricted definition of "rationality" used within the rational system perspective.

The Essential Elements

From the standpoint of the rational system perspective, the behavior of organizations is viewed as actions performed by purposeful and coordinated agents. The language employed connotes this image of rational calculation: such terms as *information, efficiency, optimization, implementation,* and *design* occur frequently. But another somewhat different set of terms also occurs within this perspective; it indicates the cognitive limitations of the individual decision maker and the effects of the organizational context in which rational choices are made. These terms—*constraints, authority, rules, directives, jurisdiction, performance programs, coordination*—imply that the rationality of behavior within organizations takes place within (some analysts would argue, because of) clearly specified limits.

It is no accident that the key features of organizations emphasized by rational system theorists are the very characteristics that have been noted to distinguish organizations from other types of collectivities. Rational system theorists stress goal specificity and formalization because each of these elements makes an important contribution to the rationality of organizational action.

GOAL SPECIFICITY

Goals are conceptions of desired ends. These conceptions vary in terms of the precision and specificity with which the criteria of desirability are formulated. Specific goals provide unambiguous criteria for selecting among alternative activities. As viewed by economists or by decision theorists, goals are translated into a set of preference or utility functions that represent the value of alternative sets of consequences. Without clear preference orderings among alternatives, rational assessment and choice are not possible.

Specific goals not only supply criteria for choosing among alternative activities; they guide decisions about how the organization structure itself is to be designed. They specify what tasks are to be performed, what kinds of personnel are to be hired, how resources are to be allocated among participants. The more general or diffuse the goals, the more difficult it is to design a structure to pursue them.

It is important to note that some organizations espouse quite vague and general goals, but in their actual daily operation are guided by relatively specific goals that do provide criteria for choosing among alternative activities and for the design of the organization structure itself. Consider the case of education. Although both educators and laypeople will argue endlessly about the true function of education and about the virtues of liberal arts versus more practical types of programs, within a given school there will be considerable agreement on such matters as what disciplines should be represented on the faculty, what courses will count toward graduation, and how many units are required for a student to graduate. With agreement on such matters as these, administrators can safely allow the faculty occasionally to debate the ultimate aims of education. Similarly, although physicians cannot agree on abstract definitions of "health" or "illness," they do successfully organize their work around such proximate outcomes as relieving pain and prolonging life.

Vague goals do not provide a solid basis for formal organizations. Either the goals become more specific and limited over time, as often happens, or the structures developed are likely to be unstable and amorphous. Collective movements such as radical political sects or protest groups may temporarily succeed in mobilizing resources and participants around vague concepts such as liberation or ecology. Indeed, their generality may broaden their appeal and enlist the support of diverse groups. But unless more specific and delimited goals emerge, we would not expect such movements to give rise to formal organizations.

The most precise description of the manner in which specific goals support rational behavior in organizations is that developed by Herbert Simon whose classic, *Administrative Behavior,* first appeared in 1945. His ideas on this subject will be summarized later in this chapter as an example of one of the major contributions to the rational system perspective.

FORMALIZATION

All rational system theorists assume the existence and presume the importance of a formalized structure, but few make explicit the contributions that formalization makes to rationality of behavior in organizations. Let us attempt to do so.

Recall that a structure is formalized to the extent that the rules governing behavior are precisely and explicitly formulated and to the extent that roles and role relations are prescribed independently of the personal attributes of individuals occupying positions in the structure. Formalization may be viewed as an attempt to make behavior more predictable by standardizing and regulating it. This, in turn, permits "stable expectations to be formed by each member of the group as to the behavior of the other members under specified conditions. Such stable expectations are an essential precondition to a rational consideration of the consequences of action in a social group" (Simon, 1957: 100).

Formalization may also be viewed as an attempt to make more explicit and visible the structure of relationships among a set of roles and the principles that govern behavior in the system. It becomes possible to diagram the organization's structure or workflow and then consciously to study and manipulate it —to design and redesign the division of responsibilities, the flow of information or materials, or the reporting relations among participants. As Gouldner notes: "Fundamentally, the rational model implies a 'mechanical' model, in that it views the organization as a structure of manipulable parts, each of which is separately modifiable with a view to enhancing the efficiency of the whole. Individual organizational elements are seen as subject to successful and planned modification, enactable by deliberate decision" (1959: 405). Thus, in a fundamental sense, the organizational structure is viewed as a means, as an instrument, which can be modified as necessary to improve performance. Organizational designers and managers draw and redraw the organizational chart; coaches attempt to improve performance by diagramming plays and giving chalk talks; and consultants are employed to recommend better arrangements for achieving business goals. In recent years, highly technical managerial systems, such as management by objectives (MBO), planning, programming, and budgeting (PPBS), performance evaluation and review techniques (PERT)—all designed to provide greater visibility and, hence, greater accountability for the critical workflows—have been developed and widely adopted to facilitate rational decision making within complex organizational systems. (See Haberstroh, 1965; Johnson, Kast, and Rosenzweig, 1967; Odione, 1965)

Formalization can contribute to rationality in other, less obvious ways. In addition to making behavior more available for conscious design, the structuring of expectations prior to interaction carries with it another distinct advantage. Laboratory research by Bales (1953) documents the strains and tensions generated when a status structure begins to emerge among individuals who entered the situation as presumed status-equals. These status battles and their associated interpersonal tensions are reduced by the pre-structuring of differentiated role expectations in which an individual is assigned a role prior to his or her participation. Thus, in an experimental study, Carter and his colleagues (1953) found that group leaders who had been appointed to their position by the experimenter spent less time attempting to assert their power and defend their position and encountered less resistance to their leadership efforts than leaders who emerged on their own. (See also Verba, 1961: 161–72)

Formalization also serves to objectify the structure—to make the definitions of roles and relationships appear to be both objective and external to the participating actors. These qualities contribute substantially to the efficacy of these systems in controlling behavior. A series of experiments conducted by Zucker (1977) demonstrates this effect. Subjects placed in an ambiguous situation were much more likely to accept influence from another when that person was defined as holding a specified organizational position (not, by the way, a position of authority but simply a named office) than when the person was described simply as "another person."

The social cement that binds and regulates activities and interactions in informal groups is the sociometric structure—the patterning of affective ties among participants. The creation of a formal structure constitutes an important functional alternative to the sociometric structure. With formalization, the smooth functioning of the organization is to some degree made independent of the feelings—negative or positive—that particular members have for one another. As Merton notes: "formality facilitates the interaction of the occupants of offices despite their (possibly hostile) private attitudes toward one another" (1975: 195). Indeed, many organizations discourage the development of positive sentiments among their members for fear that such emotional ties will undermine discipline and judgment and will interfere with attempts to deploy participants rationally.

Formalization makes allowances for the finitude of man. The process of succession—the movement of individuals into and out of offices—can be routinized and regularized so that one appropriately trained person can replace another with minimal disturbance to the functioning of the organization. In this sense, organizations can—although few actually do—achieve a kind of immortality. The Roman Catholic church may be cited as a particularly successful example.

Formalized structures are thus rendered independent of the participation of any particular individual; a related consequence is that it becomes less essential to recruit unusually gifted individuals for the key positions. The power and influence of leaders can be determined in part by the definition of their offices and not made a function of their personal qualities—their charisma. Referring to political structures, MacIver notes: "The man who commands may be no wiser, no abler, may be, in some sense no better than the average of his fellow; sometimes, by any intrinsic standard, he is inferior to them. Here is the magic of government" (1947: 13). More generally, here is the magic of formalization. To explain more clearly the alchemy of this process, Wolin draws an analogy between the formalization of structure and scientific method: "Method, like organization, is the salvation of puny men, the compensatory device for individual foibles, the gadget which allows mediocrity to transcend its limitations. . . . organization, by simplifying and routinizing procedures, eliminates the need for surpassing talent. It is predicated on 'average human beings' " (1960: 383). In the highly formalized organization, the innovating entrepreneur is supplanted by a corps of administrators and technical specialists. Leadership, even innovation, is routinized and regularized by being incorporated into the formal structure. (See Schumpeter, 1947; Galbraith, 1967)

We have reviewed some of the major contributions that formalization of structure can make to rational functioning of the organization. We must note here, however, that we have discussed only the *form* of a formalized structure; nothing has been said about its *content.* That is, we have stated that in a formalized structure positions are specified, roles are defined, and role relationships are prescribed independent of the personal attributes of participants, and we have indicated certain advantages that stem from such arrangements. But we have not concerned ourselves with the content of these specifications, definitions, and prescriptions. The content of the formal structure has also been of great concern to certain rational system theorists, as we will see when we discuss their contributions in the next section.

Selected Schools

The preceding discussion represents an effort to distill the central elements characterizing the rational system perspective. This perspective does not reflect a unitary position but includes a set of somewhat varied, historically distinct approaches. Before briefly characterizing some of these major schools, we must first acknowledge that only one of them—that associated with Simon's work —explicitly emphasizes goal specificity. The rest assume its presence. And few concern themselves with formalization per se but consider specific ways in which organizations can or should be designed to attain maximum effectiveness. That is, most of the advocates of the rational system position assume the importance of formal structure and concern themselves with specifying the nature or content of that structure. Four schools will be briefly described: Taylor's scientific management; attempts by Fayol and others to formulate administrative principles; Weber's theory of bureaucracy; and Simon's discussion of administrative behavior.

SCIENTIFIC MANAGEMENT

The scientific management approach received its primary impetus from the work of Frederick W. Taylor (1911) in the late nineteenth and early twentieth centuries but was carried forward by the contributions of others such as Frank and Lillian Gilbreth, Henry Gantt, and Charles Bedeaux. Taylor and his followers insisted that it was possible to scientifically analyze tasks performed by individual workers in order to discover those procedures that would produce the maximum output with the minimum input of energies and resources. Efforts were concentrated on analyzing individual tasks, but attempts to rationalize labor at the level of the individual worker inevitably led to changes in the entire structure of work arrangements. Ward (1964) describes the sequence of changes that resulted from Taylor's efforts to improve the efficiency of performing such menial tasks as shoveling coal and iron ore in a steel mill:

> First, a variety of kinds of shovels had to be designed to handle different kinds of materials. That also meant building shovel rooms in the various parts of the yard, so that a gang would have the proper tools at hand. To eliminate the waste motion of wandering about so large a yard, it meant, as Taylor said, "organizing and planning work at least a day in advance," so that when men checked in, they would be at that day's work. This meant, Taylor reported, building a labor office for a planning staff—a bureaucracy, as we would say. Large maps of the yard were then necessary to show at a glance the location of different kinds of work and the location of men. Furthermore, the installation of a telephone network was essential for more effective interior communication. Once the yard was mapped so that one could see at a glance the relationships in time and sequence between different jobs, it led, naturally enough, to the reorganization of the yard itself, so that materials could be delivered or dumped in a more logical sequence.
>
> One can see readily enough what happened. Taylor's attempt to make the crudest physical act of labor efficient led inexorably to a further organization of every aspect of the production process. (Ward, 1964: 64–65)

It was not only, or even primarily, the lot of workers that was to be altered by the introduction of scientific management: the role of management was also to be transformed. Taylor (1947) aspired to replace the arbitrary and capricious activities of managers with analytical, scientific procedures:

> Under scientific management arbitrary power, arbitrary dictation, ceases; and every single subject, large and small, becomes the question for scientific investigation, for reduction to law. . . .
>
> The man at the head of the business under scientific management is governed by rules and laws which have been developed through hundreds of experiments just as much as the workman is, and the standards which have been developed are equitable. (Taylor, 1947: 211, 189)

The activities of both managers and workers were to be rationalized; both were equally subject to the regimen of science.

Taylor believed that the adoption of scientific management principles by industrial concerns would usher in a new era of industrial peace. The interests of labor and management would be rendered compatible. Workers would be scientifically selected to perform those tasks for which they were best suited. Scientifically determined procedures would allow them to work at peak efficiency in return for which they would receive top wages. "Once work was scientifically plotted, Taylor felt, there could be no disputes about how hard one should work or the pay one should receive for labor. 'As reasonably might we insist on bargaining about the time and place of the rising and setting sun,' he once said" (Bell, 1960: 228). Managers would cooperate with workers in devising appropriate work arrangements and pay scales and would enjoy the fruits of maximum profits.

The underlying spirit of Taylor's approach—an amalgam of the Protestant ethic, social Darwinism, and a view of man as motivated exclusively by economic incentives—found widespread acceptance among American managers at the turn of the century. However, many were disquieted by Taylor's vision of their own new role: "After all, Taylor had questioned their good judgment and superior ability which had been the subject of public celebration for many years. Hence, many employers regarded his methods as an unwarranted interference with managerial prerogatives" (Bendix, 1956: 280). Workers for their part resisted time study procedures and attempts to standardize every aspect of their performance and rejected incentive systems requiring them to perform continuously at a peak level of efficiency. Nevertheless scientific management has had a profound and lasting effect on industrial practice and on theoretical conceptions of work organization.[1]

SEARCH FOR ADMINISTRATIVE PRINCIPLES

A second approach, developing concurrently with scientific management, emphasized management functions and attempted to generate broad administrative principles that would serve as guidelines for the rationalization of organizational activities. Whereas Taylor and his disciples proposed to rationalize the organization from the "bottom up"—changes in the performance of individual tasks affecting the larger structure of work relations—the administrative management theorists worked to rationalize the organization from the "top down." Henri Fayol, a French industrialist writing in the early part of this century, was probably the earliest exponent of this approach, but his ideas did not become widely available in this country until 1949 when his major

[1]Perhaps the most useful overview of Taylor's conception is contained in his testimony before the Special House Committee to Investigate the Taylor and Other Systems of Shop Management in 1912. This testimony is reprinted in Taylor (1947). Summaries of and commentaries on his contribution will be found in Bell (1960: 222–37), Bendix (1956: 274–81), and Mouzelis (1968: 78–87). A severe critique of Taylor's work from a Marxist perspective is provided by Braverman (1974: 85–138).

work was translated. Influential participants in this movement in the United States included two General Motors executives, Mooney and Reiley (1939), whose treatise on management principles gained a wide following, and Gulick and Urwick, who in 1937 collaborated to edit the volume *Papers on the Science of Administration.*

The various contributors to this perspective did not reach agreement as to the number of principles required or the precise formulation of many specific principles, but there was considerable consensus on the importance of two types of activities: coordination and specialization (Massie, 1965; Tausky, 1970). The major principles developed to guide coordination activities include: the scalar principle, which emphasizes the hierarchical organizational form in which all participants are linked into a single pyramidal structure of control relations; the unity of command principle, specifying that no organizational participants should receive orders from more than one superior; the span of control principle, which emphasizes that no superior should have more subordinates than can be effectively overseen (theorists were unable to agree on the precise number of subordinates who could be supervised); and the exception principle, which recommends that all routine matters should be handled by subordinates and that the superior should be free to deal with exceptional situations to which existing rules are inapplicable. Specialization issues include decisions both about how various activities are to be distributed among organizational positions and about how such positions can most effectively be grouped into work units or departments. Among the principles espoused to guide these types of decisions is the departmentalization principle, which maintains that activities should be grouped so as to combine homogeneous or related activities within the same organizational unit. Homogeneity might be based on similarity of purpose (activities contributing to the same subgoal, for example, marketing), process (activities requiring similar operations, for example, typing), clientele (activities performed on the same set of recipients, for example, a medical team organized around the care of a specific group of patients), or place (for example, services provided to individuals in a given regional territory). Also proposed is the line-staff principle, by which all activities directly concerned with achieving organizational goals are designated as line functions, to be distinguished from staff activities, which primarily provide advice, service, or support. Staff units are to be segregated from the scalar organization of power and responsible and subordinate to appropriate line units.

Note the heavy emphasis on formalization implicit in these principles. Careful specification of work activities and concern for their grouping and coordination is the hallmark of the formalized structure. Mooney (1937) makes explicit this call for formalization by distinguishing between jobs (positions) and the man on the job:

In every organization there is a collective job to be done, consisting always of the sum of many individual jobs, and the task of administration, operating through management, is the co-ordination of all the human effort necessary to this end. Such co-ordination, however, always presupposes the jobs to be co-ordinated. The job as such is therefore antecedent to the man on the job, and the sound co-ordination of these jobs, considered simply as jobs, must be the first and necessary condition in the effective co-ordination of the human factor. (Mooney, 1937: 92)

The more astute administrative theorists recognized that their managerial principles furnished at best only broad guidelines for decision making. Thus, Fayol (1949 tr.) reminds practitioners:

The soundness and good working order of the body corporate depends on a certain number of conditions termed indiscriminately principles, laws, rules. For preference I shall adopt the term principles whilst dissociating it from any suggestion of rigidity, for there is nothing rigid or absolute in management affairs, it is all a question of proportion. Seldom do we have to apply the same principle twice in identical conditions; allowance must be made for different changing circumstances. (Fayol, 1949 tr.: 19)

And Gulick (Gulick and Urwick, 1937) cautions:

Students of administration have long sought a single principle of effective departmentalization just as alchemists sought the philosopher's stone. But they have sought in vain. There is apparently no one most effective system of departmentalism. (Gulick and Urwick, 1937: 31)

In spite of such disclaimers the managerial principles enunciated by the administrative theorists came under increasing attack. Three types of criticisms have been made: (1) that the principles are mere truisms or common-sense pronouncements; (2) that the principles are based on questionable premises; and (3) that the principles occur in pairs or clusters of contradictory statements with little guidance for application to a given situation. (See Massie, 1965: 406) With respect to the first type of criticism, it is quite correct that many of the proposed administrative principles are primarily definitional in character, outlining the characteristics of a hierarchically structured formal organization, while others are sufficiently vague and imprecise as to be of little help to practitioners or researchers. In regard to the second, Massie (1965: 405) has provided a lengthy listing of questionable premises, including the assumption that individuals are motivated primarily by economic interest, that they prefer the security of a definite assignment to the freedom of discretionary activity, that they prefer not to work and so must be constrained to do so, and that managers are capable of predicting work needs in advance and establishing effective arrangements for work and its coordination. The problem is not that these assumptions are inevitably false, but that they are not made explicit enough to serve as specifications for the application of the principles. The third type of criticism has been given greatest currency by Simon, whose influential text on administration commenced with "an indictment of much current writing about administrative matters" (1957: 36). Simon, examining one after another principle, concluded variously that they involved inconsistencies, lack of specification, or "a deceptive simplicity—a simplicity that conceals fundamental ambiguities" (1957: 21).

Without gainsaying any of these criticisms, we can admire what the administrative theorists attempted to do. They were pioneers in identifying the fundamental features of formal organizational structure, audaciously clinging to the view that all organizations contain certain common structural characteristics. With the improved vision of hindsight, it is now apparent that their search was confounded not so much by their inadequate theory of motivation or by the prescriptive cast of their propositions as by their failure to develop conditional generalizations—statements that specify the limits of their applicability to particular situations or types of organizations.[2] (This is the major insight that underlies the "contingency theory" of organizations, described in chapter 5.)

WEBER'S THEORY OF BUREAUCRACY

Contemporaneous with and yet independent of the scientific management school and those who attempted to formulate administrative principles was the work of Max Weber, the influential German sociologist writing at the turn of the century. Weber's analysis of administrative structures was only a limited aspect of his much larger interest in accounting for the unique features of Western civilization. (See Bendix, 1960) In his view, what was distinctive was the growth of rationality in the West, and his active mind roamed across legal, religious, political, and economic systems, as well as administrative structures, as he searched for materials to test and extend his notions by comparing and contrasting differing cultures and historical periods. Weber's analysis of administrative systems can be fully appreciated only if it is seen in this larger context, since his listing of the structural characteristics of bureaucracy was generated in an attempt to differentiate this more rational form from earlier traditional forms—most notably patrimonial systems (Delany, 1963). The simplest way to visualize a *patrimonial* system is as a household writ large: an estate or production organization governed by a ruler-owner who relies for

[2]Massie (1965) provides a careful description and sympathetic interpretation of the contributions of the administrative theorists. As already noted, Simon (1957: 20–44) develops the most trenchant criticisms.

assistance on a variety of dependents, ranging from slaves to sons, in managing the enterprise.

As noted in our introductory comments on the concept of bureaucracy in chapter 1, Weber viewed bureaucracy as a special form of administration that was fully developed only in "the modern state" and in "the most advanced institutions of capitalism" (1946: tr.: 196). And, as described in chapter 2 in connection with the presentation of Weber's typology of authority systems, he believed that, during the last few centuries, rational bureaucratic forms have been supplanting traditional administrative systems. What did Weber identify as the distinctive characteristics of bureaucracy? In many presentations of his work, Weber's discussion appears as a simple list of administrative characteristics such as the following:

Bureaucratic organizations are characterized by:

- A fixed division of labor among participants
- A hierarchy of offices
- A set of general rules which govern performance
- A separation of personal from official property and rights
- Selection of personnel on the basis of technical qualifications
- Employment viewed as a career by participants

However, his contribution can be better appreciated if these bureaucratic elements are described in relation to the traditional features they supplanted. Thus, according to Weber (1946 tr.: 196–204; 1947 tr.: 329–36), bureaucratic systems are distinguished from traditional administrative forms by the following features:

1. Jurisdictional areas are clearly specified: the regular activities required of personnel are distributed in a fixed way as official duties (in contrast to the patrimonial arrangement in which the division of labor is not firm or regular but depends on assignments made by the leader which can be changed at any time).

2. The organization of offices follows the principle of hierarchy: each lower office is controlled and supervised by a higher one. However, the scope of authority of superiors over subordinates is circumscribed, and lower offices enjoy a right of appeal (in contrast to the patrimonial form where authority relations are more diffuse, being based on personal loyalty, and are not ordered into clear hierarchies).

3. An intentionally established system of abstract rules governs official decisions and actions. These rules are relatively stable and exhaustive, and can be learned. Decisions are recorded in permanent files. (In patrimonial systems, general rules of administration either do not exist or are vaguely stated, ill-defined, and subject to change on the whim of the leader. No attempt is made to keep permanent records of transactions.)

4. The "means of production or administration"—for example, tools and equipment or rights and privileges—belong to the office, not the office holder, and may not be appropriated. Personal property is clearly separated from official property, and working space from living quarters. (Such distinctions are not maintained in patrimonial administrative systems since there is no separation of the ruler's personal household business from the larger "public" business under his direction.)

5. Officials are personally free, selected on the basis of technical qualifications, appointed to office, not elected, and compensated by salary. (In more traditional administrative systems, officials are often selected from among those who are personally dependent on the leader, for example, slaves, serfs, relatives. Selection is governed by particularistic criteria, and compensation often takes the form of benefices—rights granted to individuals which, for example, allow them access to the stores of the ruler or give them grants of land from which they can appropriate the fees or taxes. Benefices, like fiefs in feudalistic systems, may become hereditary and sometimes are bought and sold.)

6. Employment by the organization constitutes a career for officials. An official is a full-time employee and looks forward to a lifelong career in the agency. After a trial period he or she gains tenure of position and is protected against arbitrary dismissal. (In patrimonial systems, officials serve at the pleasure of the leader and so lack clear expectations about the future and security of tenure.)

By juxtaposing Weber's list of bureaucratic characteristics and the related aspects of patrimonial systems, a clearer view emerges of Weber's central message. He viewed each bureaucratic element as constituting the *solution* to a problem or defect contained within the earlier administrative systems. Further, each element operates, not in isolation, but as part of a system of elements that, in combination, were expected to provide more effective and efficient administration. To capture both the notions of distinctive elements and their interrelation, Weber employed what is termed an *ideal-type* construct. This approach attempts to isolate those elements regarded as most characteristic of the phenomenon to be explored. The term *ideal-type* is somewhat misleading, since it does not refer to a normatively preferred type but rather to the construction of a simplified model that focuses attention on the most salient or distinctive features.

Even though Weber's model of administrative systems emphasized they were composed of many, interrelated factors, in his own analysis he gave primary attention to one particular factor: the type of authority relation that relates superiors to subordinates in the administrative structure. As discussed in chapter 2, Weber distinguished between three types of authority relations: traditional, rational-legal, and charismatic. In contrasting the rational-legal with the other two (nonrational) types, two somewhat contradictory points arise. First, the rational-legal form provides the basis for a more stable and predictable administrative structure for both superiors and subordinates. The behavior of subordinates is rendered more reliable by the specificity of their role obligations, the clarity of hierarchical connections, and their continuing dependence on the hierarchy in the short run for income and in the longer term for career progression. And superiors are prevented from behaving arbitrarily or capriciously in their demands made on subordinates.

On the other hand, the rational-legal structure permits subordinates to exercise "relatively greater independence and discretion" than is possible in the other types of administrative systems (Smith and Ross, 1978). Because obedience is owed not to a person—whether a traditional chief or a charismatic leader—but to a set of impersonal principles, subordinates in bureaucratic systems have a stronger basis for independent action, guided by their interpretation of the principles. They also have a clear basis for questioning the directives of superiors, whose actions are presumably constrained by the same impersonal framework of rules. By supporting increased independence and discretion among lower administrative officials constrained by general administrative policies and specified procedures, bureaucratic systems are capable of handling much more complex administrative tasks than could be adequately managed by traditional systems. (This general argument will be amplified in chapter 11.)

Weber's formulation, while influential, has been much criticized. We will briefly note two important criticisms. Since type of authority relation goes a long way toward determining the nature of administrative structures in Weber's conception, criticisms of his views of the type of authority prevailing in bureaucratic systems take on special significance. Both Parsons and Gouldner have suggested that Weber tended to confuse two analytically distinguishable bases of authority. On the one hand, in his discussion of the administrative hierarchy of bureaucracies, Weber notes that authority rests on "incumbency in a legally defined office." On the other hand, in his discussion of criteria for recruitment and advancement, Weber appears to argue that authority is based on "technical competence" (Parsons, 1947: 58–60). Indeed, at one point Weber states: "Bureaucratic administration means fundamentally the exercise of control on the basis of knowledge" (1947 tr.: 339) Gouldner (1954) concludes:

> Weber, then, thought of bureaucracy as a Janus-faced organization, looking two ways at once. On the one side, it was administration based on discipline. In the first emphasis, obedience is invoked as a means to an end; an individual obeys because the rule or order is felt to be the best known method of realizing some goal.
>
> In his second conception, Weber held that bureaucracy was a mode of administration in which obedience was an end in itself. The individual obeys the order, setting aside judgments either of its rationality or morality, primarily because of the *position* occupied by the person commanding. The content of the order is not examinable. (Gouldner, 1954: 22–23)

One might argue, theoretical niceties aside, whether there is a high positive correlation between a person's position in the hierarchy and his or her degree of technical competence. Such may have been the case in Weber's day when on-the-job experience was a major source of technical competence but seems far off the mark in today's world of minute specialization supported by prolonged and esoteric training in institutions separated from the work setting. Thompson convincingly portrays the ever-widening gap between ability and authority in modern organizations, asserting that: "Authority is centralized, but ability is inherently decentralized because it comes from practice and training rather than from definition. Whereas the boss retains his full *rights* to make all decisions, he has less and less *ability* to do so because of the advance of science and technology" (1961: 47). Staff-line arrangements, in which the positional authority of the line administrator is distinguished from the technical expertise of the staff specialist, appear to be not so much a solution to the difficulty—see studies by Dalton (1950; 1959) and others on staff-line conflict —as a structural recognition of the distinctiveness of the two sources of authority sloughed over in Weber's analysis.

A second criticism of Weber's formulation is that his ideal-type construct of bureaucracy is "an admixture of a conceptual scheme and a set of hypotheses" (Blau and Scott, 1962: 33), the difficulty being that Weber does not clearly distinguish definitions from propositions in his model. Weber's conception not only calls attention to what he regards as the key elements of bureaucracy— his definition of this phenomenon in terms of a set of characteristics—but also contains numerous propositions linking the various elements. For example, it is implied that organizations having a well-developed hierarchy of authority also attempt to standardize the performance of tasks by applying rules and formalized procedures, and that these same organizations also employ technical criteria in recruiting and promoting personnel, and so on. Weber's conception contains numerous propositions about the interrelations of structural characteristics in organizations, some explicit but many implicit. For a long time sociologists following in Weber's footsteps took as given the interrelations posited in his schema.

Udy (1959*a*; 1959*b*) was among the first to suggest that Weber's model could be regarded as identifying a set of structural variables whose interrelations should not be taken as a matter of definition but as a subject for empirical exploration. His lead was quickly followed by numerous others, including Hall (1963; 1968), Pugh and his colleagues (1968); and Blau and his associates (Blau, Heydebrand, and Stauffer, 1966; Blau and Schoenherr, 1971), all of whom documented the great variety exhibited by structural systems. Perhaps of greatest interest, studies by Udy (1959*a*) questioned Weber's assertion that bureaucratic organizations (in Weber's sense) were necessarily also rational in form. Employing a sample of 150 organizations from 150 nonindustrial societies (settings that afford greater variation in structural features), Udy distinguished the "bureaucratic" attributes of these organizations, including such features as the existence of a hierarchical authority structure and the presence of a specialized administrative staff, from their "rational" attributes, including the existence of specified, limited objectives, and the distribution of rewards based on performance.[3] While structural features within each of the two clusters were positively interrelated, Udy found no association between the two sets of variables: organizations that possessed more bureaucratic features were not more likely than organizations lacking them to exhibit rational features. Similarly, studies by Hall (1963; 1968) of samples of United States organizations found that an emphasis on technical qualifications was negatively correlated with other bureaucratic features, such as a hierarchy of authority, emphasis on rules, and a division of labor. This finding not only challenges Weber's ideal-type conception of bureaucracy but also lends support to the earlier criticism that Weber confused authority of office with authority of expertise. (These arguments are pursued in chapter 11.)

Although it is clearly possible to criticize and improve upon many specific aspects of Weber's formulation, he remains the acknowledged master of organization theory: the intellectual giant whose conceptions continue to shape definitions of the central elements of administrative systems, and whose historical and comparative vision continues to challenge and inform our more limited views of organizational forms.[4]

SIMON'S THEORY OF ADMINISTRATIVE BEHAVIOR

Herbert Simon, both in his early work on administration[5] and in his later collaborative work with March, has clarified the processes by which goal specificity and formalization contribute to rational behavior in organizations. (See Simon, 1957, 1964; March and Simon, 1958) We have already observed that Simon was critical of the platitudes developed by Fayol and others searching for management principles. He also criticized the assumptions made by Taylor and other early theorists about the actors in these systems. For the "economic man" motivated by self-interest and completely informed about

---

[3]Although we have no quarrel with the specific organizational features selected by Udy to represent "rational" characteristics, we are uncomfortable with the assumption that any given organizational feature can be regarded as rational irrespective of the circumstances in which it operates. In short, we believe that it is much preferable to view rationality as applicable to the *relation* between means and ends rather than to either means or ends viewed in isolation.

[4]Summaries and critical reviews of Weber's contributions to organization theory are provided by Albrow (1970), Bendix (1960), and Mouzelis (1968).

[5]Simon's basic work, *Administrative Behavior,* first appeared in 1945. However, all our references are to the second edition of this work published in 1957, which contains an extensive new introduction.

all available alternatives, Simon proposed to substitute a more human "administrative man," who seeks to pursue his self-interests but does not always know what they are, is aware of only a few of all the possible alternatives, and is willing to settle for an adequate solution in contrast to an optimal one.

Following the lead of Barnard (1938), Simon distinguishes between (a) an individual's decisions to join and to continue to participate in an organization and (b) the decisions an individual is asked to make as a participant in the organization. Only the latter set of decisions is of interest in the present context.[6] A scientifically relevant description of an organization, according to Simon (1957: 37), details what decisions individuals make as organizational participants and the influences to which they are subject in making these decisions. In general, in Simon's view, organizations both simplify decisions and support participants in the decisions they need to make.

A primary way in which organizations act to simplify participants' decisions is to restrict the ends toward which activity is directed. Simon points out that goals affect behavior only as they enter into decisions about how to behave. Goals supply the value premises that underlie decisions. *Value premises* are assumptions about what ends are preferred or desirable. They are combined in decisions with *factual premises*—assumptions about the relation between means and ends. The more precise and specific the value premises, the greater their impact on the resulting decisions, since specific goals clearly distinguish acceptable from unacceptable (or more from less accaptable) alternatives. Typically, participants higher in the hierarchy make decisions with a large value component, while lower participants are more apt to make decisions having a larger factual component. Those closer to the top make decisions about what the organization is going to do; those in lower positions are more likely to be allowed to make choices as to how the organization can best carry out its tasks. Simon (1957: 45–56) insists that quite different criteria of correctness underlie these two classes of decisions: choice of ends can only be validated by fiat or consensus; choice of means can be validated empirically.

Ultimate goals served by organizations are frequently somewhat vague and imprecise. Some organizations exist to develop and transmit knowledge, others to maintain public order, and others to care for and cure patients. Such general goals in themselves provide few clues for guiding the behavior of participants. However, as March and Simon argue, they can serve as the starting point for the construction of "means-ends chains" that involve: "(1) starting with the general goal to be achieved, (2) discovering a set of means, very generally specific, for accomplishing this goal, (3) taking each of these means, in turn,

---

[6]Factors affecting the first type of decision—decisions to participate—are discussed in Chapter 7 of this volume. See also March and Simon (1958: 52–111.)

as a new subgoal and discovering a set of more detailed means for achieving it, etc." (1958: 191). In this manner, there is established a hierarchy of goals in which each level is "considered as an end relative to the levels below it and as a means relative to the levels above it. Through the hierarchical structure of ends, behavior attains integration and consistency, for each member of a set of behavior alternatives is then weighted in terms of a comprehensive scale of values—the 'ultimate' ends" (Simon, 1957: 63).

For example, in a manufacturing organization, the assignment to an individual worker to construct a specific component of a piece of equipment such as an engine provides him with an end toward which to direct his activities. This end, viewed from the level of his supervisor, is only a means toward the creation of the engine. The supervisor's end is to ensure that all component parts are available when needed and correctly assembled to produce the engine. However, this objective when viewed from the next higher level is only a means to the end of completing the final product, such as a lawn mower, containing the engine. The completion of all component parts and assembly operations required to produce the lawn mower, while an end for the manufacturing division, is only a means at a higher level to the more ultimate end of selling the lawn mower for profit to retail outlets. Viewed from the bottom up, the rationality of individual decisions and activities can be evaluated only as they relate to higher-order decisions; each subgoal can be assessed only in terms of its consistency or congruency with more general goals. Viewed from the top down, the factoring of general purposes into specific subgoals which can then be assigned to organizational subunits (individuals or departments) enhances the possibility of rational behavior by specifying value premises and hence simplifying the required decisions at every level. From this perspective, then, an organization's hierarchy can be viewed as a congealed set of means-ends chains promoting consistency of decisions and activities throughout the organization.

The ultimate goals—making a profit, achieving growth, prolonging life— are those which, by definition, are not viewed as means to ends, but as ends in themselves. They may be determined by consensus or by decree. In either case, any challenge to these ultimate objectives is likely to be met with violent resistance. Physicians, for example, often refuse to consider the merits of euthanasia, and capitalists react with righteous indignation to any questions raised concerning their rights to profits. Apart from any considerations of self-interest, such emotional reactions are partly caused by the half-conscious realization that any challenge to the ultimate objectives calls into question the premises around which the entire enterprise is structured.

March and Simon (1958: 142–71) suggest a number of other ways in which decision making is simplified within organizations. Briefly, organizations encourage decision makers to "satisfice"—settle for acceptable as opposed to optimal solutions, to attend to problems sequentially rather than simultaneously, and to utilize existing repertories of action programs rather than develop novel responses for each situation.

Organizations also act to support participants in the decisions they must make. A formalized structure supports rational decision making by subdividing responsibilities among participants and providing them with the necessary means to handle them: resources, information, equipment. Specialized roles and rules, information channels, training programs, standard operating procedures—all may be viewed as mechanisms both for restricting the range of decisions each participant makes and for assisting the participant in making appropriate decisions within that range. As Perrow (1979: 149–53) notes, Simon's model of organizational influence stresses unobtrusive control of participants: training and channeling of information and attention play a larger role in producing dependable behavior than do commands or sanctions.

Underlying Simon's model of organizational decision making is a conception of cognitive limits of individual decision makers. Simon (1957) stresses:

> It is impossible for the behavior of a single, isolated individual to reach any high degree of rationality. The number of alternatives he must explore is too great, the information he would need to evaluate them so vast that even an approximation to objective rationality is hard to conceive. Individual choice takes place in an environment of "givens"—premises that are accepted by the subject as bases for his choice; and behavior is adaptive only within the limits set by these "givens." (Simon, 1957: 79)

By providing integrated subgoals, stable expectations, required information, necessary facilities, routine performance programs, and in general, a set of constraints within which required decisions can be made, organizations supply these "givens" to individual participants. This is the sense in which March and Simon (1958: 169–71) intend the concept *bounded rationality*—a concept that both summarizes and integrates the two key elements of the rational system perspective: goal specificity and formalization.[7]

The model developed by Simon also can be used to explain how the very structures developed to promote rationality can, under some conditions, have the opposite effect. These and other sources of organizational pathologies will be discussed in chapter 13.

[7]A good overview of Simon's contributions to the analysis of decision making in organizations is provided by Taylor (1965). An interesting critique of Simon's work is provided by Krupp (1961) and by Lindblom (1959).

Summary and Tentative Conclusions

Any conclusions reached at this point must be tentative; we cannot hope to appraise the strengths and limitations of any one perspective in isolation from the others. Nevertheless, a few general observations on the rational system approach can be made at this time.

In the rational system perspective, structural arrangements within organizations are conceived as tools deliberately designed for the efficient realization of ends. As Gouldner notes: "The focus is, therefore, on the legally prescribed structures—i.e., the formally 'blueprinted' patterns—since these are more largely subject to deliberate inspection and rational manipulation" (1959: 404–5). All theorists utilizing this perspective focus attention on the normative structure of organizations: on the specificity of goals and the formalization of rules and roles. There are, however, important differences among the various schools considered in their approach to the normative structure.

Taylor was highly pragmatic in his approach, placing his faith in a method by which, beginning with individual jobs, superior work procedures could be developed and appropriate arrangements devised for articulating the various tasks to be performed. Work planning was distinguished from work performance, the former becoming the responsibility of management. Taylor was primarily concerned with devising methods for the planning of work and working arrangements. The administrative management group was less pragmatic and more prescriptive in its approach. Members of this group believed that general principles of management could be devised to guide managers as they designed their organizations, and so busied themselves constructing lists of "do's and don'ts" as guides to managerial decision making. Weber was less concerned with discovering ways—whether pragmatic or prescriptive—for improving organizations than with attempting to develop a parsimonious descriptive portrait of the characteristics of the newly emerging bureaucratic structures. Like Weber, Simon was also descriptive in his approach but preferred to focus attention at the social psychological level rather than the structural level, examining the effect of structural features on individual decision makers within the organization. Simon's conception, in particular, enables us to understand better how thousands and even hundreds of thousands of individual decisions and actions can be integrated in the service of complex, multifaceted goals. Such rational, purposeful collective behavior requires the support of an organizational framework.

Thompson provides a simple summary of the general argument underlying this perspective: "structure is a fundamental vehicle by which organizations achieve bounded rationality" (1967: 54). The specification of positions, role definitions, procedural rules and regulations, value and factual inputs to guide decision making—all function to canalize behavior in the service of predetermined goals. Individuals can behave rationally because their alternatives are limited and their choices circumscribed.

In a larger sense, however, rationality resides in the structure itself, not in the individual participants—in rules that assure participants will behave in ways calculated to achieve desired objectives, in control arrangements that evaluate performance and detect deviance, in reward systems that motivate participants to carry out prescribed tasks, and in the set of criteria by which participants are selected, replaced, or promoted. Because of its emphasis on the characteristics of structure rather than on the characteristics of participants, Bennis has dubbed the rational system perspective one of "organizations without people" (1959: 263).

Let us not forget, however, the limited conception of rationality that is employed by this perspective. At the top of the organization, the value premises that govern the entire structure of decision making fall outside the system: so long as they are specific enough to provide clear criteria for choice, these premises can support a "rational" structure no matter how monstrous or perverted their content. And at the bottom of the organization, "rational" behavior often consists in turning off one's mind and one's critical intellectual judgment, and blindly conforming to the performance program specified by the job description (see Veblen, 1904).

We have noted the great emphasis placed in the rational system perspective on control—the determination of the behavior of one subset of participants by the other. Decision making tends to be centralized, and most participants are excluded from discretion or from exercising control over their own behavior. Most rational system theorists justify these arrangements as being in the service of rationality: control is the means of channeling and coordinating behavior so as to achieve specified goals. Few perceive the possibility that interpersonal control may be an end in itself—that one function of elaborate hierarchies and extensive divisions of labor is to allow some participants to exercise control over others. The critical or Marxist perspective calls attention to these possibilities (see Braverman, 1974; Goldman and Van Houten, 1977). We will examine this critique in more detail in chapter 7.

None of the rational system theorists took much notice of the effect of the larger social, cultural, and technological context on the structure of the organization. While it is true that Weber attempted to account for the emergence and growth of bureaucratic structures by pointing to larger societal changes (see chapter 7), he did not examine variations in structure among bureaucratic organizations and relate these to differences in social context.

Also, by concentrating attention on the normative structure, rational system analysts have virtually ignored the behavioral structure of organizations.

We learn much from these theorists about plans and programs and premises, about roles and rules and regulations, but very little indeed about the actual behavior of organizational participants. The implication is if planning is good, if decisions are sound, implementation will take care of itself. Others take some note of the need to motivate and control participants so that their actions will coincide with design, but these theorists—Taylor, for example—are criticized for holding an oversimplified view of human beings and for having inadequate knowledge of what factors will and will not prove effective in motivating behavior.

These and related criticisms gave rise to alternative perspectives on organizations. The second perspective to be considered, the natural system perspective, developed specifically in opposition to the rational system model and was designed to correct its oversimplified conception of organizational structure and its naive conception of individual participants.

chapter 4

Organizations
as
Natural Systems

> *To administer a social organization according to purely technical criteria of rationality is irrational, because it ignores the nonrational aspects of social conduct.*
>
> PETER M. BLAU (1956)

The natural system perspective developed in large measure from critical reactions to the inadequacies of the rational system model. And in our own discussion, we shall make frequent references to these criticisms. However, the natural system perspective should not be seen as merely providing a critique of another perspective. Rather, it defines a novel and interesting view of organizations that deserves to be considered and evaluated in its own right. As with our discussion of the rational system approach, we will first attempt to isolate those more general or basic ideas common to most natural system advocates and then briefly examine selected schools within this perspective.

Important Characteristics versus Distinctive Characteristics

Whereas the rational system theorists conceive of organizations as collectivities deliberately constructed to seek specific goals, natural system advocates emphasize that organizations are, first and foremost, collectivities. Thus, the rational system perspective stresses those features of organizations that distinguish them from other types of social groups, while the natural system theorists remind us that these distinguishing characteristics are not their only characteristics (Gouldner, 1959: 406). Indeed, they may not even be the most important characteristics.

We have already seen that much is made by rational system theorists of goal specificity and formalization as characteristics differentiating organizations from other types of collectivities. Natural system theorists generally acknowledge the existence of these attributes but argue that other characteristics—characteristics shared with all social groups—are of greater significance. Take first the matter of organizational goals and goal specificity.

ORGANIZATIONAL GOALS REVISITED

Organizational goals and their relation to the behavior of participants seem much more problematic to the natural than to the rational system theorist. This is largely because natural system analysts pay more attention to behavior and hence worry more about the complex interconnections between the normative and the behavioral structures of organizations. In particular, they frequently observe a disparity in organizations between the stated and the "real" goals of action, between the professed or official goals that are announced and the actual or operative goals governing the activities of participants. Indeed, simply to identify what goals are determining action in many organizations is no mean accomplishment (Perrow, 1961).

In addition to recognizing the possibility of disjunctions between the normative and behavior structures, natural system analysts have developed a more complex model of the organization itself. In some versions, we are reminded that organizations are social systems and, as such, must meet a variety of needs, only one of which is to pursue its goals (see Selznick, 1948; Etzioni, 1961; Parsons, 1960). The organization is viewed as a self-maintaining system that must satisfy a stable set of internal needs at the same time that it must adapt to influences impinging on it from an external environment (Selznick, 1948). This view suggests the appropriateness of structural-functional analysis, a theoretical model we will describe later in this section. In other versions, the greater complexity takes the form of recognizing new types of goals served by organizations: in addition to so-called *output* or product goals, organizations are seen as devoting energies to *support* or self-maintenance goals (see Gross, 1968; Perrow, 1970: 135). In both formulations, analysts insist that organizations are multifaceted systems that cannot devote all of their energies and resources to the attainment of specified goals; attention must be given to the maintenance of the system itself.

These distinctions, while useful, do not go quite far enough. They do not capture the most profound difference between these two perspectives on organizational goals. The whole thrust of the natural system view is that organizations are more than instruments for attaining narrowly defined goals; they are, fundamentally, social groups attempting to adapt to and survive in their particular circumstances. Thus, formal organizations, like all other social groups, are governed by one overriding goal: survival. Gouldner emphasizes this implication of the natural system perspective: "The organization, according to this model, strives to survive and to maintain its equilibrium, and this striving may persist even after its explicitly held goals have been successfully attained. This strain toward survival may even on occasion lead to the neglect or distortion of the organization's goals" (1959: 405). Under many conditions, organizations have been observed to modify their goals so as to achieve a more favorable adjustment. If their survivial is at stake, organizations will abandon the pursuit of their avowed objectives in order to save themselves. It is because of such tendencies that organizations are not to be viewed primarily as means for achieving specified ends, but as ends in themselves.

The earliest, and in many ways still the best, account of the processes by which an organization may be led to abandon its primary goals is that provided by Robert Michels (1949 tr.), a contemporary of Weber's writing in pre-World War I Germany. His analysis of the changes that occurred in the largest socialist party in Europe, Germany's Social Democratic party, is rightly regarded as a classic. This work is most famous for its formulation of "the iron law of oligarchy," which equates the processes by which complex administrative work is carried out in an organization with the processes by which power shifts from the rank-and-file members to a small group of leaders. "Who says organization says oligarchy" (see chapter 13). Of greater interest for present purposes are Michels's views on the consequences of these oligarchical tendencies for the professed goals of the organization. The leaders of the party continue to give lip service to its revolutionary objectives, but over time become increasingly conservative, reluctant to risk the gains they have achieved or to endanger the party, which is their source of strength. Michels gloomily concludes:

> Thus, from a means, organization becomes an end. To the institutions and qualities which at the outset were destined simply to ensure the good working of the party machine (subordination, the harmonious cooperation of individual members, hierarchical relationships, discretion, propriety of conduct), a greater importance comes ultimately to be attached than to the productivity of the machine. Henceforward the sole preoccupation is to avoid anything which may clog the machinery. (Michels, 1949 tr.: 390)

THE UNIMPORTANCE OF FORMAL STRUCTURE

If the ends that organizations are designed to serve are not pure and simple and specific in the view of the natural system analysts, neither are the structures that exist to attain them. The natural system theorists do not deny the existence of highly formalized structures within organizations, but they do question their importance, in particular, their impact on the behavior of participants. Formal structures purposefully designed to regulate behavior in the service of specific goals are seen to be greatly affected—supplemented, eroded, transformed—by the emergence of informal structures.

While there is widespread agreement as to the importance of informal structure, there is little consensus on how it is to be defined. Indeed, the distinction between formal and informal is quite confusing since so many superficially related but different meanings have been associated with this dichotomy. Some analysts equate the formal structure with the normative system designed by management—the "blueprint" for behavior—and the informal structure with the behavioral system—the actual behavior of participants. Roethlisberger and Dickson (1939: 558–62), founders of the human relations school discussed in more detail below, come rather close to this position in their pioneering discussion of these concepts. They propose that:

> The patterns of human interrelations, as defined by the systems, rules, policies, and regulations of the company, constitute the formal organization. . . . It includes the systems, policies, rules, and regulations of the plant which express what the relations of one person to another are supposed to be in order to achieve effectively the task of technical production. (Roethlisberger and Dickson, 1939: 558)

By contrast, the informal organization is described as follows:

> Many of the actually existing patterns of human interaction have no representation in the formal organization at all, and others are inadequately represented by the formal organization. . . . Too often it is assumed that the organization of a company corresponds to a blueprint plan or organization chart. Actually, it never does. (Roethlisberger and Dickson, 1939: 559)

Most analysts, however, view these structures as encompassing both normative and behavioral dimensions, so that it is possible to speak of formal norms *and* formal patterns of behavior, and of informal norms *and* informal patterns of behavior. Still, there is disagreement about the basis for distinguishing between the two types of structures. Some analysts tend to equate this dichotomy with such earlier distinctions as primary-secondary and *gemeinschaft-gesellschaft* relations (see Dubin, 1968: 104), but Blau (1955: 143) argues that relations within organizations are "clearly distinct" from either of these polar types. Another definition of these concepts is supplied by Litterer, who suggests that: "by formal is meant those aspects of organizations which have been or possibly might be, consciously planned" while "the informal organization is conceived of as being the aspects of organization that are not formally planned but that more or less spontaneously evolve from the needs of people" (1963: 10).

All of these conceptions of the distinction between formal and informal are different from the one we propose. As first discussed in chapter 1, we find it useful to equate formal structures with those norms and behavior patterns that exist regardless of the characteristics of the individual actors. Informal structures are those based on the personal characteristics or resources of the specific participants in the situation. Thus, for example, formal authority refers to those control rights that are available to and exercised by all incumbents of a given position, such as supervisor or teacher; informal authority would indicate those rights that become available to a particular supervisor or teacher because of his or her special qualities or individual resources. Obviously, one of the clearest ways to distinguish empirically between the formal and the informal elements in a given situation is to observe what happens to beliefs and behaviors when there is a change in personnel.

Regardless of differences in the specific conceptions, all natural system analysts emphasize that there is more to organizational structure than the prescribed rules, the job descriptions, and the associated regularities in the behavior of participants. Individual participants are never merely "hired hands" but bring along their heads and hearts: they enter into the organization with individually shaped ideas, expectations, and agendas, and they bring with them differing values, interests, and abilities.

Expressed through interaction, these factors come together to create a reasonably stable informal structure. One of the most important insights of the natural system perspective is that the social structure of an organization is not comprised of the formal structure plus the idiosyncratic beliefs and behaviors of individual participants but of a formal structure and an informal structure: informal life is itself structured and orderly. Participants within formal organizations generate informal norms and behavior patterns: status and power systems, communication networks, sociometric structures, and working arrangements.

In the early studies exploring informal structures, it was presumed that they characterized only the lower strata of the organization: managers and executives were immune to such developments. But empirical studies by Dalton (1959) and others dispelled such notions. Also, early studies emphasized the dysfunctional consequences of the informal structures, as private and "irrational" concerns that impeded the implementation of the elegant formal design. Thus, Roethlisberger and Dickson decided that the formal structure expresses the "logic of cost and efficiency" whereas the informal structure embraces the "logic of sentiments" (1939: 562–64). Increasingly, however, analysts have emphasized the positive functions performed by informal structures—in increasing ease of communication, facilitating trust, and correcting for the inadequacies of the formal systems (see Gross, 1953).

Greater appreciation for the functions of informal systems was coupled with increasing skepticism that formalization was conducive to rationality. Natural system analysts emphasize that formalization places heavy and often intolerable burdens on those responsible for the design and management of an organization. No planners are so farseeing or omniscient as to be able to anticipate all the possible contingencies that might confront each position in the organization. Attempts to program in advance the behavior of participants are often misguided, if not foolhardy. Such programming can easily become maladaptive and lead to behaviors both ineffective and inefficient, giving rise to the "trained incapacity" that Veblen (1904) called attention to long ago and for which some organizations have become notorious. (See also Merton, 1957:197–200) Further, formal arrangements that curtail individual problem solving and use of discretion undermine participants' initiative and self-confidence, causing them to become alienated and apathetic. Such restrictive arrangements are not only damaging to participants' self-esteem and mental health but prevent them from effectively contributing their talents and energies to the larger enterprise (Argyris, 1957; McGregor, 1960). In sum, natural system analysts insist that highly centralized and formalized structures are doomed to be ineffective and irrational in that they waste the organization's most precious resource: the intelligence and initiative of its participants.

STRUCTURAL-FUNCTIONAL ANALYSIS

Underlying the natural system perspective is a structural-functional model of analysis. The origins of this widely used model are to be found in the work of a group of British social anthropologists, most notably Malinowski (1939) and Radcliffe-Brown (1952). Merton's essay (1957: 19–84) has been the most influential statement of this approach in sociology. The paradigm is complex, and there are many variants; nevertheless, its central features can be quickly summarized. The model assumes that the social unit, in our case the organization, has certain needs or requirements that must be met if it is to persist in its present form. As we will see when specific schools are discussed, analysts vary with respect to how explicit they are in formulating the set of functional prerequisites. Specific structures that comprise the organization are analyzed in terms of the needs they meet, the functions they perform in ensuring the survival of the system. By analogy, if the human body is to survive, a continuing flow of oxygen must be supplied to the blood; the lungs perform this function. Similarly, if the organization is to survive, information about salient changes in its environment must be communicated to decision makers; the internal communication system performs this function. Showing that a given structure meets a functional need constitutes a functional "explanation" for that structure. The existence of an element is explained in terms of its consequences—the functions it performs—rather than by reference to its origins.

"Final" causes are emphasized over "efficient" causes.[1] The model also emphasizes that the structural elements are themselves mutually interdependent so that variation in one causes modification in the others. Such systems are often viewed as tending toward a state of equilibrium, following the work of Pareto as interpreted by Henderson (1935). (See Buckley, 1967: 11–17)

Many aspects of the functionalist paradigm are problematic. In the case of social systems, unlike biological systems, it is difficult to specify the essential needs; indeed, it is often difficult to specify what is meant by survival of the system. It is also not easy to link a specific structure to a particular need. As Parsons (1966: 24–25) notes, social structures vary in their degree of differentiation: some are highly developed so that each structural unit performs a highly specialized function, while others are much less developed, each structure performing a range of functions. Further, a given function may be performed by more than one type of structure—the concept of "functional equivalents or substitutes"—so that a functional explanation may not be sufficient to account for the development of a specific structural form.[2] Finally, we have already suggested that organizational forms are not as highly interdependent and as tightly coupled as biological systems, a point to be amplified in the next chapter.

In spite of all these problems and reservations, structural-functionalism provided the dominant model for organizational (and, more generally, sociological) analysis from the 1930s into the 1960s. Many of our most important insights and generalizations concerning organizations are products of this tradition; despite its flaws, it remains a popular and useful perspective from which to examine organizations.

Selected Schools

As with the rational system perspective, the natural system perspective is an umbrella under which a number of rather diverse approaches can be gathered. While they share certain generic features, they differ in important particulars. We will be content to discuss briefly three influential variants: Mayo and

[1]Blau (1955: 9–10) suggests that this theoretical postulate of the structural-functional model can be accounted for by its distinctive historical origin: social anthropologists studying primitive societies could not test historical explanations for particular structural features since there were no historical documents. To overcome this limitation, a different type of explanation was developed which emphasized the contemporary contribution made by the element to the maintenance of the larger social system. Attention shifted from a focus on origins to a concern with persistence of a particular structural feature.

[2]In addition to these theoretical and empirical problems, certain logical difficulties attend the use of this model (see Nagel, 1961: 520–35); but if carefully employed, it can be of value in analyzing self-regulating systems (see Hempel, 1959).

the human relations school, Selznick's institutional approach, and Parsons's social system model.

Mayo and the Human Relations School

We will not recount in detail the famous series of studies and experiments conducted at the Hawthorne plant of the Western Electric Company outside Chicago during the late 1920s and early 1930s. This research is meticulously described by Roethlisberger and Dickson (1939) and given its most influential interpretation by Elton Mayo (1945). Mayo, along with Roethlisberger, was a member of the Harvard Business School faculty. He was trained as an industrial psychologist, and his early work grew out of the research tradition established by Frederick W. Taylor. Like Taylor, Mayo studied individual factors such as fatigue in an attempt to determine the optimum length and spacing of rest periods for maximizing productivity. The early work in the Hawthorne plant followed the scientific management approach: the researchers set about to determine the optimal level of illumination for the assembly of telephone relay equipment. Mayo (1945) summarizes the surprising results:

> The conditions of scientific experiment had apparently been fulfilled–experimental room, control room; changes introduced one at a time; all other conditions held steady. And the results were perplexing.... Lighting improved in the experimental room, production went up; but it rose also in the control room. The opposite of this: lighting diminished from 10 to 3 foot-candles in the experimental room and the production again went up; simultaneously in the control room, with illumination constant, production also rose. (Mayo, 1945: 69)

The researchers were in confusion. Other conditions were run with similar inexplicable results. In desperation, they asked the workers themselves what was going on and learned that the workers were so pleased to be singled out for special attention that they had tried to do the best they could for the researchers and for the company! The "Hawthorne effect" was discovered.

Additional studies carried out by the Harvard group—the second relay assembly group, the mica-splitting test room, the bank wiring observation room—all served to call into question the simple motivational assumptions on which the prevailing rational models rested. Individual workers did not behave as "rational" economic actors but as complex beings with multiple motives and values;[3] they were driven as much by feelings and sentiments as by facts and

---

[3]After inspecting the results of the bank wiring observation room study at the Hawthorne plant, Mayo concluded: "It is unfortunate for economic theory that it applies chiefly to persons of less, rather than greater, normality of social relationships. Must we conclude that economics is a study of human behavior in non-normal situations, or alternatively, a study of non-normal human behavior in ordinary situations?" (145: 43)

interests; and they did not behave as individual, isolated actors but as members of social groups exhibiting commitments and loyalties stronger than their individualistic self-interests. Thus, in the bank wiring observation room, workers were observed to set and conform to daily work quotas—group norms restricting production—at the expense of their own higher earnings. And informal status hierarchies and leadership patterns developed that challenged the formal systems designed by managers (see Roethlisberger and Dickson, 1939: 379–447; and Homans, 1950: 48–155). At the social psychological level, the Hawthorne studies pointed to a more complex model of worker motivaticn based on a social-psychological rather than an economic conception of man; and at the structural level, the Hawthorne studies discovered and demonstrated the importance of informal organization.

The Hawthorne trunk has given rise to numerous research and reform offshoots, each of which has produced many individual branches. The major research issues pursued include studies of the work groups in the organizational environment, leadership behavior, and the impact of worker background and personality attributes on organizational behavior. Reform attempts include the use of personnel counselors, leadership training, job redefinition, and participation in decision making. Each of these interests merits a brief description: all of them are still flourishing.

The discovery of informal group processes in organizational settings both stimulated and received impetus from the study of small group behavior carried on by social psychologists and sociologists. Among the former, Maier (1952) and Katz (Katz, Maccoby, and Morse, 1950; Katz et al., 1951) were particularly influential; among the latter, Homans (1950) and Whyte (1951; 1959) were effective in analyzing group processes in organizational settings. A few analysts, such as Sayles (1958), attempted to understand how organizational factors affected the number, types, and tactics of groups that emerged; most focused attention not on the determinants but on the consequences of group membership, for example, the impact of group cohesiveness on individual conformity to production norms (Roy, 1952; Seashore, 1954).

From the human relations perspective, leadership is conceived primarily as a mechanism for influencing the behavior of individual participants. Early studies sought a set of leadership traits or characteristics that would stimulate individual performance in the service of organizational goals. Thus, studies by White and Lippitt (1953) reported that participants in experimental task groups performed more effectively under "democratic" than "laissez-faire" or "authoritarian" leaders. Later research stressed the relational aspects of leadership. For example, a series of studies conducted at Ohio State (Stogdill and Coons, 1957) isolated two basic dimensions of leadership behavior: "consideration," the extent to which trust, friendship, and respect mark the relation between the supervisor and his or her workers, and "initiating structure," the degree to which the supervisor is a good organizer who can "get the work out."

These dimensions were observed to vary independently, and in general, the more effective leaders—that is, leaders whose subordinates performed better and had higher morale—were those who scored high on both dimensions.

More recent efforts have emphasized that leadership characteristics vary depending on the nature of the situation (Fiedler, 1964; 1971) and the specific needs or motivations of the individual subordinates (Cartwright, 1965). Moreover, studies by Pelz (1952) suggested that a supervisor's relation to his or her own superior—specifically, the extent of his or her influence upward—is a powerful determinant of the supervisor's influence over his or her own subordinates. Likert (1961) built on this finding to create his model of the supervisor's critical function as a "linking pin" relating lower to higher levels of the hierarchy. Most of the leadership studies tend to ignore the effects of incumbency in a formal office on an individual's influence either by overlooking this aspect of the situation or by deliberately holding it constant—for example, by studying differences in leadership behavior among all first-line supervisors in a given office or factory situation (see Katz and Kahn, 1952). Blau has pointed out: "Although managerial authority in organizations contains important leadership elements, its distinctive characteristic, which differentiates it from informal leadership, is that it is rooted in the formal powers and sanctions the organization bestows upon managers" (1964: 210). It is in keeping with the natural system perspective to ignore this distinctive component of leadership in formal organizations. (We ourselves will focus on it in chapter 12).

From the very beginning, human relations analysts have emphasized the great variability of individual characteristics and behaviors and have insisted on the relevance of these differences for understanding organizational behavior. Early research demonstrated that such officially irrelevant differences as race (Collins, 1946), class (Warner and Low, 1947), and cultural background (Dalton, 1950) had strong effects on allocation to work roles and organizational behavior. More contemporary research continues to explore this theme by analyzing differences related to sex. For example, Kanter (1977a), in her intensive study of one large United States corporation, describes how men are systematically allocated to career lines allowing extended upward mobility while women tend to be placed in low-ceiling or dead-end tracks. More generally, researchers in this tradition insist that "objective" social conditions do not directly cause a given behavioral result: rather these conditions must be "processed" by individual actors who vary in their interests, values, intelligence, sensitivity, and many other properties. Hence, such factors as leadership, information, incentives, and rules do not produce a uniform but a variable effect—one contingent on interpretation by the responding actors.

The human relations school has also given rise to much effort directed at changing organizations—modifying and improving them as social environments. The original Hawthorne researchers were themselves interested in pursuing practical applications of their findings. Stressing the positive relation in their studies between worker satisfaction and productivity, they sought techniques to improve the adjustment and morale of individual workers. One approach involved the introduction of a set of personnel counselors, distinct from the line hierarchy, whose task it was to listen sympathetically to workers' complaints (Roethlisberger and Dickson, 1939: 189–376; 590–604). The interviewing techniques devised for this program contributed to the development of nondirective counseling techniques now in wide use.

Another change strategy devised by the human relations school stressed the importance of supervisory skills in promoting worker morale. Supervisors required special training if they were to become more sensitive to the psychological and social needs of their subordinates. Mayo (1945), in particular, stressed the important role to be performed by supervisors and managers whose social function it was to motivate cooperation among workers—cooperation that could no longer be assumed to be automatically forthcoming (see Bendix and Fisher, 1949). Thus, the human relations approach helped to spawn many diverse efforts in leadership training, from simple attitude change efforts to more intensive Bethel-type sensitivity or T-group training. (See, for example, Argyris, 1962; Blake and Mouton, 1964; National Training Laboratories, 1953.)

Yet another approach has focused on the need to redefine and enlarge the role definitions specified for workers. Contrary to the assumptions of the rational system model, the human relations group stressed the dangers of excessive formalization with its emphasis on extreme functional specialization. Job enlargement or, at least, job rotation, was advocated as a method of reducing the alienation and increasing the commitment and satisfaction of workers performing routine work (see Argyris, 1957). Still other reformers have stressed the importance of worker participation in decision making within the organization, particularly with regard to those decisions directly affecting them. Although given encouragement by the Hawthorne studies, more direct support linking participation to motivation and commitment has come from the experimental and theoretical work of Lewin (1948) and his colleagues (for example, Coch and French, 1948). At the current time the participation by workers in managerial decision making is given much more emphasis in certain European countries than in the United States (see Blumberg, 1968; Tannenbaum et al., 1974).

Virtually all of these applications of the human relations movement have come under severe criticism on both ideological and empirical grounds. Paradoxically, the human relations movement, ostensibly developed to humanize the cold and calculating rationality of the factory and shop, rapidly came under attack on the grounds that it represented simply a more subtle and refined form of exploitation. Critics charged that workers' legitimate economic interests were being inappropriately deemphasized; actual conflicts of interest were denied and "therapeutically" managed; and the roles attributed to managers represented a new brand of elitism. The entire movement was branded as "cow sociology": just as contented cows were alleged to produce more milk, satisfied workers were expected to produce more output (see Bell, 1960: 238–44; Bendix, 1956: 308–40; Landsberger, 1958; Strauss, 1963; Braverman, 1974: 139–51).

The ideological criticisms were the first to erupt, but reservations raised by researchers on the basis of empirical evidence may in the long run prove to be more devastating. Several decades of research have demonstrated no clear relation between worker satisfaction and productivity (see Brayfield and Crockett, 1955; Schwab and Cummings, 1970); no clear relation between supervisory behavior or leadership style and worker productivity (see Hollander and Julian, 1969); no clear relation between job enlargement and worker satisfaction or productivity (see Hulin and Blood, 1968); and no clear relation between participation in decision making and satisfaction or productivity (see Strauss, 1963: 60–70; Vroom, 1969: 227–39). Where positive relations among these variables have been observed, the direction may be opposite to that predicted: productivity producing satisfaction (Porter and Lawler, 1968) or productivity influencing supervisory style (Lowin and Craig, 1968), rather than vice versa. Even the original Hawthorne results have been reanalyzed and questioned (see Carey, 1967; Sykes, 1965).

Our brief survey of the human relations school cannot do justice to the variety of theoretical implications, empirical studies, and practical reform efforts it has generated. It is only a small exaggeration to suggest that the academic field of industrial sociology first saw the light of day at the Hawthorne plant, with Mayo serving as midwife. Moreover, sociological work on organizations well into the 1950s was shaped primarily by the human relations model—whether attempting to fill in its missing pieces or attacking its shortcomings and biases. And all of the thousands of studies concerned with motivation, morale, and leadership either have been directly stimulated by or are indirectly beholden to a tiny group of workers who kept increasing their output even though the lights were growing dimmer.[4]

SELZNICK'S INSTITUTIONAL APPROACH

Philip Selznick, a student of bureaucracy under Merton at Columbia, but an intellectual descendant of Michels, has developed his own unique natural system model. While Selznick's work is not as widely known as Mayo's, his approach is more fully developed and coherent. Selznick's work has been applied and extended by several of his students, including Burton Clark, Charles Perrow, and Mayer Zald. He has not systematically presented his

[4]For a more detailed summary and highly critical assessment of the human relations school, see Perrow (1979: 90–138).

model in any single source but has scattered his description of it through several books and articles. We will attempt to provide a short but coherent sketch of his approach.

For Selznick, "the most important thing about organizations is that, though they are tools, each nevertheless has a life of its own" (1949: 10). He agrees with the rational system analyst that the distinguishing characteristic of formal organizations is that they are rationally ordered instruments designed to attain goals. However, these formal structures can "never succeed in conquering the nonrational dimensions of organizational behavior" (Selznick, 1948: 25). The sources of these nonrational dimensions are (1) individuals, who participate in the organization as "wholes" and do not act merely in terms of their formal roles within the system; and (2) the fact that the formal structure is only one aspect of the concrete social structure that must adjust in various ways to the pressures of its institutional environment (1948: 25). In short, organizational rationality is constrained by "the recalcitrance of the tools of action": persons bring certain characteristics to the organization and develop other commitments as members that restrict their capacity for rational action; organizational procedures become valued as ends in themselves; the organization strikes bargains with its environment that compromise present objectives and limit future possibilities (1949: 253–59).

As I have noted elsewhere:

If the organization as conceived by Weber operates like a smoothly functioning professional football team, Selznick's image corresponds more closely to Alice's efforts at croquet with equipment and competition provided by the Queen of Hearts. Alice swings her flamingo mallet but the bird may duck his head before the hedgehog-ball is struck; just so, the manager issues his directives but they may be neither understood nor followed by his subordinates. (Scott, 1964: 511)

Selznick views organizational structure as an adaptive organism shaped in reaction to the characteristics and commitments of participants as well as to influences from the external environment. He explicitly embraces a structural-functional form of analysis, explaining: "This means that a given empirical system is deemed to have basic needs, essentially related to self-maintenance; the system develops repetitive means of self-defense; and day-to-day activity is interpreted in terms of the function served by that activity for the maintenance and defense of the system" (Selznick, 1948: 29). Insisting that the overriding need of all systems "is the maintenance of the integrity and continuity of the system itself," Selznick attempts to spell out certain more specific, "derived imperatives," including the security of the organization as a whole in relation to its environment, the stability of lines of authority and communication, the stability of informal relations within the organization, and a homogeneity of outlook with respect to the meaning and role of the organization. However, he regards the list as suggestive, not definitive. Acknowledging its vagueness, Selznick defends the concept of organizational need because it directs attention to the internal relevance of organizational behavior, including behaviors that are ostensibly directed outward (1948: 29–30).

To this point Selznick's model appears to be a rather conventional version of the more general natural system model described early in this chapter, but it suddenly takes an interesting turn. He proposes that we will learn more interesting things about organizations if we do not attempt to examine the satisfaction of all needs of the organism but, like Freud, focus on those needs "which cannot be fulfilled within approved avenues of expression" (1948: 32). Thus, he explicitly directs attention away from the formal structures and procedures, insofar as they are functioning smoothly, and emphasizes those organizational features created to deal in irregular ways with unmet needs. Such mechanisms include informal structures, ideologies, and cooptation.

Selznick has described this same approach in slightly different language. He argues that rather than following the lead of experimental psychologists who study routine psychological processes, we should imitate the clinical psychologists who examine the dynamic adaptation of the organism over time. Instead of focusing on the recurrent decisions made on a day-to-day basis in organizations, we should concentrate on those critical decisions that, once made, result in a change in the structure itself. The pattern of these critical decisions, viewed over time, results in the development of a distinctive character structure for each organization, just as an individual's critical decisions and typical mode of coping with problems give rise to the development of a distinctive personality (Selznick, 1957).

One final concept: Selznick refers to the process by which an organization develops a distinctive character structure as *institutionalization.* As Selznick uses the term, to become institutionalized is to become "infused with value beyond the technical requirements of the task at hand" (1957: 17). Selznick invites us to observe the process by which organizations develop distinctive structures, capacities, and liabilities; he proposes, in sum, a natural history of organizations.

If we examine some of the empirical work stimulated by Selznick's institutional model, we will obtain a clearer picture of both the strengths and weaknesses of the proposed approach. Selznick's most famous study is of the Tennessee Valley Authority (TVA), a decentralized governmental agency created during the depression to improve the economic status of the entire Tennessee Valley, a chronically depressed, flood-ravaged region. Massive federal funds—at least by the standards of the 1930s—were provided to support a broad-gauged attack on the problems of the area. Flood control, hydroelectric power, and soil conservation efforts were to be provided in an integrated manner. Top agency officials were located at the site, not in far-off Washington, so that officials would not be inclined to impose solutions from above but would work with the local inhabitants in developing acceptable projects (see Lilienthal, 1944).

As we would expect, Selznick (1949) focuses on the "internal relevance"— the consequences for the agency—of these strategies. He points out that the democratic ideology not only served to recruit and motivate talented participants but also enabled the New Deal agency to gain access to a suspicious and conservative area. Agency officials employed cooptation as a strategy to gain legitimacy and political support. *Cooptation* is a mechanism by which external elements are incorporated into the decision making structures of the organization: local leaders were recruited to participate in the agency's decision making and advisory bodies. This tactic assured that the agency would enjoy political support in the local area for its programs, but such support always comes at a price: local leaders exchanged support for a measure of influence on the agency's programs and goals. As a consequence, some public interest goals were subverted to serve private interests. For example, improved land values surrounding water projects that were supposed to benefit the public often fell into private hands, and reforested land intended as watershed was taken over by lumber interests.

Selznick's institutional approach has guided the work of a number of other researchers. Thus, Clark's (1956) study of an adult education program in Los Angeles argues that its professed goals of providing cultural and intellectual programs could not be realized because of its marginal organizational and institutional status. Lacking full legitimacy, only those parts of the program that could attract large numbers of students were retained, with other academically valuable but less popular offerings losing out to the "enrollment economy." Messinger's (1955) analysis of the Townsend movement, a pressure group developed in the 1930s to represent the economic interests of the elderly, records how the movement attempted to survive by transforming its original radical political objectives into noncontroversial recreational programs. And Zald and Denton (1963) describe the transformation of the YMCA from a religious organization performing rehabilitative and welfare services for the urban poor into a social and recreational center for suburban and middle-class young people.

These and related studies exhibit several common features. The analyst focuses on the administrative history of the organization: the structural features and programs of the organization are viewed as changing over time in response to changing conditions. The methodology employed tends to be that of the case study, and heavy reliance is placed on the analysis of organizational documents and interviews with informants knowledgeable about the organization's past history. Given this approach, most of the organizations selected for study have been relatively recently founded. Selznick insists that he is not interested in recounting the history of any given organization for its own sake but in seeking "to discover the characteristic ways in which types of institutions respond to types of circumstances" (1957: 142). However, this interest in generalization is somewhat at odds with the intensive case study approach. As Cohen notes: "As the desire to explain more and more aspects of a single study, situation, or phenomenon increases, the possibility of using this explanation outside the situation for which it was created approaches the vanishing point" (1972: 402).

Fundamentally, the institutional model seeks to explain changes in the goals of the organization—not the professed goals, but the ends actually pursued, the operative goals. The general mode of explanation is similar to that offered by Michels: to increase their own security, organizational participants modify controversial goals in the face of hostile environments. As Perrow notes, the literature spawned by the institutional school—to which Perrow himself has contributed (see Perrow, 1961)—takes on an "exposé" character: "The major message is that the organization has sold out its goals in order to survive or grow" (1979: 182). While cynicism seems often justified, Selznick's conception appears to go out of its way to inspect the seamy side of organizational life. His approach tends to focus on the forces that undermine the organization's impersonal principles and subvert its formal ends to narrow interests, rather than on those that sustain these values and bolster the distinctively rational aspects (see Gouldner, 1955). As he himself stresses, Selznick truly is a "clinical sociologist" of organizations, and like his role models, the clinical psychologists, he has chosen to focus primarily on deviance and abnormality. One learns a great deal from this literature about what makes an organization "sick" and about various forms of illness or deviance; but very little is said about those forces that sustain an organization and keep it "healthy," with its goals intact.[5]

In spite of these limitations—or, more likely, because of them—Selznick and his followers have provided us with some of the most fascinating accounts of organizations to be found in the literature. Pathology is often engrossing and can be highly instructive. And these accounts of "friction, dilemma, doubt, and ruin" (Selznick, 1948: 25) serve as a strong antidote to the paean to organizational rationality sung by some overexuberant rational system theorists.

PARSONS'S SOCIAL SYSTEM MODEL

More so than other analysts working within the natural system tradition, Talcott Parsons has developed a very explicit model detailing the needs that must be met if a system is to survive. Parson's model is the product of a lifetime devoted to perfecting a general analytic model suitable for the analysis of all

---

[5]See Perrow (1979) for a more sympathetic review and evaluation of the institutional school.

types of collectivities—from small, primary groups to entire societies (see Parsons, 1951; Parsons, Bales, and Shils, 1954; Parsons, 1966). He first applied the model to formal organizations in two papers published in the late 1950s and collected in his book on societies (1960).

We have already encountered Parsons's AGIL model in chapter 2 but will briefly review it here. According to his model, all social systems are confronted by four basic system problems: adaptation, goal-attainment, integration, and latency or pattern-maintenance. The schema is viewed as sufficiently general to be applicable to all types of social systems. In addition, it may be applied at more than one level in analyzing a given type of system. Thus, Parsons applies his model to organizations at the ecological, the structural, and the social-psychological levels. Linkages across these levels are also stressed.

First, at the ecological level, Parsons relates organizations to the functioning of the larger society. The AGIL schema is applied to the society as a whole, and as described in chapter 2, Parsons shows how subordinate social units such as organizations can be classified according to their societal function. For example, economic organizations such as firms are said to serve the adaptive needs of the larger society. Parsons points out: "What from the point of view of the organization is its specified goal is, from the point of view of the larger system of which it is a differentiated part or subsystem, a specialized or differentiated function" (1960: 19). Because of this functional linkage, the place or role of the subsystem is legitimated, and it may expect to receive societal approval and resources in accordance with the value placed in the society on the particular functions it performs.

Shifting to the structural level of analysis, each formal organization may also be analyzed as a social system in its own right; and each must develop its own differentiated subsystems to satisfy the four basic needs. Thus, each organization must develop structures that enable it to adapt to its environment and must mobilize resources needed for its continued operation. Arrangements are also needed to enable the organization to set and implement its goals. To solve its integrative problems, an organization must find ways to command the loyalties of its members, motivate their effort, and coordinate the operations of its various sectors. And mechanisms must be developed to cope with latency problems, to promote consensus on the values that define and legitimate the organization's output and system goals.

While Parsons does not insist that a specific structural unit will develop to manage each of these functional needs, he does argue that structural differentiation will tend to occur along these divisions. Functional imperatives generate the fault lines along which a social structure becomes differentiated. The explanation for this linkage between functional requirements and structural arrangements is simply that the various functional needs are somewhat in conflict, so that efforts directed at solving one functional problem interfere with efforts directed toward the others.[6] Specifically, energies devoted to adapting the organization to its environment partially conflict with efforts toward goal attainment—a problem emphasized by Selznick and his colleagues —and efforts directed toward goal attainment interfere with efforts directed toward integration—a tension emphasized by Bales (1953), and so on. A structural "solution" to these tensions is to create roles and subsystems focused on each problem area. For example, Bales and his colleagues argue that in informal groups the inherent tensions involved in goal attainment (for example, winning the game) versus integration (for example, providing satisfaction for all participants) is partially resolved by the emergence of a "task" leader, who specializes in directing and controlling goal attainment activities, and a "socio-emotional" leader, who specializes in motivating members and reducing tensions (Bales, 1953; Slater, 1955). And in formal organizations, specialized departments and roles—supervisors, maintenance workers, personnel counselors, inspectors—emerge to carry out the multiple, and somewhat conflicting, functions. This solution only simplifies the definitions of individual roles and subsystems and does not, of course, eliminate the incompatibilities: they are merely pushed to a higher level of the system for resolution. For example, at the level of the informal group, Bales (1953) argues that the differentiated leader roles provide a stable basis for group functioning only if the two leaders form a coalition of mutual support. And Lawrence and Lorsch (1967) have argued that organizations characterized by a higher level of structural differentiation are in greater need of integrative and conflict resolution mechanisms.

In moving toward a more micro or social psychological level, Parsons again employs the AGIL schema, arguing that each subsystem within the organization is itself comprised of finer subdivisions that can be distinguished in terms of the functional requirements. For example, within the goal attainment (G) subsystem—that part of the organization with the power to set and mobilize resources for goal attainment—Parsons distinguishes between:

Policy decisions—decisions concerning what goals are to be pursued and how they are to be attained (the Gg subsector—the goal attainment subsector or the goal attainment subsystem)

Allocative decisions—lower-level decisions regarding the allocation of responsibilities and resources among personnel (the Ga subsector)

---

[6]Parsons's reasoning at this point is illuminated by knowledge of the intellectual origins of the AGIL schema. His conception of these system problems grew out of his work on the "pattern variables"—basic value dichotomies representing the dimensions along which structures are arranged. The pairs of opposing values—universalism-particularism, affectivity-affective neutrality, ascription-achievement, and specificity-diffuseness—were crossclassified, producing the four system needs. Thus, values identified as most appropriate for solving the problem of adaptation are universalism, affective neutrality, specificity, and achievement; and at the opposite extreme, values appropriate for improving integration are particularism, affectivity, diffuseness, and ascription (see Parsons, 1951; and Parsons, Bales, and Shils, 1953).

Coordinative decisions—decisions about how personnel are to be motivated and
their contributions coordinated (the Gi subsector)
Supporting values—values that serve to legitimate and authorize the decision
making rights within this subsystem (the Gl subsector)

Parsons outlines how each of the other subsystems is also differentiated into
the appropriate subsectors. Finally, he also uses the four system problems as
a means of describing the relationships—in his terms, boundary processes—
between systems and subsystems (see Parsons, 1960: 22–41; see also Landsberger, 1961: 227–31).

Like all natural system models, Parson's framework emphasizes a set of
functional needs that all social systems must satisfy in order to survive. As
noted, this approach emphasizes the similarities between organizations and
other types of social systems. But unlike other natural system models, Parsons's formulation also provides a clear basis for distinguishing between organizations and other social systems. Parsons states: "As a formal analytical
point of reference, primacy of orientation to the attainment of a specific goal
is used as the defining characteristic of an organization which distinguishes it
from other types of social systems" (1960: 17). Within the Parsonian framework, this definition implies more than the widely shared view that organizations tend to pursue specific goals. Parsons's statement refers to the relative
importance placed on the goal-attainment subsystem in organizations. That is,
organizations are social systems placing greater priority on those processes by
which goals are set and resources are mobilized for goal attainment than is the
case in other social systems.

We cannot hope to summarize all of Parsons's ideas on organizations—his
framework rapidly becomes exceedingly complex—but we will review one
other useful set of distinctions. In addition to his analysis of functional differentiation that occurs along a horizontal axis at any given level of analysis,
Parsons also distinguishes among three major hierarchical levels that characterize organizational structure. At the bottom layer of the structure is the
technical system where the actual "product" of the organization is processed.
This level is exemplified by the activities of workers on assembly lines, scientists in the laboratory, and teachers in the classroom. Above the technical level
is the *managerial* system whose primary functions are to mediate between the
organization and the immediate external situation, including those who con-
sume the organization's products and supply its raw materials, and to administer the organization's internal affairs. At the top of the organization is the
institutional system whose function is to relate the organization to the larger
societal system: "the source of the 'meaning,' legitimation, or higher-level
support which makes the implementation of the organization's goals possible"
(Parsons, 1960: 63–64). Parsons makes the interesting point that there exists
a "qualitative break" in the line authority relation at the two points where the

three systems are linked (p. 65). (This distinction between levels anticipates some of the concerns of open system theorists, described in chapter 5. The significance of the break between levels is discussed in chapter 11.)

Unlike Mayo and Selznick, Parsons's approach to organizational analysis has not led to the emergence of an identifiable group of researchers who are self-consciously carrying on this tradition. Of course, Parsons's generalized social system paradigm has had considerable impact on the work of sociologists, and many of Parsons's specific concepts and ideas have influenced work in the area of organizations. We will limit ourselves to only a few general comments in assessing Parsons's contributions. On the positive side, his work attempts to develop and perfect a limited set of abstract concepts that can then be adapted for use in examining the structure and functioning of diverse types of social groupings. Using the same generic concepts helps us to see similarities in social structure and process across systems that appear on the surface to be quite different. Also, more than those of other natural system theorists, Parsons's framework is quite comprehensive, encompassing the formal and rational aspects of organizations as well as the informal. Further, Parsons is more explicit than others in defining the system needs that must be served for survival.

Problems with the Parsonian framework are numerous. They include the difficulty in translating his analytic concepts into operational variables. For example, although it is reasonably easy to give examples of roles designed to increase integration, it is often difficult to assign a given structural feature such as a role or a subunit to any single function (Morse, 1961). Landsberger (1961: 232) is correct that we should not expect concrete social structures to match closely analytical distinctions, but we do need to have a clearer set of rules for relating one to the other than Parsons provides. Finally, as many others have noted, Parsons's formulation tends to be more of a theoretical framework than a substantive theory. We are provided with numerous concepts that help us to see interesting distinctions, but given relatively few testable propositions. The functionalist paradigm underlying the approach does provide some implicit hypotheses—such as, unless the system needs are met the organization will not survive—but as already noted, such predictions are difficult to test.[7]

Summary and Tentative Conclusions

While the rational system model focuses on features of organizations that distinguish them from other social groupings, the natural system model emphasizes commonalities between organizations and other systems. The natural

[7]Useful general discussion of Parsons's social system model will be found in Morse (1961). Landsberger (1961) provides an excellent description and critique of Parsons's model applied to organizations.

system theorists do not deny that organizations have distinctive features but argue that they are overshadowed by the more generic systems and processes. Thus, the specific output goals of organizations are often undermined or distorted by energies devoted to the pursuit of system goals, chief among which is the desire to survive as a system. And the formal aspects of organizational structure that receive so much attention from the rational system analysts are treated more as faded backdrops for the "real" informal structures. More generally, it is clear that while the rational system model stresses the normative structure of organizations, the natural system model places more emphasis on the behavioral structure. And where the rational system perspective stresses the importance of structure over the characteristics of participants, the natural system perspective reverses these priorities—so much so that Bennis (1959: 266) labels this orientation as one of "people without organizations."

All of the several branches of the natural system perspective embrace a structural-functional model of analysis although they vary considerably in how explicitly and how fully they pursue its development. The human relations analysts tend to be less overt and less complete in their use of this model than is Selznick or Parsons. All schools within the natural system framework presume the existence of certain needs that must be met if the system is to survive; and all direct attention to discovering the mechanisms by which these needs are satisfied.

Varying views of the environment appear to be associated with the natural system theorists. Most of the human relations analysts simply overlook it as a factor. Like the rational system theorists, they concentrate on the internal organizational arrangements and their effects on participants, treating the organization as a closed system. This neglect is especially striking in the case of the Hawthorne studies, which were conducted during the 1930s, in the depths of the Great Depression. In the bank wiring observation room study, for example, the workers' efforts to restrict production were viewed as irrational conformity to group norms. Given the larger economic situation, however, these activities may instead have been a highly rational response to the threat of being laid off (see Landsberger, 1958: 58; Blau and Scott, 1962: 92–93). Indeed, during the period of the research there had been many layoffs at the Hawthorne plant, and in fact, the bank wiring room study had to be discontinued because so many workers were let go! (Roethlisberger and Dickson, 1939: 395).

Selznick and his students, by contrast, do consider the environment in their analyses of organizations. However, their view is a highly selective one: the environment is primarily perceived as an enemy, as a source of pressures and problems. In most of the studies in this tradition, the organization is viewed as capitulating to a tyrannical and hostile environment as the price of its survival.

In the work of Parsons we begin to have a more balanced view of the environment. Great stress is placed on the importance of the organization-environment relation, the organization being viewed as a subsystem within a more comprehensive social unit, and the environment seen more as a stabilizing element sustaining and legitimating the organization in its special mission than as a source of resistance. In many ways, Parsons anticipates the view of the open systems theorists in his treatment of the environment.

Two quite different perspectives on organizations have now been described. How could two such different viewpoints have arisen? Several explanations have been proposed. Since each sheds additional light on the subject, they will be briefly reviewed. Lawrence and Lorsch (1967: 163–84) propose that some of the differences in perspective may have been produced by variations in the experience and background of the analysts themselves. They point out that among the rational or "classical" theorists, as they label them, Fayol, Mooney, and Urwick were all practical men with managerial experience. Taylor's training was as an industrial engineer. By contrast, among the natural systems theorists, Mayo, Roethlisberger, Selznick, McGregor, and Parsons were all from academic backgrounds with experience largely in the university. (Exceptions to this division were, of course, Weber, who was a university professor —however, in terms of life style and experience he is more accurately described as a recluse scholar—and Gulick, who was also an academic.) Lawrence and Lorsch argue that these divergent backgrounds shaped the reactions of these analysts to organizations. Coming from the relatively unstructured arrangements of a university, the natural system analysts would be prone to react negatively to the formalism of an industrial plant, and might even be inclined to attribute their own needs for autonomy to workers in these situations.

A second explanation offered is that the analysts have concentrated on different types of organizations. The rational system analysts have been more likely to investigate industrial firms and state bureaucracies, while the natural system analysts have tended to focus on service and professional organizations —schools, hospitals, and the YMCA. Since it is clearly the case that the degree of formalization and of goal specificity varies greatly across the spectrum of organizations, it is quite possible that the rational system analysts have concentrated attention on the relatively highly structured end of the continuum and the natural system analysts on the less structured end.

A third but related explanation for the differences in perspectives also comes from Lawrence and Lorsch, who suggest the possibility that organizational forms vary as a function of their environments: "In simplified terms, the classical [rational] theory tends to hold in more stable environments, while the human relations [natural] theory is more appropriate to dynamic situations" (1967: 183). This important thesis is simply introduced at this point; its exploration will continue throughout the next several chapters.

Although differences in the analysts' backgrounds or in the particular organization on which they choose to focus may account for some of the variance in these two perspectives, it is our view that these points of view represent more fundamental divisions than are suggested by these explanations. Underlying the perspectives are quite basic divergences in moral and philosophical viewpoints.

The natural and the rational system theorists tend to hold differing conceptions of the actual and the proper relation of individual participants to organizations. Thus, the rational system theorists argue that only selected behaviors of participants are relevant so far as the organization is concerned and that only these "task-related" behaviors are at issue. The natural system theorists have tended to expand the definition of organizationally relevant behavior to include more and more aspects of the individual's activities and attitudes. They have done so both on the grounds that such behaviors do in fact have an impact on the task behavior of participants and because they argue that the organization as a social context has an impact on the individual participant's well-being (see Maslow, 1954; Argyris, 1957). Many of these theorists point to the dysfunctions of the partial inclusion of individual participants and argue, partly on moral grounds, that organizations should take more responsibility for the "whole person." These arguments are not without merit, but all of the morality is not on one side. It is important to recognize that formal organizations developed in part to place limits on the demands superiors could make on their subordinates. The development of formal role definitions—defining the limits of a participant's obligations—was an important step in increasing the freedom of individuals. Whether the organization's purview should incorporate more or fewer facets of the lives of its participants is a basic philosophical difference separating the two perspectives.

Finally, the two approaches are characterized by quite divergent views of the fundamental nature of social systems. These differences are reflected in the contrasting imagery or metaphors employed by the two schools. For the mechanistic model of structure of the rational system perspective, the natural system substitutes an organic model. Rational systems are designed, but natural systems evolve; the former develop by conscious design, the latter by natural growth; rational systems are characterized by calculation; natural by spontaneity. Lest we regard these viewpoints as of recent vintage, Wolin (1960: 352–434) reminds us that these images of social structure have a long history in political and social thought. The view of organizations as economic, technological, efficient instruments is associated with the work of such social theorists as Hobbes, Lenin, and Saint-Simon—the precursors of Weber, Barnard, and Simon. The view of organizations as communitarian, natural, antirational, organic systems may be traced back to the social theories of Rousseau, Proudhon, Burke, and Durkheim, the intellectual ancestors of Mayo and Selznick. With such lengthy and distinguished pedigrees, it is unlikely that either of these two lines of thought will soon end, or that their differences will be quickly resolved.

chapter 5

Organizations
as
Open Systems

*That a system is open means, not simply that
it engages in interchanges with the
environment, but that this interchange is an
essential factor underlying the system's
viability.*

WALTER BUCKLEY (1967)

The open systems perspective emerged as a part of the intellectual ferment following World War II, although its roots are much older. This general intellectual movement created new areas of study, such as cybernetics and information theory; stimulated new applications, such as systems engineering and operations research; transformed existing disciplines, including the study of organizations; and proposed closer linkages among scientific disciplines. The latter interest has been fostered especially by general systems theory. Its founder, biologist Ludwig von Bertalanffy, was concerned about the growing compartmentalization of science: "The physicist, the biologist, the psychologist and the social scientist are, so to speak, encapsulated in a private universe, and it is difficult to get word from one cocoon to another" (Bertalanffy, 1956:1). Bertalanffy and his associates argued that certain general ideas could have relevance across a broad spectrum of disciplines. In particular, they have endeavored to show that many of the most important entities studied by scientists—nuclear particles, atoms, molecules, cells, organs, organisms, ecological communities, groups, organizations, societies, solar systems—are all subsumable under the general rubric of "system."[1]

All systems are characterized by an assemblage or combination of parts with relations among them such that they are interdependent. While these features underlie the similarities exhibited by all systems, they also suggest the bases for the differences among them. The "parts" of which all systems are comprised vary from being quite simple in their own structures to being very complex, from being highly stable in their state to highly variable, and from being relatively impervious to system forces to being highly reactive to the workings of the system to which they belong. As we move from mechanical through organic to social systems, the parts of which systems are comprised become more complex and variable. Similarly, the nature of the "relations" among the parts varies from one type of system to another. In this connection, Norbert Wiener, the founder of cybernetics, notes: "Organization we must consider as something in which there is an interdependence between the several organized parts but in which this interdependence has degrees" (1956: 322). In mechanistic systems, the interdependence among the parts is such that their behavior is highly constrained and limited. The structure is relatively rigid and the system of relations determinant. In organic systems, the connections among the interdependent parts are somewhat less constrained, allowing for more flexibility of response. In social systems, such as groups and organizations, the connections among the interacting parts become relatively loose: less constraint is placed on the behavior of one element by the condition of the others. Social organizations, in contrast to physical or mechanical structures, are *loosely coupled* systems (see Ashby, 1968; Buckley, 1967: 82–83).

Also, as we progress from simple to complex systems, the nature and relative importance of the various "flows" among the system elements and between the system and its environment change. The major types of system flows are those of materials, energy, and information. And, as Buckley notes: "whereas the relations among components of mechanical systems are a function primarily of spatial and temporal considerations and the transmission of energy from one component to another, the interrelations characterizing higher levels come to depend more and more on the transmission of information" (1967: 47).

The notion of types or levels of systems that vary both in the complexity of their component parts and in the nature of the relations among the parts has been usefully elaborated by Boulding, who has proposed a classification

[1]In his monumental book on *Living Systems,* Miller (1978) identifies seven basic levels: the cell, the organ, the organism, the group, the organization, the society, and the supranational system.

of systems by their level of complexity. Briefly, Boulding identifies the following system types:

1. *Frameworks.* Systems comprised of static structures such as the arrangements of atoms in a crystal or the anatomy of an animal.

2. *Clockworks.* Simple dynamic systems with predetermined motions such as the clock and the solar system.

3. *Cybernetic systems.* A system capable of self-regulation in terms of some externally prescribed target or criterion, such as a thermostat.

4. *Open systems.* A system capable of self-maintenance based on a throughput of resources from its environment, such as a living cell.

5. *Blueprinted-growth systems.* Systems which reproduce not by duplication but by producing seeds or eggs containing preprogrammed instructions for development, such as the acorn-oak system or the egg-chicken system.

6. *Internal image systems.* Systems capable of a detailed awareness of the environment in which information is received and organized into an image or knowledge structure of the environment as a whole, a level at which animals function.

7. *Symbol processing systems.* Systems which possess self-consciousness and so are capable of using language. Humans function at this level.

8. *Social systems.* Multi-cephalous systems comprised of actors functioning at level seven who share a common social order and culture. Social organizations operate at this level.

9. *Transcendental systems.* Systems comprised of the "absolutes and the inescapable unknowables." (Boulding, 1956: 200–207)

Boulding's typology is illuminating in several respects. It quickly persuades us of the great range and variety of systems present in the world. Levels 1 to 3 encompass the physical systems, levels 4 to 6 the biological systems, and levels 7 and 8 the human and social systems. Boulding adds level 9 so that his own classification system will not be closed but open to possibilities not now understood.

Although the nine levels can be distinctly identified and associated with specific existing systems, they are not meant to be mutually exclusive. Indeed, each higher level system incorporates the features of those below it. For example, it is possible to analyze a social organization as a framework, a clockwork, a cybernetic system, and so on up to level 8, the level that captures the most complex or higher level processes occurring in organizations. Boulding argues that because each level incorporates those below it, "much valuable information and insights can be obtained by applying low-level systems to high-level subject matter." At the same time, Boulding reminds us that "most of the theoretical schemes of the social sciences are still at level 2, just rising now to 3, although the subject matter clearly involves level 8" (1956: 208). This is an important criticism of theoretical models in organizations which we need to keep before us as we review more recent attempts to develop open systems models.

Special Emphases
of the Open Systems Perspective

Broadly speaking, the contributions of the general systems perspective to organization theory up to this time have been to raise the level of our theoretical models up to level 3, where organizations are viewed as cybernetic systems, and to level 4, where they are viewed as open systems. Although Boulding's typology suggests we may still have a long way to go before our models capture the complexity of organizational behavior, the insights obtained by moving to levels 3 and 4 are of great value. Let us briefly consider each level as it applies to organizations.

ORGANIZATIONS AS CYBERNETIC SYSTEMS

Systems functioning at Boulding's level 3 are capable of self-regulation. This important feat is attained through the development of specialized parts or subsystems related by certain processes or flows. Consider the mechanical example of the thermostat related to a source of heat (see figure 5–1). The system contains three parts: (1) a mechanism for converting inputs into outputs, in this case, a heater that converts fuel into heat; (2) a mechanism for comparing the level of outputs with some desired target level and issuing instructions to the first mechanism based on any discrepancy, in our case, a thermostat that compares the temperature in the room with a desired level and switches the heater on or off accordingly; and (3) a mechanism for setting the desired target level that governs the activity of the second mechanism, in our example, a person who determines the desired temperature for the room and sets the level of the thermostat. Figure 5–1 depicts these three parts and the flows among them for the thermostat example.

Figure 5–2 diagrams the same type of system, but at a more general or abstract level. To view an organization as a cybernetic system is to emphasize the importance of the operations, the control, and the policy centers and to analyze the flows among them (Swinth, 1974). The policy center sets the goals for the system. This activity occurs in response to demands or preferences from the environment (flow 1 in figure 5–2); some of the preferences take the form of specific orders (flow 2). Note that the setting of organizational goals is based

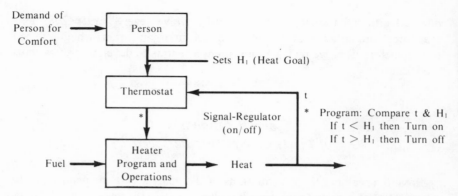

*If remove either no longer have servomechanism

Figure 5–1 Illustration of a Cybernetic System: The Thermostat and the Heater. *Source:* Adapted from Swinth (1974), figure 2–1, p. 18.

on information about preferences in the environment so that exchanges between the environment and the organization can occur. The flows out of the policy center (flow 3) are the goals of the system itself. The control center monitors the performance of the operations level, keeping its outputs in line

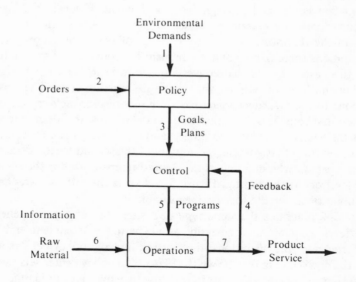

Figure 5–2 Abstract Model of Cybernetic System. *Source:* Adapted from Swinth (1974), Figure 2–4, p. 23.

106

with the goals established by the policy center. The control center also obtains information about the outputs of the operations level (flow 4). This information is compared with the standards prescribed by the goals issued by the policy center and results in a set of instructions or directive to the operations units (flow 5). As Buckley emphasizes, such feedback-controlled arrangements result in behavior that is "goal-*directed,* and not merely goal-*oriented,* since it is the deviations from the goal-state itself that direct the behavior of the system, rather than some predetermined internal mechanism that aims blindly" (1967: 53). Further, a feedback mechanism detects departures from the established goals no matter what their cause, an important control characteristic as systems become so complex that all the potential sources of disturbance cannot be identified in advance (see Beer, 1964: 29–30). The operations unit receives the raw materials (flow 6) and transforms them into products or outputs that are distributed outside the system (flow 7). The cybernetic model places great emphasis on the operational level of the organization—the level at which the production processes of the system are carried out. The analysis of these technical flows—inputs, throughputs, and outputs—is regarded as vital to an understanding of the system; indeed, the control and policy centers are examined chiefly in terms of their impact on these technical flows.

This analytic framework can be applied to the organization as a whole or to any of its subsystems. It can be used, for example, to analyze the operation of the personnel subsystem of a company, in which other subsystems place demands on the personnel department for trained employees, and this unit must control the recruitment and training of new workers and monitor their turnover (see Carzo and Yanouzas (1967: 345–47)); or it can be used to examine the working of an entire company, which respond to demands from its marketplace and oversee the production and marketing of desired products for external customers (see Clough, 1963).

While cybernetic mechanisms involving feedback loops are readily discernible in organizations, we must be aware that our discussion of them (like others in this literature) has carried us far above Boulding's level 3 model. Level 3 is that of the thermostat that regulates temperature to a given value; our discussion has included *within* the system a mechanism for selecting the desired value: the policy center. Moreover, we have assumed that this center is responsive to demands from its environment. In short, all of our examples have assumed that the system is functioning at the level of an open system.

Organizations as Loosely Coupled Systems

The cybernetic model gives the impression of a taut system—an arrangement of parts such that each is highly responsive to changes in the other. Such system elements are certainly found within organizations, but we should guard against overgeneralization. One of the main contributions of the open systems perspective is the recognition that many systems—especially social systems—contain elements that are only slightly interrelated with other elements and that are capable of fairly autonomous actions (see Ashby, 1968; Glassman, 1973).

This insight can be applied to many different components or elements of organizations and their participants. Thus, we have seen that from the standpoint of the natural system analysts, the normative structure of an organization is only loosely coupled with its behavioral structure. Rules do not always govern actions: each exhibits a capacity for autonomous action. A similar observation has been made at the social-psychological level. Some analysts have noted that an individual's goals or intentions may be only weakly linked to his or her actions (see March and Olsen, 1976a; and chapter 12). The concept of loose coupling can also be applied to the relationship among structural units such as work groups or departments. Inspection of official organizational charts may lend the impression that these units are all highly interrelated and closely coordinated, whereas observation of their actual behavior may reveal that they are only slightly and occasionally connected.

A particularly important application of the loose coupling image is that proposed by Cyert and March (1963) and adopted by Pfeffer and Salancik (1978). As noted in chapter 1, these theorists propose to view the key participants in organizations not as a unitary hierarchy or as an organic entity, but as a loosely linked *coalition* of shifting interest groups. According to Pfeffer and Salancik:

> The organization is a coalition of groups and interests, each attempting to obtain something from the collectivity by interacting with others, and each with its own preferences and objectives. (Pfeffer and Salancik, 1978: 36)

Rather than being oriented to the pursuit of consistent, common objectives, these coalitions change

> their purpose and domains to accommodate new interests, sloughing off parts of themselves to avoid some interests, and when necessary become involved in activities far afield from their stated purposes. (Ibid., p. 24)

Contrary to first impressions and to rational system assumptions, open system theorists insist that loose coupling in structural arrangements can be highly adaptive for the system as a whole (see Weick, 1976; Pfeffer and Salancik, 1978; see also chapter 11). It appears that loose coupling need not signify either low moral or low managerial standards.

The Characteristics of Open Systems

Open systems are capable of self-maintenance on the basis of a throughput of resources from the environment. As Buckley (1967: 50) notes, this throughput is essential to the system's viability. Some analysts have mistakenly characterized an open system as having the capacity for self-maintenance *despite* the presence of throughput from the environment; their assumption is that because organizations are open, they must defend themselves against the environment. This view is misleading, since interaction with the environment is essential for open system functioning. As Pondy and Mitroff argue, rather than suggesting that organizational systems should be buffered "against environmental complexity . . . it is precisely the throughput of nonuniformity that preserves the differential structure of an open system" (1979: 7).

This is not to say that open systems do not have boundaries. They do, of course, and must expend energy in boundary maintenance: but it is of equal importance that energies be devoted to activities that span boundaries. Because of their openness, determining the boundaries of organizations is always difficult and sometimes appears to be a quite arbitrary decision. Does a university include within its boundary its students? its alumni? faculty during the summer? the spouses of students in university housing? Pfeffer and Salancik (1978: 30) propose to resolve this type of problem by reminding us that individual persons are not enclosed within the boundaries of organizations, only certain of their activities and behaviors. While this interpretation helps, we all know that many actions have relevance for more than one system simultaneously; for example, a sale from the standpoint of one system is a purchase when viewed from another; and what is an act of conformity for one system can be an act of deviance for another. Moreover, as already noted, all systems are made up of subsystems and are themselves subsumed in larger systems—an arrangement that creates strong linkages across systems and confounds the attempt to erect clear boundaries between them. Finally, our determination of whether a system is open is itself a matter of how the boundaries of the system are defined. As Hall and Fagen note: "whether a given system is open or closed depends on how much of the universe is included in the system and how much in the environment. By adjoining to the system that part of the environment with which an exchange takes place, the system becomes closed" (1956: 23).

General systems theorists elaborate the distinction between closed and open systems by employing the concept of *entropy:* energy loss or energy that cannot be turned into work. According to the second law of thermodynamics, all closed systems move toward a state of entropy—a random arrangement of their elements, a dissolution of their differentiated structures, a state of maximum disorder. By contrast, open systems, which are capable of importing energy from their environment, can experience *negative entropy,* or negentropy. By acquiring inputs of greater complexity than their outputs, open systems restore their own energy and repair breakdowns in their own organization. Von Bertalanffy concludes: "Hence, such systems can maintain themselves at a high level, and even evolve toward an increase of order and complexity" (1962: 7).[2]

To emphasize these twin properties of open systems, Buckley (1967: 58–62) distinguishes between two basic sets of system processes: morphostasis and morphogenesis. *Morphostasis* refers to those processes that tend to preserve or maintain a system's given form, structure, or state. Morphostatic processes in biological systems would include circulation and respiration; in social systems, socialization and control activities. *Morphogenesis* refers to those processes that elaborate or change the system, for example, growth, learning, and differentiation. In the process of adapting to the external environment, all open systems typically become more differentiated in form, more elaborate in structure. Thus, in biological systems, organs whose sensitivities to external stimuli are coarse and broad are succeeded by more specialized receptors capable of responding to a wider range and finer gradations of stimuli. Biological organisms move toward greater complexity through the process of evolution: individual organisms are little affected, but over time as mutations occur and are selected for their survival value, species are gradually transformed. Social organizations, more variable and loosely coupled than biological systems, can and do fundamentally change their structural characteristics over time. The General Motors of today bears little if any structural resemblance to the company of the same name fifty years ago. Indeed, social organizations exhibit such an amazing capacity to change their basic structural features that researchers who study organizations over time have difficulty in determining when the units they are studying are the same organizations with reorganized structures and when they represent the birth of new organizations.

---

[2]It is interesting to note that some information theorists posit a close relation between the concepts of organization and entropy: they are viewed, in effect, as opposite states. If entropy is a state of randomness, or zero organization, it is also the state that provides maximum variety, maximum information, to someone observing the set of elements. As organization develops, constraints and limitations grow restricting the number of states that may be present among the elements. Miller elaborate this point:

> A well-organized system is predictable—you know what it is going to do before it happens. When a well-organized system does something, you learn little that you didn't already know—you acquire little information. A perfectly organized system is completely predictable and its behavior provides no information at all. The more disorganized and unpredictable a system is, the more information you get by watching it. (Miller, 1953: 3)

Based on such reasoning, information theorists Shannon and Weaver (1963) have proposed a measure of information, *H,* which assesses the amount of entropy present in a set of elements— their variation, their relative frequency of occurrence, and their interdependence. The higher the *H* level, the more information and the less organization is present (see also Buckley, 1967: 82–89).

To repeat, the source of system diversity and variety is the environment. From an open systems point of view, there is a close connection between the condition of the environment and the characteristics of the systems within it: a complex system could not maintain its complexity in a simple environment. Open systems are subject to what is termed the *law of limited variety:* "A system will exhibit no more variety than the variety to which it has been exposed in its environment" (Pondy and Mitroff, 1979: 7). Although the processes by which such "laws" operate are not clearly understood, part 3 of this volume is devoted to explicating and illustrating the interdependence of organizations and environments.

Selected Schools

As with the previous perspectives, we turn now to discuss four selected schools that exemplify the open systems approach. We will briefly describe the systems design approach; contingency theory, which can be regarded as a school contained within the systems design approach; two recently developed environmental approaches; and a social psychological model of organizing. Although open systems approaches to organizations are in their infancy, there has been much interest in this new perspective and much effort devoted to its development over the past two decades. In many respects, this work is on the cutting edge of organization theory. Hence, many of the ideas introduced in this overview are considered at greater length in succeeding chapters.

SYSTEMS DESIGN

A large and growing number of organization theorists look to general systems theory as a source of ideas to improve the design of organizations— determining proper workflows, control systems, and planning mechanisms, and their interrelations—for carrying out their designated functions (see Carzo and Yanouzas, 1967; Johnson, Kast, and Rosenzweig, 1967; Khandwalla, 1977; Swinth, 1974). Unlike some of the schools devoted to the study of organizations, the orientation of this group is pragmatic and applied: they seek to change and improve organizations as viewed from a managerial perspective, not simply to describe and understand them.

Many of the analysts attempting to apply systems ideas to organizations are aware both of the great complexity of organizations as one type of system and of the danger of misapplying or overextending analogies based on the operation of other less complex systems. Beer (1964) proposes a classification of systems ranging from those that are both simple and deterministic, such as the behavior of a block and tackle system, to those that are complex and probabilistic, such as the operation of an assembly line in a factory, to those that are "exceedingly complex" and probabilistic, such as an entire organization (for example, a company). Complex probabilistic systems, whose behavior can be generally described and predicted with statistical procedures, are the province of operations research; exceedingly complex probabilistic systems have given rise to the fields of cybernetics and systems design (Beer, 1964: 18). Because of their great complexity, the latter systems currently defy conventional mathematical modeling approaches. Instead the most widely employed technique of analysis is to simulate the operation of the system. "Here, all the variables and relationships of interest are linked as understood into a model and then the manager-analyst-researcher manipulates certain ones and observes how others change as the simulation of the system plays itself out" (Swinth, 1974: 11). Note that this approach emphasizes the importance of treating the system as a system. Complex systems cannot be understood by an analysis that attempts to decompose the system into its individual parts in order to examine each part and relationship in turn. This approach, according to Ashby, one of the founders of the general systems movement, "gives us only a vast number of separate parts or items of information, the results of whose interactions no one can predict. If we take such a system to pieces, we find that we cannot reassemble it!" (1956: 36). Simulation techniques are popular with systems analysts because they are consistent with this image of a unit whose behavior can be understood only as the resultant of complex and probabilistic interactions among its component parts. They also support the systems view that to understand organizations one must focus on the operational level of the organization. Thus, a systems design analyst would be more interested in obtaining charts depicting the flows of information, energy, and materials throughout the organization than in inspecting the formal table of organization. In examining a football team as a social system, for example, such an analyst would rather inspect the play books governing the activities of the various players during the course of a game than the formal authority arrangements between the players, coaches, managers, and owners of the club.

It is consistent with the holistic emphasis of the systems analyst that the approach deals with objects or parts of systems, the detailed structure of which is unknown or regarded as irrelevant. These basic units are the so-called black boxes, the smallest elements of the system under study (Haberstroh, 1965: 1174). For the purposes of systems analysis, all the information that is required is a description of the inputs to and the ouputs from each of the basic elements (or the relation between the inputs and the outputs). It is not necessary to know the internal workings of these system components to understand or simulate the workings of the larger system.

Among the various flows connecting system elements, the flow of information is the most critical. The gathering, transmission, storage, and retrieval of information are among the most fateful activities of organizations, and design theorists devote much attention to them. We have already described in chapter 3 Simon's views on the cognitive limits of decision makers. From the standpoint of the current perspective, Simon is pointing out the limitations of individuals as information processors.[3] Viewed in this manner, Haberstroh asserts that individuals exhibit "low channel capacity, lack of reliability, and poor computational ability." On the other hand, individuals possess some desirable features: "The strong points of a human element are its large memory capacity, its large repertory of responses, its flexibility in relating these responses to information inputs, and its ability to react creatively when the unexpected is encountered" (Haberstroh, 1965: 1176). The challenge facing the systems designers is how to create structures that will overcome the limitations and exploit the strengths of each system component, including the individual participants.

Of course, all environments do not place the same demands on organizations and their participants for information processing. Recognition of this important point has given rise to a special perspective known as *contingency theory*, which we will briefly summarize below. More generally, a number of theorists argue that the very existence of organizations is explained by the information processing limitations of individuals confronted by complex situations. These arguments, developed by Arrow (1974) and Williamson (1975), are reviewed in chapter 7.

CONTINGENCY THEORY

Jay Galbraith (1973: 2) states the two assumptions underlying contingency theory most succinctly:

1. There is no one best way to organize.
2. Any way of organizing is not equally effective.

The first assumption challenges the conventional wisdom of those administrative theorists who have sought to develop general principles applicable to organizations in all times and places. Such a quest not only overlooks the vast diversity of existing organizational forms but also fails to recognize the great variety of tasks undertaken by organizations. The second assumption challenges a "know-nothing" position that would suggest that the complexity and variety of organizations is such that it is futile to search for any underlying principles to guide their design. A third assumption can be formulated to represent the position of the contingency theorist:

[3] Simon's contributions to organizations relate as closely to these concerns of systems design as to the rational model of organizations (see Simon, 1960; 1962).

3. The best way to organize depends on the nature of the environment to which the organization must relate.

As a branch of systems design, contingency theory emphasizes that design decisions depend—are contingent—on environmental conditions.

Contingency theory is guided by the general orienting hypothesis that organizations whose internal features best match the demands of their environments will achieve the best adaptation. The challenge facing those who embrace this orientation is to be clear about what is meant by "the organization's internal features," "the demands of their environments," "best adaptation," and most difficult of all, "best match." Details of attempted answers to these questions are best postponed to part 3, but two general approaches can be briefly described to illustrate the directions pursued within this theoretical tradition.

Lawrence and Lorsch (1967), who coined the label "contingency theory" argue that different environments place differing requirements on organizations: specifically, environments characterized by uncertainty and rapid rates of change in market conditions or technologies present different demands—both constraints and opportunities—on organizations than do placid and stable environments. They conducted empirical studies of organizations in the plastics, food processing, and standardized container industries to assess the relation between these environments—ranging from high to low uncertainty—and the internal features of each type of organization. They also suggest that different segments or subunits within a given type of organization may confront different external demands. Thus, within plastics manufacturing companies, the research and development units face a more uncertain and more rapidly changing environment than do the production departments of these same companies. To cope with these varying environments, organizations and their subunits develop differentiated characteristics. For example, the normative structure may be more or less highly formalized, or the time orientation of participants may be focused on long- or short-range outcomes. The more varied the types of environments confronted by a given organization type, the more differentiated the organization structure needs to be. Moreover, the more differentiated the structure, the more effort that must be devoted to the integration of the various subunits. In sum, Lawrence and Lorsch propose that the match or coalignment of an organization with its environment occurs on at least two levels: (1) the structural features of each organizational subunit should be suited to the specific environment to which it relates; and (2) the differentiation and mode of integration characterizing the larger organization should be suited to the overall environment within which the organization must operate (see chapter 11).

Galbraith's (1973; 1977) version of contingency theory is similar to the systems design school in its stress on information processing. As in Lawrence and Lorsch's view, the environment is characterized in terms of the amount of uncertainty it poses for the organization. Galbraith connects the concepts of environmental uncertainty and information processing in the following useful manner: uncertainty enters the organization by affecting the work or tasks that organizations perform, and "the greater the task uncertainty, the greater the amount of information that must be processed among decision makers during task execution in order to achieve a given level of performance" (1977: 36). Various structural arrangements, including rules, hierarchy, and decentralization, may be viewed as mechanisms determining the information processing capacity of the system. The design challenge is to select a structural arrangement appropriate for the information processing requirements of the tasks to be performed. We will consider Galbraith's specific arguments in more detail in chapter 10.

ENVIRONMENTAL APPROACHES

Consistent with the open systems perspective, several newly emerging approaches give primary attention to the environment as a set of influences shaping the structure, functioning, and fate of the organization. The environment is identified as a force in its own right—as a source of resources and constraints controlled by actors capable of behaving independently of the organization and in ways that profoundly shape the activities and outcomes of the organization. In their useful review of these approaches, Aldrich and Pfeffer (1976) identify two rather distinct subtypes: the natural selection model and the resource dependence model.

The *natural selection* model originated in biology with the work of Darwin. Although the application of these ideas to social systems has a long and checkered history (see Hofstadter, 1945), current efforts have been stimulated by the work of Hawley (1950) and Campbell (1969). Applications of these general ideas to organizations have been developed by Hannan and Freeman (1977) and by Aldrich (1979). The natural selection model differs from other approaches to organizations in that it applies to organizations viewed as populations rather than as individual systems. That is, it is designed to explain why certain forms or types (or species) of organizations survive and multiply whereas other types languish and die. For example, this model might be employed to explain why partnerships are replaced by corporations or why mom and pop grocery stores give way to supermarkets.

As briefly noted in chapter 2, the natural selection model argues that environments differentially select certain types of organizations for survival on the basis of fit between organizational forms and environmental characteristics. Three processes are emphasized: the creation of variety, selection of some types over others, and the retention of some of these forms (Campbell, 1969). In the first stage, variety is created by some process, planned or unplanned.

In the second, a process occurs by which some types are systematically selected for survival. In stage three, the selected forms are preserved in some fashion, by reproduction or duplication. Positively selected variations survive and reproduce similar others, which then form the starting point for a new round of selection as mutants begin to appear (Aldrich and Pfeffer, 1976).

As the label suggests, the natural selection model emphasizes selection: observed patterns in the distribution of organizational forms are attributed to the action of environmental selection processes. By contrast, most of the work examining organizational-environment connections employs a *resource dependence* model. This model stresses adaptation processes. Under this perspective "subunits of the organization, usually managers or dominant coalitions, scan the relevant environment for opportunities and threats, formulate strategic responses, and adjust organizational structure accordingly" (Hannan and Freeman, 1977: 930). The organization is not passive, but active in determining its own fate. Organizational participants, particularly managers, wrestle with the environment, attempting to strike favorable bargains and to avoid costly entanglements. As an open system, the organization is dependent on suppliers of inputs and consumers of outputs; but which specific suppliers and consumers are selected as exchange partners is partly determined—at least under many conditions—by the organization itself. Astute managers are those who not only acquire the necessary customers and resources but do so in a way that does not make them overly dependent on these external parties. Dependence is the obverse of power in an exchange relation; managers seek to increase their power over critical aspects of the environment or, at least, to reduce their dependence on these units. Thus, rather than portraying organizations as the passive recipients of the actions of environments, the resource dependence model views organizations "as active, and capable of changing, as well as responding to, the environment. Administrators manage their environments as well as their organizations, and the former activity may be as important, or even more important, than the latter" (Aldrich and Pfeffer, 1976: 83).

The resource dependence approach has been developed by a number of investigators and has received a variety of labels. Zald and his colleagues refer to their version as a political economy model (Zald, 1970; Wamsley and Zald, 1973). Thompson (1967) and Jacobs (1974) pursue these ideas as an exchange or a power-dependency model. The most comprehensive develop,nent to date of the resource dependence approach is found in the work of Pfeffer and Salancik (1978). The major contribution of this literature is to discern and describe the strategies—ranging from buffering to diversification and merger —pursued by organizations attempting to relate more effectively to their environments. These strategies are reviewed and evaluated in chapter 9.

The work of the environmentalists—both the natural selection and the resource dependence groups—incorporates some of the most innovative and exciting recent contributions to our understanding of organizations. With its emergence, we begin to perceive and more adequately exploit the insights provided by the open systems model and to comprehend the power of the environment to shape the form and functions of organizations.

WEICK'S MODEL OF ORGANIZING

While the environmentalist schools have developed their version of the open systems approach at the ecological level of analysis, Karl Weick has attempted to spell out some of the implications of this approach at the social psychological level (1969; rev. 1979). We cannot do justice to his subtle and imaginative ideas in this overview but will note some of his lines of argument and attempt to capture the flavor of his work.

Weick cites with approval Bateson's (1972: 334) moto: "stamp out nouns." He argues:

> The word, organization, is a noun and it is also a myth. If one looks for an organization one will not find it. What will be found is that there are events, linked together, that transpire within concrete walls and these sequences, their pathways, their timing, are the forms we erroneously make into substances when we talk about an organization. (Weick, 1974: 358)

Rather than talking about organizations, the focus of our attention should be "organizing." This is a very explicit example of the manner in which the systems perspective attempts to shift attention from structure to process.

Weick defines organizing as "the resolving of equivocality in an enacted environment by means of interlocked behaviors embedded in conditionally related processes" (1969: 91). We will attempt to unpack this dense definition. Weick argues that organizing is directed toward information processing generally and, in particular, toward removing its equivocality. He explains:

> The basic raw materials on which organizations operate are informational inputs that are ambiguous, uncertain, equivocal. Whether the information is embedded in tangible raw materials, recalcitrant customers, assigned tasks, or union demands, there are many possibilities, or sets of outcomes that might occur. Organizing serves to narrow the range of possibilities, to reduce the number of "might occurs." The activities of organizing are directed toward the establishment of a workable level of certainty. (Weick, 1969: 40)

This work is carried out by sets of "interlocked behaviors"—"repetitive, reciprocal, contingent behaviors that develop and are maintained between two or more actors" (1969: 91). The activities are carried on in three stages: enactment, selection, and retention. It is important to note that the three stages are Weick's translation of the three phases of natural selection or evolution as developed by Campbell (1969), described previously in our review of the environmentalist approach. Weick substitutes the term *enactment* for Campbell's label of *variations* for the first stage to emphasize the more active role organizational participants carry out in defining the environments they confront. Individual information processors *create* the environment to which the system then adapts (Weick, 1979: 147–69). The process of enactment introduces information (variety) into the system, which is dealt with according to organizational rules or routines: the greater the equivocality in the information introduced, the smaller the number of rules that will be activated to deal with the input. If the input is highly equivocal, only a small number of general rules are used to attempt to structure the input; however, if the input is better understood, a greater number of rules can be applied in responding to it (1969: 73). The application of the rules reduces (by selection) the equivocality of the information. The final phase of information processing determines what information is to be retained for future reference. Although the entire process operates to reduce equivocality, some equivocal features do and must remain if the organization is to be able to survive into a new and different future. In other words, "organizations continue to exist only if they maintain a balance between flexibility and stability" (Weick, 1979: 215). The information received and selected by the organization must be both credited (retained) and discredited or questioned if the organization is to safely face a future that may resemble, but must inevitably differ from, its past.

Weick's major concern is to spell out the implications of the open systems perspective when applied to the level of individual participants and the relationships among them. The semiautonomy of the individual actors is stressed: the looseness and conditionality of the relationships linking them is emphasized. Further, familiar social psychological processes become more problematic when viewed through the lens of a systems analyst. Where the conventional view would stress the use of perceptual sets that give continuity and stability to individual responses, Weick emphasizes the importance of "attention" processes that are more variable because they take into account situational factors—the "particular here and now" that determines what is selected out and what neglected from the available cues (1969: 39). Similarly, while conventional wisdom asserts that goals precede activities, that intention precedes action, Weick (1969: 37) insists that behavior often occurs first and then is interpreted—given meaning. The view of interpersonal processes such as coordination and control is similarly affected: such "interlocked behaviors" are viewed as loosely coupled systems allowing great latitude for individual performers in interpreting and implementing directions (Weick, 1976). More generally, in his view of causation, Weick embraces and applies many of the most basic concepts of the systems analyst: for example, the concept of *equifinality*, which asserts that a given outcome may be the result of quite different processes, and the concept of *causal arc*, which insists on the likelihood of reciprocal rather than unilateral causation (Weick, 1974; see also Buckley,

1967). In these and related ways, Weick has attempted to "open up" our conception of organizational structure and behavior.

Summary and Tentative Conclusions

The open systems perspective developed late relative to the rational and natural system views, but it has gained adherents rapidly and has profoundly altered our conception of organizations, their central features and processes. The open systems view of organizational structure stresses the complexity and variability of the individual component parts—both individual participants and subgroups—as well as the looseness of connections among them. Parts are viewed as capable of semiautonomous action; many parts are viewed as, at best, loosely coupled to other parts. Further, in human organizations, the system is multicephalous: many heads are present to receive information, make decisions, direct performance. Individuals and subgroups form and leave coalitions. Coordination and control become problematic. Also system boundaries are seen as amorphous; the assignment of actors or actions to either the organization or the environment often seems arbitrary and varies depending on what aspect of system functioning is under consideration.

Open systems imagery does not simply blur the more conventional views of the structural features of organizations: it shifts attention from structure to process. Whether viewed at the more abstract level employing concepts such as enacting, selecting, and retaining processes, or at the more concrete level with concepts such as input, throughput, and output production flows and feedback control loops, the emphasis is on organizing as against organization. Maintaining these flows and preserving these processes is viewed as problematic. As Weick insists: "processes are repetitive only if this repetitiveness is continuously accomplished" (1969: 36). Both morphostatic and morphogenetic processes are of interest: the former emphasize self-maintenance and stability, the latter, development and elaboration of structure. A process view is taken not only of the internal operations of the organization but of the organization itself as a system persisting over time. The organization as an arrangement of roles and relationships is not the same today as it was yesterday or will be tomorrow: to survive is to adapt, and to adapt is to change. As Leavitt and his colleagues conclude: "The complex organization is more like a modern weapons system than like old-fashioned fixed fortifications, more like a mobile than a static sculpture, more like a computer than an adding machine. In short, the organization is a dynamic system" (Leavitt, Dill, and Eyring, 1973: 4).

The interdependence of the organization and its environment receives primary attention in the open systems perspective. Rather than overlooking the environment, as tends to be true of the rational system perspective, or viewing it as alien and hostile, as is characteristic of the natural system perspective, the open systems model stresses the reciprocal ties that bind and interrelate the organization with those elements that surround and penetrate it. The environment is perceived to be the ultimate source of materials, energy, and information, all of which are vital to the continuation of the system. Indeed, the environment is even seen to be the source of order itself.

It seems premature to attempt even a tentative assessment of the open systems perspective at this time. The general systems approach—the mother ship—was itself launched only about three decades ago, and although its applicability to social organizations has been underscored from the very beginning, the working out of its specific implications is still underway. Some problems and dangers are already apparent. There is a strong tendency to work from analogy, applying insights from one type of system to another—for example, from the thermostat-heater system to the control system of an organization. While insights can be generated by such analogies, so can errors and misconceptions. Also, more so than the other perspectives, the open systems approach seems to carry with it a large number of highly abstract and often abstruse new concepts and labels: cybernetics, morphogenesis, equifinality. New concepts appropriately understood and applied can open our eyes to new facets of reality, but sometimes open systems theorists seem bedazzled by the richness of their new vocabularies and appear to be content simply to label the various components of the organizational system under study.

Such problems, however, often accompany new intellectual developments. In general, it seems clear that the open systems perspective brings with it a much needed dimension to—if not a reorientation of—previously existing viewpoints. After the emergence of the open systems perspective, the old image of a closed, self-contained, self-sufficient system will be difficult to resurrect. The doors and windows of the organization have been opened, and we are more than ever aware of the vital flows and linkages that relate the organization to other systems. Further, we see more clearly than we did that organizations are processes as well as structures, and that some of these processes are not recurrent cycles but forces changing the existing structures.

chapter 6

Combining
the Perspectives

*Political revolutions aim to change political
institutions in ways that those institutions
themselves prohibit. Their success therefore
necessitates the partial relinquishment of one
set of institutions in favor of another.*

*Like the choice between competing political
institutions, that between competing paradigms
proves to be a choice between incompatible
modes of community life. Because it has that
character, the choice is not and cannot be
determined merely by the evaluative procedures
characteristic of normal science, for these
depend in part upon a particular paradigm,
and that paradigm is at issue. When
paradigms enter, as they must, into a debate
about paradigm choice, their role is necessarily
circular. Each group uses its own paradigm to
argue in that paradigm's defense.*

THOMAS S. KUHN (1962)

The preceding chapters of this part have de-
scribed and illustrated three perspectives on organizations. We have attempted
to present these perspectives succinctly but fairly, discussing examples of work
from each, and assessing their strengths and limitations. We have sought to
avoid treating these viewpoints as caricatures or as approaches having only
historical interest. In our opinion, each is valuable: each focuses on a set of
significant and enduring features of organizations.

In their pure form, the perspectives share many of the features of "paradigms" as described by Kuhn in his influential essay on scientific revolutions. Kuhn describes paradigms as "models from which spring particular coherent traditions of scientific research" (1962: 10). A paradigm provides a framework of assumptions and axioms within which "normal science" can proceed. Critical concepts are identified, and essential relations specified: it provides a map of the scientific terrain to be explored. A paradigm is not so much disproven as it is dislodged or supplanted by a different paradigm providing a new map of the territory—indeed, not only a new map, but new directions for map making. As Kuhn observes:

> In learning a paradigm the scientist acquires theory, methods, and standards together, usually in an inextricable mixture. Therefore, when paradigms change, there are usually significant shifts in the criteria determining the legitimacy both of problems and of proposed solutions. (Kuhn, 1962: 108).

Thus, in some respects competing paradigms are incommensurate, and the differences between them cannot be completely resolved by scientific evidence or argumentation.

Sociology has been described as a "pre-paradigmatic" discipline: we are still waiting for our Copernicus and our Newton. Thus, the three organizational perspectives are probably, at best, only primitive pre-paradigms. Nevertheless, they do supply varying models of organizational phenomena, and each rests on assumptions that cannot be verified by scientific investigation. As we have seen, one perspective does not so much invalidate another as replace or supplement it.

Given that one perspective cannot completely supplant another, is it possible that they might be combined in some manner? Many contemporary analysts have noted the selectivity of the perspectives and, hence, their incompleteness. Why embrace a theoretical perspective that is clearly limited? Why adopt a partial framework in approaching a "whole" organization? Faced with such questions, a number of theorists have attempted to develop more all-encompassing formulations, combining selected portions of the earlier traditions. We will briefly review three of these synthetic frameworks: the models of Etzioni, of Lawrence and Lorsch, and of Thompson.

In the second section of this chapter, we propose yet another basis for combining the perspectives. This discussion, which ends with brief descriptions of some of the most recent theoretical developments, prepares the way for our more detailed discussions of organization-environment relations and organization structure in part 3.

Three Attempts at Integration

A flurry of theoretical activity during the 1960s has provided us with several more comprehensive models that to a considerable extent, incorporate and reconcile previous perspectives and suggest new insights on the functioning of organizations. Many theorists have made important contributions to these developments, but we single out three efforts. Etzioni's work represents an early attempt at integration; the later work of Lawrence and Lorsch and of Thompson has greatly influenced theory and research throughout the 1970s.

ETZIONI'S STRUCTURALIST MODEL

Etzioni (1964) has proposed a "structuralist" approach as a synthesis of the classical (rational) schools and the human relations (natural) schools. Unlike the classification we have proposed, Etzioni does not regard Weber as a contributor to the classical approach but argues that Weber together with Marx provides the basis for the synthetic structuralist model. Marx and Weber both believed that regardless of the best efforts of managers and workers, their economic and social interests are inevitably in conflict. Marx (1972 tr.) viewed the factory worker as alienated from his work since he owned neither the means of production nor the product of his labor. Weber (1946 tr.: 221–24) generalized this assertion, noting that soldiers in modern armies did not own their weapons nor did research scientists own their equipment and supplies. Both assumed that those who owned the means of production could control their use. In this sense, all employees in large organizations can be viewed as alienated from their labor (see chapter 13). Thus, for Etzioni, control becomes the fundamental issue in understanding organization; and both the rational and the natural system theorists have important, and different, things to say about control systems within organizations. The rational system theorists make a contribution to the analysis of control by focusing on the distribution of power among organizational positions; the natural system theorists make their contribution by insisting that naked power only alienates, that effective power must be acceptable to the subordinates in the power relation if control attempts are to be effective.[1] Weber's work, according to Etzioni, combines both of these points of view in his examination of the distribution of power, on the one hand, and the bases on which it is seen to be legitimate by participants in the system, on the other (Etzioni, 1964: 50–51; Weber, 1947 tr.:324–

[1]Hopkins (1961) has proposed a quite similar basis for reconciliation of the two points of view.

123

29). Weber's typology based on authority and Etzioni's typology based on power and participant responses to it, both of which were discussed in chapter 2, indicate the importance of these dimensions for analyzing organizations and suggest ways in which these issues can be pursued.[2]

In addition to combining the rational and natural perspectives in the analysis of the central issue of power, Etzioni proposes that the structuralist model gives equal attention to formal and informal structures, and in particular, to examining the relations between them; to an analysis of the scope of informal groups and the relations between such groups both inside and outside the organization; to both social and material rewards and their interrelation; and to the interaction of the organization and its environment (Etzioni, 1964: 41–49). In approaching all of these matters, however, the structuralist point of view recognizes fully

> the organizational dilemma: the inevitable strains—which can be reduced but not eliminated—between organizational needs and personal needs; between rationality and non-rationality; between discipline and autonomy; between formal and informal relations; between management and workers, or more generically, between ranks and divisions. (Etzioni, 1964: 41)

In sum, the structuralist model suggests that the rational and the natural system perspectives are complementary. Each view represents a partial truth. If the perspectives seem at times to conflict, this is because the organizational elements to which they point sometimes conflict. The recognition of such conflicts is an important part of the "whole"truth about organizations, their structural features, and their functioning.

Lawrence and Lorsch's Contingency Model

We have already reported Lawrence and Lorsch's various proposals for reconciling the rational and natural system perspectives (chapter 4) and described their contingency model of organizations (chapter 5). We briefly review these ideas at this point to emphasize that they suggest a basis on which all three perspectives can be reconciled. In essence, Lawrence and Lorsch (1967) argue that if an open system perspective is taken—so that any given organization is not viewed in isolation but only in relation to its specific environment—then the rational and the natural system perspectives may be seen to focus on different organizational types; organizations vary because they have adapted to different types of environments. The rational and natural system

---

[2]These matters involving power, authority, legitimacy, and control will be more fully discussed in chapter 12.

perspectives are at variance because each focuses on a different end of a single continuum representing the range of organizational forms. At one extreme, some organizations are highly formalized, centralized, and pursue clearly specified goals; at the other extreme, some organizations are less formalized, rely greatly on the personal qualities of participants, and lack consensus on goals. The two extreme types depicted by the rational and the natural systems models should not be viewed as differing aspects of the same organization—as, for example, Etzioni's structuralist model would suggest—but rather as different forms of organizations. And, as emphasized by the open systems perspective, the nature of the form is determined by the type of environment to which the organization must adapt. Specifically, the more homogeneous and stable the environment, the more appropriate will be the formalized and hierarchical form. And the more diverse and changing the task environment, the more appropriate will be the less formalized and more organic form. Thus we arrive at the contingency argument: there is no one best organizational form but several, and their suitability is determined by the extent of the match between the form of the organization and the demands of the environment. Note that the general form of this argument is an ecological one in which it is assumed that different systems are more or less well adapted to differing environments. Environmental conditions determine which systems survive and thrive: those best adapted are most likely to prosper. By this argument, Lawrence and Lorsch attempt to account for the different forms of organizations and for the different theoretical perspectives that have developed to characterize them. The argument also explains why the rational system perspective preceded in time the natural system perspective if it is assumed, as most open system analysts would contend, that the environments of organizations were more stable in the past and have become progressively more volatile.

The open systems perspective is viewed by Lawrence and Lorsch as the more comprehensive framework within which the rational and natural system perspectives may be housed, since each constitutes only a partial view depicting particular organizational adaptations to differing environmental conditions.

THOMPSON'S LEVELS MODEL

Simultaneously with the emergence of Lawrence and Lorsch's contingency model, James D. Thompson (1967) developed a related formulation that proposes a somewhat different basis for reconciling the three perspectives. In his influential work *Organizations in Action,* Thompson argues that analysts should be mentally flexible enough to admit the possibility that all three perspectives are essentially correct and applicable to all organizations. However, they do not all apply with equal force to all organizational locations.

Thompson borrows the distinctions proposed by Parsons (1960: 60–65), that were summarized in chapter 4, identifying three organizational levels: the technical level, that part of the organization carrying on the production functions; the managerial, those activities relating to the control of the production functions and the procurement of inputs and the disposition of outputs; and the institutional level, consisting of those activities relating the organization to the larger community and institutional sectors. Thompson's argument is that the three perspectives apply differentially to the three levels of organizations.

Thompson's model in a nutshell is that organizations strive to be rational although they are natural and open systems. It is in the interest of administrators—those who design and manage organizations—that the work of the organization be carried out as effectively and efficiently as possible. Since technical rationality presumes a closed system, Thompson (1967: 10–13) argues that organizations will attempt to seal off their technical level, protecting it from external uncertainties to the extent possible. Thus, it is at the level of the core technology—the assembly line in the automobile factory, the patient care wards and treatment rooms in the hospital—that we would expect the rational system perspective to apply with most force. At the opposite extreme, the institutional level, if it is to perform its functions, must be open to the environment. It is at this level, where the environment must be enacted or adapted to, that the open systems perspective is most relevant. In the middle is the managerial level, which is required to mediate between the relatively open institutional and closed technical levels. To do so effectively requires the flexibility that is associated with the less formalized and more politicized activities depicted by the natural system theorists. It is also the managers—whose power and status are most intimately linked to the fate of the organization—who have the greatest stake in the survival of the organization as a system.

There is much to be said for, and learned from, each of these efforts to reconcile the three perspectives. In a real sense, they are all true, or what may be more important, useful: Etzioni is surely correct that all organizations embody conflicting tendencies between the formal and informal, rational and nonrational aspects of their structures; Lawrence and Lorsch are correct that some types of organizations exhibit higher formalization and goal specificity than do other types and that these differences are associated with environmental conditions; and Thompson is correct that some segments or levels of the organization are more closed or open than others. These combinations and applications of the perspectives have illuminated additional facets of organizations, and in this way, the utility of the three original perspectives has been reinforced for a new generation of students of organizations.

Another Basis for Combining Perspectives

There is yet another sense in which the three perspectives may be seen as persisting up to the present time, albeit in new combinations. Our introduction to the perspectives in earlier chapters suggested that they fell into a neat time order with the rational perspective preceding the natural system view, and the open system perspective developing most recently. We will suggest now a slightly more complex view; namely, that there have been not three but four phases created by varying combinations of the three perspectives.[3]

At the risk of considerable oversimplification, we suggest that theoretical models of organizations underwent a major shift about 1960, at the time when open systems perspectives supplanted closed system models. Analyses focusing primarily on the internal characteristics of organizations gave way at approximately that date to approaches emphasizing the importance for the organization of events and processes external to it. After 1960, the environments of organizations, conceived in terms of economic, political, cultural, social, technological, and interorganizational elements, figure prominently in attempts to explain organizational structure and behavior.

On both sides of this watershed representing the transition from closed to open system models, a second trend can be identified: a shift from rational to natural system models of analysis. It appears that this shift has occurred twice! It occurred for the closed system models in the late 1930s and early 1940s; and it seems to be occurring again for the open systems models at the present time. That is, we suggest that the dominant theoretical model for analyzing organizations up to the late 1930s was the closed, rational system model (type I). This model was succeeded by the closed, natural system model (type II) which held sway through the 1950s. The open systems models came into prominence during the 1960s. However, this perspective was quickly combined in the work of several major theorists with a resurgence of the rational system model. Rational, open systems models (type III) dominated the field well into the 1970s. Recently however, the most prominent theoretical contributions appear to represent a revival of the natural system perspective, but now combined with the open system model (type IV).

Table 6–1 summarizes this pattern and lists some representative theorists associated with each type of perspective. While there are important similarities between types I and III rational systems models and between types II and IV natural systems models, the differences generated by the transition from closed to open models are of great importance. A brief discussion of each type can

[3]An earlier statement of this view may be found in Scott (1978).

Table 6–1   Dominant Theoretical Models and Representative
Theorists for Four Time Periods

CLOSED SYSTEM MODELS		OPEN SYSTEMS MODELS	
1900–1930	*1930–1960*	*1960–1970*	*1970–*
Rational Models	*Natural Models*	*Rational Models*	*Natural Models*
Type I	*Type II*	*Type III*	*Type IV*
Taylor (1911)	Roethlisberger & Dickson (1939)	Udy (1959)	Hickson et al. (1971)
Weber (1947 tr.)	Mayo (1945) Katz et al. (1951)	Woodward (1965)	March & Olsen (1976)
Fayol (1949 tr.)	Roy (1952)	Thompson (1967)	Meyer & Rowen (1977)
Gulick & Urwick (1937)	Dalton (1959) McGregor (1960)	Perrow (1967) Pugh et al. (1969) Blau (1970) Galbraith (1973)	Pfeffer & Salancik (1978)

highlight these similarities and differences. Before reviewing each type, however, we note the relation of these four types to the organization of the present volume. To this point, our discussions of the rational and the natural systems model have emphasized their closed-system versions, types I and II. Although we have stressed the differences between a closed and an open systems perspective, we have deliberately refrained from serious attention to the new generations of rational and natural systems models, types III and IV, which have emerged since the development of the open systems perspective. These most recent contributions receive primary attention in succeeding chapters. Hence, our discussion of types I and II will serve as a brief review of the work of major theorists prior to 1960 as described in the first half of this volume. And our discussion of types III and IV will serve to preview the work of major theorists since 1960 to be discussed in greater detail in later chapters.

TYPE I—CLOSED RATIONAL SYSTEM MODELS

The representative theorists listed in table 6–1 for the closed, rational system models should by this time look very familiar: Taylor, Weber, Fayol, and Gulick and Urwick are old friends. Simon is missing since he represents a transitional case: his early work (Simon, 1957, first published in 1945) fits into type I, but his later work (for example, March and Simon, 1958) is more closely related to type III models. As emphasized in chapter 3, all of these theorists conceived of organizations as tools designed to achieve preset ends; and all of them ignore or minimize the perturbations and opportunities posed by connections to a wider environment. Thompson stresses the closed system assumptions of these theorists:

Speaking of Taylor's contributions,

> Scientific management achieves conceptual closure of the organization by assuming that goals are known, tasks are repetitive, output of the production process somehow disappears, and resources in uniform qualities are available. (Thompson, 1967: 5)

And of the work of Fayol, Gulick, and Urwick,

> Administrative management achieves closure by assuming that ultimately a master plan is known, against which specialization, departmentalization, and control are determined. (Ibid., p. 5)

And of Weber's model of bureaucracy,

> Bureaucratic theory also employs the closed system of logic. Weber saw three holes through which empirical reality might penetrate the logic, but in outlining his "pure type" he quickly plugged these holes. Policymakers, somewhere above the bureaucracy, could alter the goals, but the implications of this are set aside. Human components—the expert officeholders—might be more complicated than the model describes, but bureaucratic theory handles this by divorcing the individual's private life from his life as an officeholder through the use of rules, salary, and career. Finally, bureaucratic theory takes note of outsiders—clientele—but nullifies their effects by depersonalizing and categorizing clients. (Ibid., pp. 5–6)

Thus, in all of these models, the variety and uncertainty associated with an organization's openness to its environment is assumed or explained away.

TYPE II—CLOSED NATURAL SYSTEM MODELS

Our prime candidate for natural system theorists working predominantly with a closed system conception are the human relations theorists. As described in chapter 4, this conception originated with the empirical research of Roethlisberger and Dickson (1939) and the theoretical work of Mayo (1945) but expanded throughout the 1940s and 1950s to encompass a great deal of the sociological research on organizations (for example, Katz et al., 1951; Roy, 1952; Dalton, 1959). While it is true that because of this work our view of organizational structure became more complex and flexible, as diffuse and conflicting goals were recognized and participants were endowed with multiple interests and motives, most of the work within this tradition restricted attention to within the confines of the organization. We learn a great deal about the emergence of informal structures—interpersonal systems of power, status, communication, and friendship—and the way in which they impact on formal systems; but whether the concern was with formal or informal systems or the relations between them, the focus was primarily on the organization's internal arrangements.

This criticism does not, however, apply to Selznick's (1948) institutional model or to Parsons's (1960) social system model, which we reviewed in chapter 4. As noted, Selznick's view of the environment is a rather jaundiced one, while Parsons exhibits a more balanced view of the environment, but both of these versions of natural systems models represent more open system conceptions and, hence, are important precursors to type IV models.

TYPE III—OPEN RATIONAL SYSTEM MODELS

Beginning in the late 1950s and continuing through the mid-1970s, a new generation of theorists focused attention on the organization as a rational system, but with a difference: now the organization was also viewed as an open system. Two subtypes of studies may be identified within type III models.

One subtype is exemplified by the work of Udy (1959), Woodward (1965), Pugh and colleagues (1969) and Blau (1970), who take as their primary challenge to explain differences among organizations in their formal structures. The methodology is comparative, and the units of analysis are the organizations themselves rather than the individual participants or subgroups within them. Formal structure is viewed as the dependent variable, its characteristics to be measured and explained. A large variety of explanatory (independent) variables have been utilized—with most attention concentrated on size, technology, and uncertainty—but variables selected are primarily environmental in character. (Size is often viewed as a measure of demand.) In short, organizations are viewed as open systems. At the same time, organizations are presumed to design their structures rationally.

An assumption underlying all of these studies is that organizations are striving to develop the most effective and efficient structures. The connections between environmental demand and organizational response are mediated by positing designers or managers who are concerned with cutting costs, developing adequate arrangements to cope with environmental complexity, and creating coordinative mechanisms to manage the requirements of information processing. These are the assumptions of a rational system model, and they dominate much of the empirical and theoretical work on organizations during the 1960s.

The second subtype of the open rational system model is represented in the work of the design theorists discussed in chapter 5 (for example, Galbraith,

1973; Swinth, 1974) but also characterizes the work of Thompson (1967). Thompson is quite explicit about the rationalist assumptions that provide his theoretical underpinning: he prefaces virtually all of his empirical predictions with the phrase, "under norms of rationality, organizations seek to. . . ." As noted earlier, the problem Thompson and the design theorists set for themselves is: How can the organization function rationally, given that it is open to the uncertainties of its environment? As we already know from the first section of this chapter, Thompson's principal answer to this question is: by artificially creating some closed systems in critical parts of the organization. The sealing mechanisms and buffering strategies proposed by Thompson and others will be described in detail in chapter 9; for now, we simply note this juxtaposition of rational and open systems perspectives.

TYPE IV—OPEN NATURAL SYSTEM MODELS

It appears that we are currently on the threshold of a major shift in the types of theoretical models that guide our investigations of the structure and behavior of organizations. The open, rational models that have dominated our theories since the early 1960s are being challenged by a set of open, natural models. We are in the early stages of this development, and our announcement of the paradigm shift may be premature or incorrect, but there is clearly a flurry of activity on this front. The new models are represented by the work of such theorists as Hickson and his colleagues (1971), March and Olsen (1976), Meyer and Rowan (1977), and Pfeffer and Salancik (1978). These models place great emphasis on the importance of the environment in determining the behavior and life chances of organizations: they are clearly open systems models. However, the assumption that organizations behave as rational systems is strongly challenged in this work.

To begin, organizations are believed to place their own survival over goal attainment. Only under special—and, allegedly, increasingly rare—circumstances—does effectiveness in goal attainment contribute to survival. Or in some versions of the new model, the meaning of effectiveness is transformed. For Pfeffer and Salancik, for example: "The effectiveness of an organization is a sociopolitical question" (1978: 11). Survival is viewed as a difficult game to play because the nature of the environment has become increasingly complex and politicized. Some types of organizations operate in a highly institutionalized environment in which it is more important to conform to externally imposed rules than to produce outputs efficiently (Meyer and Rowen, 1977). And some types of organizations operate in environments in which goals are ambiguous and technologies are unclear (March and Olsen, 1976*a*). Under such circumstances there may be little connection between individual preferences and behavior, between individual actions and organizational choices, or between organizational choices and environmental responses. Rational decision models have little applicability under these conditions.

The neo-natural system models have also revived and updated natural system assumptions about the complex, social nature of participants and their interactions. Power processes, so dear to the hearts of natural system analysts, become more complex when they involve possible alliances with outsiders. Early natural system theorists outraged rationalists by proposing that organizational participants lack common interests and goals but temporarily enter into coalitions to pursue jointly advantageous objectives, but recent theorists have raised the ante. Thus, March and Olsen suggest that in some organizations "the flow of individual actions produces a flow of decisions that is intended by no one and is not related in a direct way to anyone's desired outcomes" (1976 *b*: 19).

As noted when we commenced the presentation of these types, types III and IV models are simply introduced at this point. This work is described in much greater detail in parts 3 and 4 of this volume.

Summary

The rational, natural, and open systems perspectives for analyzing organizations are pre-paradigms. They describe theoretical conceptions of organizations based on differing assumptions that render them not fully commensurable. One paradigm may replace another but cannot disprove it.

Nevertheless, some analysts have consciously attempted to reconcile the three perspectives by combining them into more complex models of organizations. And others, sometimes less explicitly, have developed varying combinations of closed or open systems models with rational and natural system perspectives. We will explore these combinations throughout parts 3 and 4 of this volume.

We conclude that knowledge of these perspectives is indispensable not only as a guide to past contributions but also as a key to understanding many of the conflicts and controversies that continue to lie close to the surface, regardless of how smooth and unruffled the theoretical covers appear to be. The perspectives exhibit great resilience: whether in an unadulterated form or in exotic mixtures, they persist and still serve to order and shape our views of organizations.

Part Three

ENVIRONMENTS, STRATEGIES, AND STRUCTURES

Three general perspectives on the nature of organizations have been described along with several attempts to combine or integrate them. If these perspectives are as useful as we have claimed, they will enable us not simply to comprehend past efforts to dissect organizations but to better fathom current work and perhaps even to discern future analytic directions.

This part combines topics that are often separated in contemporary treatments of organizations. It deals both with the ways in which organizations relate to their environments as well as with the determinants of organizational structure. With the help of the open systems perspective, we see these topics as inseparable: how an organization relates to its environment—indeed, what its environment is—is greatly influenced by the organization's structural features; and the characteristics of the organization's structure are strongly affected by the organization's environment. External forces shape internal arrangements, and vice versa.

We learn from the open systems perspective that organizations are not fortresses, impervious to the buffeting or the blessing of their environments. On the other hand, we learn from the rational and natural system perspectives that organizations are not wind tunnels, completely open and responsive to every perturbation of their context. Organizations construct and reconstruct boundaries across which they relate to the outside world. Between the organization and those outside there is not one barrier but many, and for most kinds of organizations they become higher and more impenetrable as we come closer to the organization's technical core.

This part begins by asking a fundamental, but difficult question: why do organizations exist? Chapter 7 addresses this issue from both a historical and a comparative perspective, asking, for example, what alternatives there are to organizations.

Chapter 8 informs us that, like organizations, environments may be viewed in various lights. Organization sets are distinguished from organizational populations and from organizational fields. We also ask whether it is indeed the case that the environments of organizations are becoming more complex and turbulent over time.

The strategies used by organizations to buffer their technical core and to build bridges linking them with other organizations—both competitors and exchange partners—are examined in chapter 9. The costs as well as the benefits of these techniques are described. Chapters 10 and 11 examine the structural concomitants of the organization's technology and of its buffering and bridging strategies. It is argued that technological factors are primarily associated with the structural characteristics of the core units, whereas buffering and bridging strategies are related to the characteristics of the more peripheral organizational structures: the managerial and institutional levels and the boundary units.

Environmental factors are also argued, in chapter 12, to be decisive in determining the size and composition of the dominant coalition: that subset of organizational participants who have sufficient power to set the goals pursued by the organization. And internal authority structures are legitimated by linkages to broader societal normative structures.

In all of these ways, we challenge the sharp dichotomy between inside and outside, between organization and environment. These structures and processes interpenetrate one another in interesting and unexpected ways that are revealed when we combine the open system perspective with the rational and natural system viewpoints.

chapter 7

Creating Organizations

*The distinctive features of modern life derive
from the fact that a large share of social
activity is governed by bodies of systematic
abstract doctrine.... The government of
activities by doctrines is the primary function
of bureaucracy. The foundation of the
dominance of professions in modern society is
competence in a specialized body of abstract
knowledge, systematized and taught by
scholars in professional schools. Science,
education, bureaucratic administration, the
professions—these distinctive features of
modern life are primarily concerned with
developing, transmitting, and governing
activities by bodies of systematized intelligence.
The study of modernization is, therefore, in
large measure the study of the social role of
systematized intelligence and its application to
daily affairs.*

ARTHUR L. STINCHCOMBE (1974)

In this chapter we attempt to explain how and
why organizations come into existence. It is helpful to separate this broad
question into three categories of more specific questions. The first deals with
the emergence of organizations as a distinctive type of collectivity. This category subsumes such questions as: Have organizations always existed? If not,
when did they first emerge? What are the social conditions under which
organizations develop? Note that, in general, these questions require historical
or comparative analyses. The second category assumes the existence of organizations as one type of social arrangement and asks why these arrangements
are imposed on specific activities. Here we confront such questions as: What
alternatives to organizations exist to carry out complex activities? Under what
conditions are organizations employed to carry out specific tasks? What are

the benefits and costs of using organizations? The third category assumes that the decision has been made to create a specific organization and asks how resources are mobilized for this purpose. Questions include: What resources do all organizations require for their continued functioning? Do organizations differ in their strategies of resource acquisition? What types of incentives are employed to attract and retain an organization's most precious resource—its participants?

All three sets of questions are complex; and all are just beginning to attract the attention of organizational researchers. The proposed answers are not definitive, but it is hoped they will point out fruitful areas of future inquiry. And, obviously, the three categories of questions are closely interrelated. To understand the conditions under which organizations as a distinctive social form emerge will help us to better determine why individuals choose to employ these forms in pursuing a given set of goals. And both issues have implications for the ability of an organization to garner resources.

The Emergence of Organizations

It is only in modern, industrialized societies that organizations dominate the landscape. Their emergence, proliferation, and consolidation as a ubiquitous and significant building block of society is one of the great social transformations that distinguishes the modern from the premodern world. In a quite literal sense, the history of the development of modern society is also a history of the development of special purpose organizations: organizations were both created by and helped to produce these changes. We shall not attempt to recount here this vast and complex history but will only note some of the changes scholars have identified as among the most fateful for the development of organizations.

THE CHANGING RELATIONS OF INDIVIDUAL AND CORPORATE ACTORS

When we speak of the emergence of organizations, we are not implying that previous societal arrangements exhibited disorganization. Indeed, in important ways some of the preexisting social systems exhibited higher degrees of order! The correct contrast, then, is between different types of ordered social arrangements. The principal ways in which modern social structures differ from earlier, traditional forms are (1) in the relation of individual actors to corporate actors; and (2) in the relation of corporate actors to one another.

Coleman's (1974) analysis of these differences is most illuminating. Examining the corporate bodies of the Middle Ages, he observes that the basic units

—the manor, the guild, the village—wholly contained their members and possessed full authority over them. What rights and interests individuals possessed, they acquired from their membership in these units. (Note that these bodies are the patrimonial systems dissected by Weber as described in chapter 3.) Moreover, the corporate actors were themselves organized in a strict hierarchical structure, the subordinate units being responsible to and contained within the superordinate systems in a concentric pattern (see Simmel, 1955 tr.).

Gradually and fitfully, over several centuries, these relations were altered. Individual persons were able to acquire rights and were recognized to have interests; and corporate actors were allowed to acquire rights and to pursue interests that were not simply an aggregate of the interests of their members. Coleman summarizes these developments:

> Two things happened. First, men themselves began to break out of their fixed estates, began to have rights to appear before the king's court, rights to make contracts on their own; became, in effect, persons before the law with a certain set of rights (elevated by seventeenth-century philosophers to the status of "natural rights") to engage in a variety of activities at their own pleasure. But second, and as a direct consequence of this fragmentation of the feudal structure, a different kind of intermediate organization arose in society: a corporate actor which had, under charter from the king, a variety of rights to free and expansive action. This new corporate actor became the instrument through which men could jointly exercise their new-found rights. (Coleman, 1974: 28)

Under these altered conditions, corporate actors no longer contained their individual members but only the specific resources invested in them by persons acting as owners or investors; and corporate actors no longer fully controlled their individual members but only the specific behaviors contracted for by persons who agreed to function as their participants or agents. Individuals were only partially involved in these new organizations. Also, these corporate actors or organizations were no longer themselves arranged in a concentric, hierarchical pattern, but were allowed to function somewhat independently of one another, competing for the loyalties and resources of individuals.

Coleman emphasizes the impact of individualism on the development of special purpose organizations. Simmel (1955 tr.) in his brilliant essay, "The Web of Group-Affiliations," stresses the reverse effect. When the social arrangements consist of layers of concentrically related systems, the social spaces created tend to produce homogeneous individuals: batches of individuals are likely to share the same social location and perceive themselves as holding the same social identity. However, as social arrangements shift to contain overlapping and intersecting systems, a vastly increased variety of social spaces is created, and no two individuals are as likely to share the same social location or to hold the same social identity. As Simmel explains:

The groups with which the individual is affiliated constitute a system of coordinates, as it were, such that each new group with which he becomes affiliated circumscribes him more exactly and more unambiguously. To belong to any one of these groups leaves the individual considerable leeway. But the larger the number of groups to which an individual belongs, the more improbable is it that other persons will exhibit the same combination of group-affiliations, that these particular groups will "intersect" once again in a second individual.

... As individuals, we form the personality out of particular elements of life, each of which has arisen from, or is interwoven with, society. This personality is subjectivity par excellence in the sense that it combines the elements of culture in an individual manner. ... As the person becomes affiliated with a social group, he surrenders himself to it. A synthesis of such subjective affiliations creates a group in an objective sense. But the person also regains his individuality, because his pattern of participation is unique; hence the fact of multiple group-participation creates in turn a new subjective element. (Simmel, 1955 tr.: 140–41)

Combining the insights of Coleman and Simmel, we conclude that there was an intimate, reciprocal, supportive relation between the emergence of individualism and the development of special purpose organizations. Given this historical association, it is somewhat ironic that numerous commentators in our own time perceive organizations as the enemy of individualism. (We will explore this paradox in chapter 13.)

SOCIETAL CONDITIONS FAVORING THE DEVELOPMENT OF ORGANIZATIONS

Thus far we have described some quite basic changes in societal arrangements without attempting to determine what factors brought these changes about. Drawing on the insights of Weber, Durkheim (1949 tr.), and other social theorists, Stinchcombe (1965) suggests that the capacity of a population to develop and support special purpose organizations is determined by such general factors as: widespread literacy and specialized advanced schooling, urbanization, a money economy, political revolution, and the density of social life. To these primarily economic and directly instrumental factors, theorists like Eisenstadt (1958) and Parsons (1966) add institutional and normative variables such as: increased role and institutional differentiation, allocation of roles by universalistic and achievement rather than particularistic and ascriptive criteria, and increased dissensus among societal groups concerning the priority of goals, together with increased competition among them for resources. Eisenstadt concludes: "The most important characteristics of the environment conducive to the development of bureaucracies are first, the availability of various 'free-floating' resources, and second, the development of several centres of power which compete over such resources" (1958: 111). To these characteristics, Parsons (1960: 20–21) would no doubt add that societal environments support the emergence of organizations to the extent that they are willing to legitimate their specialized functions and independent existence.

THE COORDINATION OF COMPLEX TASKS:
DEMAND AND SUPPLY

These arguments are all at a very general level: most of them describe conditions that are conducive to rationalization of the social structure in general—including such changes as the development of specialized labor markets—and do not point specifically to conditions favoring the creation of organizations. Stinchcombe (1965: 146–50) recognizes this problem and has attempted to construct more specific arguments to relate these general conditions to the creation of organizations via intermediate variables. He suggests that such general societal factors influence the development of organizations (1) by motivating individuals to form and join such social units; and (2) by improving the chances that these units once formed will survive. As an illustration of the type of arguments developed by Stinchcombe, consider the following propositions: the development of a money economy (one of the general societal factors) (1) motivates individuals to form and join organizations by (a) liberating resources so that they can be more easily acquired by new organizations; (b) simplifying calculation of the advantages of alternative ways of doing things; and (c) allowing a more precise anticipation of the consequences of future conditions. At the same time, the development of a money economy (2) improves the survival chances of new organizations by (a) facilitating the formation of free markets so that customers can transfer their loyalties; and (b) depersonalizing economic social relations.

Other specific arguments relating to the emergence of organizations have been proposed. Some of these relate to changes in the demand for organizational services; others relate to changes in their supply: that is, the ability to create effective organizational forms. With regard to demand, several of Weber's (1946 tr.: 204–14) propositions relating to the development of bureaucratic forms note the importance of increases in the scale and complexity of administrative tasks. On the importance of scale, Weber asserts: "In the field of politics, the great state and the mass party are the classic soil for bureaucratization" (Ibid., 209). Change in the complexity of administrative work is illustrated by the emergence of the welfare state, in which officials must oversee elaborate programs relating to unemployment, health, and educational services. By contrast, Boulding (1953) insists that the "organizational revolution" is best explained by changes on the supply side of the equation. In this connection, he emphasizes the importance of technical improvements in the means of transportation and communication as well as changes in the structural characteristics of organizations. Boulding argues that improvements in the means of transportation and external communication are essential if an organization (or a population of organizations) is to grow in size because of "the principle of increasingly unfavorable environment." This principle asserts that "as an organism grows it absorbs more and more of its environment, and eventually uses up the more favorable parts of its environment" (1953: 22). Improvements in transportation and communication counteract this principle by vastly extending the size of the environment to which an organization can effectively relate. Improvements in the structural characteristics of organizations, in particular, the internal communication system, are essential given increases in size because of "the principle of increasingly unfavorable internal structure." Boulding explains:

> As the size of an organization or organism increases, it is impossible to maintain the proportional structure of the organism intact.
> In the biological organism the problem arises because a uniform increase in the linear dimensions of an organism increases its surfaces by the square and its volumes by the cube of the linear increases. Thus, doubling the linear dimensions of any object increases all its areas four times and increases all its volumes eight times. (Boulding, 1953: 23)

In a biological organism, this principle is exemplified by the burdens that growth places on the circulatory or the respiratory system: "it explains why insects, which breathe mainly through the skin, cannot develop beyond a size of inches" (Ibid.). In a social organization, the principle is illustrated by the necessity of strengthening the communication system in response to organizational growth. The policy centers of the organization must receive timely and accurate information from participants on the boundaries (for example, salespeople), and the latter must receive clear and up-to-date instructions from the center if the organization is to remain effective. Such information flows become more problematic as communication lines grow longer. One solution to this problem is to make structural changes in the organization (including the communications systems). In this early work, Boulding is not very specific as to what structural changes will facilitate the flow of information. We have considerably more knowledge about such matters now, and will detail in chapter 10 some of the ways in which structure can be modified to accommodate heavier information flows.

Yet another set of analyses stresses the role played by industrialization on the emergence of organizations. One of the best and most influential statements of these connections is that developed by a group of labor economists (Kerr et al., 1964). Kerr and his colleagues attempt to identify a set of developments that are generic to the process of industrialization as well as to identify specific variants of the process that occur under differing societal and cultural conditions. Among the universal consequences, they include the creation of organizations. They assert:

The technology and specialization of the industrial society are necessarily and distinctively associated with large-scale organizations. Great metropolitan areas arise in the course of industrialization. The national government machinery expands significantly. Economic activity is carried on by large-scale enterprises which require extensive coordination of managers and the managed. A wide variety of rules and norms are essential to secure this coordination. (Kerr et al., 1964: 21)

Although Weber and Boulding and Kerr disagree on the relative emphasis to be placed on various factors, they all generally agree that organizations are called into existence by the increasing need to coordinate and control complex administrative and technical tasks. Enlarged political states, expanding markets, and improved technologies both require and are made possible by the development of organizational forms that can manage complex exchanges and coordinate diverse, interrelated activities.

INSTITUTIONALIZED ENVIRONMENTS AND ORGANIZATIONS[1]

This consensus about the primary roots of formal organizations has been challenged by Meyer and Rowan (1977). While they do not deny the operation of the organization-creating processes just described, they argue that a different type of process is also at work which, although recognized by Weber, has been neglected by most analysts. They assert that organizations have normative as well as technical and structural sources—that organizations are created by the development and elaboration of institutional rules and beliefs as well as by structural or relational complexities. Meyer and Rowan insist that these rationalized beliefs do not play merely a backstage legitimating role but often are the primary causal force creating and supporting organizational forms.

Meyer and Rowan refer to these beliefs as "rationalized myths." Note the combination of apparently contradictory terms. The beliefs are "rational" inasmuch as they are elaborated statements of rules and procedures to be followed in achieving a given end. They are "myths" because (a) they cannot be empirically verified, and yet (b) they are widely believed. Indeed, many of these beliefs are so widely shared that they are taken for granted: they are socially constructed definitions of reality (see Berger and Luckmann, 1967).

[1]Meyer and Rowan's use of the concept *institutionalized organization* is related to but not identical with Selznick's definition of the same term, discussed in chapter 4. Both usages describe a situation in which, to employ Selznick's phrase, structures and activities become "infused with value beyond the technical requirements of the task at hand" (1957: 17). However, Selznick tends to emphasize the internal organizational processes—for example, individual and organizational "commitments"—that give rise to such value whereas Meyer and Rowan stress sources of value external to the organization—belief systems and social structures that make up broader societal institutions.

Some of our beliefs about the efficacy of education may be seen to be rationalized myths. While education can and does create changes in the level of knowledge and skills of individuals, it also affects our beliefs about these individuals, bringing about changes in their status and justifying our allocation to them of special privileges and responsibilities. The former changes represent the technical contributions of education; the latter, the institutional (Meyer, 1977).

As this example suggests, all organizations are comprised of both technical and institutional ingredients, but in terms of their origins and their structural composition, some organizations are dominated by technical factors, while others rest primarily on institutional sources. (See Meyer, Scott, and Deal, 1981; for a somewhat similar formulation, see Udy, 1970) Organizations such as schools and mental health clinics are examples of highly institutionalized organizations; extraction industries, factories, and transportation companies are examples of organizations with a strong technical basis.

Rationalized myths increasingly pervade all sectors of modern societies (see Ellul, 1964). The development and penetration of law and legal procedures into virtually every sector of social life; the emergence and elaboration of professional occupations—accounting, psychology, economics; the proliferation of systems of licensure, certification, and accreditation; and the expanding jurisdiction of the political state, whose scope and influence continue to grow —these are among the more important components of rationalized institutional systems. Meyer and Rowan summarize the importance of these developments for the creation of organizations:

> The growth of rationalized institutional structures in society makes formal organizations more common and more elaborate. Such institutions are myths which make formal organizations both easier to create and more necessary. After all, the building blocks for organizations come to be littered around the societal landscape; it takes only a little entrepreneurial energy to assemble them into a structure. And because these building blocks are considered proper, adequate, rational, and necessary, organizations must incorporate them to avoid illegitimacy. Thus, the myths built into rationalized institutional elements create the necessity, the opportunity, and the impulse to organize rationally, over and above pressures in this direction created by the need to manage proximate relational networks. (Meyer and Rowan, 1977: 345)

Meyer and Rowan's views have important implications for the internal structure and functioning of organizations, but these issues are best postponed to a later point (see chapter 11).

Viewing the foregoing arguments in the light of the three general perspectives developed in part 2, we note that all analysts start from an open systems framework: organizations are viewed as creatures of their environment. But there appear to be two styles of argument within this common framework. The first and earlier stresses the function of organizations as rational tools for coordinating and controlling complex and expanding technical and administrative domains. Weber, Stinchcombe, Boulding, Kerr—all work from this basic assumption. As noted in chapter 6, these analysts combine the open and rational system perspectives. By contrast, the arguments of Meyer and Rowan grow out of the natural system—combined with the open system—perspective. These analysts stress the nonrational or mythlike nature of organization-creating forces; and as will be emphasized later, their arguments stress organizational survival—the primary concern of the natural system approach.[2]

As we consider other facets of organizational creation, we will continue to observe differences in fundamental—and unexamined—assumptions underlying the various explanations.

The Decision to Organize

Once organizational forms have been invented and become legitimated, what causes them to be chosen as vehicles for collective action? To answer this question we need to determine what alternatives to organizations are available for carrying out complex tasks. And we need to assess the comparative advantages and disadvantages of each of these alternatives as one basis for predicting which arrangement is more likely to be selected.

ALTERNATIVES TO ORGANIZATIONS

It is by no means a simple matter to generate a list of alternatives to organizations, perhaps because we see them in operation wherever we look. However, one alternative that presents itself is the informal or primary group. In addition to encompassing such systems as face-to-face peer groups, this category can be extended to include "clan" forms, networks that may or may not include kinship ties but that are based on common internalized goals and strong feelings of solidarity (see Durkheim, 1949 tr.; Ouchi, 1980). A second, perhaps less obvious, alternative to organizations for coordinating complex work is the market. Viewing organizations and markets as alternative means of organizing work was first proposed by Coase (1937), but this comparison

---

[2]We cannot refrain from observing that Meyer and Rowan's theoretical stance constitutes one of the most radical assaults yet launched against the rational system perspective. Most previous natural system analysts have been content to employ natural systems arguments to account for departures from rational system models. In Meyer and Rowan's approach, not only the departures but major aspects of the rational systems models themselves are given a natural system interpretation.

has recently been brilliantly pursued by Arrow (1974) and by Williamson (1975). Yet a third alternative to organizations is occupational structures, which provide a basis for organizing the performance of complex tasks. The clearest examples of such occupational alternatives to organizations are provided by the professions (Scott, 1966; Freidson, 1973). There are no doubt other existing and possible alternatives to organizations, but these examples will suffice for present purposes. By comparing the advantages and costs of organizations with primary groups, markets, and professional occupations, we hope to gain insight into the more general question: Why do organizations exist?

THE BENEFITS OF ORGANIZATION

Organizations versus Markets   We begin by contrasting organizations with markets. In a market system exchanges occur between buyers and sellers based on negotiated contractual agreements. These transactions are governed by the price system which, in aggregate, provides a set of signals concerning what goods and services in what quantity are desired and hence will be profitable to produce. It is presumed that all parties are governed by self-interest. Several advantages are associated with a market arrangement as a basis for organizing transactions. Adam Smith (1776) was among the first to note that relatively little knowledge is required of the participants in such transactions. Assuming that individuals know their own preferences, price signals provide a comparatively simple basis on which to make decisions. And, as symbolized by Smith's famous simile of the "invisible hand," market and pricing mechanisms do provide an overall basis for coordinating individual actions. Hence, it is not necessary to expend resources specifically to achieve coordination; no administrative "overhead" is required for planning, collective decision making, or control.

Recent analyses suggest that market transactions work well as a framework for "spot" contracts—contracts in which all obligations are fulfilled on the spot, for example, the exchange of money for a commodity in hand. They fare less well when the transactions involve future values. When goods or services are not to be delivered on the spot, but at some future time, it is often possible to draw up a "contingent claims contract." Such a document specifies the obligations of each party to the exchange, contingent upon possible future states of nature. For example, a farmer may agree to sell his grain to a warehouse if the price does not drop below a specified amount per ton. But as the future becomes more complex or uncertain, it becomes increasingly difficult and costly to draw up contracts that take into account all possible contingencies. In such circumstances, organizations are likely to be viewed as attractive alternatives to market-mediated transactions.

Arrow asserts that "organizations are a means of achieving the benefits of collective action in situations in which the price system fails" (1974: 33). The price system, viewed as a mechanism for the efficient allocation of personnel and resources to production tasks, fails when confronted with great complexity of interrelations of these factors or with uncertainty concerning future conditions. As such complexity and uncertainty increases, a greater need for information arises: more information needs to be processed in order for contracts to be negotiated and transactions conducted. Both Arrow and Williamson conclude that the specific way in which organizations are superior to markets in managing complex and uncertain economic transactions is that organizations reduce the costs of such transactions.

Williamson (1975) elaborates the argument by developing an elegant and simple model to identify the conditions under which markets tend to give way to organizations.[3] The basic elements of the model appear in figure 7–1. Williamson uses the concept bounded rationality simply to refer to the limitations of individuals as information processors. The cognitive limitations of individuals are emphasized by Simon (1957) and have already been described in chapter 5. As environments become more complex or uncertain, these limitations are quickly reached. Hence, it is only when individuals are confronted with excessive environmental demands that their own information-processing capacities become insufficient and alternative arrangements are required. Incorporating individual decision makers into organizational arrangements is one such alternative.

We have already described, in chapters 3 and 5, how organizational structures facilitate and support individual decision making. The rational system perspective is the relevant one: the organization permits problem subdivision, simplifies choices, channels information, and restricts alternatives. Goal speci-

---

[3]Williamson's terminology differs from our own and can cause confusion on first reading. He employs the term *organization* to refer to any social arrangement within which transactions are conducted. Thus, markets as well as organizations in our sense are regarded as organizations. This is why Williamson's discussion of the limitations of markets is presented as an *organizational failures framework*. Williamson's terms for organizations in our sense are, variously, *internal organization, hierarchies,* and *firms*.

HUMAN FACTORS   ENVIRONMENTAL FACTORS

Bounded Rationality ◄————————————► Uncertainty/Complexity

Opportunism ◄————————————► Small Numbers

Figure 7–1   The Market Failures Framework. *Source:* Adapted from Williamson (1975), figure 3, p. 40.

ficity and formalization function to overcome the cognitive limitations of individual actors.

Williamson's second pair of concepts—opportunism and small numbers—is used to develop a different argument regarding the relative advantages of markets and organizations. The concept of opportunism is used to note that individual actors are capable of "self-interest seeking with guile" and of making "self-disbelieved threats and promises" (Williamson, 1975: 26). In short, some individuals lie, cheat, and steal! Those of us who are honest will try to avoid entering into transactions with these disreputable types, but we may have no choice if we are faced with few alternative partners: that is, a "small numbers" condition. Williamson cogently notes that many situations not characterized in the beginning by a small number of alternative partners may become so as transactions progress because early exchange partners ("first-movers") gain decided advantages over their competitors.

The creation of organizations helps to solve the problem of opportunism among exchange partners. By bringing economic exchanges under a hierarchical structure, better auditing and surveillance systems can be constructed. Also incentive systems within an organization can be arranged so that individual participants are discouraged from behaving opportunistically. Further, arrangements by which individual performance can be more closely monitored are especially helpful when the work involves "nonseparabilities"—products resulting from highly interdependent team performance such that it is difficult to determine who has made what contributions. When outputs involve nonseparabilities it is useful to be able to inspect inputs (see Alchian and Demsetz, 1972).

Yet another difference between the market and the organization relates to the nature of the transactions that take place between exchange partners. In the case of organizations, a new type of contract comes into existence: the employment contract. The institutional economist John Commons first called attention to the special nature of this contract, noting that what the worker sells "when he sells his labor is his willingness to use his faculties according to a purpose that has been pointed out to him. He sells his promise to obey commands" (1924: 284). Under conditions of uncertainty, the advantages of this open-ended or "incomplete" contract are obvious: obedience is promised to a general range of commands,[4] the specific command being determined by the variable and unpredictable requirements of the changing situation.

---

[4]The range of commands that will be obeyed automatically in any organizational situation is, of course, restricted. Ordinarily a supervisor does not have the right to tell an employee to perform personal services or to carry out activities beyond those specified in the job description. These boundaries are also influenced by generalized social beliefs. For example, some contemporary secretaries have decided that making coffee is outside their appropriate job definition. Barnard refers to the arena within which employees will unquestioningly comply with directives as the "zone of indifference" (1938: 168–69); Simon refers to the same concept as the "zone of acceptance" (1957: 12).

These are among the considerations which, in the view of Arrow and Williamson, cause men and women to move their transactions out of the marketplace and into an organization. These arguments are well within the rational system perspective. Organizations are viewed as providing improved efficiencies over markets in terms of information processing and transactions costs, under conditions of complexity and uncertainty. Quite different arguments comparing organizations to markets have been proposed that are more congruent with the natural system perspective. Thus, both Galbraith (1967) and Pfeffer and Salancik (1978) emphasize that removing economic transactions from the market and placing them under the canopy of an organization is a means of reducing uncertainty and increasing the security of the organization. Not cost cutting and efficiency but survival is the name of the game.[5] These views are relevant to the creation of organizations but relate even more closely to the mechanisms existing organizations use in relating to the environment, and so will be discussed in more detail in chapter 9.

When organizations confront institutionalized environments rather than competitive market situations, according to Meyer and Rowan (1977), the advantage in creating an organizational framework does not lie in reducing transaction costs. Organizations are created in such situations in order to embody these rationalized myths—to become "isomorphic" with these environments—and thus to acquire the resources and legitimacy associated with them. In a society in which value and credence is placed on economic analysis, accounting procedures, and personnel management, organizations that incorporate these elements will enjoy legitimacy and support from the wider community independent of any technical advantages that may be associated with these services. In short, Meyer and Rowan postulate: "Organizations that incorporate societally legitimated rationalized elements in their formal structures maximize their legitimacy and increase their resources and survival capabilities" (1977: 352)

Organizations versus Informal Groups   Even though our theoretical definitions do not require it, most organizations exhibit a formal hierarchical structure. This is one of the principal ways in which organizations differ from informal, primary groups. A hierarchical structure incorporates several features—including status distinctions and power differences among positions—but among its most significant components is a centralized communications system. What, if any, are the advantages of carrying on work within a hierarchical structure, specifically, a centralized communications structure, as compared to a more informal and equalitarian arrangement? Experimental studies

---

[5]A question to be usefully pondered is: under what conditions do cost cutting and related efficiencies of operation contribute to the survival of the organization? A possible response is: when the organizations are themselves in a true competitive market situation. However, it is precisely Galbraith's thesis that organizations strive to avoid competition, and increasingly, succeed (Galbraith, 1967: 33–45: see also Lindblom, 1977).

of communication structures conducted during the 1950s and 1960s examined the effects of centralized versus decentralized communication networks on the task performance of groups.[6] In a technique developed by Bavelas (1951), a small number of individuals are placed in cubicles and allowed to communicate only by means of written messages passed through slots in the cubicle walls. The slots connecting each cubicle can be opened or closed by the experimenter, so that differing communication patterns can be imposed on the interacting subjects. The most frequently studied communication networks are diagrammed in figure 7–2. The circle and all-channel networks are relatively decentralized communication structures; the chain and particularly the wheel are more highly centralized structures. A typical task presented to groups of individuals placed in these networks is to provide each individual with a card

[6]Some analysts are reluctant to generalize from findings based on "artificial" experiments to behavior in real-world organizations. However, we believe that, interpreted with caution, results from experimental studies can aid our understanding of natural phenomena. The great advantage of experimental settings is that they permit investigators to isolate certain variables from others whose presence may influence the effects observed (see Zelditch, 1969). We just noted that hierarchies in organizations contain a number of components or elements only one of which relates to the formal structuring of communication flows. Experiments allow us to examine the effects of these structured flows independently of those produced by formal status and power differences. A comprehensive review of the communication network experiments is provided by Collins and Raven (1969: 137–55).

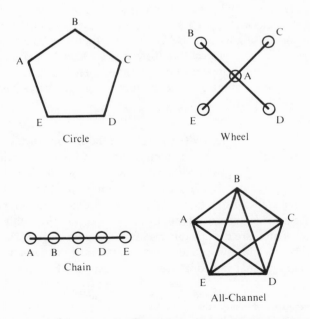

Figure 7–2   Examples of Communication Networks (five-person groups)

containing several symbols, only one of which is present on the cards of all subjects. The task is defined as completed when all participants are able to identify correctly the common symbol. Using this type of task, most studies have reported that groups working in the more centralized structures are more efficient in their performance, as measured by the speed of attaining a solution or the number of messages transmitted to arrive at a solution, than groups in more decentralized structures (See Leavitt, 1951; Guetzkow and Simon, 1955).

Vroom accounts for these findings as follows:

> The centralized structures more rapidly organize to solve the problems. Participants in peripheral positions send information to the center of the network, where a decision is made and sent out to the periphery. Furthermore, this pattern of organization tends to be highly stable once developed. In less centralized structures the organization problem is more difficult and observed interaction patterns are less stable, as well as less efficient. (Vroom, 1969: 242)

Vroom stresses the functions of formalization, as discussed in chapter 3. Arrow embraces the same conclusion, but his arguments concerning the superiority of centralized networks are based on efficiency of information processing. He notes that:

> Since transmission of information is costly, in the sense of using resources, especially the time of the individuals, it is cheaper and more efficient to transmit all the pieces of information once to a central place than to disseminate each of them to everyone. (Arrow, 1974: 68)

And noting that the gathering of information is also essential to arriving at a decision, Arrow applies the same arguments to this process, concluding: "Thus, authority, the centralization of decision-making, serves to economize on the transmission and handling of information." (Arrow, 1974: 69)

Williamson (1975: 41–54) agrees that hierarchies are superior to peer groups in the economies of communication effected. In addition, he asserts that the use of hierarchies reduces the likelihood of opportunistic behavior by improving surveillance of individual performance.

It would be incorrect, however, to conclude that hierarchies are superior to more decentralized or equalitarian arrangements under all conditions. Other studies employing the Bavelas networks have introduced more complex tasks—for example, mathematical problems—or provided subjects with more ambiguous information to process—for example, asking subjects to identify similar colors when the samples provided include unusual colors for which there are no common names (Shaw, 1954; Christie, Luce, and Macy, 1952). Such studies show that as tasks become more complex or ambiguous, decentralized nets are usually superior to centralized structures (Shaw, 1964).

Reviewing these communication network studies, Blau and I (Blau and

Scott, 1962: 116–28) concluded that formal hierarchies aid the performance of tasks requiring the efficient coordination of information and routine decision making whereas they interfere with tasks presenting very complex or ambiguous problems. Specifically, we argued that hierarchies impede work on the latter by stifling free interactions that can result in error-correction, by undermining the social support necessary to encourage *all* participants to propose solutions, and by reducing incentives for participants to search for solutions.

More generally, there appears to be a curvilinear relation between information-processing requirements and the utility of hierarchy. When little information is to be processed, there are no particular advantages to hierarchy and some clear disadvantages (for example, the costs of supporting the administrative overhead). As information-processing needs increase up to a certain point, hierarchies can be of benefit, reducing transmission costs and ensuring coordination. But as information-processing needs continue to increase, hierarchies become overloaded and the intellectual resources of peripheral participants underutilized. Such increased demands do not require a return to informal systems, but they do encourage the creation of more decentralized structures. (Specific types of decentralization strategies are described in chapter 10.)

The same type of argument can be made with respect to the relation between surveillance requirements and hierarchies. The creation of hierarchies can result in improved surveillance and control of participants up to a point, but if extraordinary demands are required for secrecy or for loyalty, formal hierarchical surveillance may have to be supplemented or replaced by clan systems relying on more diffuse, internalized controls (see Ouchi, 1980). For example, organizations confronting hostile environments, such as the FBI or the Mafia, are likely to rely heavily on procedures that induce a strong personal commitment (see Wilson, 1978) or on the creation of diffuse interpersonal ties (see Ianni, 1972) to effect tight controls (see chapter 12).

One final comment on hierarchy: it is possible to interpret this concept in a manner that does not focus on communication networks or on surveillance systems. Simon (1962) suggests that one important meaning of hierarchy is that of a nested series of systems in which complex systems are composed of subsystems that themselves contain subsystems, and so on. Simon argues that such hierarchical structures have a strong adaptive or survival capacity to the extent that the subsystems represent stable intermediate forms. In other words, hierarchy can be viewed as representing a principle of clustering in which similar or highly interdependent elements are placed together in such a manner that their interdependence is protected (see Thompson, 1967: 59). Such "nearly decomposable systems"—systems that exhibit many interconnections within each of their subsystem components but few between the subsystems —are characteristic of social organizations and are highly adaptive.[7]

---

[7]We will elaborate further on this view of organizations in chapter 11, when we discuss the advantages of loose coupling in organizations.

To this point, the arguments reviewed—whether generated from the rational or the natural system perspectives—have concentrated on the benefits derived from creating organizations, under conditions of complexity and uncertainty. From the rational system standpoint, most of these benefits related to their technical superiority or economic efficiency; from the natural system —including the institutionalized organization perspective—security and survival are stressed. We have noted that if the tasks involved become very complex or if high levels of control are required, organizational hierarchies may have to be modified in the direction of decentralization and the development of more diffuse or internalized controls. Other arguments, however, stress the costs of organization.

The most obvious costs imposed by the creation of organizations are those entailed in the development and maintenance of an administrative hierarchy —the costs of bureaucracy. With the advent of organization comes a new class of "workers"—those who are not engaged in direct productive activities but whose contributions are, at best, indirect. In a competitive market situation, it is presumed that the administrative overhead is kept at the lowest possible level to minimize these costs. However, many critics charge that, in the absence of such restraints—for example, in monopolistic situations or in the public sector—these administrative superstructures tend to become bloated, causing unnecessary costs and impairing efficiency of performance (see von Mises, 1944; Parkinson, 1957). We simply note such arguments here but will consider them in detail in chapter 11, where we examine the causes of administrative expansion, and especially in chapter 13, where we focus on pathologies associated with these processes.[8]

A second type of cost associated with hierarchical organizations relates to all of the possible deprivations that tend to be associated with low status in a hierarchy: loss of control over work decisions and activities, economic exploitation, and the associated psychic costs as reflected in low satisfaction and morale. Most of the sociological work emphasizes the importance of intrinsic rewards on the job—retaining some discretion or autonomy and some command over skills in one's work; but we should not overlook the extrinsic rewards of monetary compensation. Neither should we forget that the two types of rewards are usually positively associated: more interesting and demanding work tends also to be more highly paid. We will examine some aspects of inequality first by again briefly comparing organizations with markets and with informal groups and then, at greater length, with occupations.

[8]It seems more appropriate to consider these inefficiency costs in Chapter 13 because, in general, they tend to be "passed through" to the public. That is, these costs are borne primarily by the larger society rather than by the offending organization.

Organizations versus Markets and Informal Groups   One of the main bless-
ings of the market, according to its advocates, is the sense of freedom experienced by individual participants (see Friedman, 1962). As Arrow observes, in
the marketplace, the individual "is free to act within the system; there is no
direct order telling him what to do" (1974: 21). That this sense of freedom may
be "somewhat illusory" given great disparities in resources or poor market
location does not negate the point that many individuals value situations
permitting self-directed conduct. Organizations place constraints on such conduct. A similar concern is voiced by some analysts conducting experiments
with communication networks. They observe that while the centralized networks are superior to the less centralized systems in promoting effective performance (under the conditions noted), the centralized systems are also associated
with low satisfaction among peripheral participants (Leavitt, 1951; Trow,
1957). These experiments call attention to the negative consequences of hierarchical structure for the morale of subordinate members. Thus, in comparison
with either markets or primary groups, hierarchical systems curtail the autonomy of subordinate participants and can engender low morale and feelings of
alienation (see chapter 13).

Certainly the most famous and devastating critique of the human costs of
industrial organization is that produced by Karl Marx. Marx asserted that in
the production organizations of capitalist systems, the workman "becomes an
appendage of the machine, and it is only the most simple, most monotonous,
and most easily acquired knack, that is required of him" (Marx and Engels,
1955 tr.: 65). Marx argued that the type of division of labor developed in these
organizations destroyed the craft skills of workers:

> Hence, in the place of the hierarchy of specialized workmen that characterizes
> manufacture, there steps, in the automatic factory, a tendency to equalise and
> reduce to one and the same level every kind of work that has to be done by the
> minders of the machines. (Marx, 1954 tr.: 420)

Marx observed that complex tasks were being subdivided, simplified, and
mechanized and that discretion was being removed from workers and transferred to managers and their staff. And, of course, Marx insisted that it was
not only discretion that was being removed and transferred: the surplus value
of labor was stripped from workers and passed along to manager-capitalists.

Kerr and his colleagues insist that Marx's dark descriptions and dire predictions have not been borne out by the actual course of industrialization. They
note:

> Industrialization in fact develops and depends upon a concentrated, disciplined
> industrial work force—a work force with new skills, and a wide variety of skills,
> with high skill levels and constantly changing skill requirements. . . . The indus-

trialization process utilizes a level of technology far in advance of that of earlier societies. . . . The industrial system requires a wide range of skills and professional competency broadly distributed throughout the work force. (Kerr et al., 1964: 17)

But Braverman (1974) has recently challenged this picture as misleading, insisting that the net effect of industrialization as it has progressed in the twentieth century has been the "deskilling" of a large segment of the population. He reviews considerable data bearing on job requirements at varying levels and concludes:

Clearly the "average" scientific, technical, and in that sense "skill" content of these labor processes is much greater than in the past. But . . . the question is precisely whether the scientific and "educated" content of labor tends toward *averaging,* or, on the contrary, toward *polarization.* . . . The mass of workers gain nothing from the fact that the decline in their command over the labor process is more than compensated for by the increasing command on the part of managers and engineers. (Braverman, 1974: 425)

Moreover, Braverman argues that much of the upgrading of occupational groups does not reflect real changes in skill level but is an artifact of distinctions made by census categories that, for example, label workers who have any type of contact with a machine as "operatives" or "semiskilled" and that regard any type of office or clerical employment as superior to blue-collar work. Braverman also observes that the fastest growing occupational sectors are those involved in service work, sales, and clerical positions. These positions are less affected by industrialization, require lower skills, and generally, are associated with lower pay. And these are the positions into which women— a vast new labor pool—are primarily drawn.

Organizations versus Occupations   Marx and Braverman appear to prefer broad political solutions to the problems they pose, but it is worth noting that both implicitly contrast organizational systems with occupational arrangements in which workers are able to retain control over the skills and judgments required to perform their work. The craft associations and guilds of earlier times provide examples of such occupational control systems (see Pirenne, 1949); and some residues of these systems persist to the present (see Stinchcombe, 1959). Without doubt, however, the most obvious contemporary instance of such occupational systems is provided by the professions. Eliot Freidson, in numerous writings, has given us the clearest picture of how professional occupations provide an alternative to administrative organizations. Most of his specific analyses have concentrated on occupations within the medical care arena and, specifically, on physicians (see Freidson, 1970*a*; 1970*b*).

Freidson (1973) explicitly contrasts the organization of work governed by an "administrative principle" as opposed to an "occupational principle." Under the administrative arrangement, as noted by Marx and others, the division of labor is determined by an organizational hierarchy, work is minutely subdivided, and the individual worker loses control over the definition of the tasks to be performed and the manner of their performance. By contrast, under the occupational principle, the occupational group "obtains the exclusive right to perform a particular kind of work, control training for and access to it, and control the right of determining and evaluating the way the work is performed" (Freidson, 1973: 22). The most highly developed professional groups are set apart from other occupations by the degree to which they "have gained the organized power to control themselves the terms, conditions and content of their work in the settings where they perform their work" (Freidson, 1977: 22).

Such occupations develop special arrangements for controlling individual practitioners that do not depend on hierarchical systems. Individual professionals are subjected to a prolonged period of socialization and training in which they are expected to internalize standards, acquire a repertory of skills, and master a general set of theoretical principles that will enable them to make decisions and act autonomously in a responsible and expert fashion. These internalized controls are reinforced by collegial watchfulness and, under extreme conditions, by formal sanctions reinforced by occupational associations (Goode, 1957; Merton, Reader, and Kendall, 1957; Scott, 1966). Although there is considerable evidence that such controls are often not employed or are not very effective (Editors of the Yale Law Journal, 1954; Freidson and Rhea, 1963; Freidson, 1975), the norms enforced by these groups are sufficiently strong to ward off most attempts by lay (nonprofessional) persons to control professional performance.

Professional occupations are able to exercise considerable control over their work activities whether they work as independent practitioners or as organizational employees. As Freidson points out:

> The effectively organized professional occupation controls even the determination and demarcation of tasks embodied in jobs supported by employers. . . . Through their influence on regulatory agencies, the organized professions (and the crafts) are often responsible for writing the job descriptions for their members and determining the employer's training and educational requirements as well as the kind of special skill imputed to the qualified worker. (Freidson, 1977: 24)

Moreover, although these host organizations contain hierarchies for the coordination and control of support and auxiliary functions, the professional actors are largely immune from these administrative systems. A sharp distinction is drawn by professionals between "administrative" and "professional" work, and while professionals may reluctantly accept directives in the former arena, they strongly resist any administrative encroachment into their professional sphere. Of course, considerable variation exists among various professional groups in the scope of their professional domains: in the case of secondary school teachers and social workers it may be relatively small; in the case of physicians and scientists it is usually quite large (see Scott, 1965*b;* Hall, 1967).

In general, comparative studies of worker satisfaction show that the greater the level of variety, autonomy, and meaningful responsibility associated with one's job, the higher the level of individual satisfaction (see Blauner, 1960; Sheppard and Herrick, 1972; Special Task Force, 1973). Since professionalized occupations serve to legitimate and protect these types of job characteristics, it is not surprising that the satisfactions of workers in the professions tend to be quite high. Further, their material rewards are commensurate with their psychic benefits.

There is disagreement over whether the relative advantages in variety of work and discretion and income enjoyed by the members of the professions are due to inherent differences in the types of work performed (a rational system explanation) or to the exercise of power (a natural system explanation). Most early students of the professions insisted that the explanation lay in the special nature of the tasks performed by these occupations: their social importance and their high level of complexity require specialized intellectual techniques (see, for example, Flexner, 1915; Carr-Saunders and Wilson, 1933; Parsons, 1939). More recent analysts have questioned these explanations and instead pointed to the importance of political or power processes (see Friedman, 1962; Wilensky, 1964; Krause, 1977). Thus, Freidson argues that the ability of an occupational group to attain control over its work "presupposes a successful political organisation which can gain the power to negotiate and establish favourable jurisdictions in an organised division of labour, and to control the labour market" (1977: 23). And the power of professional occupations is not exclusively political. It can also operate in a primarily normative fashion, providing guidelines and standards to its members even in the absence of state certification or licensure provisions (see Reeves, 1980).

Occupational groupings and categories are important building blocks for organizations. The more they exist and lay claim to prerogatives independently of employing organizations, the more negotiating space exists for these groups and their members. The professions represent a special case of this general pattern in that they bequeath to their members a "vertical vision" of their future (Bledstein, 1976) that enables them to structure their career lines within and across existing organizations.

In summary, the costs and benefits of organizing are not distributed equally throughout the hierarchy. Whether all or most individuals participate in the growth of knowledge and skills and wealth that attends the development of industrialization remains in dispute. Some occupational groups—most notably, the professions—have successfully resisted subordination to an administrative hierarchy. Their ability to fend off administrative domination may be due in part to the importance and complexity of the tasks which they perform; but it is also a result of their ability to organize and mobilize social and political support to back their territorial claims (see chapter 10).

Before leaving the topic of professions and organizations, we wish to make one more general point. To argue that there is some conflict between professional and administrative principles of organization is not to conclude that these two arrangements are incompatible in all respects. On the contrary, professional and administrative principles share numerous common features: both emphasize the use of universalistic standards; both place value on specialization as the key to expertise; both stress a need for an affectively neutral orientation toward work; and both emphasize the importance of technical qualifications (see Parsons, 1951; Blau and Scott, 1962; 60–62). In short, they represent alternative paths to the rationalization of a field of action—and at this general level, the two approaches are compatible. Professionals and organizations are not only compatible in theory; they are frequently found together. An emphasis on relatively independent professional groups such as physicians can lead us to overlook the many instances in which professional groups and organizations have developed in close association. For example, it is hard to imagine priests or ministers, teachers, scientists or accountants operating apart from an organizational base. The widespread existence of professionals can, however, have important effects on the *form* of organizations which we consider in chapters 8 and 10.

The Mobilization of Resources

Oberschall provides a useful definition of *mobilization*— "the process of forming crowds, groups, associations, and organizations for the pursuit of collective goals" (1973: 102). Organizations do not spontaneously emerge but require the gathering and harnessing of resources—materials, energy, information, and personnel. The availability of such resources varies from place to place and from time to time. In traditional societies, material resources are locked into landholdings and individuals into caste and kinship systems; in modern societies, to repeat the observation of Eisenstadt (1958), resources are more "free-floating" and easier to mobilize into the service of specialized goals. We have already reviewed, in the first section of this chapter, the general societal factors that facilitate the creation of these conditions.

No organization is self-sufficient; all must secure a continuing supply of resources from the environment, and all must compete for the resources they require. Even the most "sacred" organization and the most well entrenched government bureau must compete for resources: although vested interests may exist, they must still be continuously defended and supported. The fact that organizations do not entirely control all of the resources necessary for goal attainment or survival leads them to become interdependent with other systems, as Pfeffer and Salancik (1978) note. Such interdependence places important constraints on and poses significant opportunities for organizations. The strategies used by organizations to manage these interdependencies are examined in chapter 9.

INITIAL RESOURCE MIX

Each specific type of organization presents a particular combination of resource requirements—economic and technical as well as social. The technological base on which the organization rests must be in place; labor, trained and movable, must be available; capital is required from individuals willing to risk it; and an appropriate organizational form must have been invented. Larger cultural norms must support the venture: the goals of the enterprise together with the means employed in their pursuit must be regarded as legitimate.[9] Any given combination of requirements cannot always be met. Appropriate conditions come together at certain periods creating new possibilities for the support of organizations that could not exist under different circumstances. This accounts for the pattern of organizational founding noted by Stinchcombe, who points out that

> an examination of the history of almost any type of organization shows that there are great spurts of foundation of organizations of the type, followed by periods of relatively slower growth, perhaps to be followed by new spurts, generally of a fundamentally different kind of organization in the same field. (Stinchcombe, 1965: 154)

Stinchcombe cites numerous United States examples: the founding of savings banks and the first factory industry, textiles, in the 1830s; the development of railroads and steel companies in the 1850s and 1870s; the founding of universities and labor unions from the 1870s to the 1900s; the development of department stores in the 1850s and mail-order houses in the 1970s; the growth of the oil, rubber, and automobile industries in the 1920s; the emergence of the airline manufacturing and transportation companies during and after World War II; and the recent development of data processing and electronic equipment in the 1960s and 1970s (Ibid., 154–55).

---

[9]Recall that Weber's (1958 tr.) most famous essay, "The Protestant Ethic and the Spirit of Capitalism," deals with the role of religious values and belief systems, particularly Christian asceticism such as Calvinism, in legitimating the accumulation and investment of capital and effort in economic enterprise.

Given the similar resource requirements confronting each of these types of organizations, it should come as no surprise that each cohort of organizations of the same type is quite similar in its occupational composition and structural features. As Stinchcombe observes, "organizations which are founded at a particular time must construct their social systems with the social resources available" (Ibid., p. 168). What is remarkable is that once established, an organization of a given type tends to retain the basic characteristics present at the time of its founding. Organizational forms tend to be *imprinted:* they are likely to retain the features acquired at the time of their origin. Stinchcombe (Ibid., pp. 155–69) cites a variety of types of evidence to support this conclusion: for example, industries comprised of small firms at the outset tend to retain this characteristic; industries relying heavily on unpaid family workers tend to continue to do so. And only those firms established during the last few decades use professional staffs extensively. Both rational and natural system explanations may account for this association between organizational characteristics and time of founding. The characteristics may provide a competitive advantage over alternative arrangements (a rational system argument); they may be preserved by a set of "traditionalizing forces" including vested interests; or these organizations may not confront competitive forces and so are free to continue to exist without major changes or technical improvements (natural system explanations). Whatever the case, it is instructive to realize that the form and shape organizations acquire at the time of their founding is likely to be the structure they retain over the course of their life span. The mix of initial resources out of which an organizational structure is created has lasting effects on the attributes of that structure.

BALANCING CONTRIBUTIONS AND INDUCEMENTS

Of all the many resources required by organizations, the most vital are the contributions of its human participants. Not only are these contributions themselves of infinite variety; they are also the ultimate means by which all other resources are acquired. More than other early theorists, Barnard (1938) stressed the importance of an organization's ability to motivate participants so that they will continue to make contributions—of time, resources, effort—to it rather than to some competing system. Barnard's concerns were pursued by Simon (1957), resulting in the Barnard-Simon theory of "organizational equilibrium."[10] Since equilibrium refers to the organization's ability to attract essential contributions, it deals with the crucial question of the organization's survival. The basic postulates of the theory are as follows:

[10]Recall as discussed in chapter 3 that Barnard and Simon distinguish between the decisions a particpant makes to join and continue to participate in an organization and those that he or she makes *as* a participant in the organization. The current discussion deals with the first category of decisions.

1. An organization is a system of interrelated social behaviors of a number of persons whom we shall call *participants* in the organization.

2. Each participant and each group of participants receives *from* the organization *inducements* in return for which he makes to the organization *contributions*.

3. Each participant will continue his participation in an organization only so long as the inducements offered him are as great or greater (measured in terms of *his* values and in terms of the alternatives open to him) than the contributions he is asked to make.

4. The contributions provided by the various groups of participants are the source from which the organization manufactures the inducements offered to participants.

5. Hence, an organization is "solvent"—and will continue in existence—only so long as the contributions are sufficient to provide inducements in large enough measure to draw forth these contributions. (Simon, Smithberg, and Thompson, 1950: 381–82)

While pointing to an essential truth about the survival of organizations, as Simon himself observes, the theory "verges on the tautological" (March and Simon, 1958: 84). It is difficult to measure the balance of inducements and contributions independently of the individual's decision to stay with or leave the organization. Also, as noted by Krupp, since the concept of organizational inducement includes techniques for changing an individual's values or needs, it is difficult to distinguish between inducements that "win participation because they create satisfactions at a given level of willingness and inducements that shift the level of willingness" (1961: 107). Further, it is difficult to determine what utilities or values are attached by individual participants to the contributions they are asked to make and the inducements they are offered. Indeed, one of the major contributions of the human relations school in attempting to counteract the myth of economic man is its demonstration of the diversity of factors to which individuals attach importance—for example, working conditions, tools, skills, personal relations, office furnishings, raw materials (see Whyte et al., 1955). And related work emphasizes that level of satisfaction is not assessed on an absolute scale but depends on choice of reference or comparison group; that is, how one worker assesses his or her own benefits depends on those received by others regarded as comparable (see Adams, 1965; Homans, 1961; Patchen, 1961).

One of the most useful approaches to understanding how organizations attract and reward participants for their contributions is based on a simple typology developed by Clark and Wilson (1961: 134–36; see also Wilson, 1973). Clark and Wilson differentiate between three types of incentives:

Material incentives—tangible rewards; rewards with a monetary value: for example, wages, interest, fringe benefits, patronage

Solidary incentives—intangible rewards derived from the act of association: for example, sociability, status, identification

Purposive incentives—intangible rewards related to the goals of the organization: for example, satisfaction obtained from the election of a candidate supported by one's party; pleasure from the results of a beautification project to which one has contributed.

Like Etzioni (1961), whose similar typology was developed at the same time, Clark and Wilson (1961: 137–49) suggest that while all organizations make use of all three types of incentives, it is usually possible to identify a predominant type for each. And associated with each type are important structural and operational differences. Organizations that rely primarily on material incentives are labeled *utilitarian organizations,* for example, business firms, trade unions, and political machines. Clark and Wilson predict that such organizations will explicitly seek material rewards for their members and develop fairly precise cost-accounting machinery. Executives will devote their energies first and foremost to obtaining the material resources needed to provide incentives; central conflicts within the organization will center on their equitable distribution. The substantive goals pursued by the organization will be of only secondary importance. Such organizations can be flexible about their goal-related activities: these "activities may change without disrupting member participation as long as material incentives continue to be available" (Clark and Wilson, 1961: 140).

Solidary organizations include most service-oriented, voluntary associations and social clubs. Members make contributions in return for sociability and status. Executive efforts must be devoted to obtaining these inducements— additional organizational prestige, publicity, or good fellowship. The goals of such organizations need to be noncontroversial and socially desirable. Solidary organizations are tactically less flexible than utilitarian organizations: the means utilized must be acceptable to powerful participants, and projects must often be carried on publicly to stimulate the flow of approvals and publicity.

In many ways, *purposive organizations* represent the most interesting case. These organizations "rely almost exclusively on their stated purposes as incentives to attract and hold contributors" (Ibid., p. 146). This would appear to be the ideal organizational arrangement: members join because they wish to help in achieving the goals espoused by the organization; and the organization, in achieving its goals, supplies inducements to its members securing their continuing contributions. Wilson's (1962; 1973) analyses, however, suggest that this "ideal" is very difficult to realize. Executives in these organizations —like their counterparts in other organizations—must secure a continuing flow of inducements to sustain the interests of members; but many of the types of goals sought by purposive organizations are difficult to achieve. Political parties do not always succeed in electing their candidates; religious organizations do not always succeed in transforming the world or converting the heathen; and social movements may not succeed in achieving their specific goals—which range from achieving equality for racial groups to banning nuclear warheads. Sometimes goals in such organizations may be only vaguely stated—in order to appeal to a large number of potential adherents; but when the time comes for action and goals are more specifically defined, many participants may feel betrayed or, at least, sense that their interests are not being served. Alternatively, specific goals can serve as a guide to action but may only appeal to a narrow minority and prevent the organization from growing by attracting new recruits. Most purposive organizations are forced to set up intermediate objectives—for example, political clubs hold meetings in which their members debate and "endorse" specific positions in order to "manufacture" inducements for participants. Such contrived inducements can undermine the attainment of the organization's original goals. Thus, the club's endorsements of controversial political positions often embarrass, unduly constrain, or help to defeat candidates in the general election (Wilson, 1962).

Olson (1965) suggests yet another reason why purposive organizations are difficult to sustain. Under the classical economic assumption that individuals attempt to behave rationally and to pursue their own self-interests, Olson points out that no individual should be expected to join an organization in order to achieve common or public interests. Rational persons will realize that their own act of joining, except under very special conditions, will not appreciably affect the chances of the organization to succeed in its mission. And these individuals will also observe that because the goals served represent a collective good—one that cannot be unequally distributed but is available to all—they will share in the benefits of the organization's success whether or not they have contributed to its attainment.

Thus, both the analyses by Clark and Wilson and by Olson conclude that purposive organizations—those attempting to equate organizational goals with individual motives—are difficult to manage and to maintain. Except for the most ideologically pure or the more extreme redemptive varieties (see Wilson, 1973: 45–51), purposive organizations typically supplement their primary incentives with material inducements—to retain a core staff—and solidary incentives to help sustain rank-and-file participants through the dry spells.

ACQUIRING RESOURCES

How difficult it is to garner the necessary resources to support an organization depends greatly on the nature of the organization and its goals. Much recent work has been devoted to describing the situation of protest or social

movement organizations that pursue controversial or change-oriented programs. Such organizations face a decidedly uphill struggle in their search for
resources—including adherents and constitutents—and, more often than not,
fail in their attempt to survive (see Oberschall, 1973; Gamson, 1975, McCarthy
and Zald, 1977). Similarly, small businesses such as restaurants and specialty
shops, which face a highly competitive market with small capital reserves, are
much more likely to fail than to survive.

At the other end of the spectrum, the institutionalized organizations described by Meyer and Rowan may have a much easier time. They select their
purposes precisely because they are socially valued and choose their organization ingredients—including professionals, procedures, and categories of service—because they are socially validated. To repeat Meyer and Rowan's
summary of the situation: "After all, the building blocks for organizations
come to be littered around the societal landscape; it takes only a little entrepreneurial energy to assemble them into a structure" (1977: 345).

The expansion and penetration of the state in modern societies is another
major facet of the growth of institutionalized environments having important
consequences for organizational growth and maintenance. As Aldrich asserts:

> The role of the state is perhaps the single most important factor in accounting
> for patterns of organizational creation, for state support and protection consti-
> tute an overwhelming advantage for organizations receiving state blessing, di-
> rectly or indirectly. (Aldrich, 1979: 188)

And, unlike restaurants, organizations enjoying direct support from the state
—governmental bureaus—are likely to survive for long periods of time (Kaufman, 1976).

Summary

Organizations, as we know them, have not always existed. They evolved
during the past few centuries as part of a dual process: the same social changes
that brought about the development of individualism—the freeing of individuals from all-absorbing social structures—are responsible for the growth of
organizations—the freeing of resources, including individuals, which can be
mobilized in the service of specialized purposes.

Organizations are called into existence by increases in the need to coordinate and control complex administrative and technical tasks. Improvements
in transportation and communications systems—including internal communications capabilities—enable organizations to respond to these needs. Organizations are also created by the development and elaboration of institutional rules
in modern societies.

The costs and benefits of creating organizations are more easily evaluated if organizations are compared to alternative social forms for carrying on complex work. Organizations are viewed as having advantages over market mechanisms when the tasks to be carried out are sufficiently complex and uncertain so as to exceed the information-processing capacities of individuals, and when so few potential buyers or sellers exist that they may attempt to take advantage of one another. Under these conditions, organizations offer mechanisms for reducing transaction costs and for constraining opportunistic behavior. Organizations are viewed as superior to informal, peer groups as mechanisms for overseeing and coordinating complex work. However, conventional hierarchies in organizations may function poorly on ambiguous or highly complex tasks that require the exercise of individual discretion and the exchange of large amounts of information. Occupations—in particular, professional occupations—constitute an alternative social structure for the management of complex work. Under these arrangements, individual performers retain considerable discretion and command over a broad range of skills. They exhibit higher satisfaction than their counterparts in conventional organizations. Such arrangements may reflect differences in the complexity of the tasks performed; they certainly reflect differences in the power of the performers.

All organizations must secure a continuing supply of resources—including participants—from their environment. The initial mix of resources that are mobilized at the time of the creation of a particular organizational form are critical in that they constitute a structural pattern that tends to persist—imprinting the organization with characteristics that are preserved across succeeding generations of that form. What types of incentives are held out to induce the contributions of participants has important consequences for the stability and the flexibility of the organization.

chapter 8

Conceptions
of Environments

*For a given system, the environment is the set
of all objects a change in whose attributes
affect the system and also those objects whose
attributes are changed by the behavior of the
system.*

*The statement above invites the natural
question of when an object belongs to a system
and when it belongs to the environment; for if
an object reacts with a system in the way
described above should it not be considered a
part of the system? The answer is by no means
definite. In a sense, a system together with its
environment makes up the universe of all
things of interest in a given context.
Subdivision of this universe into two sets,
system and environment, can be done in many
ways which are in fact quite arbitrary.
Ultimately it depends on the intentions of the
one who is studying the particular universe as
to which of the possible configurations of
objects is to be taken as the system.*

A. D. HALL AND R. E. FAGEN (1956)

Since the emergence and increasing promi-
nence of open systems models, investigators are no longer able to comfortably
ignore the effects of environments on organizations. To examine these causal
connections, it is necessary to develop some working conceptions of environments themselves: ideas as to how to circumscribe them and how to identify
and assess their relevant features. This chapter describes the major conceptions

that are beginning to take shape and that currently guide investigations in this area.

Analyzing Environments

Before considering some of the ways in which organizations relate to their environments, we need to determine how we are to approach the concept of environment. Although we have referred to this concept many times throughout this volume, we have not attempted to define it systematically or, more important, to describe how the concept is treated in organizational analysis. We will discover that there is not much consensus on how environments are to be defined, described, or measured. This is, perhaps, not surprising given that, in a general sense, the environment of a system consists of "everything else"—that is, everything that is not-system. Treating environments as a residual category suffices when we wish to focus attention on the organization itself, but not when we wish to treat the environment as a causal force influencing the structure or activities of organizations—as a set of independent or interdependent variables.

We focus attention first on the cultural environments of organizations, acknowledging that relatively little progress has been made in this area in spite of its obvious importance. However, there is no shortage of interesting hypotheses. After considering how cultural effects may be produced and illustrating some possible differences among organizational types in differing societies, we turn to discuss some more analytical attempts to conceptualize the environments of organizations. We note that variations in conceptions of the environment stem from three primary sources: differences in which components or dimensions are singled out for attention; differences in levels of analysis; and differences in the degree of independence attributed to environments.

CULTURAL DIFFERENCES

The most neglected aspect of environment-organization relations is the analysis of the impact of cultural factors. Up to the present time, most of the work in this area has been descriptive and concrete, focusing on specific belief patterns and their impact in particular situations. Several early studies conducted in non-Western settings (for example, Abegglen, 1958; Berger, 1957) called attention to the importance of cultural differences for the structure and functioning of organizations, but these issues have not been systematically pursued. Only a few cross-cultural studies have been conducted in which similar data were gathered on organizations in different societies (see Udy, 1959*b*, Landsberger, 1970; Lammers and Hickson, 1979*c*).

Lammers and Hickson suggest that culture patterns can affect organizations in three ways:

1. through the existence of generalized social values, norms and roles, often embedded in legal requirements and governmental regulations, which influence the ways in which organizations are evaluated and the responses of their significant publics;

2. through the existence of social models and premises concerning what organizations "can and should be" that influence the conceptions of those who design and redesign organizational systems; and

3. through the beliefs and actions of both elite and rank-and-file participants who "perform their roles and relate to one another in ways which stem from values, norms and roles 'imported' from the outside." (Lammers and Hickson, 1979*b:* 403)

They suggest that these types of influence from the surrounding culture penetrate organizations so that salient variables and relationships are affected. Four types of effects are distinguished:

1. *differences of degree* in a particular variable—for example, some studies show that American organizations of a given type exhibit higher levels of formalization than their British counterparts (McMillan et al, 1973)

2. *trait differences,* in which particular variables are highly constrained by cultural restrictions—for example, prohibitions against the hiring of particular ethnic groups

3. *relational differences,* as variables are observed to interact in distinctive ways due to cultural effects—for example, workers in the United States have been observed to react negatively to close supervision while Peruvian workers were noted to react favorably to such tactics (Williams, Whyte, and Green, 1966)

4. *type differences,* which involve distinctive combinations or distributions of sets of variables by culture—for example, the suggestion that differing organizational forms prevail in different cultural systems. (Lammers and Hickson, 1979*b:* 404–9)

The last effect, type differences, is, of course, the most far-reaching and significant, assuming that it exists. Given the paucity of systematic research, it is not possible to cite convincing evidence of such type differences, but several theorists argue that they are likely and several studies point to their possible existence. For example, Lammers and Hickson (1979*a*) summarizing several studies aimed at detecting cross-cultural differences in organizational types, conclude that current evidence points to at least three distinctive cultural forms: a *Latin* type, exemplified by French, Italian, and Spanish organizations, characterized by relatively high centralization, rigid stratification and sharp inequalities among levels, and conflicts around areas of uncertainty (see

Crozier, 1964; Clark, 1979; Schoenherr and Vilariño, 1979); an *Anglo-Saxon* type, exemplified by British, United States, and Scandinavian organization, marked by more decentralization, less rigid stratification, and more flexible approaches to the application of rules (see Clark, 1979; Schoenherr and Vilariño, 1979); and a *traditional* type, found in third-world, developing countries, characterized by paternalistic leadership patterns, implicit rather than explicit rules, and lack of clear boundaries separating organizational from non-organizational roles (see Berger, 1957; Negandhi, 1979).

Van Dorn (1979) argues that the types of organizations that arise—the distinctive mix of organizational forms—can be related to the value patterns which characterize a particular society. He notes that the emergence of large scale, formal, bureaucratic organizations in the military, industrial, and public sectors was

> not only favored by the rise of organizational elites but also conditioned by the existence of a vast lower class with virtually no social or political influence. The social machines of the time were able to draw upon large reservoirs of powerless and voiceless masses, ready to subordinate themselves to the depersonalized and hierarchical structure of the organization (van Dorn, 1979: 68).

By contrast, voluntary associations are

> a product of the rise of the urban population and particularly of the nineteenth-century middle class which organized itself in associations to maximize its political and economic influence and to become active in the spheres of culture, education and welfare. If formal organizations grew out of the various managerial revolutions, voluntary associations emerged from the American and French revolutions and their aftermath, which set the scene for the political participation of the citizen. (Ibid., p. 68)

Voluntary associations are not to be found in societies lacking an urbanized middle class and a strong commitment to human rights and individual freedom.

One of the most interesting lines of argument relates organizational forms to differences in societal stratification patterns and educational institutions and values. These connections may be pursued at varying occupational levels, (see Maurice, 1979), but we will focus on professionals. Ben-David (1963) has pointed out that in contrast to Europe, the United States has produced a much larger number and greater variety of university-trained professionals. This country more than most has emphasized the cultural value of individualism; and the absence of an entrenched elite here allowed a strong middle class to assume control of the educational institutions and transform them from bulwarks of the cultural tradition of restrictive upper elites into "pragmatic institutions of teaching and research in a growing variety of basic and practical fields" (Ben-David, 1963: 276). The number and variety of professionals—which in turn is related to more basic societal factors including cultural values and the class structure—has important implications for the type of organizations that develops. Meyer argues:

> Many variants of modern culture can produce rationalized organizations—but the level at which rationalization occurs may vary. . . . Cultures emphasizing diffuse interpersonal solidarity will tend to create organizations that have low vertical and horizontal mobility, infrequent work evaluations, elaborate rituals of groups and organizational community, relatively fixed but implicit definitions of roles, and the dominance of rules of seniority and status. Cultures emphasizing individual task achievement will create organizations with high mobility, explicitly defined roles, frequent and output-based evaluations, and few rituals of diffuse solidarity. (Meyer, 1978: 354)

All of the foregoing arguments, while interesting and often plausible, are lacking in firm empirical support. We know little, and need to learn much more, about the interactions of organizations and their cultural environments.

DIMENSIONS OF ENVIRONMENTS

Organization theorists have attempted to identify some more general and abstract features of the environment which ignore more substantive cultural distinctions or institutional differences. Two widely employed approaches are (1) to conceive of the environment as a source of information; and (2) to view the environment as a stock of resources (Aldrich and Mindlin, 1978). Investigators emphasizing the informational aspects of environments focus primary attention on the degree of uncertainty confronting the organization; those stressing the resource aspect of environments focus on the degree to which the organization is dependent on others for vital resources. Both uncertainty and dependency are viewed as problematic situations confronting organizations; and much attention has been devoted to examining the types of strategies and mechanisms organizations use to cope with these difficulties. But before turning to attempted "solutions," we need to inquire into the general conditions that give rise to these states.

Several general dimensions have been proposed by investigators as affecting either organizational uncertainty or dependence. Without attempting an exhaustive summary, we will present here the major variables and their expected effects:

DIMENSIONS AFFECTING UNCERTAINTY

1. Degree of homogeneity-heterogeneity
—extent to which the environmental entities to which the organization must relate are similar to one another, for example, the number of different types

of clients relating to a service organization. Other labels: complexity, diversity (see Dill, 1958; Thompson, 1967).

2. Degree of stability-change
— extent to which the entities are undergoing change, for example, the rate of product innovation within the industry category to which a given firm belongs. It is possible to differentiate between the rate of change and its evenness or fluctuation (see Lawrence and Lorsch, 1967; Thompson, 1967).

3. Degree of interconnectedness-isolation
— extent to which the organization is linked to many other environmental entities whose actions may impinge on it, for example, the number of different suppliers from whom a manufacturing company must buy its inputs (see Pfeffer and Salancik, 1978).

4. Degree of organization-nonorganization
— extent to which the organization confronts a set of environmental entities whose actions are coordinated or structured. For example, does a seller face a set of independent grocery stores or a chain of supermarkets? (see Jurkovich, 1974).

In general, we would expect that the greater the degree of heterogeneity, the higher the rate of change or instability, the larger the degree of interconnectedness, and the lower the degree of organization within the environment, the higher will be the uncertainty facing the organization.

DIMENSIONS AFFECTING DEPENDENCE

1. Degree of munificence-scarcity
— extent to which the resources required by the organization are available in its environment, for example, the availability of petroleum to a chemical company. Other labels: environmental capacity (see Pfeffer and Salancik, 1978; Aldrich, 1979).

2. Degree of concentration-dispersion
— extent to which the resources required are evenly spread throughout the environment, for example, economic concentration has been defined as the proportion of an industry's sales controlled by the largest four or eight firms (see Nutter, 1968; Pfeffer and Salancik, 1978).

3. Degree of organization-nonorganization
— extent to which the organization confronts a set of environmental entities whose actions are coordinated or structured. For example, does a seller face a set of independent grocery stores or a chain of supermarkets?

The greater the scarcity of resources, the higher the degree of concentration, and the greater the degree of organization exhibited by entities within the environment, the greater the dependence of the organization.

Note that the two dependent variables, uncertainty and dependence, do not necessarily co-vary in response to a given environmental state. Thus, a higher degree of environmental organization is expected simultaneously to decrease the organization's uncertainty but to increase its dependence. A similar prediction might well be made for level of concentration.

We believe that the identification of a number of environmental dimensions at this level of generality represents a significant advance in organization theory. The operationalization of such variables, however, has proved to be a difficult and often frustrating business. This is partly due to the abstract nature of the concepts and to the great variability in types of organizations and, hence, in the kinds of environments to which they relate. But the task of application is rendered particularly difficult by the differentiated nature of organizations: different components or subunits of an organization may confront quite different environmental sectors. For example, Lawrence and Lorsch (1967) investigated variation in the characteristics of some of the environmental sectors confronting different departments within plastics manufacturing organizations. Their measures revealed that the scientific environment to which the applied research departments related was more uncertain than the marketing environment the sales department confronted. Of course, other specialized units or departments relate to still other environmental sectors. To state the problem as succinctly as possible: every organization relates to a number of different environments, and these environments may exhibit differing characteristics. And any attempt to determine *the* characteristics of *the* environment requires respondents or investigator to arrive at a summary judgment that may conceal a great deal of variance.

LEVELS OF ENVIRONMENTS

Another source of variation in environmental conceptions stems from the level of analysis selected. In chapter 1 we distinguished between the social psychological, structural, and ecological levels. Since our current concern is with conceptions of organizational environments—the ecological level—all the distinctions to be proposed at this point are within this level.[1] It is helpful to identify three sublevels within the ecological level.

At the most general level, we have the *ecological community* (Hawley, 1950) or the *interorganizational field* (Warren, 1967). At this level, the investigator focuses on the relations linking a collection of organizations (and perhaps other types of social units) within a delimited geographical area.

---

[1] This does not mean that the other levels of analysis are not relevant to examining the relation between organizations and environments. Thus, when boundary roles are considered (see chapter 10) the level of analysis often employed is the social psychological; and when organizational strategies and structural modifications are examined as modes of organizational adaptation to environments (see chapters 9 and 10), the level of analysis is the structural. The concern at this point, however, is to determine variations in the way in which environments of organizations are circumscribed, so that all of the alternative conceptions are at the ecological level.

Emphasis is not on the individual organizational units, but on the pattern or network of relations connecting them. A number of investigators have worked at this level: Litwak and Hylton (1962), Warren (1967), and Turk (1977) have all examined the nature of linkages that may develop among similar or diverse organizations located within the same community or metropolitan area;[2] and Clark (1965) and Stern (1979) have examined influence and control processes among schools in the United States—Clark by describing the development and adoption of a new science curriculum and Stern by examining the creation of the National Collegiate Athletic Association. Emery and Trist's (1965) widely employed typology of environments is also formulated at this level of analysis. They distinguish among four types of fields: placid, randomized environments in which the resources required by an organization are unchanging and randomly distributed; placid, clustered environments in which resources are unchanging but clustered so that location becomes an important factor in survival; disturbed-reactive environments in which the availability of resources is determined by the actions of organizations, and an organization's survival is dependent on the use of strategies that take into account the behavior of competitors; and turbulent environments, in which all organizational actors are interconnected, and the organizational field or network itself becomes a force in the situation. Note that this typology employs a number of the dimensions previously identified: stability-change, connectedness-isolation, organization-nonorganization, concentration-dispersion. Indeed, Emery and Trist's seminal typology is one of the primary sources of these distinctions.

Finally, a number of investigators have noted the relevance of network analysis as a useful approach for analyzing interorganizational fields (see Aldrich, 1979; Stern, 1979). Use of these mathematical and graph techniques in analyzing complex social structures is illustrated in Laumann and Pappi (1976) and in Boorman and White (1976).

A second level identified by analysts is referred to as the *population* of organizations (Hannan and Freeman, 1977). This concept is used to refer to aggregates of organizations that are alike in some respect, for example, institutions of higher education or newspapers. As noted in chapter 2, the notion of a population of organizations is analogous to that of species in biology. Also noted were the difficulties confronted by analysts in devising rules for classifying organizations. Various criteria have been proposed to identify the members of the population set, including common structural features, similar patterns of activity, similar functions performed for the societal system, or similar responsiveness to environmental variations. Aldrich and Pfeffer (1976) rightly stress that an investigator's rules for classifying organizations can strongly

[2]Both Warren and Turk promote the assumption that identifying the pattern of interorganizational linkages within a community is a useful approach to describing the structure of that community (see Warren, 1963; Turk, 1970).

influence the findings. By way of illustration, they point to Stinchcombe's (1965) conclusions concerning the stability of the structural characteristics of organizations over time, work we summarized in the previous chapter. Stinchcombe employed the definitions of industries supplied by the Bureau of the Census and therefore classified organizations such as railroads and air transport into different categories. His data led him to conclude that the structural characteristics of railroads, for example, have changed very little since the time of their founding in the mid-nineteenth century. However, had he decided to focus on all organizations providing transportation, his conclusion would have been quite different. Aldrich and Pfeffer complete the argument:

> A different outcome might emerge if organizations were classified by their functional niche in the interorganizational division of labor. . . . One could argue for the functional continuity of certain industries that Stinchcombe separated. Thus, water, rail and air transport might be considered evolving forms of transportation. . . .
>
> If such a reclassification is made, different inferences emerge from Stinchcombe's data. Now there is evidence of forms evolving toward more bureaucratic structures. . . . If the argument is correct, then newer forms should be gradually displacing older forms and achieving a larger share of the market. . . . The stability of forms uncovered by Stinchcombe may not be an accurate portrayal of the evolutionary process that is actually occurring. (Aldrich and Pfeffer, 1976: 99–100)

In spite of the problems of definition and categorization noted here and in chapter 2, the emergence and growing popularity of the natural selection model of organization—a model best applied at the population level—ensures that this level of analysis will be increasingly employed by organizational analysts.

The third level to be identified is that of the organization *set* (see Blau and Scott, 1962: 195–99; Evan, 1966). Both Blau and I and Evan acknowledge that the concept of organization set was developed by analogy from Merton's (1957: 368–80) concept of role-set. Merton noted that a single social position such as "mother" is associated with not one but a cluster of different roles depending on the identity of the counterpositions. Thus, a mother has a number of specific role obligations with respect to her children; other obligations with respect to her husband; still other obligations with respect to the child's teachers, and so on. Similarly, a given organization participates in a variety of relations depending on the identity of its specific partners. For example, a small grocery store will relate in one manner with its suppliers, another with its customers, yet another with its regulatory bodies, and so one. The fundamental idea is a simple one, but its implications are quite rich. One is led to ask questions about the relative size of the organization set, the extent to which one group of role partners is aware of the demands made by another, the extent to which expectations held by partners coincide, and so on.

One of the more useful concepts to emerge at the level of the organization set is that of organizational *domain* (Levine and White, 1961; Thompson, 1967). An organization's domain refers to the claims it makes regarding products or services provided and populations served. These claims immediately relate it to a number of other organizations—suppliers, customers, competitors —that affect its behavior and outcomes. An important consideration for any organization is the degree of consensus among members of its set regarding its proper domain.

Note that the primary difference between the concept of organization set and that of either organizational field or population is that in the former approach the environment is viewed from the standpoint of a specific ("focal") organization. Relations or connections between other ("counter") members of the set are of no concern unless they affect the activities or interests of the focal organization. Analysts employing the resource-dependence approach, as described in chapter 5, typically work at the level of the organization set. It is from this level that the interests, the resources, the dependencies of a given organization are best examined and its survival strategies probed. The great majority of recent studies of organization-environment connections has been conducted at the organization set level of analysis.

At the organization set level, a healthy controversy has developed about the relative merits of employing subjective (perceptual) versus objective measures of environmental characteristics. A number of analysts (Dill, 1958; Lawrence and Lorsch, 1967; Duncan, 1972) argue that it makes sense to measure the environment in terms of the perceptions of participants within the focal organization since only factors that are perceived can enter into the decision-making behavior of participants. Weick's (1969) formulation is even stronger. His concept of enactment, as discussed in chapter 5, stresses that participants do not react to environmental stimuli but enact them. Not only do individuals engage in this creative process as a function of what they attend to or select and how they process in-coming information; the structure of the organization and its systems for collecting and processing information has profound effects on what is received. On the other hand, Pfeffer and Salancik (1978: 62–63) correctly argue that what participants don't know *can* hurt (or help) them— that although environments must be perceived in order to influence organizational actions, they can influence organization outcomes whether or not they have been perceived. Thus, one's measurement strategy should depend on what is being predicted: perceptual measures are necessary if we wish to predict the choices or behavior of organizational participants, but they are not sufficient if we wish to predict the outcome of these choices, since outcomes are a product of many forces, some of which are outside the control of the organization. For example, perceptions of the market held by recording studio executives can better predict what types of vocal artists are given contracts than how well their records will sell.

The Interdependence of Organizations and Environments

The distinction between objective and subjective views of organizational environments, treated as a measurement controversy, masks a more fundamental theoretical issue that needs to be recognized. Weick's concept of enactment touches on this issue because it stresses that what is understood by the environment of an organization is as much—Weick would argue more—a function of the organization, its participants, and information systems, as it is of the external situation. This argument can be extended beyond the point where it is viewed simply as a question of perceptual differences among individuals or selectivity in information processing. Even if we prefer to develop objective measures of an organization's environment, we need to take into account the characteristics of the organization in order to evaluate what aspects of the external situation are likely to be salient. The environment for a church and factory in the same general setting will not be the same. The demands a specific organization makes on the environment will vary with each type of organization. Hence, one cannot describe "objectively" the environment of an organization without knowledge of the organization.

We must be careful not to overstress the subtlety and complexity of the information systems devised by organizations to respond to their environments. Recall in this connection Boulding's (1956) typology of system levels described in chapter 5 of this volume. Organizations are capable of responding to their environments at levels 7 and 8 by creating complex consensual images of environmental processes as a basis for their response. But much organizational information gathering and interpretation takes place at levels 2 and 3 —the level of clockworks and cybernetic response. Ashby (1952) stresses the highly adaptive behavior of which simple systems are capable as they monitor one or a few particular variables linked to one or a few response rules: witness the "intelligence" of the thermostat. Simon (1962) suggests some language which helps to distinguish between these lower and higher level responses. He proposes that a cybernetic response works on the principle of the "recipe": feedback variables trigger the carrying out of a specified sequence of activities. Steinbruner amplifies: "The simplest cybernetic mechanisms do not confront the issue of variety at all, for they make no calculations of the environment. The mechanisms merely track a few feedback variables and beyond that are perfectly blind to the environment" (1974: 57). By contrast, higher level responses entail the construction of what Simon terms a "blueprint": an image of the environment which provides the basis for the formulation of a response.

In stressing the interdependence of the organization and its environment, we need to take into account systems mechanisms for simplifying the environment as well as mechanisms for codifying its complexity.

Not only are organizations conceptually related to their environments; they are causally interdependent. The actions of organizations affect their environments—sometimes profoundly, as in the case of monopolies—and the characteristics of environments affect organizations, both their actions and their structure. We began to report arguments and evidence in support of this view of reciprocal influence in chapter 7 and will continue to do so in succeeding chapters.

Finally, we have already noted the open system assertion that the boundary separating the organization from its environment is somewhat arbitrarily drawn and varies according to what flows or activities are being examined. For example, if we wish to study the authority system regulating faculty members at a university, we will probably want to include professional colleagues from other universities who serve as significant evaluators (see Hind, Dornbusch, and Scott, 1974). Hence, systems that for some purposes are usefully analyzed as parts of an organization's environment are for other purposes included within the organization itself. Also, even arbitrarily set boundaries change over time. What today is a functioning system operating outside the framework of a given organization may tomorrow be incorporated as a subsystem by that organization. As we will have occasion to describe below, one of the most prevalent strategies employed by organizations in relating to some aspect of their environment is to absorb it. With increasing frequency, organizations acquire—and disaffiliate from—other systems. In this sense, organizational executives, like researchers, take a pragmatic view of the boundary separating organizations and environments.

The Evolution of Environments

After generating so many distinctions—dimensions, levels, types of measures—we are hesitant to conclude this chapter by commenting on the general direction of environmental change. Since commentators increasingly disagree on this subject, however, we feel somewhat protected from the dangers of overgeneralization.

Until quite recently the prevalent view was that first enunciated by Emery and Trist: "the environmental contexts in which organizations exist are themselves changing, at an increasing rate, and toward increasing complexity"

(1965: 21). Except for noting that these conditions are occurring "under the impact of technological change" (Ibid., p. 30), Emery and Trist are content to describe these developments rather than to explain them. Terreberry cites a considerable number of empirical studies of organizations that, in her opinion, lend support to Emery and Trist's thesis that

> these systems are increasingly finding themselves in environments where the complexity and rapidity of change in external interconnectedness gives rise to increasingly unpredictable change in their transactional interdependencies. This seems to be good evidence for the emergence of turbulence in the environments of many formal organizations. (Terreberry, 1968: 598)

However, Terreberry's major argument supporting Emery and Trist's thesis is a conceptual rather than an empirical one. Her reasoning is as follows: organizations are, by definition, open systems. All open systems tend to evolve from less to more complex states. The environment of any given organization is increasingly comprised of other organizations. Hence, it follows that organizational environments are evolving from less to more complex states. Two corollaries are developed: for any given focal organization (1) "these trends mean a gross increase in their area of relevant uncertainty" (Emery and Trist, 1965: 26); and (2) "the evolution of environments is characterized by an increase in the ratio of externally induced change over internally induced change" (Terreberry, 1968: 599).

We are not convinced by these arguments that all environments of organizations are moving toward greater turbulence—increased uncertainty and interdependency. While Terreberry is correct that open systems evolve from more to less complex states, increased complexity need not be synonymous with increased uncertainty. Indeed, as Galbraith (1967) and others have noted, differentiation permits specialization of function, and specialization, in turn, permits the application of scientific or engineering knowledge to the problem at hand. Thus, differentiation contributes to rationalization and routinization of a field of action and, in this manner, to increased certainty. Similarly, the spread of organizations into more arenas of activity often results in increased standardization and predictability. Why trust the uncertainty of small-town cuisine when you can count on the certitude of a Big Mac?

> On the modern McDonald's grills, winking lights tell countermen when to flip over the hamburger.... A small group of equipment makers furnished McDonald's with a stream of such continually updated gadgets designed to automate the serving and cooking of food to the ultimate degree: premeasured scoops, ketchup and mustard dispensers, computer-run fryers, infrared warning lights, instruments for testing the solidity of raw potatoes and the fluffiness of shakes.

Nothing—as Hamburger Central proudly boasts—was left to chance. (Boas and Chain, 1977: 40–41)

Increased interconnections among organizations in the environment also does not always lead to increased uncertainty: it can lead to the creation of unitary or of federative contexts (Warren, 1967; see also chapter 2 of this volume) in which coordination and common goals supplant competition.

Not only are there important factors creating certainty among technical organizations. Organizations relating to institutional environments, as defined in chapter 7, often confront relatively certain or predictable environments. Thus, Meyer argues that "in post-industrial societies, rationalized states expand their dominance over more and more aspects of social life, increasing centralization and homogeneity in these domains." He insists that through the creation of rationalized myths, modern societies produce "vast new forms of certainty, which organizations may obtain by the mere process of conformity to environmental specifications" (1978: 361, 363.)[3] Since Meyer stresses increased certainty in institutionalized environments, we will strike the opposing note. Although new laws, administrative agencies, and professional occupations are continually created, giving rise to new rationalized myths that provide a basis for organized action where none existed before, we should not overemphasize the amount of certainty that results. Laws are often ambiguous and variously interpreted; state and federal bureaus represent an increasingly vast and diverse collection of interests and programs that are often contradictory or competing, and professional occupations challenge one another's visions of truth.

While some arenas of action are probably moving toward increasing certainty—whether because of the routinization of technical operations or the widespread acceptance of rationalized myths—we also see evidence of increased uncertainty in many areas of social life. Given these contradictory processes—of standardization and rationalization on the one hand, and uncertainty and turbulence on the other—it seems inappropriate to make any assumption about the general direction of change in the environments within which organizations function. Empirical investigations, not *a priori* assumptions, should determine the rate and direction of environmental change.

[3]It is of interest to note that Emery and Trist, the authors who see the future of organizations as increasingly turbulent, simultaneously espouse a different view which, although little recognized, bears a striking resemblance to Meyer's conception. They argue that a possible solution for organizations in turbulent fields is represented by "the emergence of values that have overriding significance for all members of the field." These values "can be rational as well as irrational" and are likely to become more rational as "the scientific ethos takes greater hold in a society." The emergence of these commonly accepted values creates a field "which is no longer richly joined and turbulent but simplified and relatively static" (Emery and Trist, 1965: 28). In short, their vision of future organizational fields includes some circumstances—including the emergence of rationalized values—that result in more rather than less certainty for organizations.

Summary

Determining how the environments of organizations can be usefully characterized and circumscribed are issues that confront analysts embracing the open systems perspective. Relatively little empirical work has been carried out, but there has been much speculation about the ways in which the cultural environments of organizations may differ and their implication for organization variables, relationships, and forms.

Two widely accepted abstract characterizations of organization environments are (1) as sources of information and (2) as stocks of resources. Analysts viewing environments as information sources emphasize the dimension of certainty-uncertainty; those viewing environments as resource pools emphasize the dimension of power-dependence. It is increasingly recognized that, since organizations are themselves differentiated systems, each aspect of the organization may confront a different type of environment.

Conceptions of environments also vary by level of analysis; three levels have been identified which provide differing bases for circumscribing their boundaries. The first, labeled the interorganizational field, encompasses the relations that link together all of the organizations within a delimited geographical area. The second, labeled the population of organizations, focuses on all organizations that are alike in some respect. And the third, the organization set, identifies the environment from the point of view of a single, focal organization. These conceptions should be viewed as complementary: they aid us in asking and answering different, but equally important, questions about organization-environment connections.

Most observers argue that the environments of organizations are becoming more complex and uncertain over time. Increasing differentiation and interconnections of organizations cause increased uncertainty and interdependency for them. However, other processes—routinization, standardization, the creation of rationalized myths—operate to create new islands of certainty. We conclude that the extent and the direction of change in the environments of organizations is a matter to be settled not by assumption but by empirical investigations.

chapter 9

Boundary Setting
and
Boundary Spanning

*The organizational world bubbles and seethes.
Observed for a lengthy interval, the
configuration of organizations within it changes
like the patterns of a kaleidoscope.
Organizations expand, contract, break up, fuse.
Some surfaces become thick and opaque,
reducing exchanges between their interior
contents and the external environment, while
others etherealize and permit heavier traffic in
one or both directions. Shapes are altered.
Some processes are depressed, some intensified.
Levels of activity rise and fall. Organizations
disintegrate and vanish as others form in
droves, and the birth and death rates vary over
time and space. Nothing stays constant.**

HERBERT KAUFMAN (1975)

The central insight emerging from the open
system model is that all organizations are incomplete: all depend on exchanges
with other systems. All are open to environmental influences as a condition
of their survival. By contrast, both the rational and the natural system perspectives insist that organizations, as a condition of their existence, must maintain
boundaries that distinguish them from their environments. In the absence of
distinguishable boundaries, there can be no organizations as we understand
that term. In this chapter we explore the interdependence and the independence of organizations; and we examine the types of mechanisms used to set
(and reset) and to span their boundaries.

*Excerpt from The natural history of human organizations by Herbert Kaufman is
reprinted from *Administration and Society* Vol. 7, No. 2 (August 1975) p. 143 by permission of
the Publisher, Sage Publications, Inc.

The Social Boundaries of Organizations

The problems confronting organizations in setting and policing their boundaries are complex and subtle. Given the essence of organizations as open systems, their boundaries must necessarily be sieves, not shells, admitting the desirable flows and excluding the inappropriate or deleterious elements. Determining what is desirable or harmful can be a difficult decision, in part because the criteria can vary from time to time and from location to location in the organization. To explicate these issues, we will first concentrate attention on the social boundaries of organizations, examining the various indicators used to mark those boundaries and the criteria employed by organizations in determining who to admit or reject.

THE BOUNDARIES OF COLLECTIVITIES

Early in chapter 1, after laboring over the concepts of normative and behavioral structure, we quietly slipped in the concept of *collectivity*. This concept serves to bring together the two components of structure but also adds a new element: the notion of boundary. We view a collectivity as a specific instance of social organization—an identifiable "chunk" of the social order. As noted, the criteria for determining the existence of a collectivity are: (1) a *delimited* social structure, that is, a *bounded* network of social relations; and (2) a normative order *applicable to the participants* linked by the network. All collectivities—including informal groups, communities, organizations, and entire societies—possess, by definition, boundaries that distinguish them from other systems.

Many different indicators can help to identify the boundaries of collectivities. Some focus attention on the behavioral structure and some on the normative. A widely used behavioral indicator is interaction rates. While no collectivity is completely separated from its environment, Homans suggests that it is possible to locate group boundaries where the web of interaction shows "certain thin places" (1950: 85). (More systematic, but still somewhat arbitrary criteria for placing individuals in groups according to interaction rates have been devised by network theorists.) Alternatively, we may focus on the nature or content of the activities being carried out: we would expect to observe a change in the activities performed by individuals as they cross the boundaries between collectivities. Also, group activity always requires both space and time, and organizations in particular establish spatial barriers (for example, doors and walls, guards, and secretaries) and temporal systems (for example, working hours, activity schedules, and meeting times) to contain and protect activity clusters. Finally, the boundaries of collectivities may be measured as a gradient of influence. Thus, Pfeffer and Salancik suggest that organizational boundaries are coterminous with activity control:

The organization is the total set of interstructured activities in which it is engaged at any one time and over which it has discretion to initiate, maintain, or end behaviors. . . . The organization ends where its discretion ends and another's begins. (Pfeffer and Salancik, 1978: 32)

While behavior control is an important and useful indicator, we would not choose to adopt it as the sole or even the primary criterion of organizational boundaries. In our view, normative criteria should not be ignored.

Most groups, and particularly organizations, carefully differentiate between members and nonmembers, developing explicit normative criteria for determining who is to participate in the organization. Why is this true? What is the importance of membership boundaries for the functioning of organizations?

Relevant Recruitment Criteria: Dealing with Multiple Participant Roles

Rational system theorists are quite certain that they understand the functions of organizational boundaries: boundaries contribute to organizational rationality. Several of the characteristics Weber (1947 tr.: 334–35) identified as defining rational-legal systems may be viewed as bounding or insulating the organization from its social context. For example, his stipulation that officials be appointed by free contract according to their technical qualifications is intended to ensure that selection criteria are organizationally relevant and that the selection process will be relatively free from the influence of other social affiliations, whether religious, economic, political, or familial. Udy's (1962) study of 34 production organizations located in 34 different nonindustrialized societies lends strong credence to Weber's concerns. Udy asked how the internal features of organizational structure are related to the type of recruitment criteria used by each organization. His measures of structure are rather crude because the data are drawn from a systematic file of secondary data sources —the Human Relations Area File—based primarily on anthropological field studies. However, because the sample of organization is drawn from nonindustrialized societies, it contains much greater variation in environmental and organizational characteristics than would be present in a comparable sample of organizations in industrialized societies. Udy differentiated among five types of recruitment ranging from those who participated in a production organization because of "voluntary self-commitment and self-defined interest" (high *social insulation*) to those who participated because it was "required by compulsory political ascription" (high *social involvement*). To assess the structural characteristics of these organizations, Udy developed a scale that measured the extent to which they reflected rational principles of organization. The presence or absence of seven indicators—including whether the organization was pursuing limited objectives, whether rewards were based on performance criteria, the presence of specialization, and whether rewards were controlled by superiors—assessed the degree of structural rationality within each organization. Analysis of the data revealed that the higher the degree of social insulation achieved by the organization, the more likely it was to exhibit a rational structure.

Udy's findings do not seem surprising. Consider the case of a family that decides to run a retail store. The father might feel obliged to pay the older son a higher wage, in recognition of his superior status in the family structure, even if he does not contribute as much as others toward achieving the goals of the organization. The more an organization is insulated from its social environment—in this case an externally defined kinship structure—the more it can select, deploy, and reward its participants according to organizationally relevant criteria.

Organizationally controlled recruitment criteria are but one important mechanism fostering insulation of the organization from its social environment; Weber (1947 tr.) pointed to the need for others. His insistence that officials, once recruited, should regard their office as their sole, or at least their primary, occupation indicates his recognition that other occupational affiliations of members may affect their performance within organizations. And it is not only other occupational demands that may create claims on participants that may conflict with those of the focal organization. As the kinship example emphasizes, any social identity may become the basis of conflicting expectations and behavior patterns. Externally reinforced status characteristics such as age, sex, ethnic status, and social class are one important source of these expectations and obligations (see Hughes, 1958: 102–15; Dalton, 1959). And as the number and variety of other special purpose organizations grows, membership in them supplies new identities and sources of power that may impinge on the participant's role performance in the organization. Salient identities can also develop as the result of interactions and exchange processes occurring among participants within the organization, and these give rise to informal status distinctions (see Homans, 1961; Blau, 1964).

The external identities of individual participants play a relatively small role in rational system views of organization: they are viewed primarily as a problem to be managed by appropriate recruitment criteria and control mechanisms. By contrast, the many faces and facets of participants are of great interest to natural system analysts. To begin, from a natural system perspective, it is impossible for any organization to eliminate completely these sources of "disturbance": social identities—externally validated roles, qualities, interests—are among the most portable of baggage. Some extreme types of organizations do attempt to eliminate the external status connections of a subset of their participants. This is the case for such "total institutions" as prisons, mental hospitals, monasteries, and army barracks. As Goffman explains:

> The barrier that total institutions place between the inmate and the wider world marks the first curtailment of self. In civil life, the sequential scheduling of the

individual's roles, both in the life cycle and in the repeated daily round, ensures that no one role he plays will block his performance and ties in another. In total institutions, in contrast, membership automatically disrupts role scheduling, since the inmate's separation from the wider world lasts around the clock and may continue for years. Role dispossession therefore occurs. (Goffman, 1961: 14)

In addition to these time and physical barriers, many such institutions forbid all contact with outsiders, strip the inmate of personal possessions, segregate sex or age groups, issue institutional garb, and restrict interaction among inmates. It is possible to view these measures as constituting a set of mechanisms for ensuring that organizations will be buffered from the disturbing effects of the external roles occupied by participants. However, in our view they are sufficiently rare and extreme that they serve better to remind us how difficult it is for any organization to eliminate the influence on its participants of their nonorganizational roles and relationships. Total institutions are best viewed as a limiting case—as defining one extreme end-point on a continuum. Most organizations do not erect excessive barriers or engage in elaborate stripping tactics; hence, we should expect most organizations to be comprised of participants who possess multiple identities and behave accordingly. Certainly, natural system analysts embrace this view. We have already noted (in chapter 4) the interest taken by human relations investigators in the effects of sex, class, and ethnicity in the allocation of workers to roles and on worker behavior. And Selznick's analysis of individual "commitments" and the constraints they place on the rational deployment of personnel (also reviewed in chapter 4) is highly germane to these issues.

Most natural system theorists do not emphasize the disruptive and constraining effects of participants' other roles; indeed, they insist that these characteristics are a vital resource for the organization. Even within a rational-system, performance-oriented context, natural system analysts point out that most organizations do not themselves train their members to talk, to think, or to use specialized tools: these fundamental skills are typically acquired in different settings and imported into the organization. But, from the natural system perspective, goal-attainment considerations are secondary to survival; and many participants are recruited precisely because they possess extraorganizational characteristics viewed as valuable to this end. For most organizations—and especially for those labeled by Meyer and Rowan (1977) as institutionalized organizations—it is important to recruit the "right" participants for symbolic as well as for technical considerations. Schools need to hire certificated instructors; nursing homes, licensed administrators; universities, instructing staffs with Ph.D.'s; and financial organizations, certified public accountants. Such personnel characteristics assure legitimacy and increased confidence in the organization. Organizations also conform to the expectations of their social environments by maintaining some consistency between their own status systems and the stratification criteria in use in the larger society

(Anderson et al., 1966). For example, women have not frequently been promoted to high managerial positions in most United States corporations partly because their special social identities are viewed by their male colleagues as introducing additional sources of uncertainty into transactions requiring high trust (Kanter, 1977*a*), but also because organizations wish to inspire confidence in outsiders with whom they conduct business, and so try not to violate widely shared community norms. Further, for certain types of boundary-spanning roles, such as a member of the board of directors, an individual's selection may depend entirely on his or her external roles and connections. Thus, a banker may be asked to serve on the board of directors of a hospital because of his or her ties with the financial community. (Such connections are discussed in more detail in the final section of this chapter.) The general point is that the external identities and connections of participants—far from being disruptive and restrictive—are, under many conditions, a primary resource for the organization, providing skills, legitimacy, and connections with the larger social environment.

SOCIAL INSULATION AND SOCIAL ENGULFMENT

The strategic question facing all organizations is how to recruit participants and harness their associated roles and resources in the service of organizational goals (whether goal attainment or survival), while avoiding or minimizing the danger of becoming captive to participants' external interests or personal agendas. Once pipelines are established, resources may flow in either direction! Katz and Eisenstadt (1960) discuss this issue from a less organization-centered point of view. They note that problems can occur from either type of imbalance —from an organization imposing too many or too few restrictions on the types (and imputed relevance) of other roles held by its participants. When nonorganizational roles impinge on organization roles inappropriately, then we have the problem of "de-bureaucratization." The simplest examples are those of nepotism or political corruption. The reverse problem occurs when organizational roles improperly assume priority over nonorganizational roles, leading to "over-bureaucratization." Examples of this process are provided by Whyte's (1956) best seller, *The Organization Man*, which describes the unreasonable requirements placed by some corporations on the personal lives of upwardly mobile managers and their wives. It is by no means always a simple or noncontroversial matter to determine when external roles are or are not properly impinging on organizational roles and vice versa. Clearly, value judgments are involved; and depending on which normative system provides the standard, different judgments are likely to be made. Courts of law and regulatory agencies often are asked to resolve these controversies.

The extreme case of de-bureaucratization involves the disappearance of the organization. An organization no longer exists when it does not produce a delimited network of social relations to which a distinctive normative order is applicable. Diamond (1958) provides an interesting case study of a disappearing organization: the famous Virginia Company associated with the founding of the Jamestown colony.[1] This company was established in 1607 to exploit the riches of a new continent and the labors of its native peoples. Virginia proved to be different from previous sites in that native labor refused to be mobilized and mineral wealth was not to be found. It became necessary to establish an agricultural community based on voluntary labor imported from England. Over time, the company was forced to supply more and more inducements to its colonists: land became easier to acquire, women were recruited to become the wives of settlers, and company discipline was limited as representatives of the settlers acquired some voice in government. Diamond summarizes these changes:

> At one time in Virginia, the single relationship that existed between persons rested upon the position they occupied in the Company's table of organization. As a result of the efforts made by the Company to get persons to accept that relationship, however, each person in Virginia had become the occupant of several statuses, for now there were rich and poor in Virginia, landowners and renters, masters and servants, old residents and newcomers, married and single, men and women; and the simultaneous possession of these statuses involved the holder in a network of relationships, some congruent and some incompatible, with his organizational relationship. (Diamond, 1958: 471)

Gradually, settlers came to regard their roles outside the company as the more important and were no longer willing to accept their organizational position as the primary basis of legitimate order. Thus, a society emerged where before there had been only an organization.

Note that we have now located both ends of the continuum of organizational control over the relevant properties of participants. The continuum of "social involvement," to use Udy's phrase, stretches from one end at which the organization is highly insulated from its social environment, the limiting case being that of the "total institution" as defined by Goffman. At the other end, the organization is highly involved in its social environment, the extreme case being the "engulfed organization," exemplified by the Virginia Company as described by Diamond.[2] Of course, the majority of organizations are somewhere between these two extremes, able to exert some control over the multiple

[1]This account is paraphrased from an earlier summary written with Blau (see Blau and Scott, 1962, p. 234).

[2]Note that Katz and Eisenstadt have in mind a different continuum. One end point, debureaucratization, is the same as Udy's high social involvement but the other end point, overbureaucratization, extends beyond the point where the organization insulates itself from the environment (as a total institution) to include situations in which the organization imposes its normative system on formerly autonomous systems.

roles participants bring into the organization or informally develop within its confines, but rarely in a position to completely eradicate or dominate them. In most cases organizations do not wish to eliminate these external roles but to mobilize them in the service of the organization.

MOBILITY PROCESSES AND STRATIFICATION SYSTEMS

Some investigators are more interested in examining the ways in which organizational processes bring about changes in their environments: they focus on external rather than internal effects of personnel policies. A new generation of labor economists and sociologists is beginning to challenge on both theoretical and empirical grounds the comfortable assumptions of the neoclassical economists that labor markets are fluid and responsive so that earnings and mobility are an accurate reflection of worker investments in skills and education and productivity (see Montagna, 1977: 65–90). It is increasingly recognized that labor markets are themselves highly segmented and stratified by industry, by whether employers are in the core or the periphery of the economy (Averitt, 1968), and by the extent to which occupational groups are sheltered from competition (Freedman, 1976). One of the most relevant distinctions for our purposes is that between "internal" and "external" labor markets. Doeringer and Piore define internal markets as those existing within "an administrative unit, such as a manufacturing plant, within which the pricing and allocation of labor is governed by a set of administrative rules and procedures" (1971: 1). Within these settings, "internal"—that is, organizational—processes dominate market mechanisms as individuals are recruited, allocated to positions, dismissed, retained or promoted, and compensated according to organizationally managed criteria. Surprisingly, there has been relatively little research on the processes by which organizations carry out these processes.

A large number of empirical studies have investigated the relation between individual background, personal characteristics such as ethnic status and intelligence, and education, occupation, and earnings (see, for example, Blau and Duncan, 1967; Sewell and Hauser, 1975). Economists have begun to add to these models measures that reflect labor market segmentation. For example, Rees and Shultz (1970) have shown that the effect of personal characteristics on earnings varies across occupations; and Bluestone and colleagues (1973) have reported that the effects of individuals' characteristics vary depending on the properties of the industry in which they are employed, such as degree of unionization or of capital intensity. Only recently have analysts begun to explicitly introduce organizational variables into these models. Stolzenberg (1978) has shown, using data from a national employment survey, that size of employer (establishment) exerts a strong effect on the relation between individual worker education and occupational status and earnings. Specifically, the larger the organization, the stronger the impact of education on position and earnings. Stolzenberg interprets these data as consistent with the expectation that larger organizations exhibit a higher degree of formalization and place greater reliance on universalistic indices of achievements such as education.[3] And Talbert and Bose (1977), examining survey data on retail clerks from a single metropolitan area, observed that, in addition to the characteristics of individual workers, such organizational characteristics as the degree of work routinization, type of clientele served, and status of merchandise handled affect employees' wages. Since women and men are differentially located in these organizational spaces, a substantial portion of the disparity in their earnings is attributable to sex segregation among store types and departments within stores. Although federal legislation now prohibits overt job discrimination by race or sex, we know far too little about the intraorganizational processes by which employees, once hired, are routed to different organizational locations that, independent of individual abilities, have a major impact on potential earnings and long-term career opportunities. Kanter's (1977a) description of the maze of traps, dead-ends, escalators, and fast-tracks making up career patterns in the "Industrial Supply Corporation" suggests how intricate and subtle are the processes at work in contemporary organizations.

Taking a somewhat broader historical perspective, there is no doubt that organizations have helped to bring about basic changes in societal stratification systems. Returning to the simple example of the family-run retail store, to the extent that the father does not honor the expectations generated by the kinship system in his distribution of rewards among family members, the kinship structure has lost power over the economic system. One of the "great transformations" of the last few centuries has been the increasing autonomy enjoyed by economic organizations in relation to other institutional sectors (Polanyi, 1944). Many excellent historical accounts describe the gradual, halting process by which ascriptive, hereditary stratification systems have given way to more competitive, open-class systems, and this change is partially attributable to the increasing use of organizationally relevant recruitment criteria (see Tout, 1916; Barker, 1944; Rosenberg, 1958). Individually, and in the short run, most organizations adapt to the demands of their social environments; collectively, and taking a longer view, organizations gradually transform their environments.

[3]Stolzenberg acknowledges that the findings are also consistent with the view that larger organizations place greater emphasis on educational attainment because of the symbolic value placed on education, independent of its relation to job performance (see Miller, 1968; Collins, 1979). In Meyer and Rowan's terms, large organizations may be expected to be more highly institutionalized.

Managing Task Environments

Dill uses the term *task environment* to refer to all aspects of the environment that are "potentially relevant to goal setting and goal attainment" (1958: 410). This very broad definition is rather quickly reduced to focus on four major sectors to which most types of organizations must relate: (1) customers, including distributors and consumers; (2) suppliers of materials, labor, capital, equipment, property; (3) competitors for both markets and resources; and (4) regulatory groups, including governmental agencies, interfirm associations, professional bodies, and labor unions. The conception of task environment emphasizes that most organizations are created to perform some type of work. It also emphasizes a point first made in our discussion of the mobilization of resources in chapter 7: no organization is self-sufficient—all must secure resources from their environment. Since no organization generates all the resources necessary for its goal attainment or survival, organizations are forced to enter into exchanges, becoming interdependent with other environmental groups, typically other organizations. Unequal exchange relations can generate power and dependency differences among organizations, so that organizations are expected to enter into such transactions cautiously and to pursue strategies that will enhance their own bargaining position. This general perspective, labeled the *resource dependence approach* (see chapter 5), has given rise to considerable theoretical and empirical work during the past decade, as organizational researchers describe and analyze these strategies. The level of analysis most often associated with this approach is that of the organization set: the environment is viewed as it relates to and impinges on some particular organization, which serves as the primary focus of the analysis.

We will review in this section the main concerns and contributions of the resource dependence theorists, in particular Thompson (1967) and Pfeffer and Salancik (1978). In general, two lines of work may be distinguished. The first focuses attention on the central work processes of the organization and asks how they may be protected from disturbances arising from the task environment. The strategies considered are those that attempt to *buffer* the organization's technical core. This work emphasizes the need to close the system artificially to enhance the possibilities of rational action.[4] The second enlarges the view by asking more generally how organizations relate to their task environments. Not only the core, but the peripheral structures are involved. Organizations are not simply regarded as technical systems but as social and political systems; and the concern is not primarily how to achieve technical efficiency but how to ensure organizational survival and, if possible, enhance the organization's

[4]Some kinds of task demands are such that it is not possible to exclude uncertainty from the technical core. Structural accommodations for dealing with these situations are examined in chapter 10.

bargaining position vis-a-vis other systems. The strategies employed are basically boundary-spanning or *bridging* strategies that forge connections between
organizations and their exchange partners or competitors. Thus, between the
two strategies, both the concerns of the rational and the natural system analysts are addressed.

BUFFERING THE TECHNICAL CORE

Organizations may be viewed as technological systems—as mechanisms for
transforming inputs into outputs. It is almost always possible to identify one
or more central sets of tasks around which the organization is built. Teaching
in schools, surgery and patient care in hospitals, laboratory work in research
organizations, line work in assembly plants, legislating in Congress—these are
examples of central tasks in varying types of organizations. Following Thompson (1967), we will refer to the arrangements developed to perform these
central tasks—including the skills of personnel employed to carry them out—
as the *core technology* of the organization.

A key proposition formulated by Thompson is that "under norms of rationality, organizations seek to seal off their core technologies from environmental influences" (1967: 19). This proposition follows from Thompson's attempt
to reconcile the rational, natural, and open system perspectives, as described
in chapter 6. In his view, the rational system perspective is most applicable at
the technical level of the organization. Here, if anywhere, there is expected to
be a concern with the careful selection of means to pursue ends and an attempt
to reduce to a minimum the extraneous forces that can upset these connections.
The purest example of these tendencies, which are expected to be present to
some degree in all organizations, is supplied by organizations that are able to
develop a "long-linked technology," exemplified by the assembly line in a
manufacturing company (Thompson, 1967: 15–16).[5]

Long-linked technologies can be created only when certain conditions are
met. They require (1) a clear understanding of the cause-effect relations linking
inputs with outputs, so that by carrying out the proper activities it is possible
to produce the desired effect regularly; (2) a stable supply of appropriate
inputs; and (3) a continuing demand for the standardized outputs produced.
The last two conditions require the organization to deal with its environment.
The long-linked technology, while effective and efficient for achieving limited
objectives, is quite inflexible and, hence, vulnerable to change or uncertainty.
Galbraith has described how the application of scientific principles to technical
tasks results in increasing inflexibility, using as an example an automobile

---

[5]Thompson's typology of technologies, of which the long-linked system is one category, is
described in chapter 2.

assembly line. As noted in chapter 8, he argues that scientific knowledge can only be applied if the work is subdivided in such a manner that

> it begins to be coterminous with some established area of scientific or engineering knowledge. Though metallurgical knowledge cannot be applied to the manufacture of the whole vehicle, it can be used in the design of the cooling system or the engine block. . . .
>
> Nearly all of the consequences of technology, and much of the shape of modern history, derive from this need to divide and subdivide tasks and from the further need to bring knowledge to bear on these fractions and from the final need to combine the finished elements of the task into the finished product as a whole. (Galbraith, 1967: 12–13)

The consequences of such intensive work subdivision accompanied by scientifically based rationalization of techniques include:

- An increasing span of time between the beginning and the completion of any task. Because ordinary steels could be used in the manufacture of the earliest cars, they were readily available from local warehouses. By contrast, the steels used in today's cars are specifically designed for this purpose and so must be ordered months if not years in advance.
- An increase in the capital that is committed to production tools. Specialized machinery is developed to perform highly intricate tasks.
- With increasing technology, the commitment of time and money tends to result in greater inflexibility, as all parts of the system are geared to the production of a specific product (see Galbraith, 1967: 13–17).

Given these consequences, organizations with long-linked technologies are highly motivated to secure enough stability, determinateness, and certainty to be able to function efficiently and effectively in the face of environments that contain unknowns and uncertainties. Organizations seeking to buffer their technical flows from environmental perturbations may pursue a number of strategies.

BUFFERING STRATEGIES

Buffering strategies come in many forms and guises, but they all may be regarded as intraorganizational techniques aimed at reducing uncertainty for the technical core. As with all strategies, there are potential costs as well as gains for the organization, and in our brief review we will touch on both.

Coding   Organizations can classify inputs before inserting them into the technical core. Preprocessing of inputs aids their proper routing and, if necessary, their exclusion. If inappropriate or inadequately processed inputs inadvertently gain entry, they can cause delays, create machinery problems, or require special attention, often from supervisory personnel. For example, on an automobile assembly line, the separate component parts are carefully inspected and rejects are culled before they are placed on the conveyor belt. Coding is not restricted to long-linked technologies or even to industrial concerns: for example, human service agencies classify clients as a means of determining eligibility for service and to facilitate their routing to the appropriate service units. On the other hand, the costs of coding should not be overlooked. The coding process itself consumes resources and is always imperfect. No set of codes can capture all of the relevant properties of the raw materials; codes always simplify, sometimes in useful, but sometimes in distorting or biasing ways. Also, we should recall Weick's (1979) admonition: organizations need to reduce equivocality (by coding) in order to ensure some stability, but they also need to retain some equivocality in order to learn how their environment is changing and to retain flexibility (see chapter 5).

Stockpiling Organizations can stockpile raw materials or products and by this means control the rate at which inputs are inserted into the technical core or outputs released to the environment. Organizations are likely to stockpile critical resources, resources whose supply is uncertain, or resources whose price fluctuates greatly over time. The hope is that regardless of vicissitudes on the supply side, the organization will be assured of a continuous flow of resources. Similarly, on the output side, products may be held in warehouses in order to be released on the market at the most propitious time. But the capital tied up in reserves is not productive, and the costs of stockpiling include storage costs and possible loss through spoilage, damage, deterioration, or obsolescence. The problem confronting all organizations is how to ensure that inventories are sufficient to meet all needs—both on the supply and demand sides—while defending against the possibility of obsolescence as needs or customer demands change.

Leveling Leveling or smoothing techniques involve attempts by the organization to reduce fluctuations in its input or output environments. Whereas stockpiling is a relatively passive technique, leveling entails a more active attempt to reach out into the environment to motivate suppliers of inputs or to stimulate demand for outputs. Organizations may use advertising to stimulate demand for their products; retail stores may schedule sales during slack periods, and colleges may hold conferences in the summer to use idle facilities. Even hospitals may smooth their workflow by scheduling elective surgery during slack periods. The costs associated with such efforts are self-evident: seeking out suppliers or customers consumes energy and resources; and many of the techniques used, such as advertising, tend to combine high costs and high risks.

Forecasting If environmental fluctuations cannot be handled by stockpiling or by leveling, organizations may have to settle for forecasting: anticipating changes in supply or demand conditions and attempting to adapt to them. Environmental changes are often patterned, exhibiting a weekly or a seasonal trend. Organizations taking account of such regularities can often accommodate to them. For example, taxi companies can anticipate changes in demand for their services over a 24-hour period and arrange drivers' schedules accordingly; and beaches or amusement parks can make educated guesses about crowd size based on school and holiday schedules. Costs associated with forecasting, in addition to those entailed in guessing wrong, include the difficulties of expanding and contracting capacity, in particular, the problems and inefficiencies of using part-time or short-term help.

Growth One of the most general strategies employed by organizations involves a change in scale of operations, an expansion of the technical core. (We postpone to the following section a discussion of growth by merger with other existing organizations.) Technological factors may encourage growth: there are favorable economies of scale for virtually every kind of technical process, and Thompson argues that organizations will tend to expand "until the least-reducible component is approximately fully occupied" (1967: 46). Other probably more compelling factors encourage growth as well. Distinct advantages accrue to the firm that is large and, in particular, large in relation to its market. Large organizations are better able to engage in "planning," in Galbraith's sense of that term: "much of what the firm regards as planning consists in minimizing or getting rid of market influences" (1967: 25). Thus, large firms are better able to set prices, control the amount produced, and influence the decisions of related organizations. Pfeffer and Salancik summarize the advantages of size:

> Organizations that are large have more power and leverage over their environments. They are more able to resist immediate pressures for change and, moreover, have more time in which to recognize external threats and adapt to meet them. Growth enhances the organization's survival value, then, by providing a cushion, or slack, against organizational failure. (Pfeffer and Salancik, 1978: 139)

We have argued that buffering strategies are employed to help seal off or cushion the technical core from disturbances arising from the environment. The strategies described are particularly useful for organizations employing long-linked technologies, but as we have noted, other organizations often use some variant of them. Organizations also use bridging strategies, some of which perform a buffering function, protecting the technical core. More often, however, these strategies are oriented more generally toward enhancing the security of the organization in relation to its environment. Safety, survival, and an improved bargaining position are the sought-after prizes that motivate bridge building rather than simply increased certainty for the organization's technical operations.

BRIDGING STRATEGIES

Virtually all of the formulations of power and exchange relations among organizations build on the conception of power developed by Emerson (1962). Emerson emphasizes that one actor's power over another is rooted in the latter's dependency on resources controlled by the former. As expressed by Emerson: "The power of A over B is equal to, and based upon, the dependence of B upon A" (1962: 33). Further, the dependence of one actor on another varies as a function of two factors: B's dependence on A (1) is directly proportional to the importance B places on the goals mediated by A; and (2) is inversely proportional to the availability of these goals to B outside the A-B relationship. Obviously, the actors involved may be individuals, groups, or organizations. (See also chapter 12)

Emerson's formulation is useful when applied to a given organization and the set of organizations to which it relates for several reasons (see Thompson, 1967). Power is not viewed as some generalized capacity but as a function of specific needs and resources that can vary from one exchange partner to another. Thus, it is possible for an organization to have relatively little power in relation to its suppliers, but considerable power in relation to its buyers. Further, we would expect each supplier's power to vary as a function of the importance of the resources it supplies and the extent to which alternative suppliers are available. The approach avoids a "zero-sum" view of power in which it is assumed that when one actor gains power another must lose it. Rather, it becomes possible for two actors to both gain in power over each other—by increasing the extent of their interdependence.

Bridging strategies may be viewed as a response to increasing organizational interdependence. Such situations occur when two or more organizations that are differentiated from one another exchange resources. This is known as *symbiotic* interdependence and can give rise, as noted, to power differences if the resources exchanged are not of equal importance. Interdependence also occurs when two or more similar organizations compete for the resources of a third party. This is known as *competitive* or commensalistic interdependence. Competitive interdependence is often resolved by differentiation, former competitors becoming exchange partners (Blau and Scott, 1962: 217–21). For example, an automobile manufacturer may be unable to compete successfully in that market but can continue to survive by supplying parts to other automobile companies. The most complete analysis of bridging strategies to date is that provided by Pfeffer and Salancik (1978); our summary draws heavily on their work. Their general thesis is simply stated: "The typical solution to problems of interdependence and uncertainty involves increasing coordination, which means increasing the mutual control over each other's activities. . . ." (Ibid., p. 43). Although all bridging strategies share this feature, they are quite varied in the strength of the coordinate links forged and the nature of the connections. Following are some of the more common types of bridging strategies:

Bargaining We use the term bargaining to refer not to one, but to a large family of strategies by means of which the focal organization attempts to ward off dependence. To be compulsively precise, bargaining is not really a bridging but a pre-bridging strategy: things to do before calling in the bridge builders or while waiting for them to arrive. They are competitive as opposed to cooperative techniques (see Thompson, 1967: 32–37), aimed at assisting the organization to retain its independence. Examples of bargaining strategies include attempts by the focal organization to develop alternative suppliers of critical resources; and selective disclosures of conflicting demands being made by two or more members of the organization set—for example, a company may call the attention of its regulators to a union's wage demands in the hope of enlisting the regulator's support in resisting the union. Pfeffer and Salancik (1978: 92–111) provide an excellent guide to these types of bargaining strategies including the more subtle tactics, such as organizations that "help" the various members of their set to define their demands vis-a-vis the focal organization and organizations that gain control over the determination of when a demand made on them has been met.

Contracting Following Thompson, we regard contracting as "the negotiation of an agreement for the exchange of performances in the future" (1967: 35). For present purposes, contracts may be more or less formally drawn up and more or less legally binding. The critical point is that they represent attempts by organizations to reduce uncertainty by coordinating their future behavior, in limited and specific ways, with other units. As we have already learned from Williamson (1975), there is a limit to how much uncertainty can be hedged or handled by contracts (see chapter 7), but Williamson himself notes (pp. 90–95) that contracts can be modified to handle considerable uncertainty—for example, through the use of such devices as contingent claims contracts, incomplete long-term contracts, and sequential spot contracts. The negotiation of contracts with labor unions and principal suppliers and buyers is one of the chief ways in which organizations assure themselves of some degree of certainty as they face a changing future.

Cooptation   As defined in chapter 4, cooptation entails the incorporation of representatives of external groups into the decision-making or advisory structure of an organization. The significance of this practice in linking organizations with their environments was first described by Selznick (1949), who also noted its possible costs. Selznick argued that by coopting external representatives, organizations were, in effect, trading sovereignty for support. Most investigations of cooptation have focused primarily on boards of directors. Pfeffer and Salancik (1978) regard board appointments to be among the most flexible and easiest mechanism available to organizations to establish linkages with their environments. Of course, not all board members function as environmental representatives; some are there to provide specialized expertise or administrative guidance; and not all organizations are equally dependent on board-mediated linkages with their environments. Studies by Pfeffer of 80 randomly selected non-financial corporations (1972a) and of 57 Illinois hospitals (1973) provide empirical support for the expectation that board appointments are often used by organizations to establish linkages with important segments of their environments but that the need for such linkages varies by type of organization. For example, the corporations that exhibited a higher debt/equity ratio had a higher proportion of representatives from financial institutions on their boards; similarly, hospitals with larger budgets, which received a higher proportion of their capital budgets from private donations and which lacked federal or religious affiliations, were more likely to stress the importance of fund raising as a criterion for selecting board members.

Cooptation is also in wide use among federal reform and service agencies. From the early 1960s era of the "Great Society" programs down to the current period, we have witnessed the development of a great many new federally sponsored organizations whose hallmark is decentralized decision making combined with mandated participation of representatives from the areas affected. Such programs include community action agencies, model cities programs, community mental health programs, area agencies for the aged, and health systems agencies (see Binstock and Levin, 1976; Musto 1975; Hudson, 1974; Piven and Cloward, 1971; Sundquist, 1969). It is difficult to generalize from the experience of these agencies because each has a different domain and each must adapt to a different environment. Some studies suggest that federal bureaucrats and reformers use the participation ideology as a smoke screen to cloud their strategy of coopting local elements simply to legitimate federal intervention (see Krause, 1968). Others suggest that cooptation is indeed occurring, but that it is the local interests that are capturing and subverting the reform-oriented goals of the program (see Moynihan, 1970). Probably the truth of the matter is that both processes are occurring: each group is to some extent using the other to achieve its own objectives, and both are somewhat constrained by the need to accommodate to the other's interests. Cooptation as a bridging mechanism provides a two-way street with both influence and support flowing sometimes in one direction, sometimes in the other, and more often, in both.

Joint Ventures A joint venture occurs when two or more firms create a new organization to pursue some common purpose. Joint ventures differ from mergers, to be discussed below, in that they entail only a limited pooling of resources by the participating organizations. For example, several wholesale companies may combine resources to purchase a trucking operation, or a wholesale company may combine assets with a farmers' cooperative to build a canning company. As these examples suggest, joint ventures may occur either among competitors or exchange partners. Testing the hypothesis that joint venture activities tend to reflect resource interdependencies, Pfeffer and Nowak (1976) examined data from 166 joint ventures occurring over the span of a decade. In support of the hypothesis, they found that the greater the volume of exchanges between different industry groups, as measured by interindustry sales figures, the more likely firms from these industries were to enter into joint ventures. Pfeffer and Nowak also tested the prediction that firms within industry groups facing higher competition would be more likely to develop joint ventures as a means of reducing competitive pressures. Again, the data were supportive in that joint ventures were found to be more frequent within industries exhibiting an intermediate level of concentration, a situation of maximum competitive pressure.[6]

Mergers One of the most drastic strategies used by organizations in relating to critical units of their environment involves the absorption of these units: the merging of two or more independent organizations so that they become a single collective actor. Three major types of mergers are identified.

1. *Vertical integration,* in which organizations engaged in related functions but at different stages in the production process merge, backward or forward, with one another. Vertical integration, of course, involves the merger of exchange partners, of organizations that are symbiotically related. For example, organizations engaged in logging operations may merge with others who process lumber and lumber byproducts.

2. *Horizontal merger,* in which organizations performing similar functions merge to increase the scale of their operation. For example, two car dealer-

---

[6]Industry groups with high concentration ratios are those dominated by a relatively small group of firms. These firms are likely to have developed an "understanding" with each other; and together they control the conditions of survival for the smaller firms within the industry. On the other hand, industry groups with low concentration ratios are, by definition, comprised of a great many small firms, no one of which is able to generate great competitive pressures on its neighbors.

ships that formerly handled only one line of automobiles each may merge into one dealership handling two or more brands.

3. *Diversification,* in which one organization acquires one or more other organizations that are neither exchange partners nor similar organizations in competition with each other, but organizations operating in different domains. For example, in the 1960s International Telegraph and Telephone, an electronics manufacturing company, acquired a rent-a-car company, a major hotel chain, a home-building company, a baking company, a producer of glass and sand, a consumer lending firm, and a data processing organization. The extreme form of diversification is the creation of a *conglomerate.*

This country has experienced several waves of mergers, each of a differing type. Drucker (1970) argues that most mergers occurring at the turn of the century involved horizontal or vertical integration as a dominant industrialist or financier attempted to gain control within a single industry. Mergers occurring in the 1920s represented a "defensive" reaction to these earlier developments as smaller companies jockeyed for position in the second tier. Most recent mergers involve the creation of conglomerates, either as a result of organizations attempting to diversify through merger or as a result of their being "taken over" by aggressive asset managers who promise stockholders a better return on capital.

Research by Pfeffer (1972*b*) supports the expectation that mergers involving vertical integration are more likely to occur among companies in industries that are engaged in frequent transactions. His study of 854 large mergers of companies in manufacturing and mining shows that mergers tended to occur more often among types of firms highly interdependent in their resource flows. Further, his findings related to the effects of competitive interdependence replicated those reported for joint ventures: horizontal mergers were more likely to occur among firms located in industries exhibiting intermediate levels of concentration—situations of maximum intraindustry competition. Finally, Pfeffer and Salancik argue that mergers involving diversification are most likely to occur "when exchanges are very concentrated and when capital or statutory constraints" limit the use of other options for managing interorganizational interdependence (1978: 127).

As we have seen, Pfeffer and Salancik emphasize the extent of interorganizational resource flows and the degree of market concentration as the basis for generating predictions about mergers in general and vertical integration in particular. Williamson (1975: 82–116) has proposed that his "market failures" framework can also be used to explain the emergence of vertically integrated firms. After all, decisions about whether or not to merge with another firm are, fundamentally, decisions about where to draw organizational boundaries, as discussed in chapter 7. If boundaries are drawn in a constricted manner, then a given set of functions will be viewed as part of one's environment, as an independent business with whom one must negotiate for services or supplies. Redrawing the boundaries in an inclusive manner will bring the functions under one's own roof. Williamson argues that the resolution of these "make or buy" decisions that confront all organizations will be influenced by—you guessed it—the magnitude of the associated transaction costs. The higher the costs for negotiating contracts with suppliers or buyers, the greater the benefit to the organization in incorporating those transaction partners, turning a problematic environmental constraint into a domesticated internal unit. Further, Williamson asserts that the same basic combination of variables—complexity/uncertainty combined with bounded rationality, and small numbers of potential exchange partners combined with opportunism—determines the level of transaction costs. Williamson's arguments are not inconsistent with those developed by Pfeffer and Salancik. They may be viewed as representing a further specification of the conditions under which organizations involved in exchange interdependencies will seek to bring these exchange partners inside the walls of the organization.

Associations   Associations are arrangments that allow similar (and, occasionally, diverse) organizations to work in concert to pursue mutually desired objectives. They operate under many names, including trade associations, cartels, coordinating councils, and coalitions. Trade associations typically arise to allow similar or competitive organizations (and professionals) to establish generalized norms restraining competition and to allow the population of organizations to act in a concerted manner to advance or defend their common interests. Formal trade associations are more likely to arise in industries with low levels of concentration, serving as a device of communication and modest coordination under such circumstances (Pfeffer and Salancik, 1978: 177). Informal linkages tend to arise in more concentrated markets to allow similar firms to act in concert to protect their mutual interests. Such linkages are widespread and constitute an important element in structuring the relationships among organizations. Galbraith's well-known theory of countervailing power proposes that they have become more important than competition in regulating transactions among firms. He argues:

> The long trend toward concentration of industrial enterprise in the hands of a relatively few firms has brought into existence not only strong sellers . . . but also strong buyers. . . . The fact that a seller enjoys a measure of monopoly power, and is reaping a measure of monopoly return as a result, means that there is an inducement to those firms from whom he buys or those to whom he sells to develop the power with which they can defend themselves against exploitation. . . . Competition which, at least since the time of Adam Smith, has been viewed as the autonomous regulator of economic activity and as the only avail-

able regulatory mechanism apart from the state, has, in fact, been superseded. . . . In the typical modern market of few sellers, the active restraint is not provided by competitors but from the other side of the market by strong buyers. (Galbraith, 1952: 118–19)

Both similar and diverse organizations enter into associational forms at the community or regional level. We find many examples of associations combining similar organizations—for example, hospital councils and associations of retail merchants—as well as some examples of associations combining diverse organizations—for example, chambers of commerce. Although such arrangements impinge on specific organizations, and so can be examined at the level of the organization set, it is also helpful to shift levels, examining the structure of these associations at the level of the interorganizational field. Recall in this connection Warren's (1967) typology of interorganizational fields, which focuses on the degree of coordination and concerted action prescribed among the participating organizations, briefly described in chapter 2.

Increasingly, organizational associations attempt to influence not their counter-organizations but those organizations that define and regulate the context within which all transactions occur: the government in all its various forms. Since not only associations but individual organizations can engage in such activities, we treat them as a separate example of bridging strategies.

Governmental Connections　Governments affect transactions among organizations in at least three ways. (We limit discussion to governmental action at the federal level, but the same ideas apply at the state and local levels.) First, government helps to determine the overall context of organizational action, defining what actions are legal and which transactions will be supported by law. In addition, the government increasingly imposes on all organizations— regardless of their specific goals—constraints and requirements expected to benefit the larger society in one or more of the following ways: (a) raising general tax revenues; (b) providing insurance protection for work-related accidents and retirement income for employees (for example, workmen's compensation, disability and social security requirements); (c) protecting society from "external costs"—costs generated by organizational actions that are not reflected in prices—(for example, pollution controls); (d) protecting organizations against unfair competition (for example, laws prohibiting cartels); and (e) protecting consumers from their own ignorance (for example, pure food and drug laws; occupational licensure regulations). Federal policies in such areas as these are spelled out—sometimes in numbing and confusing detail—in the form of legislative statutes, administrative regulations, and judicial interpretations. Individual organizations or associations of organizations are affected not only by the general policies but by the specific wording of the statutes and regulations or their court interpretations, and so are motivated to influence them. Thus, when tax laws are being revised, organizations will see to it that their concerns and interests are expressed in testimony before congressional committees, in lobbying efforts with individual congressmen, and in commentaries on the "feasibility" and fairness of proposed administrative regulations; and when the tax laws are being enforced, organizations will court the favor of administrative officials and seek expert legal counsel to define and defend their interests in litigation.

Second, governments place special constraints on selected organizations, or on selected activities of certain organizations. Many types of organizations confront governmental regulatory bodies that monitor closely the quality of products or services provided or the transactions among exchange partners and competitors. Airline companies, railroads, and banks, for example, have long lived under the close scrutiny of federal regulatory bodies. Numerous observers, however, have concluded that the operation of such regulatory agencies benefits chiefly the organizations being regulated: competitive pressures are restrained, rival organizations are constrained from entering the market, and prices are managed in a manner that often sacrifices public interest to provider comfort (see Kohlmeier, 1969; Pfeffer, 1974; Stigler, 1971). Although a satisfactory accommodation may be worked out between the regulators and the regulatees over time, organizations first feeling the pinch of federal constraints—and there are an increasing number of them in the last three decades—usually complain loudly about the activities of the intruders. For example, private universities in this country have long operated relatively free from governmental constraints, but these days appear to be rapidly passing. The president of Harvard (Bok, 1980) described the situation at the beginning of the 1980s:

> Universities have worked for generations to establish their autonomy over academic affairs, and [Justice] Frankfurter plainly spoke for all of higher education when he declared: "For society's good, political power must abstain from intrusion into this activity of freedom, except for reasons that are exigent and obviously compelling." Despite these words each of the university's "four essential freedoms" has become the subject of increasing federal scrutiny and regulation. In the selection of students, Congress has outlawed discrimination based on race, color, or national origin; quotas have been imposed on medical schools to secure the entry of Americans studying abroad; and the Supreme Court has trimmed the power of admissions officers to prefer minorities in choosing their students. In hiring faculty, universities must comply with affirmative-action requirements as well as rules forbidding discrimination based on race, sex, national origin, religion, or age. Congress has moved upon the curriculum by using the power of the purse to encourage dental schools to compel their students to train for six weeks in a medically underserved area, and government agencies have been considering the training requirements that medical schools should provide for primary-care physicians in order to qualify for federal funding. In the laboratory,

federal law prohibits certain types of fetal experiments; HEW has imposed detailed procedural safeguards for all investigations involving human subjects; and Congress has actively debated the use of comprehensive guidelines to regulate recombinant DNA research. (Bok, 1980: 81–82)

As the examples, if not the arguments, make clear, one reason why private universities are increasingly operating under federal scrutiny is that they are the recipients of more, and more kinds of, federal support in the form of research funds, training grants, and loans and scholarships to individual students. In short, for many organizations, the government is not only a source of general and specific regulations and constraints but also a fountain of resources.

Hence, a third way in which government influences the operation of organizations is as a provider of resources. Some resource flows are indirect, coming in the form of tax breaks or exemptions; others are more direct, involving outright transfers of funds in the form of subsidies or grants; and still others involve the government's acting not as an interested third party, but as a direct participant in the transaction—as a buyer of products or a client of services. Some branches of the federal government, such as the Pentagon, are the primary purchasers of the products of a vast complex of organizations, in this case, defense-oriented manufacturers. And some families of organizations, for example, applied research organizations such as RAND or SRI, exist largely on contracts to conduct studies and provide services for a large range of governmental agencies. While it is often argued that organizations selling services to government exist in a highly concentrated market, in fact the operations of the government are becoming increasingly differentiated, so that sellers often find several different governmental units of the same kind bidding for their services.[7]

Most large organizations in this country are as of this time heavily involved with governmental operations in all of the ways just described. So much is this the case that observers are beginning to question the familiar distinction between private and public organizations. For example, the influential political scientist, Robert Dahl, has argued:

Nothing could be less appropriate than to consider the giant firm a private enterprise. . . . General Motors is as much a public enterprise as the U.S. Post Office. With gross receipts approximately equal to Sweden's Gross National

---

[7]Competition among governmental units has long existed at the level of state and local governments, as individual jurisdictions compete with each other—using tax incentives, land grants, tax-exempt bonds, and labor policies—in the hope of attracting business enterprises to their area. In recent years, as indicated, the federal government has become large and fragmented enough so that a similar kind of competition has developed among its several branches and departments.

Product; with employees and their families about as large as the total population of New Zealand; with outlays larger than those of the central government of France or West Germany, wholly dependent for its survival during every second of its operations on a vast network of laws, protection, services, inducements, constraints, and coercions provided by innumerable governments . . . General Motors is de facto the public's business. (Dahl, 1970: 120)

Several theorists have recently begun to examine the ways in which private organizations, because of their increasing size and power, act like governments —as well as the reverse process: the ways in which modern governments, because of their increasing complexity and fragmentation, act like market organizations (see Hirschman, 1970; Lindblom, 1977).

The tactics organizations employ to influence governmental organizations are not the same as those used in relating to private organizations. In particular, as Pfeffer and Salancik (1978: 192) have noted, private organizations requesting special treatment from governmental agencies must justify their private claims as serving the public interest. Thus, universities seek to preserve academic freedom not primarily because professors and university administrators prefer unconstrained decision making but because academic freedom must be preserved "for society's good," to use Justice Frankfurter's argument, quoted approvingly by President Bok. And the Chrysler Corporation's successful pursuit of $1.5 billion in loan guarantees from the federal government was justified in the name of preserving competition in the automobile industry and safeguarding the jobs of American workers.

Institutional Linkages Perhaps the most highly developed bridging strategies on the current scene are those employed by institutionalized organizations, as defined by Meyer and Rowan (1977) and described in chapter 7. In their pure form, these organizations not only rely on external connections to assure their supply of critical resources and outlets: they depend on these linkages to provide the "rational myths" that support their existence. The acceptance and legitimacy of their operations depends on the extent to which they are properly connected with those external structures that define and validate their functions. Linkage is everything, since the organization is nothing more than an embodiment of these externally defined meanings.

As an extended example of the manner in which institutionalized organizations connect to their environments, consider the following description of public elementary schools:

School organizations go to the greatest lengths, not to accomplish instructional ends, but to maintain their legitimate status as schools. They seek *accreditation,* which depends on structural conformity with a set of rules that are professionally specified and legally mandated, and react in panic when it is threatened. They hire *teachers* who are properly *credentialled.* Persons lacking such certification will not be employed regardless of their knowledge and instructional abilities. These teachers are assigned to carefully defined *students* who are classified in *grades* that are given standardized meanings throughout the country (although there is enormous educational heterogeneity in any given grade). The teachers apply to the students a curriculum, which is in turn organized into a large number of fairly standardized categories (e.g., reading, mathematics, social studies) that are given some specification at the district and school levels, but are rather homogeneous in their meaning and content across the country. . . . Instruction occurs in buildings and classroom spaces whose characteristics and contents must conform to state laws.

This apparatus is managed by *principals* and *superintendents,* whose roles are also defined (and sometimes credentialled) by the wider environment. . . .

The larger point here is that individual school organizations conform to institutional rules defining what a school is. As illustrated, some of these rules are generalized cultural beliefs (e.g., definitions of roles such as teacher and elementary student and categories such as reading and mathematics), some are requirements enforced by occupational associations (e.g., tenure rules) and others are mandated by state or federal legislation (e.g., certification and accreditation requirements). Schools conform to these rules because it is adaptive for them to do so: their survival and resources depend upon their conformity with instructional requirements. Schools which are in any way suspect in terms of their legitimacy or accreditation status suffer drastically lowered survival prospects, irrespective of what evidence they have regarding their instructional effectiveness. (Meyer, Scott, and Deal, 1981)

As we noted in chapter 7, all organizations have institutionalized aspects: all must maintain connections with their legitimating sources which supply those understandings and agreements that undergird all types of stable, collective action.

RATIONAL VERSUS NATURAL SELECTION

Our discussion of the buffering and bridging strategies employed by organizations has been conducted primarily within the theoretical framework of the resource-dependence framework. We have emphasized that this approach works at the level of the organization set, examining how the world appears from the windows of a specific focal organization and asking what strategies are available to that organization as it seeks at least to survive and, if possible, to thrive in its environment. We have not emphasized to this point a second important characteristic of this approach: it assumes that organizational structures can be modified, that they are subject to manipulation by participants who are attempting to improve their adaptation. The strategies we have reviewed presume the presence of decision makers who survey the situation, are confronted by alternatives as well as constraints, and select a course of action. They presume, in short, that organizational structures can be changed by *rational* selection processes.

These assumptions are challenged by advocates of the population ecology approach, who suggest that much of the variation among structural forms is due to environmental or *natural* selection rather than rational calculation (see Aldrich and Pfeffer, 1976; Aldrich, 1979). This alternate view is supported by arguments regarding the inertia of the structural features of organizations. Hannan and Freeman (1977: 931–32) cite a large number of constraints that prevent or inhibit change in organizational forms. Their list includes such internal limitations as the organization's investment in capital equipment and trained personnel, constraints on the transfer and processing of information, the costs of upsetting the internal political equilibria, and the conservative forces of history and tradition. Equally important are the external constraints on structural change, including legal and fiscal barriers to entry and exit from markets, environmental limitations on the flow of information, and the difficulty of securing external political and social support needed to legitimate any change. Evidence regarding the stability of organizational structures over time is provided by Stinchcombe's (1965) analysis, described in chapter 7, of the link between time of founding and current structural characteristics of organizations. Stinchcombe's thesis of organizational imprinting is consistent with the view that organizations do not easily or quickly change their structural features.

The natural selection view, which is best applied at the population level, presumes that much of the observed structural variation is due to an environmental selection process in which the "fittest" forms persist, while the ill-suited forms disappear. While "learning" and structural modification by individual organizational forms is not precluded, it is not regarded as the major selection process at work.

At the risk of appearing to be Janus-faced, we see merit in both perspectives. Specifically, the natural selection perspective seems to us to be particularly useful in focusing attention on the core features of organizations, explaining the life chances of smaller and more numerous organizations, and accounting for changes in organizational forms over the long run. By contrast, the rational selection or resource dependency approach emphasizes the more peripheral features of organizations, is better applied to larger and more powerful organizations, and stresses changes occurring over shorter periods of time. Let us briefly amplify each of these sources of divergence.

The natural selection approach rightly emphasizes that there are important constraints on the variability and adaptability of organizational structure. This applies particularly to those characteristics that are closely associated with the core technology:[8] it is here that we find the major investments in capital equipment and skilled personnel, investments not readily changed. On the other hand, the resource dependency advocates are correct in pointing out the many possibilities open to organizations in modifying their peripheral structures—their buffers and bridges. To label these structures as "peripheral" is not to regard them as superficial or of little adaptive consequence. As we have tried to argue throughout this chapter, the strategies employed by organizations to buffer and bridge can have profound effects on their chances for survival and level of functioning.

The natural selection perspective is more readily applied to relatively small and numerous organizations that are not individually in a position to exert much effect on their environments. The approach can usefully be applied to such organizations as colleges, hospitals, and to small businesses such as newspapers and restaurants.[9] The larger and more powerful the organizations under investigation, the more likely it is that they will be able to influence their environments; hence, the more difficult it is to sustain the argument that environments select organizations.

Finally, the natural selection perspective is best suited to explain changes in the distribution of organizational forms over the long run—over a period of decades or centuries. For example, it is better used for explaining changes over time in the numbers of junior colleges in relation to other organizational forms in higher education than for explaining structural changes made by one college in reacting to some environmental challenge. The resource dependence approach is best employed to account for adaptive responses of specific organizations over a relatively short period of time.

Thus, we regard both points of view as valuable. However, we do take sides in the controversy to this extent: we believe that a single organization is capable of extensive structural change and elaboration over both shorter and longer time periods. In our opinion, some population ecologists have overemphasized the structural rigidity or inertia present in organizations. Perhaps this is because many of their general ideas and models are adapted from the work of biological ecologists. Although there are important analogies between biological and social forms, we side with the open system theorists in insisting that an important hallmark of the latter is their unusual capacity for structural modification and elaboration. Substantial portions of chapter 10 are devoted to examining these significant and distinctive organizational processes.

---

[8]The emphasis placed by natural selection models on the core production processes of organizations is exhibited in their criteria for constructing organizational typologies, as discussed in chapter 2.

[9]Hannan and Freeman regard restaurants as the "fruit flies" of the organizational world. Since their expected life span is so brief, it is possible to observe changes more easily in this species of organizations over several "generations."

Summary

At one and the same time, organizations must be open to their environments and attentive to their boundaries. This poses an intricate problem with respect to the recruitment of participants. Organizations require some control over the criteria by which individuals are admitted and rewarded, and in some extreme cases organizations hold sufficient power to eliminate characteristics or identities held by participants based on their involvement in other social systems. In the more usual case, however, organizations have neither the power nor the desire to eliminate such identities, which can be put to use by the organization. How to mobilize these characteristics in the service of organizational goals while preventing participants from using organizational resources in the service of other goals is a continuing challenge for managers of all organizations.

Two broad classes of strategies have been identified by which organizations relate to their task environments. Organizations employ buffering techniques —coding, stockpiling, leveling, forecasting, and growth—in an attempt to seal off their technical core from the influence of environmental disturbances. Organizations use bridging techniques—bargaining, contracting, cooptation, joint ventures, mergers, associations, governmental connections, and institutional linkages—to enhance their security by increasing the number and variety of linkages with competitors and exchange partners. Analysis of such strategies is most readily conducted at the level of the organization set and presumes that organizational managers can shape and fashion its activities to enhance its security or effectiveness. This assumption is challenged by analysts working at the population level, who emphasize the inertia of organizational behavior and insist that most change occurs because of natural selection—the differential survival of different organizational types—rather than because of rational selection—conscious design by organizational managers. Both approaches—which are addressed to different levels, time periods, and types of organizations—appear useful for examining organization-environment interdependencies.

chapter 10

Sources
of Structural Complexity:
The Technical Core

> The characteristic of living systems which
> distinguishes them most clearly from the
> nonliving is their property of progressing by the
> process which is called evolution from less to
> more complex states of organization. . . . The
> parallel between learning and evolution arises
> as a corollary to this principle since it can be
> shown that both in evolution and in learning
> there is an increase in the complexity of the
> organism.
>
> J. W. S. PRINGLE (1951)

Whether by natural or rational selection—by evolution or learning—organizations tend to move toward higher levels of complexity. This thesis will be amplified at two levels. First, in this chapter we examine the sources of structural complexity that develop within the technical core of an organization. The prime source of core complexity is seen to be the nature of the work being carried out—the demands made by the technology on the structure. Second, in chapter 11 we consider the sources of structural complexity that occur outside the technical core, in the peripheral sectors of the organization, including the managerial and institutional levels. These structures are viewed as responding in particular to demands posed by the size or scale of the organization and to the task environment. At the conclusion of chapter 11 we examine the relation between the core and peripheral structures.

Contingency theory provides the primary orienting framework for these topics. As described in chapter 5, this approach insists that there is no single best way in which to design the structure of an organization. Rather, what is the best or most appropriate structure depends—is contingent—on what type of work is being performed and on what environmental demands or conditions confront the organization. The contributions of Lawrence and Lorsch (1967) and of Jay Galbraith (1973, 1977) are central to this approach, and inform our own discussion of structural complexity. We turn now to the primary subject of this chapter: accounting for the complexity of the technical core.

To the extent possible, organizations will attempt to seal off their technical core, protecting it from environmental disturbances. This central proposition developed by Thompson (1967) helps to account for the defensive behavior of many types of organizations. The specific strategies devised by organizations to buffer their technical core have been reviewed in the previous chapter. But what if the buffers are inadequate so that uncertainty penetrates the technical core? As organizations take on more complex and unpredictable tasks, we cannot assume that all traces of uncertainty will be buffered out of the core. How can the structure of the technical core be modified so as to accommodate these more demanding tasks? Before dealing with this question, we need to develop a clearer conception of how we are going to define and measure the nature of the work performed in the technical core.

Defining and Measuring Technology[1]

As we pointed out in chapter 1, *technology* is the term that has evolved to refer to the work performed by the organization. This concept is broadly defined by organization theorists to include not only the hardware used in performing work but also the skills and knowledge of workers, and even the characteristics of the objects on which work is performed. We must acknowledge at the outset that there is considerable overlap between *technology, task environment,* and *environment* as these terms are employed by organizational analysts. Environment is the more inclusive term and incorporates political, technological, and sociocultural aspects of organizational context. Task environment emphasizes those features of the environment relevant to its supply of inputs and its disposition of outputs but also includes the power-dependence relations within which the organization must make its exchanges. Technology, as defined above, is the more restricted term. However, it is important to emphasize the extent to which an organization's technology—although an "internal" element—links the organization to its environment: the environment not only is the source of inputs and the recipient of outputs but also is

[1]The following discussion draws on my previously published description of the characteristics of technology and relation between technology and structure (see Scott, 1975).

the major source of the work techniques and tools employed. Most organizations do not themselves invent their technologies but import them from the environment. Also, given the degree of overlap between the concepts of technology and environment, it should not surprise us to find many of the same analytical dimensions being used by analysts to identify their relevant features.

Earlier students of industrial and organizational sociology have noted the importance of technical and production features of the work process for worker behavior and work group structure (for example, Sayles, 1958; Trist and Bamforth, 1951; Walker and Guest, 1952; Whyte, 1948). But it was the empirical research of Woodward (1958, 1965) and a theoretical article by Thompson and Bates (1957) that first called attention to technology as a general determinant of organizational structure. Woodward's conception of technology as applied to industrial organizations was broadened and generalized by Thompson (Thompson and Bates, 1957; Thompson, 1967), by Litwak (1961), and by Perrow (1967, 1970) so as to be applicable to all types of organizations. Typologies developed by Woodward, Perrow, and Thompson to assess technologies employed by organizations are described in chapter 2.

An examination of the many recent attempts to define and measure technology indicates that the concept has been viewed very broadly to include (1) the characteristics of the *inputs* utilized by the organization; (2) the characteristics of the *transformation processes* employed by the organization; and (3) the characteristics of the *outputs* produced by the organization. Alongside this view of technologies varying by stage of processing, Hickson, Pugh, and Pheysey (1969) point out that approaches to technology vary by whether analysts emphasize (1) the nature of the *materials* on which work is performed; (2) the characteristics of the *operations* or techniques used to perform the work; or (3) the state of *knowledge* that underlies the transformation process. If these two sets of distinctions are combined, they allow us to both classify and summarize many of the specific measures that have been employed to assess organizational technologies. The classification together with illustrative measures appears in table 10–1.

The variety of measures summarized in table 10–1 suggests that there is no dearth of variables with which to assess technology. Indeed, we have an embarrassment of riches! Although we have found examples of all the types suggested by the classification schema, some types of measures are much more popular than others. As the examples suggest, the largest number of measures has been developed to assess the characteristics of throughput operations; the next most popular measures are those developed to gauge the characteristics of materials at the input stage. Measures emphasizing knowledge employed in the throughput process are also frequently employed. Note that an emphasis on knowledge as compared to materials or operations marks a shift from an objective to a more subjective conception of technology. A conception based on knowledge takes into account the characteristics of the performer as well

Table 10-1. Classification of Technology Measures. Source: Adapted from Scott (1975), pp. 5-6.

FACETS OF TECHNOLOGY	STAGE OF PROCESSING			
	Inputs	*Throughputs*		*Outputs*
Materials	Uniformity of inputs (Litwak, 1961) Hardness of materials (Rushing, 1968) Variability of stimuli (Perrow, 1970)	Number of exceptions (Perrow, 1970) Interchangeability of components (Rackham and Woodward, 1970)		Major project changes (Harvey, 1968) Homogenizing vs. individuating settings (Wheeler, 1966) Multiplicity of outputs (Pugh et al., 1969) Customization of outputs (Pugh et al., 1969)
Operations	Preprocessing, coding, smoothing of inputs (Thompson, 1967)	Complexity of technical processes (Udy, 1959b; Woodward, 1965) Workflow integration (Pugh et al., 1969a) Routineness of work (Hage and Aiken, 1969) Automaticity of machinery (Amber and Amber, 1962) Interdependence of work units (Thompson, 1967)		Control of outputs through stockpiling, rationing (Thompson, 1967) Value added in manufacture
Knowledge	Predictability (Dornbush and Scott, 1975) Anticipation of fluctuations in supplies (Thompson, 1967)	Knowledge of cause-effect relations (Thompson, 1967) Analyzability of search processes (Perrow, 1970) Information required to perform task compared to information possessed (Galbraith, 1973)		Time span of definitive feedback (Lawrence and Lorsch, 1967) Anticipation of fluctuations in demand (Thompson, 1967)

as those of the work to be performed. For example, materials that are the object of work processes may be objectively variable in their behavior or response to a performer's efforts to transform them, but they may also be more or less predictable depending on the knowledge or experience of the performer. For example, a physician can confront a disease process that is highly variable across its several stages of development and yet follows a known pattern and so is predictable in its behavior (see Dornbusch and Scott, 1975:79–82). (We will examine the implications of subjective versus objective conceptions of tasks in the final section of this chapter.) There have been relatively few attempts to develop variables based on measures of organizational outputs.[2]

Although a great many specific measures of technology have been generated, we believe that it is possible to identify three general variables or underlying dimensions that encompass most of the more specific measures and, more to the point, isolate the most critical variables needed to predict structural features of organizations.[3] These three dimensions are complexity or diversity, uncertainty or unpredictability, and interdependence. We will discuss each briefly.

Complexity or Diversity   This dimension refers to the number of different items or elements that must be dealt with simultaneously by the organization. Specific measures such as multiplicity and customization of outputs and variety of inputs tap this dimension.

Uncertainty or Unpredictability   This dimension refers to the variability of the items or elements upon which work is performed or to the extent to which it is possible to predict their behavior in advance. Some of the general factors affecting the degree of uncertainty of the organization's task environment described in chapter 8 are also relevant here. Specific measures of uncertainty include uniformity or variability of inputs, the number of exceptions encountered in the work process, and the number of major product changes experienced.

Interdependence   This dimension refers to the extent to which the items or elements upon which work is performed or the work processes themselves are

[2]A large number of output measures has been developed by the Aston group (see Pugh et al., 1969:99–102). These researchers regard their measures as relating to the concept of "charter"—the social function or goals of the organization—rather than to its technology. Nevertheless, many of their specific measures relate to the characteristics of outputs, for example, multiplicity of products and degree of customization, and so from our point of view are appropriate measures of technology.

[3]The stage of processing distinction illustrated in table 10–1 is also useful for predicting structural features since it indicates *where* in the technical core work-processing demands are likely to be heavier. Input units that must deal with a large amount of uncertainty will be differently structured than input units that handle only a small amount of uncertainty.

interrelated so that changes in the state of one element affect the state of the other. Thompson (1967:54–55) has proposed a useful typology for assessing the degree of interdependence. Three levels are identified: (1) *pooled* interdependence, in which the work performed is interrelated only in that each element or process contributes to the overall goal (for example, selecting fabrics and color schemes for the inside decor of a jet airplane is related to its aerodynamic design only in that both contribute to the overall objective or final product); (2) *sequential* interdependence, which exists when there is a time-dependent sequence such that some activities must be performed before others can be (for example, component parts of a jet engine must be produced before they all can be assembled into a single functioning unit); and (3) *reciprocal* interdependence, which is present to the degree that elements or activities relate to each other as both inputs and outputs (for example, design decisions regarding the weight and thrust of a jet engine and the aerodynamic design of the fuselage and wings must be made taking each other into account). Thompson points out that the three levels of interdependence form a Guttman-type scale in that elements or processes that are reciprocally interdependent also exhibit sequential and pooled interdependence; and processes that are sequentially interdependent also exhibit pooled interdependence.

As indicated, these variables are of interest because they can be employed to predict the structural features of organizations.

Technology and Structure

Since matters can rapidly become complicated, we will state at the outset the major linkages we expect to exist between an organization's technology and its structure. We note these main effects, recognizing that the interaction effects—the effects produced by two or more of the variables in combination —are more powerful and are frequently of greater interest. Our predictions are:

1. The greater the technical complexity, the greater the structural complexity. The structural response to technical diversity is organizational differentiation.

2. The greater the technical uncertainty, the lower the degree of formalization and the lower the degree of centralization.

3. The higher the degree of technical interdependence, the more resources must be devoted to coordination. More specifically, Thompson (1967:55–56) argues that pooled interdependence can be managed by *standardization,* the development of rules or routines; sequential interdependence requires the development of *plans* or *schedules,* which specify timing and order in the work processes; and reciprocal interdependence requires the use of *mutual adjustment*

or coordination by feedback, in which the interrelated parties must communicate their own requirements and be responsive to the needs of the other group. Each coordination strategy is increasingly costly in terms of resources expended.

Galbraith (1973; 1977) has usefully argued that one way in which the varying kinds of demands made by technologies on structures can be summarized is to ask how much information must be processed during the execution of a task sequence. He argues that information requirements increase as a function of increasing diversity, uncertainty, and interdependence of workflows. Using this simple formula to gauge information processing demands, Galbraith then outlines a series of structural modifications organizations can make in their technical core as a means of adapting to increased demands for the processing of information. Beginning with the simpler structures and moving to the more complex forms, the following structures may be employed to manage the workflow.

COORDINATION MECHANISMS

Rules and Programs   Organizations performing the simplest and most routine tasks rely primarily on rules and performance programs to secure acceptable outcomes. And, of course, organizations carrying on even the most complex types of work perform many activities that can be regulated by rules and programs. These structural devices represent agreements about how decisions are to be made or work is to be processed that predate the work performance itself. They can be made to handle considerable complexity and some uncertainty, particularly as regards sequence of events. For example, it is possible to develop rules for carrying out specified task activities and to add "switching rules" that signal which of several clusters of activities is to be performed or the order of their performance (see March and Simon, 1958:142–50).

Schedules   Schedules are necessary when different kinds of activities are to be carried on in the same location or when sequential interdependence is present. To information concerning the what and how of task performance, schedules add the dimension of when. Schedules also specify the time period they are in force, and so are subject to modification. Galbraith suggests that increasing uncertainty can be handled by shortening the "plan-replan cycle" —that is, the period during which a given set of rules and schedules is in force.

Departmentalization   One of the most difficult and critical of all decisions facing organizations is how work is to be divided: what tasks are to be assigned to what roles and what roles to departments. As described in chapter 3, early administrative theorists suggested that homogeneous activities should be placed in the same organizational units, but critics noted that there are often several, competing bases for determining homogeneity (see March and Simon, 1958:22–32). Thompson (1967:57) has proposed that organizations will seek to group tasks according to their degree of interdependence, with reciprocally related tasks placed in the same or closely adjacent units, then sequentially related tasks, and last, tasks exhibiting pooled interdependence. Organizations are expected to behave in this manner because the type of coordination mechanism needed to cope with reciprocal tasks—mutual adjustment—is the most costly in terms of organizational resources; schedules, which are used to cope with sequential tasks, are the next most costly, and so on. In short, Thompson argues that organizations attempt to group tasks so as to minimize coordination costs. It is instructive to note that Thompson's principle of minimizing coordination costs as an explanation for the location of departmental boundaries can be viewed as a special case of Williamson's (1975) principle of minimizing transaction costs as an explanation for the location of organizational boundaries (see chapter 7).[4]

Hierarchy Hierarchy can be used to respond to increased information flows in two ways. First, as Fayol and other administrative theorists emphasized early in this century (see chapter 3), officials can be used to deal with unexpected or irregular occurrences on an "exception" basis. Of course, this practice can only provide a satisfactory solution if the exceptions do not arise too frequently. Second, as suggested in chapter 7, hierarchies are structural devices for grouping tasks (Simon, 1962). According to Thompson:

> It is unfortunate that hierarchy has come to stand almost exclusively for degrees of highness or lowness, for this tends to hide the basic significance of hierarchy for complex organizations. Each level is not simply higher than the one below, but is a more inclusive clustering, or combination of interdependent groups, to handle those aspects of coordination which are beyond the scope of any of its components. (Thompson, 1967: 59)

As the amount of interdependence among organizational tasks increases, it becomes more difficult to handle it by departmentalization—to contain, for

[4]Williamson's concept of transaction costs is broader than Thompson's concept of coordination costs because it includes the costs of negotiations between prospective exchange partners who are trying to decide whether or not to engage in exchanges as well as the negotiations needed to coordinate exchanges once an agreement has been established. Within most organizations the former negotiations do not occur: one department is not allowed to determine whether or not to enter into exchanges with another unit in the same organization. However, in some very large organizations an attempt is made to simulate a market situation, and departments are allowed to decide whether to enter into exchange agreements with other internal units or to seek more favorable exchange rates externally.

example, all of the instances of reciprocal interdependence within an organizational unit. As interdependence overflows departmental units, a heavier burden of information processing is placed on hierarchical officers who are expected to provide links across units. For example, consider a manufacturing firm that begins to perform more customized work, fitting the product to the customer's particular requirements. We would expect the interdependence between the sales and the production departments to increase and to be reflected in higher levels of information to be processed during task performance: for example, specifications of desired products, information about cost and feasibility, and requirements for and predictions concerning delivery date. Under these circumstances, we would expect the sales and production units to be clustered under a common superior who would facilitate the flow of information between departments as a means of coordinating their work.

Delegation   Rather than attempting to regulate closely the work of all participants and insist that all decisions be made above the level of performers, organizations confronting increased complexity and uncertainty can delegate some autonomy to workers. Galbraith (1973) refers to this arrangement as "targeting" or "goal setting," indicating that coordination is secured not by minute descriptions of work procedures but by specification of the desired outcomes. In the example of the manufacturing firm performing more customized work, a manager could provide the production department with a detailed specification of the desired product together with cost and time constraints but allow participants to exercise their own judgments and skills in arriving at a product that would satisfy these requirements. Delegation is present to some extent and for some positions in most organizations. However, it reaches its most highly developed form in the case of professional organizations, a form to be discussed more fully later in this chapter.

Rules and programs, schedules, departmentalization, hierarchy, and some delegation: these are the ubiquitous features of complex formal organizations. By means of these conventional structural mechanisms, organizations are able to respond to task demands posing moderate information-processing requirements. But what if the levels of diversity, uncertainty, and interdependence are higher still so that conventional solutions prove inadequate? Galbraith argues that organizations confronting excessive levels of task complexity and uncertainty can choose one of two general responses: an organization may elect to (1) act in ways so as "to reduce the amount of information that is processed"; or (2) act in ways "to increase its capactiy to handle more information" (1973: 15). Although the responses push in different directions, they are not necessarily incompatible, and an organization may pursue more than one of the following options.

Strategies designed to reduce information processing are described first.

Slack Resources An organization can reduce its information-processing demands simply by reducing the required level of performance (see Galbraith, 1973). Higher performance standards increase the need for coordination, while lowered standards create slack—unused resources—which provides some ease in the system. For example, if delivery deadlines are not set so as to challenge the productions units, then the need for information processing is reduced. If there are few constraints on inventory levels, then rapid response to changes in supply and demand messages is less essential. And, to use a nonmanufacturing example, if every third-grade teacher uses the first several weeks to reteach the second grade, then the sequential interdependence between second- and third-grade teachers is reduced, and there is less need for coordination of their efforts. Of course, some slack in the handling of resources is not only inevitable but essential to smooth operations. All operations require a margin of error to allow for mistakes, waste, spoilage, and similar unavoidable accompaniments of work. The question is not whether there is to be slack but how much slack is permitted. Excessive slack resources increase costs for the organization that are likely to be passed on to the consumer. Since creating slack resources is a relatively easy and painless solution available to organizations, whether or not it is employed is likely to be determined by the amount of competition confronting the organization in its task environment.

Self-Contained Tasks We have noted that information-processing costs can be reduced by placing highly interdependent tasks in the same or adjacent work units. This principle underlies the creation of product-based departments. For example, a publishing organization may begin with a departmental structure based on function or process criteria: an editorial, a production, and a marketing division. Suppose that two product lines develop: college texts and "trade" or commercial bookstore publications. At some point, the costs of attempting to handle the information that must accompany these quite different types of products across the three divisions may become sufficiently high that the company decides to reorganize on a product basis. Now we have two divisions: text and trade, and each division has its own separate departments of design, production, and marketing. The diversity of information processing required by the former structure has been substantially reduced by a shift from process to product organization.

The costs accompanying the creation of self-contained tasks are primarily those associated with the loss of economies of scale. The scale of each unit has been reduced, and this may prevent the use of specialized personnel or machinery that can only be supported by a large volume of work. Product-based organization also reduces the likelihood that the benefits of variety—stimulation, transfer of learning, overlap of domains—will be available to enrich the organization or its participants.

The remaining strategies are intended to increase the information-processing capacity of the organization.

Augmented Hierarchies   Many analysts have observed that although hierarchies can assist the coordination of work by imposing patterns and constraints on the flow of information, if the messages sent become too numerous or the content too rich, a hierarchical system can quickly become overloaded (see chapter 7; also Guetzkow, 1965; Rogers and Agarwala-Rogers, 1976). The capacity of the hierarchical system can be increased in two ways. The first is to improve the methods by which information is gathered and transmitted to the decision-making centers. In earlier times, and at the present time for many functions, this is accomplished by adding specialized administrative and clerical personnel—inspectors, accountants, secretaries—charged with gathering and summarizing information needed for decision making. More recently, some of these functions have been taken over by the development of increasingly sophisticated electronic monitoring, transmission, and data-reduction systems. The design of systems that will permit the rapid transmission of relevant, "on-line" information through feedback loops to appropriate decision centers is one of the major aims and achievements of the modern systems design movement (see Simon, 1960; Myers, 1967; House, 1971).

The second method for increasing the system's capacity to process information is to work, not on the receptors or the transmitters, but on the decision centers, the nodes of the system. One of the earliest and most widely used structural modifications of the simple hierarchy—the creation of the staff-line distinction—may be viewed as a means of increasing the information-processing and problem-solving capacity of the system without formally decentralizing or sacrificing the unity of command principle. Staff "experts" give technical assistance and specialized advice to generalist managers who are empowered to make the final decision. However, we know from a large number of studies that although the staff-line distinction may preserve the appearance of a unified command system, much actual power passes from the hands of line officers to staff associates (see Dalton, 1959; Goldner, 1970). In addition to these staff-line arrangements, the modern executive is likely to be surrounded and supported not only by technical specialists but also by a variety of "assistants," "assistants-to," and "associates" who perform stable or shifting duties but always act on behalf of and subject to the approval of their superiors. All, however, contribute to the capacity of the system to process information.

Lateral Connections   Consider the following situation: an aircraft company has reorganized to group workers within divisions by product, and one of the divisions is responsible for the development and testing of new types of jet engines. Departments are created on a functional basis to house scientists and engineers responsible for design, a production department comprised of mechanical engineers and technicians responsible for building prototype engines, and another departmental group of scientists and engineers responsible for evaluating and testing the models. Clearly this situation involves high levels of task complexity, uncertainty, and interdependence and will require the exchange of large amounts of information as the work is carried on. In such situations, the development of lateral connections across work groups and departments is an obvious response to handling the heavy information flow. That is, rather than sending information up and over through hierarchical channels, lateral connections allow information to flow more directly among the participants in the interdependent departments or work groups. While the opening of such channels may seem both simple and obvious, it represents an organizational revolution! Informal communications and arrangements among interdependent workers exist in virtually all organizations and undoubtedly often save them from floundering because of inadequacies of the vertical channels. But we are dealing here not with informal but formal structures: we are discussing the official legitimation of connections among workers across departmental boundaries. To permit such developments is to undermine the hierarchical structure: department heads are no longer fully in control of, and so cannot be held fully accountable for, the behavior of their subordinates. This is why organizations—even organizations facing fairly high degrees of uncertainty and interdependence—are reluctant to develop formal lateral connections. If and when the decision is made to do so, several alternate mechanisms exist to support the lateral exchange of information (see Galbraith, 1973; 1977). They include:

• a. Direct Contacts. This approach legitimates the creation of direct channels of information among rank-and-file workers in the interdependent work groups or departments. This type of "all-channel" network is likely to be associated with both deformalization of the various roles and decentralization of decision making. Burns and Stalker have labeled such arrangements "organic systems" and provide the following description:

> Organic systems are adapted to unstable conditions, when problems and requirements for action arise which cannot be broken down and distributed among specialist roles within a clearly defined hierarchy. Individuals have to perform their special tasks in the light of their knowledge of the tasks of the firm as a whole. Jobs lose much of their formal definition in terms of methods, duties and powers, which have to be redefined continually by interaction with others participating in a task. Interaction runs laterally as much as vertically. Communication between people of different ranks tends to resemble lateral consultation rather than vertical command. (Burns and Stalker, 1961:5,6)

Although legitimating direct contacts among interdependent workers might seem the simplest method of opening lateral channels, it is, in fact, one of the most extreme approaches in terms of its structural implications. Other mechanisms are less disruptive of the hierarchical structure.

• b. Liaison Roles.   Rather than opening up all channels among participants, specialized positions or units may be created to facilitate interchange between two or more interdependent departments. The responsibilities of such integrating roles may include trouble-shooting, conflict resolution, and anticipation of problems. These positions are similar to staff roles except that they relate to two or more managers rather than to one. Lawrence and Lorsch (1967) examine the functions of such positions for organizations and discuss the characteristics of successful individuals in these positions. Their work is discussed more fully in chapter 11. Note that the creation of liaison roles makes for a more complex management structure but does not undermine the hierarchical principle.

• c. Task Forces.   A task force is by definition a temporary group that is given a specific problem to solve or project to handle. The expectation is that the group will be dissolved once its work is completed. The task force may involve its participating members full or part time. Participants are drawn from several departments, and frequently from several levels, and are selected not only because of their interest or ability with respect to the work of the task force but also because of their stature in their own departments. In the case of the jet engine division, a task force involving representatives from all three departments might be created to codify the technical terms and symbols used by members of the division. The strength of the task force is that it allows multiple representatives to interact intensively over a short period of time to achieve a specific objective. Status distinctions that hinder free interaction are typically suspended during the course of the group's existence. The fact that they are present but ignored contributes to its special atmosphere (see Miles, 1964).[5] However, because the task force is defined as temporary, its existence is compatible with the maintenance of the hierarchy. Indeed, such devices may function as safety valves reducing tensions and solving problems generated by the continuation of the hierarchy.

• d. Project Teams.   While task forces are temporary systems created to solve nonrecurring problems, project teams are groupings of personnel across de-

[5]A particularly interesting and dramatic example is provided by President Kennedy's creation of a task force—the Excom, composed of trusted advisors and associates—to make recommendations to him on the course of action to be pursued during the Cuban missile crisis of 1962. The best account of this group's structure and deliberations is provided by the President's brother, Robert Kennedy (1969).

partmental lines to carry on some portion of the regular work of the organization. In the jet engine example, a team comprised of several members from each department could be built around the design and testing of a highly experimental prototype engine. Members would be released from their regular duties over an extended period of time in order to better contribute to this effort. The typical project team would have a leader or manager responsible for planning and coordinating the work of the team so long as it performed as a unit. Departmental officers would, in effect, delegate authority to the project manager to act on their behalf during the duration of the project but would see to it that their own personnel were being used and treated appropriately.

• e. Matrix Organization. A matrix structure may be developed when most or all of the organization's work is carried on within a shifting set of project teams. This type of structure is illustrated in figure 10–1, which depicts the formal structure of the rocket division of a space agency. The hallmark of the matrix is the simultaneous operation of vertical and lateral channels of information and of authority. The vertical lines are typically those of functional departments that operate as "home base" for all participants; the lateral lines represent project groups that combine and coordinate the services of selected functional specialists around particular projects. All participants are responsible to their functional superior and one or more project leaders. Generally speaking, the conflict that exists in at least a latent form in all organizations between function and product is elevated by the matrix organization into a structural principle. While the institutionalization of conflict in this manner does not resolve it, it does ensure that both the functional and the product interests receive managerial attention. Matrix organizations are to be found in the more highly innovative industries such as contract research, electronics, and aerospace.

Both project teams and matrix structures suffer the same diseconomies of scale as other types of product-based systems: each project group tends to duplicate the capacities of the others. Also, these systems presume enormous flexibility of resources and personnel as teams are continually initiated, discontinued, and reconstituted.

Organizations built around a core staff of highly trained workers, together with those that legitimate lateral relationships, constitute the new generation of organizational forms. As we have attempted to illustrate, a number of different structural forms are in use—including organic systems, project teams and matrix—but all move us away from hierarchical arrangements, "beyond bureaucracy," or "from bureaucracy to ad-hocracy." Futurists and social commentators such as Bennis (1966), Bennis and Slater (1968), and Toffler (1970) agree that the new organizational forms require highly educated, self-directed, and flexible participants in order to function. They are less clear

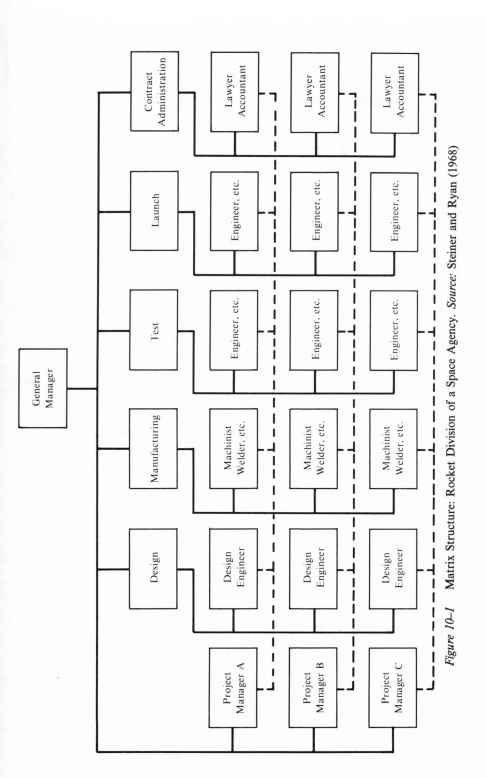

Figure 10-1 **Matrix Structure: Rocket Division of a Space Agency.** *Source:* **Steiner and Ryan (1968)**

about whether our schools and families are capable of preparing individuals to cope with such high levels of social—and organizational—change.

PROFESSIONALS IN ORGANIZATIONS

We began the discussion of technology and structure by stating three general principles relating characteristics of technology and of structure; specifically, that greater technical complexity is associated with greater structural complexity, that greater technical uncertainty is related to lower formalization and centralization, and that greater interdependence is associated with more elaborate coordination structures. We now call attention to an important exception to the first principle. Technical complexity does not invariably give rise to greater complexity of structure; alternatively, it may give rise to greater "complexity" of the performer. That is, one way to manage greater task complexity is not to subdivide the work and parcel it out among differentiated work groups or departments, but to confront the complexity with more highly qualified and flexible performers—with professionals. This response is particularly effective when: (1) the work is also uncertain, a condition that mitigates against preplanning and subdivision; and (2) the work does not involve high levels of interdependence among workers. For example, the teaching by faculty members in universities, the work of lawyers in law firms, and the work of physicians in clinics as customarily performed tend to involve relatively little interdependence. Whether complexity and uncertainty of work give rise to complex organizations or to complex performers is partly determined by the characteristics of the work itself but is also influenced by the political and social power of the performer group. We made this point in chapter 7 in discussing occupations versus hierarchies, and we will amplify it in our discussion of variations in task conceptions in the final section of this chapter.

Professionals perform the core tasks of the organization under two general types of arrangements. The first, which we have labeled the *autonomous* professional organization, exists to the extent that "organizational officials delegate to the group of professional employees considerable responsibility for defining and implementing the goals, for setting performance standards, and for seeing to it that standards are maintained" (Scott, 1965:66). The professional performers organize themselves—as a "staff" in hospitals, as an "academic council" in universities—to assume these responsibilities. A fairly well demarcated boundary is established to distinguish between those tasks for which the professional group assumes responsibility and those over which the administrative officials have jurisdiction. Even when a professionally trained person occupies the administrative positions, as is often the case, the boundaries tend to remain intact so that the professional officials exercise authority with respect to administrative procedures but are not granted direct control over professional tasks (see Goss, 1961). Rather, considerable discretion and autonomy are delegated to individual professional performers, and they are subject only to collegial review and control systems, some formally mandated but others operating only informally. Examples of types of professional organizations likely to conform to the autonomous pattern include general hospitals, therapeutic psychiatric hospitals, medical clinics, elite colleges and universities, and scientific institutes oriented to basic research (see Stanton and Schwartz, 1954; Clark, 1963; Smigel, 1964; Freidson, 1975).

We have labeled the second type the *heteronomous* professional organization because in this arrangement "professional employees are clearly subordinated to an administrative framework," and the amount of autonomy granted them is relatively small (Scott, 1965:67). Employees in these settings are subject to administrative controls, and their discretion is clearly circumscribed. Unlike their autonomous counterparts, they are subject to routine supervision. This type of professional organization is exemplified by many public agencies —libraries, secondary schools, social welfare agencies—as well as some private organizations such as small religious colleges, engineering companies, applied research firms, and public accounting firms (see Bidwell, 1965; Etzioni, 1969; Kornhauser, 1962; Miller, 1967; Montagna, 1968). Also, as Hall (1968) has pointed out, the distinction between autonomous and heteronomous structures can be applied to organizational departments as well as to entire organizations. Thus, the research and development department of a manufacturing company is likely to be organized as a heteronomous structure.

The structure of heteronomous professional organizations is in many respects similar to the arrangements already described in which organizations handle somewhat complex and uncertain tasks by *delegation.* The work of the professional participants takes place within a structure of general rules and of hierarchical supervision, but individual performers are given considerable discretion over task decisions, in particular, decisions concerning means or techniques. Thus, individual teachers make choices regarding instructional techniques, and individual engineers make decisions concerning design or construction strategies. Given that performers are expected to exercise more autonomy, we might expect to observe savings in supervisory costs: lower ratios of managers to performers or larger spans of control for supervisors. Several empirical studies, however, report just the opposite. In a study of 30 departments within a community hospital, Bell (1967) found that the greater the complexity of work performed by departmental participants, the smaller the spans of supervisory control—the fewer workers a supervisor could manage. Similarly, in a study of 252 public personnel agencies, Blau, Heydebrand, and Stauffer (1966) found that the higher the qualifications of staff members, the higher the managerial ratio. (See also Pugh, Hickson, and Hinings,

1969:118–19) Blau and colleagues interpret these unexpected findings in terms that are now familiar to us: higher ratios of managers are needed to handle the larger amount of information that must be communicated upward. Blau (1968) also points out that higher ratios of supervisors or managers reduce the centralization of decision making. These analyses suggest that the more complex work carried on in heteronomous professional organizations is managed by both delegation and *augmentation of the hierarchy.* The hierarchy is augmented by the simple expedient of hiring more managers and reducing the span of control. Note, however, that both the terms *manager* and *span of control* are misleading in this context because the managers are themselves professionals and the proportional increase in their numbers signifies not increased closeness of supervision but an attempt to improve the transmission of information and the decision-making capacity of the organization.

The organization of autonomous professionals takes many forms depending, in particular, on the degree of interdependence among the individual performers and performer groups. One of the primary strengths of the full-fledged professional is that he or she is deemed capable of independent decision making and performance, and this includes coordinating work with others as required by the situation. Thus, in many kinds of autonomous professional organizations we would expect to see coordination via *direct contacts* supplementing the formal organization of the professional staff with its elaborate committee structures—the whole functioning much in the manner of Burns and Stalker's (1961) *organic system.* However, more explicit structural forms to coordinate work are required as professionals themselves become more highly specialized and are expected to coordinate not only their own work but the work of a growing number of paraprofessional workers and as interdependence among work groups and departments increases. In many cases *project teams* are used. Thus, in hospitals teams may be built around a particular type of surgical procedure—open-heart surgery is a dramatic example—or around the care of a particular group of patients—for example, the treatment of children with cancer (see Fox, 1959; Beckhard, 1972). And faculty members in universities conduct an increasing amount of their research in teams or project groups, each of which has a coordinator or leader, often designated as the principal investigator. These arrangements support collaborative effort across disciplinary or departmental lines. *Matrix designs* are common in research organizations such as RAND (Smith, 1966) and are used in some hospital departments (Neuhauser, 1972). Thus, in confronting the most complex, uncertain, and interdependent tasks, complex performers who can individually handle some of the demands made by the work are used, and they are placed within complex structures that can elicit and coordinate the contributions of many performers who collectively endeavor to meet the challenges posed.

Problems in Relating Technology
and Structure

In the previous sections, we argued that characteristics of the work being performed—in particular, its complexity, uncertainty, and interdependence—are associated with the characteristics of the structure devised to organize the work—for example, the extent of structural differentiation, decentralization, and modes of coordination. With the help of Galbraith and others, we attempted to illustrate ways in which structural arrangements can be adjusted to accommodate differences in task demands. But although we have argued and illustrated, to this point little in the way of evidence has been presented. When we turn to the empirical studies relating technology and structure, we find that the evidence is, at best, mixed. Although some studies do support the arguments (for example, Woodward, 1965; Hage and Aiken, 1969; Khandwalla, 1974; Van de Ven, Delbecq, and Koenig, 1976), others report at best weak and often conflicting evidence (for example, Hickson, Pugh, and Pheysey, 1969; Mohr, 1971; Child and Mansfield, 1972).

Some of the confusion in research findings is due to the variety of different measures employed for assessing both technology (see table 10–1) and structure: there is not much consensus on what variables to measure or how to operationalize those selected. Another source of difficulty relates to differences in the types of data gathered and in the level at which information is collected (see Scott, 1977b). The data employed may be obtained from documents and records, informant reports, or from individual responses to surveys; and in Lazarsfeld and Menzel's (1961) terms, defined in chapter 1, the measures developed based on these data may be analytical, structural, or global. Substantial problems of reliability and validity attend each of these data sources, and in the case of collective measures based on the aggregated response of individual participants, it is difficult to determine how weights should be assigned to each response.[6] Moreover, there is sometimes little agreement among different types of measures of the same variables. For example, Pennings (1973) used a variety of types of measures of structural variables, such as centralization and formalization, in a study of ten organizations. When

---

[6]For example, participants may be asked to describe where decisions of various types are made in the organization as an indicator of centralization. A common procedure in organizational studies is to combine all responses to the question and calculate a mean, which, in effect, gives the same weight to each response. However, as I note elsewhere

Equal weighting flies in the face of everything we know about social structure—both formal and informal—the most important characteristic of which is differentiation: differentiation of knowledge, of competence, of influence, of commitment, of power, etc. (Scott, 1972: 141).

measures of these variables based on the judgments of officials acting as informants were compared with measures of the same variables based on aggregated survey data from rank-and-file participants, intercorrelations among them proved to be very low and, in some cases, negative, indicating the low convergent validity of the indicators employed.

In addition to these important methodological problems, several unresolved theoretical issues generate disagreement among investigators and militate against the cumulation of consistent empirical findings. We will review three of these issues: inconsistencies in the organizational levels at which the predictions relating technology to structure are formulated and tested; disagreements over the conception of technology; and differences in hidden or implicit assumptions that underlie research in this area.

VARYING ORGANIZATIONAL LEVELS

The relation between technology and structure has been studied at differing organizational levels including (1) attempts to characterize the technological and structural characteristics of the organization as a whole (for example, Woodward, 1965; Hickson, Pugh, and Pheysey, 1969; Khandwalla, 1974); (2) attempts to measure technology and structure at the level of the work group or department (e.g., Bell, 1967; Lawrence and Lorsch, 1967; Grimes and Klein, 1973; Hrebiniak, 1974; Van de Ven and Delbecq, 1974); and studies of work characteristics and work arrangements at the level of the individual participant (Hrebiniak, 1974; Dornbusch and Scott, 1975).

Efforts to relate technical and structural measures at the organizational level are extremely hazardous because organizations tend to employ a variety of technologies and to be structurally complex. Some analysts have attempted to resolve the difficulty by what might be termed a "Mixmaster" method: data on technology and structure are gathered from various participants and work units and then combined to produce overall scores for the two subsystems. Thus, the Aston group (Hickson, Pugh, and Pheysey, 1969) aggregated data gathered by interviews with chief executives and a number of department heads into a single measure, workflow integration, to characterize the technology of the organization as a whole. And Hage and Aiken (1969), while careful to give greater weighting to the reports of the supervisory staff, combined worker and supervisor responses across departments to arrive at a single measure of routineness of work for each organization in a sample of health and welfare agencies. Similarly, structures that are likely to exhibit considerable diversity in centralization or in formalization, for example, are characterized by an average score reported for the organization. A different approach to the problem of technical and structural heterogeneity is exemplified by the work of Woodward (1965) and Khandwalla (1974) who restricted their studies to the "production systems" of the organizations surveyed. But the structure of one department or division should not be taken as representative of the entire organization.

Analysts studying technology and structure at the departmental level confront less severe, but similar, problems caused by technical and structural heterogeneity. Many work groups and most departments include different types of work, particularly in the case of product-based organizational structures. Further, studies (for example, Bell, 1967; Mohr, 1971) that measure the characteristics of tasks performed by individual workers and aggregate them to form measures of some modal task characteristics may not only cause the analyst to overlook variance across individual workers but fail to capture those characteristics of technology that are distinctive to the group level, such as measures of work variety or complexity at the departmental level (see Comstock and Scott, 1977).

Only a few studies have focused on the relation between technology and structure at the level of the individual worker. Dornbusch and I (Dornbusch and Scott, 1975), in collaboration with a large number of graduate student colleagues, conducted a series of studies at the level of the individual participant by focusing attention on the participants' conception of the nature of the work performed and their perception of the work arrangements governing them. Studies of diverse types of workers in varied settings, including school teachers in public and alternative schools, university faculty members, football players, assembly bench workers, Catholic priests, and members of a hospital house staff, convinced us that most workers perform a variety of tasks and work under a number of structural arrangements. How much uncertainty is confronted, how much interdependence is present, how complex are the demands posed—all vary depending on what tasks or aspects of a given participant's work are being singled out for attention.

In summary, given the great diversity and complexity of types of work and structures encompassed by most organizations, we should not be surprised to learn that many specific studies report varying and contradictory findings. When the subject of study is variable and complex, findings will be highly susceptible to differences in the variables and indicators employed, the sample drawn, the level of organization studied, and similar research decisions.

Choice of the level of organization at which to conduct the study is particularly critical because organizational levels often relate in a complementary fashion: that is, uncertainty may be relatively low at one level *because* it is high at another. Thus, it is quite possible for individual workers to be confronted by complex and uncertain tasks within the framework of a relatively simple administrative system, for example the work of physicians in a small group practice clinic. Conversely, individual workers may carry out a few simple tasks as part of a technology that is highly complex when viewed at the departmental level, as is the case with workers on an assembly line (see Mohr, 1971). The level of complexity and uncertainty at two adjacent organizational levels may vary dramatically. Indeed, an important aspect of organizational design is to decide where to locate such demands.

Given these conditions, in our opinion, if progress is to be made, researchers must exhibit greater sensitivities to the complexities of organizational systems. Our measures and predictions should allow for differences in the relation between technology and structure at the individual, work group, and organizational level. Thus, Comstock and I (Comstock and Scott, 1977) in a study of the organization of 142 patient care wards in a sample of 16 hospitals showed that the predictability of the tasks confronting individual nurses was more closely associated with the characteristics of the nursing personnel on that unit (for example, level of qualifications, professionalism) than with the characteristics of the control system of the ward itself (for example, degree of formalization, centralization). The latter were more closely associated with measures of complexity and uncertainty at the *ward* level, for example, ward size, the extent of staff differentiation, and the level of workflow predictability. By analogy, the same type of argument applies when one attempts to characterize the structure of the organization as a whole. Rather than treating organizational structure as some kind of average of the characteristics of its work activities and work units, it would seem more appropriate to treat it as an overarching framework of relations linking subunits of considerable diversity, and to develop measures that capture the distinctive characteristics of this suprastructure.

VARYING TASK CONCEPTIONS[7]

Most investigators assume that organizational participants agree on the characteristics of the technology in use: on the nature of the materials, the operations, and the state of knowledge. Presumably such consensus exists because these technological traits are real and objective, determined by the state of the environment. By contrast, we believe that the characteristics of technologies are much less solid than they at first appear, that they are often socially determined and can vary from participant to participant, or, more interestingly, from one set of participants to another. Thus, given the same set of task objects, it is possible for participants to emphasize their uniformity or their diversity, their unpredictability and complexity, or their certainty and simplicity. For example, historical and comparative accounts of treatment of the mentally ill demonstrate that conceptions of the raw materials—in this case, mental patients—have varied enormously over time and place. Under such circumstances, Perrow (1965) has suggested that ideology substitutes for

---

[7]This discussion draws heavily on a previously unpublished article written with a number of colleagues (see Scott et al., 1971; see also Dornbusch and Scott, 1975: 76–91).

technology. Similarly, conceptions of students' characteristics vary somewhat from one teacher to another, but vary even more from one type of school to another—for example, the conceptions of students held by traditional public schools versus those that prevail in alternative schools (see McCauley, Dornbusch, and Scott, 1972; Swidler, 1979). In a like manner, participants may disagree on the characteristics of the operations performed. where one sees repetitive activities another sees ingenuity and artful adaptation. Thus, Freidson (1970b) has pointed out that physicians are likely to insist on the problematic and unpredictable nature of many aspects of their work that others regard as relatively straightforward and routine. And although the differences might not be so large, we would expect some disagreements in task conceptions among participants working with physical or material objects and techniques.[8]

As indicated, we find differences in task conceptions among groups of participants of more interest than those among individuals. We have already noted that different forms of the same organizational type, such as varying forms of mental hospitals or schools, may be associated with differing conceptions of the task objects or operations. Another difference of interest may develop between performers and administrators within a given type of organization. The conceptions of performers are relevant inasmuch as they must relate directly to the task objects and perform the task operations; the conceptions of administrators are of interest because they are responsible for designing the structure within which the work is to be carried out. We begin with the premise that there is always some tendency for dissension between these two categories of participants. We would expect that, in general, participants more closely associated with the actual conduct of task activities will be more likely to emphasize the uncertainty and the complexity of the task performed. And as we move from the work location to administrative levels, perceived variability tends to diminish. In addition to variation in task conceptions rooted in distance from the work, performers and administrators often differ in their views of the scope of the definition of the task. Performers are more apt to concentrate on individual cases, while administrators will be more concerned with classes of objects or events. For example, a classroom teacher may view the task of teaching as reacting appropriately to the differing needs and problems of individual students. School administrators, however, are more likely to be concerned that all students perform sufficiently well to move smoothly from one class or grade to another.

Variations in conceptions of work are expected to be associated with variations in *preferred* work structures. Performers who view their work as more uncertain and complex will desire more discretion and work autonomy; and

---

[8]We had presumed that the task of making beds in a hospital was relatively simple and certain, but many nurses' aides informed us that this job was highly variable and often very difficult, depending on the location of the bed in the room, the attitude and the weight of the patient, the quality of the sheets, and so on.

administrators who view the work of performers under their control as more predictable and routine will prefer work arrangements that are more formalized and centralized. Given that there can be discrepancies between the conceptions of work held by performers and administrators, how are these resolved?

Hidden Assumptions

To answer this and related questions regarding the relation between technology and structure, it is necessary to expose some hidden or implicit assumptions underlying much of the work in this area. Certainly, one of the most pervasive assumptions made by investigators in this area is that of rationality of decision making. We have already noted that Thompson prefaces all of his propositions relating technology and structure with the phrase "Under norms of rationality." Theorists such as Galbraith presume that structures are designed to match information-processing needs of the tasks performed. And even Perrow, whose work is primarily grounded in the natural system perspective, embraces a rationalist orientation when he focuses on this topic. He writes: "We must assume here that, in the interest of efficiency, organizations wittingly or unwittingly attempt to maximize the congruence between their technology and their structure" (1970:80). Contingency theorists may not assume rationality of intent, but they are likely to assume rationality of outcome by positing that those structures that are better suited to meet the demands made by their technical systems or task environments will be more effective and, in the end, be more likely to survive (see Lawrence and Lorsch, 1967). In short, rationality of fit between technology and structure is assumed to occur either by direct rational selection (design) or by indirect natural selection.

By contrast, our work on task conceptions suggests that participants may hold varying conceptions of the work performed by the organization and, consequently, varying preferences for structural arrangements. It is important to note that these views may not be disinterested ones but work to the advantage of the perceiver. If performers desire greater autonomy and discretion over their work, they are likely to emphasize the complex and uncertain nature of the tasks for which they are responsible. Alternatively, if managers prefer to retain control over the work place by centralizing decisions and promulgating rules, they will attempt to define the work as predictable and respond to complexity by differentiation (which results in the deskilling of individual performers). Whose task conceptions prevail—whether performers or administrators—is more likely to be determined by power than by rational discourse. As Benson argues:

> The ideas which guide the construction of the organization depend upon the power of various participants, that is, their capacity to control the direction of

events. Some parties are in dominant positions permitting the imposition and enforcement of their conceptions of reality. Others are in positions of relative weakness and must act in conformity with the definitions of others. (Benson, 1977:7)

We believe that such conflicts occur in all types of organizations. However, they are particularly visible in organizations employing professional workers (see Scott, 1972). Such occupational groups are more likely to develop divergent task conceptions, these notions being transmitted by external socializing organizations, and reinforced by peer-group processes (see chapter 7). Because specific alternative task conceptions are collectively held by performers, these shared conceptions and expectations concerning appropriate work arrangements become important unifying forces for occupational groups across varying settings (see Reeves, 1980). In addition, a more or less tight monopoly over the performance of some aspects of the work, plus, in some cases, the ability to regulate the supply of performers, assures that professional groups will be in a relatively powerful position vis-à-vis organizational managers.

A second assumption governing most work on this topic is that technology causes structure, not the reverse. But if conceptions of technology are socially determined, as we believe they are, then it seems clear that one of the most powerful influences on these conceptions must be the structural arrangements within which the work is performed. Whoever controls the structure can have a powerful effect on performers' task conceptions. This appears to be one of the most important factors distinguishing the work situation of semiprofessional occupations such as nursing, engineering, and public school teaching from professional occupations such as scientists and physicians. The latter, as noted, exercise considerable control over their task conceptions and retain the right to determine what characteristics of the task objects are to be regarded as meriting attention. The former lack this control and are obliged to work within heteronomous arrangements designed by administrators. They are less able to specify what characteristics of the task objects (for example, clients) are salient and are to be taken into account in the provision of services (see Scott, 1969; Street, Martin, and Gordon, 1979). By officially specifying the nature of the raw materials and the types of activities to be carried out, structures can have a powerful effect on performers' conceptions of their work. Note that "work" in this sense is closely related to goals, so that we have here a specific instance of the way in which structures can help to shape the goals toward which performers direct their energies.[9]

[9]Most analysts stress the interdependence of goals and formal organizational structures. Note, however, that the causal direction of the relation between goals and structures may vary from that expected. Under the assumptions of the rational system perspective, we would expect specific goals to provide design criteria for organizational structures. However, following the present line of argument, and consistent with natural system assumptions, organizational structures may be created reflecting power disparities, and these structures then shape organizational objectives (see chapter 12).

Structures affect the characteristics of work in even more direct ways. How uncertain or complex work is at a given point in the system is, in large measure, a question of how the structure is designed. We have seen that through differentiation, complex tasks can be subdivided and made simple; alternatively, through professionalization, complex tasks can be retained and delegated to individual performers. Similarly, we have seen that how much interdependence is present in a given system is, in part, a matter of structural design. The interdependence of work groups can be reduced by a product-based division of labor and increased by a functional structure. So does technology determine structure or structure determine technology? The answer must be that the relation is reciprocal but variable. Presumably technology always exerts some general constraints on the shape of the structure, but within these limits market conditions and power processes may be expected to play an important role (see chapter 7).

A third assumption that guides studies of technology and structure is that this relation is primarily determined by intraorganizational forces. This assumption is challenged by most of the previous discussion, which argues that market forces and occupational systems external to the organization help to shape both the participants' conceptions of work as well as the outcomes of struggles between performers and administrators for control over work structures. It is also called into question by examples such as the following. The major incentive for many organizations to develop a project management structure came not from within as a rational response to information processing demands but from outside the organization. The Department of Defense required its contractors to use this structural arrangement in the 1950s as a condition for obtaining financial support! (Wieland and Ullrich, 1976:39). Government contract officers were tired of getting the runaround from functional department heads, each of whom had only partial control over any given project. The development of a project management format gave these officers someone they could more easily relate to and hold responsible for the successful and timely completion of the project. We should never overlook or underestimate the effect of environmental forces on "internal" structures and processes.

Summary

Most efforts to explain the structural complexity within the technical core of an organization focus on the characteristics of the work being performed —on the technology. A great many specific measures of technology have been proposed, some emphasizing different phases of the work process—inputs, throughputs, or outputs—and some focusing on different facets of the process

—materials, operations, or knowledge. Most important for explaining differences in structural characteristics of organizations are three dimensions of technology: complexity, uncertainty, and interdependence. In general, we expect technical complexity to be associated with structural complexity or performer complexity (professionalization); technical uncertainty, with lower formalization and decentralization of decision making; and interdependence, with higher levels of coordination. Complexity, uncertainty, and interdependence are alike in at least one respect: each increases the amount of information that must be processed during the course of a task performance. Thus, as complexity, uncertainty, and interdependence increase, structural modifications need to be made that will either (1) reduce the need for information processing, for example, by lowering the level of interdependence or by lowering performance standards; or (2) increase the capacity of the information-processing system, by increasing the channel and node capacity of the hierarchy or by legitimating lateral connections among participants.

Empirical studies of the relation between technology and structure show mixed and often conflicting results. Among the factors contributing to this confusion are methodological problems such as lack of consensus on measures or on measurement strategies; and theoretical problems, including misspecifications of the level of analysis at which the measures apply, disagreements among participants about the nature of the technology employed, and lack of clarity about the causal connections between technology and structure.

chapter 11

Sources
of Structural Complexity:
The Peripheral Sectors

*The device by which an organism maintains
itself stationary at a fairly high level of
orderliness . . . really consists in continually
sucking orderliness from its environment.*

ERWIN SCHRÖDINGER (1945)

The division between the technical core and
the peripheral sectors of an organization is admittedly somewhat arbitrary. It
is intended to emphasize that organizations are comprised of different units
that respond to different forces. The previous chapter emphasized those portions of the organization—labeled the technical core—that carry on its primary work. We argued that the characteristics of the work performed are
related to the characteristics of the structures created to contain the work.
(Whether work characteristics produce structural characteristics or the reverse was a question raised and discussed but not fully resolved.) Attention was
limited to the characteristics of those structures that contain, control, or are
in the near vicinity of the organization's central workflow.

In the current chapter the focus broadens to include structures less directly
tied to the technical core. They are "peripheral" in this sense and only in this
sense: *peripheral* is not synonymous with *marginal*. The peripheral structures,
for present purposes, encompass many aspects of the managerial and the
institutional levels as defined by Parsons (see chapter 4). We will examine, in
particular, the structural changes at these levels that accompany the organization's attempt to buffer its technical core and construct bridges connecting it
with other social units. These changes accompany the organization's efforts to
adapt to and to modify its task environment. We also will examine structural

features associated with the size of the organization. As we will learn, the meaning of size is far from clear, but its importance as a determinant of structural characteristics is well established. In the final section, relations between the core and peripheral structures are discussed.

A brief methodological note: Examinations of the structural features of organizations, their determinants, and interrelations require the collection of data from a large sample of organizations. In these studies, the organizations are themselves the units of analysis. Ideally, what is required is a large sample of organizations randomly drawn from a population of independent organizations. The two major series of studies to date—the research by Blau and his associates in the comparative organizations research project and the studies in England conducted by the Aston group—only partially meet these requirements, as will be discussed subsequently. Nevertheless, these pioneer projects constitute an important beginning to the systematic comparative study of organizational structure.

Size and Structure

DEFINING AND MEASURING SIZE

What is size? Some analysts treat it as a dimension of organizational structure like formalization or centralization—one of several structural properties of an organization that may be seen to co-vary (for example, Hall and Tittle, 1966). Others treat size more as a contextual variable, measuring the demand for an organization's services or products, which provides opportunities for and imposes constraints on the organization's structure (for example, Blau and Schoenherr, 1971; Pugh et al., 1969). Like technology, size appears to be a variable that is on the interface between the organization and its environment: both variables are, on the one hand, internal features interacting with other structural properties and, on the other, features strongly shaped by external conditions. And, because it is externally driven like technology, size is more likely to be treated as an independent variable acting to shape and determine other structural variables. If technology assesses what type of work is performed by the organization, size measures how much of that work the organization carries on—the scale on which the work is conducted.

As Kimberly (1976) notes, several different indicators of organizational size have been employed by researchers, and each measures a somewhat different aspect of size. Thus, some indicators, such as square footage of floor space in a factory or number of beds in a hospital, measure the physical capacity of an organization to perform work. Indicators such as sales volume or number of clients served during a given period focus less on potential capacity and more on current level of performance. And indicators such as net assets provide a measure of discretionary resources available to the organization.

Most studies of the relation between organizational size and structure have used number of participants (usually, employees) as an indicator of size. The advantages of this measure are that it tends to reflect both the capacity of the organization for performing work as well as the current level of actual performance. Also, most of the dependent variables of interest—formalization, centralization, bureaucratization—are measures that relate to methods for controlling and coordinating people, so that numbers of individuals are of more relevance than other possible indicators of size. However, using number of participants as an indicator of size poses some problems. As previously discussed, it is often difficult to determine how to set the boundary between participants and nonparticipants; also, comparisons of number of participants across different types of organizations can be misleading since some types of organizations are much more labor-intensive than others.[1]

We turn now to consider the major predicted and empirical relations between size and structure.

Size, Bureaucracy, and Differentiation

Early interest in the effects of size focused on its relation to the degree of bureaucratization, defined as the relative size of the administrative component. A number of critics, for example, Parkinson (1957), have asserted that large organizations are overbureaucratized, devoting a disproportionate amount of their staff resources to administration. Empirical investigations of the relation between organization size and bureaucratization conducted during the 1950s reported contradictory results: some studies found that the administration was disproportionally large in larger organizations (for example, Terrien and Mills, 1955); some that the proportion of administrators was smaller in large organizations (for example, Melman, 1951; Bendix, 1956); and some that there was no association (for example, Baker and Davis, 1954). One important reason for the absence of any clear results is noted by Rushing (1966*b*). He points out that the administrative component of an organization is not a unitary structural element but is, in his terms, a "heterogeneous category" comprised of varying types of participants performing quite different functional roles. If the administrative component is separated into its constituent occupational categories—for example, managerial, professional and technical, clerical—numerous studies have shown that these categories relate differently to size. In general, the proportion of managers tends to decline with increases in size,

---

[1]For an extended discussion of conceptual and empirical difficulties associated with current definitions and measures of size, see Kimberly (1976).

while the proportion of technical and clerical personnel is positively associated with size (see Rushing, 1966; Blau and Schoenherr, 1971; Kasarda, 1974). The general point, however, is that the administrative component is comprised of various occupational groups that may relate differently to size.

A second basic reason for the absence of consistent associations between organizational size and administration is that size produces two different effects, which have opposing consequences for the size of the administrative component. (1) Organizational size is positively associated with structural differentiation. Studies of a wide variety of organizations show reasonably consistent and positive associations between size of organization and various measures of structural differentiation, including number of occupational categories, number of hierarchical levels, and spatial dispersion of the organization, for example, number of branch offices (see Blau, 1973; Blau and Schoenherr 1971; Hall, Haas, and Johnson, 1967b; Meyer, 1972; and Pugh et al., 1969). Larger organizations tend to be structurally more complex. On the other hand, (2) size is positively associated with the presence of more activities of the same general type. Size involves an increase in the *scale* of operations, which means not necessarily more kinds of operations (that is, differentiation) but more operations of the same kind. As noted, these two effects of size have opposing consequences for the size of the administrative component. In a remarkable series of propositions, Blau (1970) attempts to summarize and resolve these conflicts, as follows. Large size is associated with structural differentiation, and differentiation, in turn, creates pressures to increase the size of the administrative component. This occurs because differentiation increases the heterogeneity of work among the various subunits and individuals, creating problems of coordination and integration. The administrative component expands to assume these responsibilities. On the other hand, organizational size is associated with increases in the average size of units, within which the work performed is relatively homogeneous. The larger the number of persons engaged in similar work, the smaller the number of administrative personnel needed to supervise them. In sum, larger organizational size, by increasing structural differentiation—that is, by increasing the number of different types of organizational subunits—increases the size of the administrative component, which must coordinate the work of these units; and at the same time, larger organizational size, by increasing the volume of homogeneous work within organizational subunits, reduces the size of the administrative component, which must supervise work within these units.

In their analysis of the 53 state employment security agencies, Blau and Schoenherr conclude that:

> Large size, by promoting differentiation, has the indirect effect of enlarging the managerial component, but the savings in managerial manpower resulting from

a large scale of operations outweigh these indirect effects, so that the overall effect of large size is a reduction in the managerial component. (Blau and Schoenherr, 1971: 91)

Such a conclusion may well hold for the type of organization studied, but in our opinion, should not be generalized to other types of organizations. Whether the administrative component is, on balance, affected positively or negatively by size would seem to depend primarily on what type of differentiation is involved—for example, differentiation that merely creates new units of the same type (segmentation) would be expected to have a less positive effect on the administrative component than functional differentiation that creates new types of units—as well as how much differentiation is involved. And the latter issue would seem to be determined primarily by what type of work the organization is performing, that is, by its technology.[2]

Size, Formalization, and Centralization

We have defined formalization as the extent to which roles and relationships are specified independently of the personal characteristics of occupants of positions. Most empirical studies of formalization emphasize the extent to which rules such as formal job definitions and procedural specifications govern activities within the organizations. A Weberian model of structure would lead us to expect that the larger the size of the organization, the more formalized would be its structure, and indeed, most empirical studies support this prediction. Hall, Haas, and Johnson (1967b) report only moderate but fairly consistent positive correlations between size and six indicators of formalization, including "concreteness" of positional descriptions and formalization of the authority structure. Blau and Schoenherr's (1971) study of state employment security agencies reports a positive association between organizational size and the extent of written personnel regulations in the state's civil service system.[3] And the Aston group (Pugh et al., 1969) in their study of 46 work organizations reports a strong positive correlation between size and scales measuring formalization and standardization of procedures for selection and advancement.

The conventional view of the bureaucratic model of organizational structure would also lead to the prediction that large organizations will have more highly centralized systems of decision making (see Hage, 1965). However, the

[2]For a more complete discussion of the relation between size, differentiation, and the administrative component, see Scott (1975).

[3]Noting that this relation might better be tested at the state rather than the agency level, Blau and Schoenherr (1971: 58–59) also report a strong positive correlation between the total number of all state employees, as an indicator of the size of the state government, and the extent of formalized personnel regulations in the state's civil service system.

studies by Blau and Schoenherr and the Aston group do not support this expectation. Rather, in both studies, organization size was negatively correlated with several indicators of centralization (for example, Blau and Schoenherr used measures of the decentralization of influence to division heads and the delegation of responsibility to local office managers, and Pugh and his colleagues developed scales to determine the level in the hierarchy where executive action could be taken subject to only pro forma review). Consistent with the positive association between size and formalization, centralization was negatively associated with most of the measures of formalization. This pattern of results was also reported by Child (1972), who applied the scales developed by the Aston group to a national sample of 82 business organizations in Britain. And Mansfield (1973) reanalyzes these data to show that although the relationships are not very strong, the negative association between measures of centralization and standardization or formalization persist when the effects of size are controlled.

Blau and Schoenherr explain this unexpected pattern of results by suggesting that centralization and formalization may be viewed as alternative control mechanisms: more formalized arrangements permit more decentralized decision making. They argue:

> Formalized standards that restrict the scope of discretion make decentralized decisions less precarious for effective management and coordination, which diminishes the reluctance of executives to delegate responsibilities way down the line to local managers far removed in space as well as in social distance from top management at the headquarters. (Blau and Schoenherr, 1971: 121)

Mansfield, perhaps with the aid of hindsight, scolds his colleagues for expecting a positive relation between formalization and centralization in the first place, arguing that Weber has been misread:

> It can be argued, paradoxically, that the only method by which the directorate in large organizations can retain overall control of the organization's functioning is by decentralizing much of the decision making within the framework of bureaucratic rules. It is reasonable to interpret Weber as implying a moderate negative relationship between the bureaucratic variables and the centralization of decision making. This proposition, however, runs counter to everyday notions of bureaucracy. (Mansfield, 1973: 478)

Mansfield's interpretation of Weber's view is supported by our conclusion (in chapter 3) that Weber's model of rational-legal authority provides a structure of roles that supports the exercise of relatively greater independence and discretion, within specified constraints, than other types of administrative arrangements. The extent of bureaucratization and centralization is also affected by the organization's technology and, especially, by the degree of staff professionalization, and we will discuss these relations after we briefly comment on some problems in determining the effects of size on structure.

Problems in Relating Size and Structure

A number of problems attend studies of the relation between size and structure. Kimberly (1976) has addressed many of the more important issues. In addition to the fundamental question of the theoretical status of size—what does size measure?—the causal status of this variable is problematic. One reason why we know little about the causal relation between size and structure is that virtually all of the studies conducted have relied on cross-sectional data. Some recent longitudinal studies suggest that inferences based on cross-sectional studies of organizations regarding the effects of organizational growth or decline on structure may prove to be quite misleading. Holdaway and Blowers (1971), using data from 41 urban school systems in western Canada, report that examined cross-sectionally, the relation between organization size and administrative ratio exhibits the expected negative relation, but that viewed longitudinally, administrative ratios do not decline as a function of increasing size in most districts examined over a five-year period. And a study by Freeman and Hannan (1975) based on data from 769 California school districts suggests that different relations obtain between size of organization and the administrative component depending on whether the organization is in a period of growth or decline. Their analysis reveals that the size of this component increases along with size of the organization during periods of growth, but that during periods of decline, the size of the administration does not decrease at the same rate as does the rest of the organization. This disparity in rates leads Freeman and Hannan to be skeptical about attempts to develop generalizations relating organization size and administration from cross-sectional studies since these studies will inevitably combine data from both growing and declining organizations.

Technology, Size, and Structure

Professionals and Structure

We have already discussed the relation between the presence of professionals and the structural features of the technical core. We have also noted that the presence of professional workers can affect the characteristics of more remote administrative structures (see chapter 10). Thus, we cited findings from the study of public personnel agencies that those with a greater proportion of highly educated workers were characterized by higher managerial ratios (Blau, Heydebrand, and Stauffer, 1966). Similar results are reported in a study of United States hospitals (Heydebrand, 1973). Data from the finance department study also indicate that decision making was more decentralized in organizations with more highly qualified workers (Blau, 1968).

Hall's (1968) study of varying occupational groups in 27 different organizations provides more complete information concerning the relation between professional employees and organizational structure. Hall assessed six structural features of these organizations: hierarchy of authority (defined as the extent to which the locus of decision making is prestructured); the division of labor (extent of functional specialization); presence of rules; extent of procedural specification; impersonality (degree of formalization); and technical competence (extent to which universalistic standards such as qualifications and education are used in selection and promotion). Reasonably strong, positive correlations were found among all of these dimensions with the exception of technical competence. This variable was negatively correlated with all of the other structural attributes! Moreover, dividing the sample of organizations according to our distinction between autonomous and heteronomous types revealed that, as expected, the former organizations were much lower than the latter in the levels of each of the structural variables with the exception of level of technical competence. The more highly professional groups were found in those organizations that exhibited fewer "bureaucratic" attributes, as Weber defined the term: organizations with lower levels of centralization, task specialization, formalization, and standardization.

These results suggest that whether or not work is simplified and subdivided among less highly skilled participants or assigned to workers with higher skills who are granted more autonomy of action has implications not only for the immediate structure of the technical core but for the more remote, general structural characteristics of organizations. They also should remind us of the criticisms by Parsons, Gouldner, and others of Weber's model of bureaucracy as tending to overlook the difference between authority based on office and that based on expertise or technical qualifications, described in chapter 3. Further, the results suggest that Udy (1959a) was correct to insist that Weber's ideal type model of bureaucratic structure should be subjected to empirical validation. Udy's early study, based on a sample of 150 production organizations in 150 different nonindustrial societies, indicated the separation of a highly intercorrelated set of bureaucratic (hierarchical) characteristics from a second set of intercorrelated characteristics that measured the presence of limited objectives and a performance emphasis—a cluster of "rational" characteristics. These results indicated that rational organizations may or may not assume a hierarchical form (see chapter 3; Blau and Scott, 1962: 206–9; and Blau, 1968).

We conclude that one of the great watersheds in the design of organizations is the decision concerning whether work is to be subdivided and hierarchically coordinated or left intact and delegated to a professionalized work force. Both are instances of rational organization. But each is associated with a different overall structural form.

Technology versus Size

With two externally driven factors affecting the structural characteristics of organizations, the question naturally arises as to which is the more powerful. Both Blau and his colleagues and the Aston group argue for the overriding importance of size as a determinant of structure. Thus, early in the presentation of findings on the employment security agencies, Blau and Schoenherr summarize the conclusion to which their data point: "Size is the most important condition affecting the structure of organizations" (1971: 57). It is difficult to accept this sweeping generalization because of the design of this and other studies carried out in Blau's program of comparative studies. In each of several studies—of employment security agencies, of public finance departments, of colleges and universities, of industrial firms—a single type of organization was selected for study. This has the effect of not allowing technology to vary meaningfully across organizations, since they are all performing basically the same tasks or functions, while at the same time permitting size to vary freely, since both large and small organizations of the same type were included within the sample. Focusing on a single type of organization also reduces variation in other important environmental factors such as the political and economic context within which the organization operates. (The effects of these environmental factors on organizational structure are examined in the following section of this chapter.) It is not appropriate to make comparative assertions as to the relative power of classes of variables under circumstances in which certain of them—in this case, technology and task environment—are arbitrarily restricted in variation or excluded from consideration.

The studies conducted by the Aston group seem better designed in this respect (Pugh et al., 1963; 1968; 1969). Concerned with the limitations of focusing on one or a few selected variables, they defined and measured a large number of structural and contextual variables. These measures were then applied to a heterogeneous, random sample of 46 organizations in the Birmingham area in the original study and to a similar national sample of 82 British organizations in Child's (1972) replication. However, the Aston studies are difficult to interpret and, in particular, to compare with other studies because of the way in which the measures of structure and technology were treated. The approach has already been briefly described in chapter 2, because the Aston data were used to generate an empirically derived typology of organizations; but we will quickly review it here. After carefully developing complex scales and sub-scales to measure a number of widely recognized structural dimensions including specialization, standardization, formalization, centralization, and configuration (the shape of the hierarchy), the analysts examined the interrelations of all of the scales. Rather than retaining the original theoretically based dimensions, a factor analysis was performed to determine what scales were sufficiently highly correlated so as to suggest the presence of a common underlying dimension or factor. Three major factors emerged from this empirical procedure: the first, labeled *structuring of activities,* emphasized the co-variation of those scales measuring specialization, standardization, and formalization; the second, labeled *concentration of authority,* emphasized measures of centralization; and the third, *line control of workflow,* emphasized control over work by line officials rather than impersonal mechanisms. The nature of the factor analysis used was such that the resulting factors are orthogonal—relatively independent of each other. These factors were then related to such "contextual" variables as size and technology. And as previously noted in chapter 10, technology itself was measured by a complex series of scales combined to measure what the analysts termed *workflow integration.*

As already reported, size was found to exhibit strong and positive associations with the factor structuring of activities but was not correlated with the other two factors (Pugh et al., 1969). Technology, as measured by workflow integration, showed "modest but distinct" correlations with all three factors, positive with structuring of activities and line control of workflow, negative with concentration of authority. But after a more detailed analysis of these data including multiple correlations in which technology was combined with other variables, Hickson, Pugh, and Pheysey conclude:

> Operations technology as defined here is accounting for but a small proportion of the total variance in structural features. Other variables contribute more. On this sample, the broad "technological imperative" hypothesis that operations technology is of primary importance to structure is not supported. . . . The present data suggest that operations technology has only a limited specific effect compared with size. (Hickson, Pugh, and Pheysey, 1969: 388–89)[4]

Although the Aston group's design appears better suited to compare the relative effects of size and technology, a number of problems reduce confidence in their conclusions. The use of factor scores disrupts the connection between

[4]Hickson and his colleagues intend this generalization to apply only to the relation between technology and peripheral organizational structure. They did find associations between technology and some aspects of the technical core structures and suggest that the pervasiveness of these effects is a function of organizational size. They argue:

> Structural variables will be associated with operations technology only where they are centered on the workflow. The smaller the organization the more its structure will be pervaded by such technological effects: the larger the organization, the more these effects will be confined to variables such as job-counts of employees on activities linked with the workflow itself, and will not be detectable in variables of the more remote administrative and hierarchical structure. (Hickson, Pugh, and Pheysey, 1969: 394–95)

theoretically defined variables and empirical measures so that it is often difficult to interpret measures of relations. Also, the measure of technology, workflow integration, seems to be both narrow and to combine measures of work and workflow inappropriately across levels, so that it also is difficult to interpret or accept. In addition, there are problems with the samples developed. The first sample was drawn exclusively from the Birmingham area and so can hardly be regarded as a representative sample of independent—that is, unrelated—organizations.[5] Further, as Child (1972) has noted, the sample contained a large number of branches, in contrast to independent companies, and this may have resulted in an inflated score for centralization and affected the observed relation between structuring of activities and centralization. The second sample used in the replication study was drawn from a broader sampling frame—all of Britain—but was restricted by type to business organizations. We suggest that McKelvey's (1975) advice about the critical importance of sample selection in developing empirical typologies of organizations, noted with approval in chapter 3, should also be applied to studies attempting to discover the relative importance of external factors such as size and technology in determining the structure of organizations. Finally, the problems with this research are not only methodological but theoretical. Aldrich (1972) has shown that the specific empirical findings reported by the Aston group may be used to support quite varying interpretations of the relations among size, technology, and structure. The correlational data are consistent with models in which technology is presumed to influence structure directly as well as indirectly through size as well as with models in which size is assumed to have causal priority. Therefore, empirical results from cross-sectional studies alone cannot resolve the issue of the relative importance of size and technology as determinants of organization structure.

Task Environment and Structure

BUFFERING, BRIDGING, AND STRUCTURAL COMPLEXITY

Chapter 9 was devoted to describing some of the specific mechanisms used by organizations to both buffer their technical cores from disturbing environmental influences and build bridges to link themselves to essential exchange partners and allies. Such organizational responses to the environment are not

---

[5]The same criticism can be made of Woodward's (1965) sample of industrial firms, all of which were drawn from the same region of South Essex and of Hage and Aiken's (1969) sample of 16 health and welfare organizations, all of which were located in the same metropolitan area (see Scott, 1977b).

a simple matter of utilizing selected techniques or mechanisms. Associated with their use are fundamental changes in the structure of the organization.

Mapping Environmental Complexity What changes may be expected when organizations employ one or more of the several buffering techniques described: coding, stockpiling, leveling, or forecasting? Carrying on such activities will require the development or recruitment of personnel with new and different skills from those employed in the technical core itself. These new participants will require additional space and special equipment. In short, as the need for such buffering techniques grows, we would expect to observe the development and growth of new specialized roles and departments at either end of the technical core, buffering units that interface with the input and output environments of the organization.

Consider also the use of the simpler bridging techniques such as bargaining, contracting, and cooptation. As the task environment itself becomes more differentiated and active with the development of segmented labor markets, rapid scientific developments, many potential buyers and sellers, competitors to be watched and bargained with, and an increasingly complex legal and political environment to relate to, the organization's response is to add new types of occupational groups and specialists to deal with each of these environmental sectors. Organizations hire personnel officers and labor relations experts to deal with more complex labor markets, scientists and engineers and research administrators and patent lawyers to participate in and keep pace with scientific developments, purchasing agents and marketing specialists to relate to the input and output environments, market researchers and industrial spies to look after competitors, and lobbyists and lawyers to attend to the legal and political environments. Most of these additions to the organizational structure involve the creation of new staff or support departments attached to the managerial level of the organization. Structural elaboration may also occur at the institutional level as the size of boards of directors is increased to allow for the addition of new types of board members, connecting the organization with sectors or units of importance in their environment; or as advisory structures are created to broaden the linkage of the organization to its task environment. Thus, the increasing complexity of the task environment is adapted to by increased structural complexity—differentiation—on the part of the organization.

This adaptation occurs not only in response to technical environments but also, according to Meyer and Rowan, as a reaction to institutional environments. They argue that organizations in such environments enhance their own chances for survival and resource acquisition by adhering closely to the institutionally defined patterns, by incorporating them in their own structures, by becoming structurally isomorphic with them. Meyer and Rowan argue, for example:

The rise of professionalized economics makes it useful for organizations to incorporate groups of economists and econometric analyses. Though no one may read, understand, or believe them, econometric analyses help legitimate the organization's plans in the eyes of investors, customers (as with Defense Department contractors), and internal participants. Such analyses can also provide rational accountings after failures occur: managers whose plans have failed can demonstrate to investors, stockholders, and superiors that procedures were prudent and that decisions were made by rational means. . . .

Thus, organizational success depends on factors other than efficient coordination and control of productive activities. Independent of their productive efficiency, organizations which exist in highly elaborated institutional environments and succeed in becoming isomorphic with these environments gain the legitimacy and resources needed to survive. (Meyer and Rowan, 1977: 350, 352)

Whether differentiation of organizational structure occurs as a rational system response to support the buffering and bridging activities of organizations attempting to regulate critical resource flows or as a natural system response to coalign the structure with its institutional environment to ensure its survival, the more general processes at work here are best depicted by the open systems perspective. This approach insists that an organization as an open system adapts to more complex environments by itself becoming more complex: that it is a type of system "whose persistence and elaboration to higher levels depends upon a successful mapping of some of the environmental variety and constraints into its own organization on at least a semipermanent basis" (Buckley, 1967: 63).

It is important to stress that the organization's "mapping" or incorporation of portions of the "environmental variety" into its own structure introduces new and different, and sometimes alien and hostile, elements into its own system. For example, the hiring of a labor relations specialist by a personnel department presumably introduces a person with expertise in, and experience with, labor unions. Such persons are hired because of their ability to understand, communicate, and negotiate with unions and their representatives. They may be more similar in background and training and attitudes to their counterparts in the unions than they are to their colleagues in the personnel department (see Goldner, 1970). The same is true for hundreds of other types of occupational groups whose services are required by the organization but whose value depends on their marginality to the system and on their connections with similar groups in other organizations. These associations between persons in similar occupational groups—accountants, computer specialists, labor lawyers, public relations experts, advertising managers—across different organizations are among the most important bridges linking contemporary organizations. The flow of traffic as individuals move back and forth across these bridges sometimes creates problems for the larger society (see chapter 13) but always creates problems for the host organization, which must attempt to control and integrate their activities and resolve their conflicts.[6]

Integration and Loose Coupling The study by Lawrence and Lorsch (1967) of the plastics manufacturing companies, which has been referred to several times throughout this volume, illustrates many of the major points we wish to emphasize.[7] As will be recalled, their research showed that (1) the task environments confronting the plastics manufacturing companies were highly varied depending on whether one focused on research or production or marketing; (2) this environmental variety was mapped into the structure of the organization, resulting in the creation of separate departments to confront these diverse environments; (3) the more closely aligned were the structural characteristics of each of these departments with the characteristics of the task environments they confronted, the more effective was the organization;[8] (4) hence, the more differentiated the organization's departments—the more unlike their structural characteristics—the more effective the organization; (5) however, the more differentiated the departments within each organization, the more likely were disagreements and conflicts to develop and the more difficult the problems of coordinating and integrating their work; and (6) therefore, the more differentiated the departments *and* the more successful the organization in integrating their efforts, the more effective the organization.

The primary integrating mechanism used in the plastics companies studied was that of liaison roles: special roles were created to help to integrate the work of the three basic departments and resolve conflicts among them. Lawrence and Lorsch (1967: 54–83) report that the more successful integrators were those who possessed attributes and orientations intermediate to those of the units they bridged, exercised influence based on technical competence, were oriented to the performance of the system as a whole, and enjoyed high influence throughout the organization. Walton and his colleagues (Walton, Dutton, and Fitch, 1966; Walton and Dutton, 1969) have also studied interdepartmental conflict in organizations and examined strategies for resolving it. They note that such conflicts often develop out of mutual task dependence, task-related asymmetries, conflicting performance criteria, dependence on

[6]The implication of these connections between similar occupational groups across organizations for the generation of power differences is discussed in chapter 12.

[7]The results of interest in the present context are based on a study by Lawrence and Lorsch of only six plastics companies. Since the organizations themselves were the units of analysis, this is a very small sample on which to base any firm conclusions. We prefer to treat their research as a stimulating exploratory study that is of value chiefly for the ideas generated, not for the hypotheses confirmed.

[8]Lawrence and Lorsch (1967:40) combined objective measures of change in profits, sales volume, and number of new products with subjective ratings by managers of how well their companies were performing to arrive at a composite rating of effectiveness. We will examine these and other measures of effectiveness in chapter 14.

common resources, communication obstacles, and ambiguity of goals as well as organizational differentiation. Such conflicts can be met with varying responses, from structural redesign to third-party consultation and attempts at reeducation of participants (see Blake, Shephard, and Mouton, 1964; Likert and Likert, 1976; Walton, 1969).

Note, however, that it is a rational system perspective that underlies most of these concerns with the integration of structurally differentiated departments. The assumption is made that the organization is primarily a production system and that when conflicts occur among subunits, they must be resolved. Conflict interferes with goal attainment; and its resolution is associated with greater effectiveness of performance. A quite different view of conflict and conflict resolution processes is associated with the natural system perspective, which presumes that intradepartmental conflict is not primarily a product of error, ambiguity, and ignorance but results from quite fundamental divergences in group interests; and that the struggles are not concerned simply with means but concern the goals to be served by the organization. These matters will be discussed in chapter 12.

Also, the assumption that integration is required because differentiation is present is also consistent with the rational system model, which presumes that the various parts of the organization should be tightly coupled, each harnessed in the service of unified objectives. By contrast, the open systems model of organizations envisages a system of more or less loosely coupled elements, each capable of autonomous action (see chapter 5). Weick (1976) has pointed out that the phrase *loose coupling* may be applied to numerous connections relevant to the study of organizations, but we shall restrict attention here to connections among departmental units. Weick notes a number of ways in which loose coupling of these structural elements may be highly adaptive for the organization, particularly when confronting a diverse, segmented environment. To the extent that departmental units are free to vary independently, they may provide a more sensitive mechanism to detect environmental variation. Loose coupling also encourages opportunistic adaptation to local circumstances; and it allows simultaneous adaptation to conflicting demands. Should problems develop with one departmental unit, it can be more easily sealed off or severed from the rest of the system. Moreover, adjustment by individual departments to environmental perturbances allows the rest of the system to function with greater stability. Finally, allowing local units to adapt to local conditions without requiring changes in the larger system reduces coordination costs for the system as a whole.

Obviously some organizations effect tighter coupling among their departmental units than do others; and within a given organization we will see variation in the degree of coupling. In general, we would expect to observe tighter coupling between units within a technical core linked by serial or reciprocal interdependence than between core units and those operating on the boundaries. Nevertheless, two conclusions merit emphasis: first, the extent of interdependence, coordination, or coupling present among any two organizational subunits is a matter for empirical determination, not assumption; second, whether looser or tighter coordination or coupling is adaptative for the organization depends on the specific circumstances confronted, and is also a matter for investigation, not prejudgment.

From Unified to Multidivisional Structures In considering the structural consequences of buffering and bridging strategies, two techniques remain to be considered: growth and merger. Both represent changes in the scale of the organization and, based on our discussion in the previous section, we would expect increased size to be associated with increased structural differentiation. But we can be more specific than this. Chandler (1962) and Williamson (1970; 1975) argue that when firms grow beyond a certain point, not just further differentiation, but a structural reorganization is likely to take place. This shift is described as a change from a unified to a multidivisional structure. The unified structure is the conventional organizational form comprised of a central office and several functionally organized divisions. The multidivisional structure is depicted in figure 11–1. It consists of a general office and several product-based divisions, each of which contains functionally differentiated departments. These departmental units may be further subdivided into work units that are distributed on a geographical or product basis.

Chandler (1962) points out that the multidivisional form first appeared on the scene in this country shortly after World War I, and that it appears to have been independently developed at about the same time by a number of major companies including Du Pont, General Motors, Standard Oil of New Jersey and Sears, Roebuck. Chandler's arguments are complex and varied, but in brief, he identifies four phases of growth for American industrial enterprise. The first period, just after the Civil War, was a time of rapid expansion and resource accumulation. This was the age of the larger-than-life entrepreneurs who expanded their organizations, most often through vertical integration. In the second phase a new generation of professional managers developed "methods for managing rationally the larger agglomerations of men, money, and materials" (Ibid., p. 388). Attention was concentrated on the reduction of unit costs and the coordination of the diverse functional activities. Phase three, lasting from the turn of the century to the first World War, witnessed the filling out of existing product lines as firms continued to expand. And, in order to ensure the continuing and expanded use of their resources, firms began to diversify. In the final phase, after World War I, companies that had diversified and were attempting to manage several different product lines found it necessary to reorganize in order to assure the efficient employment of their resources. The form that emerged was the "decentralized" or multidivisional structure, the chief advantage of which was that it permitted the clear separation of entrepreneurial from operating decisions (Ibid., p. 11). Entrepreneurial decisions, which are concerned with the allocation or reallocation of resources

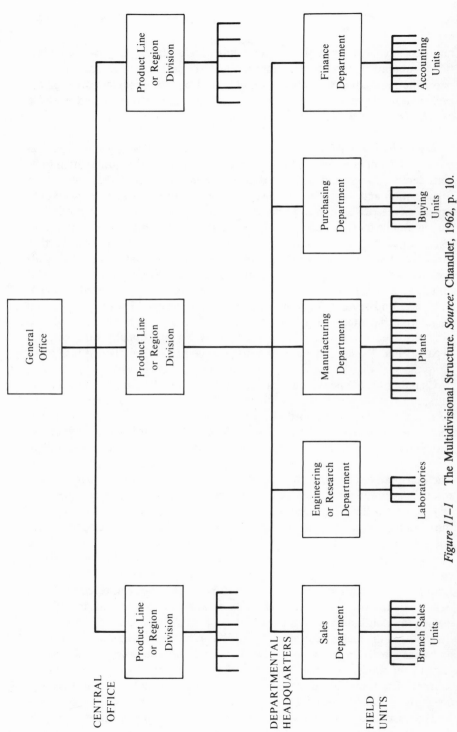

Figure 11-1   The Multidivisional Structure. *Source:* Chandler, 1962, p. 10.

and with long-range planning, are reserved for the general office level; operating decisions, which relate to the proper use of allocated resources and to a shorter time horizon, are delegated to the managers at the divisional level (see figure 11–1). Chandler summarizes the argument as follows:

> Unless structure follows strategy, inefficiency results. This certainly appears to be the lesson to be learned from the experience of our four companies. Volume expansion, geographical dispersion, vertical integration, product diversification, and continued growth by any of these basic strategies laid an increasingly heavy load of entrepreneurial decision making on the senior executives. If they failed to re-form the lines of authority and communication and to develop information necessary for administration, the executives throughout the organization were drawn deeper and deeper into operational activities and often were working at cross purposes to and in conflict with one another. (Chandler, 1962: 314–15)

Williamson (1975: 132–54) points out that Chandler's historical account of the problems accompanying growth, whether through simple expansion, vertical integration, or diversification, and the solutions that emerged are consistent with his predictions based on the "market failures" framework (see chapter 7). He argues that the principal problem created by continued growth is that it creates increasing complexity and uncertainty—this time *within* the organization rather than in the environment—up to a level that exceeds the information-processing and decision-making capacity of the managers. The structural development that occurs is one that simplifies the informational and decision situations by clearly differentiating between the long-range policy decisions to be handled by the general office and the short-run operational decisions to be determined at the divisional level. Also, since companies within a diversified structure may be expected to buy from each other where possible, a small numbers situation prevails that may motivate opportunistic behavior at the divisional or departmental levels. To curb these natural tendencies, an elite staff is attached to the general office to perform both advisory and auditing functions and in this manner to secure greater control over the behavior of the operating divisions (see Williamson, 1970: 120–21). As might be suspected, the multidivisional structure, which combines centralized policy control with decentralized operational decision making, is the form most frequently employed by multinational corporations (see Vaupel and Curhan, 1969; Robock and Simmonds, 1973; Blake and Walters, 1976).

EXPLAINING ORGANIZATIONAL STRUCTURE

Just as we did in our examination of the relation between technology and the core structures of the organization, we need to make explicit the assumptions underlying attempts to account for the characteristics of the organization's peripheral structures. Most analysts who have examined the relation between technology and structure, size and structure, or task environment and structure attempt to account for these associations using rational system arguments. Blau, Galbraith, Lawrence and Lorsch, Thompson, Chandler, Williamson—all explain their empirical findings or justify their predictions on the basis of improved performance or reduced costs or other language that implies that organizations are fundamentally goal attainment systems seeking to maximize effectiveness and efficiency. Thus, Thompson argues that the variation in organizational structure to a large extent "can be accounted for as attempts to solve the problems of concerted action under different conditions, especially conditions of technological and environmental constraints and contingencies" (1967: 74). Structure is viewed as a "joint result" of adaptations to technology and environment.

Child criticizes most of the research relating technology, size, and structure on the grounds that it allows insufficiently for the exercise of choice on the part of those who design the organization. He points out that these studies

> attempt to explain organizational structure at one remove. They draw attention to possible constraints upon the choice of effective structures, but fail to consider the process of choice itself in which economic and administrative exigencies are weighed by the actors concerned against the opportunities to operate a structure of their own and/or other organizational members' preferences (Child, 1972: 16)

Certainly, Chandler (1962) insists on the importance of choice. His study of the development of multidivisional forms by selected United States firms summarized above stresses the role of "strategy"—the setting of goals and objectives—and the uncertain relation between "strategy and structure"—the design of a satisfactory organizational form. He notes that even in the four innovative organizations—du Pont, General Motors, Standard Oil, and Sears, Roebuck

> there was a time lag between the appearance of the administrative needs and their satisfaction. A primary reason for delay was the very fact that responsible executives had become too enmeshed in operational activities. (Chandler, 1962: 315)

His survey of 70 other large industrial companies, some of which adopted the structural changes and others of which did not, revealed that although "expansion did cause administrative problems which led, in time, to organizational change and readjustment," any fundamental "reshaping of administrative structure nearly always had to wait for a change in the top command" (Ibid.,

p. 380). Such comments remind us of the importance of organizational inertia, a feature stressed by the populational ecologists (see chapter 9). Child and Chandler stress that organizations change—and fail to change—because of choices made by organizational participants.

Contingency theory—which predicts a relation between structure-environment match and performance—is consistent with either the rational selection view that successful managers design their structures to fit environmental contingencies or with the natural selection view that environments select organizations so that only those best matched to their environments survive.

If organizational change or its absence reflects not only external constraints but also internal choices, we may still ask what determines the choices made by organizational participants. Most analysts would embrace the assumption of, at least, intended rationality: members may not always behave rationally because of misinformation or ignorance or a lapse of attention, but they are believed to be motivated to serve the goals of the organization. However, natural systems analysts, as we already know, would challenge this view.

Natural system researchers have over the years devoted their efforts to accounting for the departure of behavior from the dictates of formal structure or describing the emergence of the informal structure (see chapter 4). However, they have recently begun to enter the discussion concerning the determinants of the formal structure itself. As we know, some of these theorists following Cyert and March (1963) view the organization as comprised of a coalition of groups, each pursuing its own interests (see chapter 1). Pfeffer has attempted to spell out the possible implications of this view for explaining organizational structure:

> If we take seriously the conceptualization of organizations as coalitions, then a critical issue is not just what the consequences of various structural arrangements are, but who gains and who loses from such consequences. Structure, it would appear, is not just the outcome of a managerial process in which designs are selected to ensure higher profit. Structure, rather, is itself the outcome of a process in which conflicting interests are mediated so that decisions emerge as to what criteria the organization will seek to satisfy. Organizational structures can be viewed as the outcome of a contest for control and influence occurring within organizations. (Pfeffer, 1978: 36)

Similar to our own discussion in the previous chapter, Pfeffer points out that the relation between technology and structure may result from power processes rather than from rational design decisions: powerful participants defend the definitions of their work as uncertain and hence prevent its routinization. He also suggests that the relation between environmental diversity and structural differentiation may be explained simply by the organization's tendency to incorporate external interest groups into its own structure as a means of coopting or placating them. And the same argument is used to explain the relation between organizational size and differentiation: size is associated with diversity of interests encountered by the organization, and differentiation is its response to this diversity. While these and related arguments require refinement and verification, they appear sufficiently plausible as to suggest that many features of organizational structure can be explained by nonrational power or conflict models as well as, if not better than, by rational models (see also Silverman, 1971; Benson, 1977).

Connecting the Core and Peripheral Structures

TIGHT AND LOOSE COUPLING

Much of what passes for organizational structure are varying types of mechanisms for controlling the behavior of participants. Hierarchy, formalization, centralization, modes of coordination—all are devices to help ensure that the organizational managers can shape and influence the behavior of other participants charged with carrying on the production activities of the organization. Indeed, a primary justification for the existence of managers is in terms of the impact of their ideas and decisions and designs and plans on the behavior of other participants. Many accounts of organizational structure—or, alternatively, many types of organizational structure—emphasize the tight coupling of managerial and performer's behavior. Managers decide, performers implement; managers command, performers obey; managers coordinate, performers carry out specialized tasks. Organizations or segments of organizations of this type certainly exist, particularly in situations in which work activities have been subdivided and routinized. Rational system analysts emphasize this view of organizational structure.

By contrast, early natural system analysts, with their interest in behavioral rather than normative structures, looked more carefully at the operation of these systems and failed to observe the presence of the taut command systems described by the textbooks in administrative science. Rather, their studies revealed that workers were reluctant to accept close supervision and likely to develop protective work group mechanisms or understandings with their supervisors that allowed them some leeway and breathing space in defining and meeting requirements (see Roethlisberger and Dickson, 1939; Roy, 1952;

Gouldner, 1954; Rushing, 1966a). The control systems were less tightly coupled in operation than in theory.

All formal structural devices, however, do not connote tight coupling of activities. Decentralization, delegation, professionalization, even the creation of the staff-line distinction—these are mechanisms for ensuring *some* coordination and control but also for legitimating and supporting the exercise of independence. They build in flexibility and encourage initiative in the technical core of the organization and so reduce its dependence on and its responsiveness to hierarchical directives. Moreover, as Parsons (1960:65–66) pointed out when he distinguished between the technical, managerial, and institutional levels of organization, a qualitative break in the line authority relation exists at the points where the three levels connect (see chapter 4). Parsons argues that only within a level can a superior directly supervise the work of subordinates and assume responsibility for it since differences in the nature of the work performed at each level are too great to permit direction of the lower by the higher levels. Thus, board members functioning at the institutional level would not be expected to exercise direct, routine line authority over managers but to grant them considerable freedom in exercising their managerial responsibilities; and managers, in turn, would not ordinarily exercise direct line authority over the technical functions of workers. In short, the functions performed at each level are seen to be relatively distinct and not readily linked to one another. Thus, even the relatively conventional views of rational and natural system theorists recognize the presence of considerable loose coupling as an important structural and operational feature of most organizational systems.

Meyer and Rowan (1977) take a more extreme view of the possibilities of loose coupling in organizations. They suggest that institutionalized organizations (as defined in chapter 7) will be inclined to selectively *decouple* their formal structures from the activities carried on in their technical core. The rationalized myths that provide meaning and legitimacy to the formal structures often do not provide clear and consistent guidelines for technical activities. The result is that the organization conforms closely to the ritually defined meanings and categories supplied by the environment but does not attempt seriously to implement them at the operational level. For example, Meyer and Rowan argue that educational organizations adhere closely to the ritual categories of education: "There seem to be centralized and enforced agreements about exactly what teachers, students, and topics of instruction constitute a particular school" (1978: 84). But at the operational level, there is little organizational coordination or control over instructional activities. These activities are delegated to professionals, and there is little or no attempt to evaluate and control their performance—either hierarchically or collegially—or to collect and use data on outputs, such as student performance scores, as a means of improving teacher performance.[9] The solution of decoupling is particularly effective in situations where environmental rules impose conflicting requirements on organizations. Thus, schools may be simultaneously required to give special treatment to educationally handicapped children but at the same time to "mainstream" them, not to differentiate them from their fellow students. Organizations can adapt to conflicting demands by creating appropriate programs and offices at the administrative level that can create the required reports but then decoupling these offices from the operational level.

In a closely related discussion, Marshall Meyer (1979) argues that changes in organizational structure can serve as an important signaling mechanism to the organization's constituencies. For example, the creation of an office for affirmative action can signal to interested parties an organization's commitment to the goals of this program independent of whether or not affirmative action policies are pursued. Meyer points out that such signals are taken seriously by outsiders because changes in structure are highly observable and do cost money (unlike pronouncements of goals or policy statements, which are relatively inexpensive and hence discounted), but are still much less costly than actual changes in rules together with the imposition of inspection and sanctioning procedures to detect conformity with the new program.

The arguments of these institutional organization theorists are novel because they suggest that the formal structures of organizations have meaning and importance *regardless of whether they affect the behavior of performers in the technical core.* Formal structures can symbolize meaning and order. As Marshall Meyer observes: "The fact, established in research, that people carry rational, consistent, and orderly images of organizations underscores the usefulness of structure as a signaling device" (1979:495). And, as John Meyer and Rowan have emphasized, structures that conform closely to institutional meanings "maximize their legitimacy and increase their resources and survival capabilities" (1977: 352).

---

[9]As Meyer and Rowan note, the problem is not typically the absence of data on student outputs:

> Schools use elaborate tests to evaluate pupils and to shape the course of their present and future lives. But the same data are almost never aggregated and used to evaluate the performance of teachers, schools, or school systems. (Some data of this kind are made available for school and district evaluation in California, but only under the pressure of the state legislature, not the local school system.) (Meyer and Rowan, 1978:88–89)

Meyer and Rowan cite numerous benefits associated with these practices including increased commitments of school participants, both teachers and students, the shielding of ritual classifications from uncertainties arising in the technical core, and the provision of mechanisms allowing schools to adapt to inconsistent and conflicting institutionalized rules (Ibid., pp. 98–104).

It is certainly obvious that over the eight decades of this century, organizational forms have become more and more top-heavy. As Bendix (1956) and others have pointed out, the proportion of administrators to production workers has grown continuously throughout this period (see chapter 1). A number of factors contributing to this result have been described in previous portions of this volume: the augmentation of the hierarchy to increase the information-processing capacity of the organization as the tasks performed become more complex and uncertain; the elaboration of managerial and staff positions in response to the need to buffer core departments and build connections with other units in the task environment; the incorporation of representatives from external units at the managerial or institutional level in order to relate more adequately to these interests, either as exchange partners or symbolically. All of these developments imply the growth of peripheral roles and structures in relation to the technical core. However, only some of them orient the managerial level in and down toward the activities of the technical core. Many direct their attention up and out through the institutional level to the larger task, social, and political environment. Managers of today's organizations must devote as much time and energy to "managing" their environments as to managing their production system.

In one sense, the increasing power of external systems weakens the influence of organizational managers. As Terreberry (1968) notes, increasingly organizational change is externally rather than internally induced (see chapter 8). On the other hand, external challenge and adversity can strengthen the hand of organizational leaders. There seems little doubt that the power of hospital and university administrators over their own organizations has increased as a direct result of the increasing demands made on these organizations by regulatory, fiscal, and organized constituency groups.

One of the more critical decisions managers must make in responding to environmental demands is not simply how to respond but where—in what part of the structure—the response should be made. It is possible to respond to an external demand by adding a representative of that group at the institutional level (for example, on the board of directors), adding an office at the managerial level to relate to the external unit (for example, adding a program officer to relate to a governmental agency), or by adding personnel or procedures at the operating level (for example, adding new rules and inspectors to meet some new governmental requirement). Sometimes changes are made at all three levels, sometimes at only one—for example, a change at the institutional level serving to successfully buffer the demand. Whatever the decision, we may expect it to have implications not only for the organization's relation to the environmental unit, but also for the distribution of power within the organization. The latter effect is examined in chapter 12.

Summary

This chapter has examined some of the factors affecting the larger structure of the organization: the extent of its bureaucratization, centralization, formalization, and differentiation. Although the characteristics of the organization's core technology influence its peripheral features, the latter also respond to other forces, in particular, the organization's size and its task environment. A number of empirical studies show that larger organizations are more highly differentiated and more formalized than smaller organizations. However, these studies also reveal that larger organizations tend to be less bureaucratized and centralized in their decision-making structures. It is suggested that reductions in bureaucratization occur because of administrative economies resulting from managing more of the same type of work, although these savings are counteracted and may be offset by increased administrative costs associated with greater differentiation. Decentralization is both necessary, because of information overload at the top caused by increased size and differentiation, and possible, because formalization promotes consistency of decision making. Technology also affects the characteristics of peripheral structures; in particular, the subdivision and routinization of work is associated with higher levels of differentiation, formalization and bureaucratization, while the delegation of work to professional personnel is associated with the opposite structural effects. Whether the effects of size or technology dominate in determining structural features of organizations cannot be determined by reviewing existing studies: longitudinal studies designed to test explicit causal models based on better samples of organizations are required.

The peripheral structures of organizations are also affected by the buffering and bridging strategies employed by organizations in relating to their task environment. Associated with all of these specific techniques are structural modifications—additions of new roles and departments and representatives of external interests. Open systems map critical features of their environments into their own structures as a major adaptive strategy. Structural reorganization is also associated with organizational growth.

The extent to which managerial units control and coordinate work in the technical core varies by type of organization but has probably been overstated. Considerable looseness of coupling has not only been observed in most organizations in the behavior of supervisors and workers but is legitimated by many types of formal arrangements. Recent analysts have called attention to some of the adaptive features of loosely coupled systems—whether the coupling involves boundary units relating to specific environmental segments, connections among boundary units, or connections between boundary and core units. The symbolic importance of structure has also been noted. Changes in structure at the institutional or managerial level are important whether or not they are associated with changes in procedures or behaviors within the technical core.

Managers must expend as much time and energy in relating to environmental demands as in directing the internal affairs of the organization. Balancing and reconciling—as well as buffering and segregating—are the primary administrative tasks in contemporary organizations.

chapter 12

Goals, Power,
and
Authority

*Group decision-making extends deeply into the
business enterprise. Effective participation is
not closely related to rank in the formal
hierarchy of the organization. This takes an
effort of mind to grasp. Everyone is influenced
by the stereotyped organization chart of the
business enterprise ... Power is assumed to
pass down from the pinnacle. Those at the top
give orders; those below relay them on or
respond.*

*This happens, but only in very simple
organizations—the peacetime drill of the
National Guard or a troop of Boy Scouts
moving out on Saturday maneuvers. Elsewhere
the decision will require information. Some
power will then pass to the person or persons
who have this information. If this knowledge is
highly particular to themselves then their power
becomes very great.*

JOHN KENNETH GALBRAITH (1967)

The subjects of goals and of power have re-
curred frequently enough throughout the preceding chapters of this volume
that their importance must by now be established. Although we have touched
on both topics in many places—and have skirted around them in others—we
have not yet confronted either directly. We begin by discussing the concept of

organizational goals, indicating some of the reasons why it has proved so obstreperous. We will find that it is helpful to change the questions, What are goals, and Do organizations have goals? to the question, Who set the goals in organizations? It is here that the questions of goals and power come together. It is also instructive to ask whether there are organizations that lack goals and, if so, what effect this situation has on their structure and functioning.

We also examine power and authority systems in organizations. What are the sources of power, and how does power become authority? How is authority used to regulate performance in the service of organizational goals? We will also comment on some of the limitations of conventional authority systems and speculate about some emerging types of authority in formal organizations. In a curious and unexpected way, goals are seen as providing a basis for control in some of the newer organizational forms.

Goal Setting in Organizations

PROBLEMS IN CONCEPTUALIZING ORGANIZATIONAL GOALS

The Varying Uses of Goals   The concept of organizational goals is among the most slippery and treacherous of all those employed by organizational analysts. Many factors contribute to the state of confusion in this area. A brief description of some of them may not resolve all of the questions but at least will clarify some of the issues confronted. One source of difficulty is that statements of organizational goals are used in a number of ways by organizations. Thus, rational system analysts emphasize that goals provide criteria to generate and to select among alternative courses of action (Simon, 1957; 1964). These analysts stress the *cognitive* functions of goals as they provide directions for and constraints on decision making and action. Natural system analysts, such as Barnard (1938) and Clark and Wilson (1961), emphasize that goals serve as a source of identification and motivation for participants. And Selznick (1949) notes that goals may be employed as ideological weapons with which to overcome opposition and garner resources from the environment. These analysts all emphasize the *cathectic* (emotional) properties of goals as they serve as bases of attachment for both organizational participants and external publics. Note that a goal statement that is satisfactory for analysts concerned with their cathectic properties may be unsatisfactory for analysts interested in their cognitive contributions. Vague and general descriptions of goals may suffice for motivational purposes—indeed, they may be especially suited to this function—but be unsatisfactory for cognitive guidance. For example, colleges may be able to attract students or funds with the claim that they are "preparing tomorrow's leaders," but such goal statements will provide little help in designing the curriculum or hiring the faculty.

Still other analysts have challenged the conventional view of behavior in which goals precede actions. Weick has insisted on the relevance of dissonance theory as formulated by Festinger (1957) and others to decision making in organizations. Weick argues:

> Rationality seems better understood as a postdecision rather than a predecision occurrence. Rationality makes sense of what has been, not what will be. It is a process of justification in which past deeds are made to appear sensible to the actor himself and to those other persons to whom he feels accountable. (Weick, 1969: 38)

In short, behavior sometimes precedes goals; and goal statements can serve as a *justification* for the actions taken (Staw, 1980). March reaches a similar conclusion:

> It seems to me perfectly obvious that a description that assumes goals come first and action comes later is frequently radically wrong. Human choice behavior is at least as much a process for discovering goals as for acting on them (March, 1976: 72).

Goal statements also serve as the basis for *evaluating* the behavior of participants or of entire organizations (see Scott, 1977*a*). They provide criteria for identifying and appraising selected aspects of organizational functioning. We will examine goals used as evaluation criteria applied to individual performance later in this chapter and applied to organizational performance in chapter 14. The criteria used to evaluate performance may or may not be the same as that employed to direct it.

More generally, the various types of goal statements—goals used to direct behavior, to motivate it, to justify it, or to evaluate it—may not coincide closely not only because they serve different functions but because they emanate from different sources. Cathectic goals are likely to be promulgated at the institutional level of the organization, which seeks to legitimate organizational purposes by stressing their larger social functions. Managers are likely to emphasize the cognitive functions of goals since it is the primary way in which they can shape and direct the performance of their subordinates. Performers will be most likely to employ goals statements as justifications for their past performance—behaviors they have carried out and now are asked to explain. Finally, evaluative goals are most likely to be employed by managers who are expected to appraise the performance of their subordinates and by external constituencies who depend on the organization for some sort of output (see chapter 14).

Other reasons for complexity and confusion in the analysis of organizational goals have been noted throughout this volume. Our current discussion will be better informed if we pause here to collect distinctions previously made. The distinction between product or output goals and maintenance or system goals proposed by natural system analysts (see chapter 4) is a useful one. It reminds us both that organizations are complex systems that can expect to devote only a portion of their resources to goal attainment and must expend energies in self-maintenance and renewal, and that organizations can become strongly committed to a particular way of doing things. These commitments to means constitute as real a set of guidelines for or constraints on organizational actions as do commitments to ends.

Individual and Organizational Goals Simon (1957; 1964) has most forcefully urged the distinction between individual goals that govern the decision to join or remain in an organization, and organizational goals that are expected to govern the decision of individuals as participants (see chapters 3 and 7). Simon proposes that for the sake of clarity such individual goals should be labeled "motives." This rational system conception of a relatively clear distinction between individual motives and organizational goals is challenged by the natural system perspective, which insists that individuals are not completely contained within their roles but may be expected to impose their own preferences on the choice of opportunities that confront them as participants. Simon (1964) does not deny the operation of such processes but insists that the distinction retains value. He notes, for example, that many requirements organizations impose on their participants are orthogonal to their motives—for example, it is a matter of indifference to individuals who have accepted employment as secretaries whether they type one letter rather than another. More generally, one would need to deny the existence of social roles and their impact on individual behavior in order to maintain that organizational goals are indistinguishable from individual motives. The separation of these concepts is also aided by Clark and Wilson's (1961) discussion of incentive systems (see chapter 7). Their typology reminds us that in only a limited subset of organizations—which they label "purposive"—do individual motives and organizational goals coincide. In most organizations the goals toward which participants direct their behavior are different from the goals that motivate them to participate in the organization.

One implication of these considerations is that we will not want to survey individual participants and then aggregate their individual objectives to arrive at a description of the organization's goals. In escaping from this type of error, however, we must be careful not to go to the opposite extreme and posit the existence of some type of metaphysical corporate mind in which collective goals are formulated. To do so is inappropriately to reify the organization, granting it anthropomorphic properties it does not possess. We can avoid both types of fallacies by reformulating our question. Instead of asking, Do organizations have goals? we will ask the questions, Who sets organizational goals, and How are organizational goals set?

THE DOMINANT COALITION

The most satisfactory answer to date to the question of who sets organizational goals is that provided by Cyert and March (1963). They note that the classic economist's response to this question is to point to the goals of the entrepreneur, and to equate the organization's goals with this person's objectives: the firm as the shadow of one powerful actor. A second proposed solution is to presume that goals are consensually defined: that all participants share in goal setting. Both of these models of goal setting are rejected as exceptional patterns found only rarely in nature. Cyert and March (1963: 27–32) propose the alternative conception of organizational goals being set by a negotiation process that occurs among members of dominant coalitions. We will briefly summarize this important conception.

Organizations are viewed as being comprised of coalitions—groups of individuals sharing certain interests. Each coalition will attempt to impose its preferences (goals) on the larger system, but in the typical case, no single coalition will be able to determine completely what goals are to be pursued. Coalition members seek out other groups whose interests are similar as allies, and they negotiate with those groups whose interests are divergent but whose participation is necessary. One coalition will make a "side-payment" to another to secure its cooperation; that is, it will accede to that group's demands. For example, a management group, to secure its goal of continued growth, will agree to provide a given level of return on investment to its stockholders and will agree to pay a specified level of wages to its employees. Note, however, that what is a goal for one group is viewed as a side-payment by another group, and vice versa. Each coalition whose interests must be taken into account helps to define the goals of the organization. Each negotiated agreement provides guidance to the organization and places constraints on what may be regarded as an acceptable course of action. In this sense, all coalitions powerful enough to impose conditions on organizational decision making and action may be regarded as helping to set the goals of the organization. And the goals themselves are complex statements that summarize the multiple conditions any acceptable choice must satisfy. Simon amplifies this latter point:

> In the decision-making situations of real life, a course of action, to be acceptable, must satisfy a whole set of requirements, or constraints. Sometimes one of these requirements is singled out and referred to as the goal of the action. But the choice of one of the constraints, from many, is to a large extent arbitrary. For

many purposes it is more meaningful to refer to the whole set of requirements as the (complex) goal of the action. (Simon, 1964: 7)

Simon points out that the complexity of these goal statements provides yet another reason why there is often disagreement over whether organizations may be said to have goals. He argues:

> If we use the phrase organization goals broadly to denote the constraint sets, we will conclude that organizations do, indeed, have goals (widely shared constraint sets). If we use the phrase organization goals narrowly to denote the generators [preferences held by individual coalition participants used to propose satisfactory alternatives], we will conclude that there is little communality of goals among the several parts of large organizations. (Ibid., p. 9)

The conception of the dominant coalition, while certainly not the last word on the subject, does help to avoid many of the problems that have plagued earlier formulations. We embrace this conception because of the following features:

- The problem of reification is avoided: individuals and groups have interests, and the process by which these preferences come to be imposed on the organization is specified.
- Although individuals are allowed to specify the goals of the organization, there is no presumption that they do so on an equal footing, nor is it assumed that individual participants hold common objectives.
- Although individuals impose goals on the organization, in most cases no single individual is powerful enough to determine completely the organization's goals; hence, the organization's goals are distinct from those of any of its participants.
- Allowance is made for the presence of differences in interests among participants; some, but not all, of these differences may be resolved by negotiation, so at any time, conflicting goals may be present.
- It is recognized that the size and composition of the dominant coalition may vary from one organization to another and within the same organization from time to time.

Coleman (1975) points out that yet another advantage to this general approach to goal setting in organizations is that it easily permits the analyst to shift levels of analysis from, for example, focusing on the individual coalitions and their interests to attending to the organization as a unit comprised of these interests. He asserts:

> If we conceive of this system as an actor at the next level (which I shall call a "corporate actor"), then its interests are given by the values of events at the lower

level. In such an integrated system, the organization acts as if it were a single actor, and the directions in which it acts are given by the values of events generated at the lower level. . . .

Thus the shift between levels in this theory is accomplished by conceiving of organizations as continuing systems of action, subject to internal analysis, and also as corporate actors, with interests derivable from that internal analysis. (Coleman, 1975: 86)

Coleman's explication helps to clarify the model, but in so doing calls attention to a major weakness.

With all of its advantages over previous conceptions, the coalition model of goal setting remains basically an aggregative model. Individual actors and even groups are allowed to have genuine interests, but organizations are not: they are viewed simply as collections of interests, or in Pfeffer and Salancik's terms: "as settings in which groups and individuals with varying interests and preferences come together and engage in exchanges" (1978: 26). Such a conception may suffice for a coalitional or open-systems theorist but cannot be expected to be acceptable to a rational or natural system analyst. Wallace voices their concerns in his critique of Coleman's view that " 'interests' are fixed in individuals" and that "causal dominance" is located at the bottom rather than the top of the hierarchy.

Thus Coleman apears to deny or ignore the reverse possibility that the values of events at the higher level may "give" the interest of the individual actor; he also appears to overlook the possibility that genuinely new interests may emerge from a new arrangement (especially a hierarchical arrangement) of individual actors.

Coleman's rejection of corporate determination of individual interest and his apparent choice of interest-aggregation over interest-emergence between the individual and the corporate levels seem clearly to constitute psychological reductionism. (Wallace, 1975: 127)

Although interests are certainly brought to the organization and imposed on it by some powerful participant groups, it seems entirely plausible that interests also are generated within the organization. Managers who stand to profit from economies realized by increased scale or technical innovation may be expected to coalesce around these "new" interests; and others whose power is closely associated with the condition and survival prospects of the larger enterprise may be expected to champion the interests of the organization as a whole. Thus, we need to allow for the possibility that new interests and new coalitions may emerge over time in response to the opportunities and dangers created by the existence of the organizational structure itself. The dominant coalition model appears able to accommodate these more unified conceptions of goal-setting arrangements posited by the rational and natural system analysts.

As noted, all organizations are not expected to look alike in the size and composition of their dominant coalitions. We need to examine what factors may account for these differences.

SIZE AND COMPOSITION
OF THE DOMINANT COALITION

What accounts for the distribution of power within organizations? This obviously important question has not received much attention until quite recently. Perrow (1970: 87–88) draws on Woodward's typology of production systems (see chapter 2) to argue that the relative power of the various functional groups in organizations varies depending on what type of technology is employed. Thus, in the unit and small batch systems, power seems to reside in the research and development units; in the large batch and mass systems, the most powerful group is typically the production department; and in the process companies, power seems to flow to those who manage the marketing of the product. However, other than indicating that the powerful group in each case was performing the "most important function" and that importance varies with technology, Perrow is not very explicit about the determinants of power.

The connection between the technical or functional role of a work group or department and its power have been elaborated and clarified by Hickson and his colleagues (1971). Like Thompson, Hickson explicitly embraces Emerson's (1962) view of power as flowing from exchange relations and as rooted in the exchange partner's dependency (see chapter 9). Power is defined as "the determination of the behavior of one social unit by another" (Hickson et al., 1971: 218). Hickson's formulation is also indebted to Crozier's (1964) intensive case study of the French tobacco manufacturing industry. Crozier's analysis suggests that work in this industry is so highly mechanized and standardized that little is left to chance. About the only area of uncertainty that remains is the possibility of machine breakdown. This situation is one in which the mechanics, who can deal with this source of disturbance, have considerable power— much more than would be predicted on the basis of their formal position in the organization.

Hickson and colleagues propose three general propositions relating to the development of power by subunits within organizations. The first, following Crozier's insight, is that subunits that cope more effectively with environmental uncertainty are more likely to acquire power. The importance of external uncertainty for internal power is illustrated by Goldner's study of the industrial relations (IR) unit in a manufacturing organization. Goldner writes:

> The major source of IR's power over specific plant-level issues was . . . the use
> of the union as an outside threat. Recognition that their nominal antagonists
> were the source of their internal power was even made explicit by one IR

manager: "As I told one of the (other IR) guys who was damning the unions—Don't bite the hand that feeds you." (Goldner, 1970: 104–5)

Uncertainty is not a constant but is subject to change over time. For example, improvements in technology can lead to increased routinization of work and, hence, to reductions in uncertainty. Thus, in the corporation studied by Goldner:

> The dominant theme in the recent history of the operations unit has been its steady loss of power, which had accompanied the increased rationalization of the organization. Those in operations were subject to the effect of more extensive decision-making by others on matters that directly affected operations. They had lost autonomy and resented it. (Ibid., p. 109)

However, the main contribution of the Hickson proposition is its insistence that it is not the presence of uncertainty alone but the *successful coping with uncertainty* that produces power for the subunit. Only if the subunit can effectively manage the uncertainty confronted, and in doing so protect the other units from its disturbing effects, can the subunit parlay uncertainty into power. In Goldner's example, for the IR unit to profit from the threat posed by the union, it must be able to cope with that threat, thereby reducing uncertainty for the rest of the organization.

Hickson's second proposition is "the lower the *substitutability* of the activities of a subunit, the greater its power within the organization" (1971: 221). This prediction is a direct application of Emerson's principle that power is inversely affected by alternative sources. In operational terms, this variable can be measured by the extent to which an organization can obtain alternative services to those provided by the unit or by the extent to which the personnel within the unit are replaceable. The third proposition relates to the *centrality* of the subunit which is defined as having two components: pervasiveness: "the degree to which the workflows of a subunit connect with the workflows of other units"; and immediacy: "the speed and severity with which the workflows of a subunit affect the final outputs of the organization" (Ibid., pp. 221–22). Hickson and colleagues predict that the higher the centrality—pervasiveness and immediacy—of the subunit, the greater its power.

These researchers have operationalized and tested their predictions in a study of the four principal subunits—engineering, marketing, production, and accounting departments—in each of seven small manufacturing organizations, 28 subunits in all (Hinings et al., 1974). A sample of organizations was selected so as to vary the uncertainty faced by the subunits, in particular, marketing. Independent variables were measured using scales based on both questionnaire and interview responses. The dependent variable, power, was measured in several ways: perceived influence attributed to the subunits over a variety of task areas; perceived formal authority over the same task areas; and reported participation in decision making. The several power indicators showed, in general, high and positive intercorrelations. Generally speaking, the data provided support for the three propositions. In terms of relative importance, coping with uncertainty was observed to have the greatest impact on power, followed, in order, by immediacy, nonsubstitutability, and pervasiveness.

These arguments suggest that as environmental conditions vary, we may expect power to shift within an organization from one group to another. Thus, Perrow's (1961) case study of a community hospital documents the gradual transition of power from the owners and trustees to the physicians, as a result of the increasing ability of the latter group to effectively cope with medical uncertainties presented by patients; and the more recent shift of power from the physicians to the professional administrators, as a result of the importance of internal coordination and external boundary management and the administrator's capacity to deal with these problems.

These arguments also help to explain why the size of the dominant coalition has increased in most types of organizations. Rather than highly centralized hierarchies in which one or a few persons exercise most of the power and make most of the decisions, most contemporary organizations exhibit power and decision-making structures that include a substantial number of individuals. Galbraith (1967) argues that one of the most fundamental changes that has occurred in the organization of the modern corporation is a shift from an entrepreneurial mode in which a single powerful person dominates the enterprise to a "technostructure" in which power is widely diffused. According to Galbraith the technostructure consists of

> the association of men of diverse technical knowledge, experience or other talent which modern industrial technology and planning require. It extends from the leadership of the modern industrial enterprise down to just short of the labor force and embraces a large number of people and a large variety of talent. [It constitutes the] new locus of power in the business enterprise and in the society. (Galbraith, 1967: 58)

More so than Galbraith, Thompson (1967: 127–36) makes clear the reason for the increasing size of the organization's power structure. Consistent with the views of Crozier and Hickson, Thompson argues that the number of positions of power within the organization, and hence the size of the dominant coalition, is affected both by the nature of the organization's technology and its task environment. The more uncertain the technology and the greater the number of sources of uncertainty in the organization's task environment, the more bases for power there are within the organization and the larger will be the dominant coalition. When organizations embrace more uncertain technologies, as in professional organizations, and when the sources of uncertainty increase in the technical environment of the organization, we may expect those who cope with these problems to demand and receive a place in the decision-making councils of the organization.

What difference, if any, does it make when power shifts from one group to another or is shared with a larger proportion of the participants? The difference should be reflected, of course, in the goals pursued by the organization. Admission to the dominant coalition is an empty victory if the new partners cannot affect the definition of the goals to be served. And, on the basis of his case study of the community hospital, Perrow (1961) asserts that, as doctors replaced trustees, hospital goals shifted from community welfare concerns to business-professional objectives including research; and as the administrators gained dominance over the physicians, the hospital's goals shifted to emphasize the role of the hospital as the medical center for the community. And in the coalitions of interests present in the modern corporation, Galbraith argues that although the stockholders must receive their side-payment of a satisfactory return on their investment, the maximization of profits associated with the entrepreneurial regime has given way to a new set of goals preferred by the now-dominant coalition of technical and managerial specialists: "the greatest possible rate of corporate growth as measured in sales." This goal is valued by the technostructure because "expansion of output means expansion of the technostructure itself . . . including more jobs with more responsibility and hence more promotion and more compensation" (1967: 171).

In more differentiated and loosely coupled systems such as universities, power differences among subunits may be reflected not so much in direct attempts to redefine the goals of the larger system but in efforts to lay claim to a disproportionate share of the organization's resources. This process is well illustrated in a study by Pfeffer and Salancik (1974) of the allocation of general university resources among 29 academic departments examined over a 13-year period. These researchers convincingly show that the greater the power of individual departments, as measured by indicators such as perceived influence and representation on powerful university committees, the greater the proportional allocation of general university funds they received. Although such budgetary decisions may appear remote from the general goals of the university, they are in reality highly relevant: the allocation of scarce resources among diverse university programs is one of the clearest indicators available of the "real" goals of the institution.

ORGANIZATIONS LACKING CLEAR GOALS

Both the bureaucratic-administrative model of the rational system perspective and the coalitional-bargaining model of the natural/open systems perspective provide for the development of a set of goals by which organizational decisions can be made. Both allow for the construction of relatively clear criteria or preference orderings in terms of which priorities can be set and selections made among alternative courses of action. But classes of organizations—and more importantly, classes of decision situations within many organizations—exist in which no clear preference orderings have been determined. Such organizations are on the fringe if not beyond the pale of those collectivities included within the conventional definitions and theories of organizations (see chapter 1). Yet they present both interesting and instructive cases.

Thompson and Tuden (1959) focus on these situations by constructing a typology that combines two dimensions: (1) how much agreement there is among participants of the organization about the goals or preferred outcomes of the system; and (2) how much agreement there is about the means or the causal processes by which these outcomes can be realized. The cross-classification of this simple ends-and-means distinction produces four types of decision contexts, each of which is argued to be associated with a different decision strategy, as follows:

PREFERENCES ABOUT OUTCOMES

BELIEFS ABOUT CAUSATION	Agreement	Disagreement
Agreement	*Computation*	*Compromise*
Disagreement	*Judgment*	*Inspiration*

We are most interested in the right-hand column involving situations in which participants lack consensus on goals, but let us briefly comment on the simpler and more familiar situations in which such agreement is present. Thompson and Tuden use the term *computation* to denote the typical bureaucratic decision-making structure which, as we have often noted, is most suited to situations in which goals are clearly defined and the technology is relatively certain. The term *judgment* is employed to refer to the strategies required when agreement on goals exists but the means of achieving them is uncertain. This situation is best confronted with a collegium and is well illustrated, in our opinion, by the structure of professional organizations previously described.

Turning to the column of interest, Thompson and Tuden argue that there are sometimes situations in which participants agree about how to accomplish some objective or about the expected consequences of available alternatives but disagree over which alternative is preferable. A mild version of this situation is provided by the coalitional view of decision making—which, as we have described, is resolved by negotiation and bargaining. More extreme instances of disagreement and conflict can sometimes be resolved through the creation of representative bodies which allow for the expression of differences and the engineering of compromises. Most such forums—for example, the United Nations, the United States Congress—presume the existence of substantive differences in preferences but rely on procedural agreements for resolving them.

The fourth and final decision situation is characterized by the absence of agreement about either ends or means. Thompson and Tuden suggest that these anomic situations are more commonly found in and among organizations than conventional theories suggest. They propose that such circumstances, if they are not to be followed by complete system disintegration, call for "inspiration," perhaps of the type suggested by Weber's (1947 tr.) description of the charismatic leader. This is not inconsistent with Weber's own views, described in chapter 2, in which charismatic leaders are viewed as more likely to emerge in crisis situations—during times when conventional goals are being challenged and established procedures are not working. And, like Weber, Thompson and Tuden expect such leadership to give rise over time to a computational (bureaucratic) structure based on a new definition of goals and accepted procedures, as charisma is routinized.

March and his colleagues (March and Olsen, 1976a; Cohen, March, and Olsen, 1972, 1976; Cohen and March, 1976; March, 1978) have also examined decision making under conditions of "inconsistent and ill-defined preferences," "unclear technologies," and "fluid participation"—the shifting involvement of members in decision situations (Cohen, March, and Olsen, 1972: 1). They label these conditions *organized anarchies.* But unlike Thompson and Tuden, March and associates do not view these circumstances as crises or as transitory states. Rather, they insist that they have been "identified often in studies of organizations," "are characteristic of any organization in part," and "are particularly conspicuous in public, educational, and illegitimate organizations" (Cohen, March, and Olsen, 1976: 25).

The portrait of organized anarchies is set within a more general framework that stresses the ambiguity in decision making. March and Olsen comment on their approach:

> We remain in the tradition of viewing organizational participants as problem-solvers and decision-makers. However, we assume that individuals find themselves in a more complex, less stable, and less understood world than that described by standard theories of organizational choice; they are placed in a world over which they often have only modest control. (March and Olsen, 1976b: 21)

The organizational world depicted here is similar to that described by Weick (1969; also see chapter 5): individual decision makers have cognitive and attention limits; external conditions constrain alternatives and affect outcomes but often go unnoticed; and choices by individuals in decision-making positions may not eventuate in organizational action. Under such conditions, all choices are somewhat ambiguous.

> Although organizations can often be viewed conveniently as vehicles for solving well-defined problems or structures within which conflict is resolved through

bargaining, they also provide sets of procedures through which participants arrive at an interpretation of what they are doing and what they have done while in the process of doing it. From this point of view, an organization is a collection of choices looking for problems, issues and feelings looking for decision situations in which they might be aired, solutions looking for issues to which they might be the answer, and decision makers looking for work. (Cohen, March, and Olsen, 1972: 2)

Under the conditions of organized anarchy, the ambiguity of choice present in all decision-making situations reaches its apex. Here problems, solutions, participants, and choice opportunities are viewed as flows that move relatively independently into and out of the decision arena—metaphorically labeled a "garbage can." Which solutions get attached to which problems is largely determined by chance—by what participants with what goals happened to be on the scene, by when the solutions or the problems entered, and so on. Although the system described seems bizarre and even pathological when compared with the conventional model of rational decision making, it does produce decisions under conditions of high uncertainty: that is, some solutions do get attached by some participants to some problems.

Cohen, March, and Olsen (1972) have developed and examined some implications of their garbage can model under varying assumptions using computer simulation techniques. However, this model of decision making was originally suggested to them on the basis of observations of decision-making processes in colleges and universities:

Opportunities for choice in higher education can easily become complex "garbage cans" into which a striking variety of problems, solutions, and participants may be dumped. Debate over the hiring of a football coach can become connected to concerns about the essence of a liberal education, the relations of the school to ethnic minorities, or the philosophy of talent. (Cohen and March, 1976: 175)

Perhaps it is due specifically to the characteristics of universities, or perhaps they intend their comments to apply more generally to all organized anarchies, but unlike Thompson and Tuden, Cohen and March (1974; 1976) do not look for a charismatic leader to ride in on horseback bringing inspiration for new goals. They perceive the role of leaders—for example, university presidents— in such situations in much more problematic and pessimistic terms. They do suggest that leaders can improve their performance if they take into account the unusual nature of decision-making situations in these organizations. By careful timing of issue creation, by sensitivity to shifting interests and involvement of participants, by recognizing the status and power implications of choice situations, by abandoning initiatives that have become hopelessly entangled with other originally unrelated problems, by realizing that the planning function is largely symbolic and chiefly provides excuses for interaction, leaders in organized anarchies can maintain their sanity and, sometimes, make a difference in the decision made.

While ambiguous goals and unclear technology may provide occasions for charismatic creativity and for the random association of solutions with problems, in our own view two other types of responses are more likely. Both have been described earlier in this volume. First, we see these situations as occasions for the creation of institutionalized organizations as defined by Meyer and Rowan (1977; see also chapter 7). Ritually defined categories can provide order and meaning, and rational myths can supply rationales for choice and action. Widely understood roles—for example, teacher and student—can offer a basis for legitimate action in the absence of specific organizational guidelines and controls (Meyer et al., 1978). Second, we believe that ambiguous goal statements are often replaced by more specific, proximal and often, procedural goal statements that provide a basis for making decisions and achieving order (see chapter 3). Thus, in universities, disagreements over the aims of education may be resolved by agreements on the number of course units required for graduation. Although some critics of organizations view such goal transformation processes as pathological (see chapter 13), we must acknowledge that they do permit the construction of coherent organizational systems in arenas where they otherwise would be difficult if not impossible to sustain.

GOAL SETTING AND THE ENVIRONMENT

Before leaving the topic of goals, in keeping with the theme of this part of the volume, we need to underline the importance of the connection between organizational goals and the environment. We have previously discussed, in chapters 1 and 2, Parsons's (1960) useful conception of organizations as subsystems of larger societal systems. Viewed in this manner, an organization's goals may be seen as only a subgoal serving a specialized function within the larger system. Recall also that the amount of support in the form of legitimacy and resources accorded to the organization may be expected to reflect the value placed on its functions in the larger social system. This assertion may have been easier to accept earlier than now since our conception of goals and systems has grown more complex; but in our opinion, it contains an important element of truth. Organizations cannot command resources: in the final analysis they acquire them because of the value that external groups place on the goods and services they provide.

In the present chapter, another important basis of connection between goals and environments has been developed. We have argued that the existence of environmental uncertainty provides the possibility of an important power base to organizational actors who can cope with it adequately. Such uncertainty is typically caused by some new environmental group—a regulatory agency, a union, a consumer organization—that is in a position to make some sort of demand on the organization. The successful creation of such an internal power base, we have argued, leads to modifications in organizational goals. Although we have, to this point, regarded this as a "victory" for the new member of the coalition, it is surely no less a "victory" for the environment, which has succeeded in modifying the organization both in its structure and its goals.

Power and Authority

CONTROL SYSTEMS IN ORGANIZATIONS

All collectivities control their members. As we have previously argued in defining them, if collectivities do not show evidence of a distinctive normative structure and some regular patterns of participant behavior, we cannot even establish their existence. But, as Etzioni has argued, the problems of control in organizations are especially acute:

> The artificial quality of organizations, their high concern with performance, their tendency to be far more complex than natural units, all make informal control inadequate and reliance on identification with the job impossible. Most organizations, most of the time cannot rely on most of their participants to internalize their obligations to carry out their assignments voluntarily, without additional incentives. Hence, organizations require formally structured distribution of rewards and sanctions to support compliance with their norms, regulations, and orders. (Etzioni, 1964: 59)

Perhaps this explains why so many of the topics discussed in connection with organizations relate more or less directly to the subject of control. Consider the following list: administration, authority, automation, boundaries, bureaucratization, centralization, contracts, coordination, decision premises, discipline, evaluation, formalization, hierarchy, incentives, integration, performance programs, power, procedures, routinization, rules, sanctions, specialization, supervision—these are some of the specific manifestations and instruments of control.

We wish in this section to focus on the interpersonal control system—the structure of power and authority in organizations. This system of "personal" controls is often contrasted with a set of less obtrusive, impersonal control mechanisms used in organizations. Thus, Gouldner (1954) and Rushing (1966a) have emphasized the advantages of impersonal systems of rules in comparison with personal supervision. And Blau and I (Blau and Scott, 1962: 176–83) have reviewed the effects of three differing types of impersonal control arrangements—the assembly line, statistical records of performance, and automation—on worker autonomy and satisfaction and on relations between superiors and subordinates. And Perrow (1979: 149–50) has contrasted "direct and obtrusive" control systems such as giving orders and exercising surveillance with "fully unobtrusive" controls in which participants internalize decision premises that govern their performance. While the distinction between personal and impersonal control systems has been much employed and calls attention to an important dimension of control, we believe that it leads to confusion in the analysis of formal authority systems. On the one hand, these are systems of "personal" control; but in another sense, this is precisely what they are not. An emphasis on formalization and authority may be regarded as an attempt to reduce the personal component in interpersonal control systems. We will amplify this argument in our discussion of power and authority in organizations.

POWER

A great many pages have been filled with discussions of power, and many definitions of this important concept have been proposed (see Cartwright, 1965; Schopler, 1965). One of the simplest and most satisfactory approaches to this topic is that taken by Emerson, who suggests:

> It would appear that the power to control or influence the other resides in control over the things he values, which may range all the way from oil resources to ego-support, depending upon the relation in question. In short, power resides implicitly in the other's dependency. (Emerson, 1962: 32)[1]

This approach emphasizes that power is not to be viewed as a characteristic possessed by an individual but, rather, as a property of a social relation. To say that a given person has power is meaningless unless we specify over whom he or she has power. We must take into account the characteristics of both the superordinate and the subordinate individual in describing a power relation. The power of superordinates is based on their ability and willingness to sanction others—to provide or withhold rewards and penalties; but we must recognize that what constitutes a reward or a penalty is ultimately determined by the goals or values of subordinates in the relation. To use two extreme examples, a gunman has no power over the individual who does not value his life, nor does a person with money have power over another who does not value money or the things it will buy. Emerson's formulation also provides a means of determining the degree of power in a relation: recall his suggestion that A's power over B is (1) directly proportional to the importance B places on the

---

[1] An important advantage to this approach is that it is applicable to relations among varying types of units: individuals, groups, organizations. In the current context we apply the conception to relations among individuals; in Chapter 9, we used it to examine power relations among organizations.

goals mediated by A; and (2) inversely proportional to the availability of these goals to B outside the A-B relation (1962: 32).

It is consistent with this approach that power can have many bases. An individual's power is based on all the resources—money, skills, knowledge, strength, sex appeal—that he or she can employ to help or hinder another in the attainment of desired goals. What types of resources will function as sanctions will vary from one individual to another and from situation to situation. Thus, if workers in an office value the quality of their technical decisions, then expertise becomes an important resource that can be used as a sanction in this situation (see Blau, 1955); and if boys in a camp situation prefer to avoid black eyes and to be on winning teams, then such characteristics as strength and athletic prowess will become important bases of power in those settings (see Lippitt et al., 1953).

Emerson's formulation also allows for the possibility of mutual dependency. The power relations can be reciprocal: one individual may hold resources of importance to another in one area but be dependent on the same person because of resources held by the latter in a different area. And just as the degree of individual dependence may vary by situation, so may the degree of mutual dependence, or interdependence.

We will define interpersonal *power* as the potential for influence that is based on one person's ability and willingness to sanction another person by manipulating rewards and punishments important to the other person. That is, power has its origin in the dependency of one person on resources controlled by another, but power itself is best defined as a potential for influence. We turn now to discuss briefly the emergence of power structures in informal and formal systems.

Power in Informal Groups and Formal Organizations During the 1950s a large number of studies examined the operation of power in informal groups and, in particular, the emergence of power differences in previously undifferentiated task groups. The emergence of power was examined in field studies (Lippitt et al., 1953; Sherif and Sherif, 1953) as well as in the laboratory (Bales, 1952; Bales and Slater, 1955). These studies describe the way in which certain personal qualities or characteristics that differ among members become the basis for differences in sanctioning ability. As analyzed by Homans (1961) and Blau (1964), the process of differentiation occurs through a series of exchanges among group participants. Over a period of time, some members emerge who are both more willing and more able to make important contributions to goal attainment—whether to the goals of individual members or of the group as a whole: they can manipulate sanctions of importance to others. And if they so choose, as Blau notes: "A person who commands services others need, and who is independent of any at their command, attains power over others by making the satisfaction of their need contingent on their compliance" (1964: 22). Both Blau and Homans see the origin of power structures as a product of unequal exchange relations that occur when some individuals become increasingly dependent on others for services required in reaching their objectives. A person lacking resources to repay the other for these services, who is unwilling to forgo them and unable to find them in other relations has but one alternative: "he must subordinate himself to the other and comply with his wishes, thereby rewarding the other with power over himself as an inducement for furnishing the needed help" (Ibid., pp. 21–22). In this manner, exchange processes that involve asymmetries give rise to a differentiated power structure.

Power in informal groups is based on the characteristics of individuals—individual differences that can function as resources allowing some to reward and punish others. It is the differential distribution and use of such characteristics-resources that give rise in informal groups to a power structure. By contrast, power in formal organizations is at least in part determined by design. Most organizations are designed in such a manner that a hierarchy of positions is created: one position is defined as controlling another. A supervisory position, for example, is defined as being more powerful than that of a worker; and in accordance with this definition, sanctioning powers are attached to the position. Thus, supervisors may be allowed to evaluate the work of their subordinates, determining by these evaluations who receives what rate of pay and who is to be recommended for promotion. Such powers are attached to the position: they are available to any individual who occupies it, regardless of his or her personal qualities.

Rational system theorists emphasize the importance of formal power structures in the functioning of organizations. They argue that it is possible to design power structures in such a manner that sanctioning power may be made commensurate with responsibilities and distributed so as to facilitate the organization's requirements for coordination and control of participants' contributions. They also note that although the theoretical range of subordinates' values and, hence, of power bases is quite broad, the actual range is quite narrow; certain values are widely shared so that it is possible to identify resources, such as money and status, that will function as sanctions for most participants most of the time. They further note the quite palpable advantages associated with the formalization process itself which results in the "domestication" of power. Thus, tensions associated with the generation of power differences are avoided; the organization is freed from the necessity of finding "superior" individuals to fill superior positions; and power is more readily transferred from one person to another as position occupants come and go (see chapter 3). Formalization is one of the important ways in which the "personal" element is removed from interpersonal control systems.

Natural systems theorists insist, on the other hand, that no organization ever succeeds in completely controlling all sources of power or in rationally allocating power among its positions. There are three reasons for this. First, we come again to the chief thesis of the natural system perspective: positions are filled by persons, and persons possess diverse and variable characteristics, some of which may become the basis for informal power differences in formal organizations. Differences among individuals in intelligence, motivation, training, skills, attractiveness, and other respects can serve as resources that sometimes supplement and sometimes contradict and erode the formal distribution of power. Second, in the organization's allocation of resources to positions, some participants inevitably obtain access to resources that can be used in ways not intended by the organizational designers. For example, access to information is an important resource that can become the basis for sanctioning and controlling others. A position such as secretary can make its occupants privy to sensitive information that they can use to enhance their own power and influence (see Mechanic, 1962). Third, as we have learned from Hickson and associates (1971), a person or a position's capability of dealing with uncertainty impinging on the organization from its task environment can also be an important unanticipated source of sanctions and hence of influence.

Research by Tannenbaum and associates (Tannenbaum, 1968; Tannenbaum et al., 1974) supplies evidence to support the general expectation that amount of control or influence is positively associated with position in the formal hierarchy. If individuals are asked to describe how much influence is associated with each type of position in the organization, then it is possible to construct a "control graph" that depicts how centralized or decentralized is the distribution of power in the organization. The centralization of power varies from organization to organization largely as a function of differences in ideology or goals that directly affect the formal definitions of how power is to be distributed: for example, power was more evenly distributed in the League of Women Voters, a voluntary agency emphasizing member participation, and in Yugoslavian companies emphasizing worker participation than in more traditional United States business and industrial concerns. (However, as Tannenbaum emphasizes, power was somewhat centralized in all of these organizations, ideology and preferences notwithstanding.) Of more interest is Tannenbaum's demonstration that, aside from its distribution, the *total amount* of control exercised varies from one organization to another. That is, in some organizations none of the positions is perceived as exercising very much influence over others, whereas in other organizations all of the positions are seen to exercise considerable power. This finding underlines our earlier point that organizations may be expected to vary in the amount of mutual dependence or interdependence they display.

AUTHORITY

Weber has pointed out that in his experience no organization

voluntarily limits itself to the appeal to material or affectual motives as a basis for guaranteeing its continuance. In addition, every such system attempts to establish and to cultivate the belief in its "legitimacy." (Weber, 1947 tr.: 325)

In other words, no organization is likely to be content with establishing a power structure; in addition, it will attempt to create an authority structure. Most social scientists define authority as legitimate power. *Legitimacy* refers to a set of social norms that defines situations or behaviors as correct or appropriate. Thus, to speak of legitimate power is to indicate (1) a set of persons or positions linked by power relations and (2) a set of norms or rules governing the distribution and exercise of power and the response to it.

In informal groups, we refer to the exercise of power as legitimate to the extent that there emerges a set of norms and beliefs among the members subordinate to the power wielder that the distribution and exercise of power is acceptable to them and is regarded as appropriate. The emergence of such norms significantly alters the control structure, as Blau and I have argued:

> Given the development of social norms that certain orders of superiors ought to be obeyed, the members of the group will enforce compliance with these orders as part of their enforcement of conformity to group norms. The group's demand that orders of the superior be obeyed makes obedience partly independent of his coercive power or persuasive influence over individual subordinates and thus transforms these other kinds of social control into authority. (Blau and Scott, 1962: 29)

In sum, a set of dyadic power relations between the superior and each subordinate is transformed by the emergence of legitimacy norms into a multiperson control structure with each subordinate now participating in the control of each of his or her colleagues. Peer group controls are harnessed in the support of the power structure. Another way of describing these important developments is to say that a stable role structure has emerged that guides the expectations of participants, making it possible for a leader to lead and for followers to follow without the generation of disruptive emotional responses. Further, the emergence of legitimacy norms helps to render power relations more impersonal and reduces the tensions associated with the exercise of interpersonal power. As Thibaut and Kelley suggest, in an authority structure, in contrast with a power structure,

> nonadherence is met with the use of power to attempt to produce conformity, but the influence appeal is to a supra-individual value ("Do it for the group" or "Do it because it's good") rather than to personal interests ("Do it for me" or "Do it and I'll do something for you"). (Thibaut and Kelley, 1959: 129)

For all of these reasons—involvement of subordinate participants in the control system, development of differentiated expectations among participants, impersonalization of power processes with consequent reduction of interpersonal tensions—authority structures tend to be much more stable and effective control systems than are power structures. Like formalization, authority helps to clothe personal power in impersonal garb.

There is, however, another equally important consequence of the legitimation process. The emergence of social norms not only allows a greater measure of control of subordinates by the power wielder but also operates to regulate and circumscribe the exercise of power by the power wielder. Emerson (1962) points out that the emergence of legitimacy norms among subordinates allows them to act as a coalition vis-à-vis the power wielder, defining the arena within which he or she can appropriately exercise power. Subordinates are individually weaker but collectively stronger than the superior, allowing them to place some limits on his or her power. Legitimacy norms specify the orders to which subordinates are expected to comply—hence, supporting the exercise of power —but also identify demands that the power wielder cannot appropriately make of subordinates—hence, limiting the exercise of power. In sum, legitimacy norms cut both ways: they permit greater and more reliable control of subordinates within certain limits, defined as appropriate areas of control—Barnard (1939) referred to this area as the "zone of indifference"—and they restrict the exercise of power to this specified area. We conclude that *authority is legitimate power and that legitimate power is normatively regulated power.*

Two Types of Authority: Endorsed and Authorized Power   Dornbusch and I (Dornbusch and Scott, 1975) have raised a question that has not been explicitly asked by previous students of authority. Having determined that social norms that regulate power relations provide the basis for legitimate control structures, we sought to determine who—what group of participants —defines and enforces these norms. In most informal groups, there is only one possible source: the set of participants who are subject to the exercise of power and hence are subordinates of the power wielder. We have noted how, by acting as a coalition, this subordinate group can limit and regulate the exercise of power over them by a superordinate. We label this type of situation *endorsed power* or authority by endorsement. A number of theorists—in particular, Barnard (1938)—view the enforcement of norms by subordinates, or endorsement, as the basic mechanism underlying authority in formal organizations. While we do not deny that this process operates in organizations, in our opinion it is secondary to another source in these situations.

An important characteristic of formal organizations is the presence of persons superordinate to as well as subordinate to a given power wielder. Most hierarchies are multi-level so that norms may be developed and enforced by persons superior to the power wielder. Indeed, this is one of the primary features of a hierarchy of offices. As Weber states:

> The principles of office hierarchy and of levels of graded authority mean a firmly ordered system of super- and subordination in which there is a supervision of the lower offices by the higher ones. (Weber, 1946 tr.: 197)

A familiar safeguard built into most hierarchies is the principle of appeal by which, if subordinates feel that their superior is making unfair or unreasonable demands on them, they may turn to their superior's boss with the expectation that he or she will enforce authority norms that curb the superior's power. We label a situation in which power is regulated by those superior to the power wielder *authorized power* or authority by authorization.[2]

For authorization to operate as a source of normative control, there must be a level of the hierarchy above that of the person or position whose exercise of power is at issue. What happens at the very top of the hierarchy where there is no superordinate level to regulate the exercise of power? In the usual case, as Parsons (1960) has pointed out, the managerial hierarchy ends with its top position being responsible to a different type of office: the institutional level, exemplified by the board of directors or board of trustees. These offices are defined as legitimated by—normatively regulated by—some different, non-hierarchical principle. Often, they are legitimated by some type of electoral process (for example, officers elected by stockholders); or officers are appointed to represent the interests of the ultimate beneficiaries, for example, the owners or the citizenry. It is important to emphasize that a principal function of the institutional level—one noted at several times throughout this volume—is to secure the legitimation of the organization's hierarchy. This is accomplished by linking the norms and values supporting the hierarchy to broader institutionalized normative systems, demonstrating their congruence and consistency. Weber's famous typology of authority systems, described in chapter 2, is based on differences in the types of norms that legitimate power systems. Recall that he distinguished between traditional, charismatic, and bureaucratic systems, each of which justifies and regulates an existing structure of power on a different basis. Both Weber (1947 tr.) and Bendix (1956) have examined how these broadly accepted normative beliefs change over time, causing and reflecting changes in power arrangements within specific administrative systems. For example, the legitimacy of the nation state is no longer likely to be justified by the doctrine of the divine right of kings, but is instead supported by beliefs in its consistency with constitutional documents or the "people's will." Similarly, the authority systems of more limited organizations are justified by beliefs in property rights, or procedural correctness, or the legitimacy of specialized expertise.

Returning to our basic distinction, it is possible for some control attempts to be authorized—that is, supported by superiors of the power wielder—but not endorsed—that is, not supported by subordinates of the power wielder—or

---

[2]Another possible source of the creation and enforcement of norms in organizations is the colleagues or equals of the power wielder—those occupying the same formal position in the organization. This source may be expected to be of particular importance in professional organizations, and is labeled *collegial power*.

vice versa. It is also possible for control attempts to be both authorized and endorsed. An instance of the first type would be the authority exercised by a police officer in an urban neighborhood whose residents are suspicious or hostile toward police activities; the second type is illustrated by the authority exercised by an informal leader in a work group. The third type—authority that is both authorized and endorsed—is represented by an individual serving as supervisor who is also a natural leader. Authority that is both authorized and endorsed may be said to enjoy greater legitimacy and may be expected to be more effective and more stable than that which receives support from only one source (Dornbusch and Scott, 1975: 56–64).

We do not equate formal with authorized and informal with endorsed power systems: these pairs of concepts are analytically distinct. However, we would expect them to be empirically associated. Consider the relation between authorized and formal power. Managers attempting to regulate the control attempts of the supervisors under their charge are more likely to attempt to treat them equally—to emphasize the power of position rather than the power of person—partly because of equity and precedent considerations and partly because the possibility of turnover in personnel is always present. By contrast, subordinates typically relate to only a single superior and are likely to have some difficulty in separating personal from official characteristics. If comparisons are made, they are more likely to focus on those features that differentiate their own supervisor from others of whom they have knowledge. For these reasons, informal power is likely to be associated with endorsed power. It is striking that virtually all of the empirical studies of supervision and control in organizations tend to focus attention on informal and endorsed power, often termed "leadership" to the neglect of formal and authorized systems of control.[3]

Authority and Evaluation My colleagues and I have also examined the manner in which authority within organizations can be used to implement organizational goals (see Scott et al., 1967; Dornbusch and Scott, 1975). Briefly, we attempt to develop a conception that will allow for the identification of types of authority in a specific enough manner to be empirically useful but in an abstract enough manner to be applicable to a broad range of organizations. Our model is designed to focus on the control of participants engaged in the performance of organizational tasks.

Organizational goals are defined as conceptions of desired end states determined by members of the dominant coalition. A task is simply a set of activities carried out by a participant to attain a goal. The basic premise underlying our conception is that if power is to be employed to control the behavior of participants who are working on organizational tasks, then some type of

[3]For a detailed review of empirical studies of power and authority in both informal groups and formal organizations, see Dornbusch and Scott (1975: 45–56).

evaluation, however crudely performed, is necessary.[4] Because evaluation is central to the control of performance, its phases or component elements are used as the basis for our typology of control acts. Four activities are distinguished:

> *Allocation:* the act that determines who is to perform a given task and, hence, specifies who is to be evaluated for it
>
> *Criteria-setting:* the act of specifying the task properties, their weights (relative importance), and the standards to be employed in evaluating the task
>
> *Sampling:* the act of determining what indicators are to be employed in inspecting the work and what sample of work is to be drawn
>
> *Appraising:* the act of comparing the observed values on the indicators with the standards specified for such tasks in order to arrive at a performance evaluation

These activities are not separated simply as a logical exercise but because they are often distinguished in organizations and form the basis for differentiation of the control system. For example, a supervisor may be granted the right to allocate tasks, a testing department the right to set standards, inspectors the right to select performance indicators and determine the sample, and all this information fed back to the supervisor, who carries out the appraisal. In order to be regarded as a part of the control (power) system, the resulting performance evaluations must have some impact on the distribution of organizational sanctions to the performer. Assuming that this is the case, then all those who participate in the evaluation process—by setting criteria, sampling performances, and so on—are involved in the control system. And to the extent that these control attempts are authorized—legitimated by officials superior to those who carry out the control activities—then the control system may be regarded as an authority system.

Figure 12–1 contains a model of the evaluation process as we envisage it. The lines between the various components of the process denote the links that must exist among the several components for the process to be carried out; thus, if a different person were to perform each function, then the lines would illustrate the minimum set of communication linkages among the members of the control system. For example, task allocators need to communicate information about the nature of the task not only to the performer but also to the criteria setter; the criteria setter needs to specify to the sampler the relevant

---

[4]It is recognized that all control systems in organizations do not attempt to control directly the performance of organizational tasks. Some organizations, for example, are content to control the characteristics or "qualities" of their participants under the assumption that such indirect control will ensure acceptable levels of performance. Institutionalized organizations and organizations employing professionals are especially likely to rely heavily on controlling qualities rather than performances (see Dornbusch and Scott, 1975: 97–99; Meyer and Rowan, 1977: 356–59).

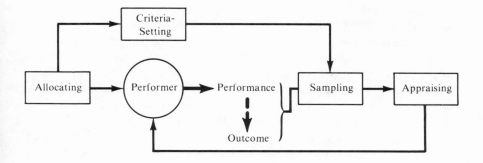

Figure 12–1 A Model of the Evaluation Process. *Source:* Dornbusch and Scott (1975: 144)

task properties; the sampler needs to provide the appraiser with information on the observed performance values; and for the entire process to have meaning as a control attempt, the appraiser needs to communicate the performance evaluation to the performer either directly or indirectly. We call attention to the resemblance between figure 12–1 and figure 5–2, the diagram of the organization as a cybernetic system. As Dornbusch and I note:

> In our view, the melding of the traditional sociological approaches to the study of power and authority with the newer approaches to control developed by the systems analysts is one of the strengths of this model. (Dornbusch and Scott, 1975: 144)

Following a review of studies conducted on performance evaluation systems in organizations, Haberstroh draws two major conclusions:

> First, performance reporting is omnipresent and necessarily so. Second, almost every individual instance of performance reporting has something wrong with it. (Haberstroh, 1965: 1182)

Our own studies lead us to embrace both conclusions. Most organizations do attempt to monitor in some manner the performance of their participants. Of the many types of organizations examined by our surveys—hospitals, schools, electronics firms, basic research agencies, universities, Catholic parishes—all had developed formal, authorized systems of performance evaluation. (The most elaborate system of performance evaluation was found in connection with the management of a college football team!) We also found problems or deficiencies in all of the control systems examined. Indeed, the major portion of our research is devoted to the development and testing of a series of propositions relating incompatibility—problems or inadequacies in existing authority systems—to instability—attempts to change these systems (Dornbusch and Scott, 1975: 243–331).

The problems of interpersonal control systems based on performance evaluations are particularly acute under conditions of excessive task complexity and interdependence, lack of goal clarity, and high uncertainty. The more difficult it is to determine whose performance has contributed to a particular outcome, or to determine what sort of outcome is desired, or to predict how a given desired outcome may be accomplished, the more difficult it is to design an adequate system of control that bases sanctions on performance. Under such conditions every component of the evaluation process becomes highly problematic (see Dornbusch and Scott, 1975: 145–62). Nevertheless, as described in previous chapters, a number of contemporary organizations face precisely these conditions. How do they deal with the need for control?

The Authority of Goals

We don't know the answer to the question just posed, but we may know where to look for it—or at least for one kind of answer. Several analysts appear to be converging on a rather similar formulation. Each, of course, uses slightly different language, but the central message appears to be that a new basis of authority is not to be found in the rules or the offices but in the goals of the organization. We will briefly review several versions of this emerging thesis.

Satow (1975), following the suggestion of Willer (1967), argues that it is possible to construct a fourth type of authority by extending Weber's arguments. Weber (1947 tr.), in addition to describing legal, traditional, and charismatic norms that legitimate social action, suggested a fourth type of normative belief system: value rationality, or action that is oriented toward the realization of an absolute goal. Satow suggests that this belief system can support a different type of authority system in which:

> Obedience is given to an ideology; that is, to ideological norms rather than formal laws or rules. Those in authority are therefore obliged to obey the norms in giving orders and the content of the orders are legitimized by their relationship to the goals of the ideology. (Satow, 1975: 527)

Satow proposes that professional organizations—in particular, autonomous professional organizations—represent an important instance of a contemporary organizational form in which the primary belief system legitimating the structure of decision making and power is commitment to a set of generalized, professionally defined goals. Such goals take on a moral character. She also suggests that in its pure form "a value-rational orientation involves commitment to an absolute goal regardless of consequences to the organization" (Satow, 1975: 528). This helps to account for one of the primary structural features of professional organizations: the existence of an administrative structure, differentiated from the professional staff, charged with the responsibility of maintaining the organization.

Quite a different type of organization is singled out by Rothschild-Whitt (1979), who focuses on collectivist organizations: various types of alternative organizations, such as free medical clinics, free schools, and cooperatives, which challenge established forms. Such organizations vary from their more conventional counterparts in a number of ways, but Rothschild-Whitt argues that their most critical differentiating feature relates to the basis of authority:

> The collectivist-democratic organization rejects rational-bureaucratic justifications for authority. Here authority resides not in the individual, whether on the basis of incumbency in office *or* expertise, but in the collectivity as a whole. (Rothschild-Whitt, 1979: 511–12)

Decisions are arrived at through a consensus process that emphasizes that their legitimacy depends on the extent to which they represent the will or goals of the organization as a whole. Thus:

> Only decisions which appear to carry the consensus of the group behind them, carry the weight of moral authority. Only these decisions, changing as they might with the ebb and flow of sentiments in the group, are taken as binding and legitimate. (Ibid., p. 512)

Although these collectivist, alternative organizations may seem remote from the autonomous professional systems and, indeed, in many instances are created to challenge these "elitist" institutions, both contain sets of participants who are committed to the pursuit of a value "for its own sake" and who elevate substantive value commitments over procedural, instrumental norms (Ibid., pp. 509–10).

Ouchi (1980) follows a different path to arrive at a similar conclusion. He reviews with approval Williamson's framework comparing markets and hierarchies (see chapter 7) but goes on to explore the inadequacies of hierarchies for controlling highly uncertain and interdependent work, such as that currently carried on in high technology industries. Ouchi argues that the costs of monitoring these complex transactions by conventional organizational authority systems is prohibitive and will increasingly give rise to "organizational failures" and the search for alternative approaches to control. One alternative emphasizes the importance of goal congruity among organizational participants and gives rise to a "clan" type of structure. As noted in chapter 7, Ouchi's concept of clan includes groups that may or may not be linked by kinship ties but are based on common internalized goals and strong feelings of solidarity. Examples include professional occupations, some types of labor unions, certain ethnic groups (see Light, 1972), Japanese organizations which stress lifetime commitment of employees (see Abegglen, 1958; Dore, 1973), and some types of American corporations that pursue policies of long-term employment, slow and diffuse evaluation and promotion, holistic concern for participants, and consensual decision making (see Ouchi and Jaeger, 1978). Ouchi stresses the role of common, internalized goals as the basis for control in these systems:

> Common values and beliefs provide the harmony of interests that erase the possibility of opportunistic behavior. If all members of the organization have been exposed to an apprenticeship or other socialization period, then they will share personal goals that are compatible with the goals of the organization. In this condition, auditing of performance is unnecessary except for educational purposes, since no member will attempt to depart from organizational goals. (Ouchi, 1980: 138)

As a final example of this emerging point of view, Swanson argues that "management by objectives" is becoming the new basis for order and authority in postindustrial organizations.

> Size, complexity, and competitive pressures favor not only management by objectives but management solely for the sake of objectives. Everything is considered of value only for its contribution to the attaining of objectives. Everything is subject to being discarded or changed in the interest of attaining objectives. This includes the way in which an organization is arranged to conduct its work, the kind of personnel it hires and retains, the sort of skills and personalities it finds appropriate, the criteria for judging a performance to be good, and all other aspects of its activities. When this approach is rigorously pursued, nothing but a handful of objectives is taken as given and even these are constantly reexamined in a search for their essence. (Swanson, 1980)

As should be clear from this statement, Swanson is not referring to the relatively narrow set of prescriptions for organizational design formulated by Odione (1965), but to a broad group of innovations emphasizing the overriding importance of objectives. These include all attempts to de-emphasize structural rigidities and status distinctions as well as efforts to incorporate more facets of the person in the work role, a stress on participative management and collective decision making, on spontaneity and authenticity, and the use of outside consultants to probe and correct misunderstandings and myopic visions of the future. Swanson argues that only a shared set of objectives can provide an adequate framework for the collaboration of the multiple specialists — each with their own base of expertise and their own claim or autonomy in the selection of means—on which the contemporary organization is dependent. Common goals can also provide a sense of continuity and unity to counteract the structural flux as participants shift from one task group to another and from one temporary system to the next.

To repeat, we are struck by the similarity in conclusions reached by this rather diverse set of analysts.[5] We must point out that most of the work is rather speculative and that the types of organizations cited as examples remain either on the fringe—collectivist organizations—or in the minority—high technology industrial and professional organizations. Nevertheless, the ideas seem to us intriguing, and although the organizations described are currently a small subset, they may embody the future as we move into the postindustrial era.

Summary

Goals are put to many uses by organizational participants. They serve cognitive functions, guiding the selection of alternative courses of action; they have cathectic properties, serving as a source of identification and commitment for participants and external constituencies; they provide present justifications for actions taken in the past; they provide criteria for the evaluation of performances, participants, and programs of action; and under some conditions, they provide ideological guidance for the contributions of participants. Moreover, individual participants bring their own private goals or motives with them into the organization, and these rarely coincide with those of the organization.

The concept of a dominant coalition that determines goals in organizations solves some of the mysteries of goal setting. It helps to avoid reification of the organization as a single purposeful actor but at the same time allows the organization's goals or preference structures to differ from those of all its human agents. The concept allows for the possibility that individuals, groups, and participants have different interests and agendas and indicates how, through negotiation and the making of side-payments, bargains are struck and a basis for common action developed. The concept of dominant coalitions also reminds us that individual participants do not have equal power in decision making and that the preferences and interests of some will receive more attention than those of others. Although individuals and groups bring preferences and interests with them into the organization, organizations are more

---

[5]Some of these analysts argue that such changes have important implications not only for the authority system of the organizations but for the individual participants as well. These arguments will be reviewed in the following chapter.

than a setting where existing interests come together: they are places where new interests are created.

The size and shape of the dominant coalition changes over time in response to the changing external conditions to which the organization must adapt. As new sources of uncertainty and challenge develop in its environment, the organization creates offices to deal with them. Officers who can successfully cope with such problems may be expected to acquire power within the organization since others are dependent on them for critical services. As environments become more complex and turbulent, the dominant coalition grows in size, and its shape changes to incorporate more and different specialists capable of managing one or another boundary problem. And as the composition of the membership of the dominant coalition undergoes change, the goals of the organization also change, reflecting these shifts in power.

Some organizations lack clear goals or efficacious technologies. Such conditions are not very hospitable to the formation and maintenance of organizations, but when they exist several alternative strategies are possible. Organizations may suffer and hope for the millennium, awaiting the appearance of a charismatic leader who will clarify ends and supply means. They may attune themselves to high ambiguity, recognizing that almost-random connections among streams of problems, participants, and solutions will produce some decisions. Some will seek to create institutionalized organizations in which meaning and matter are supplied by rationalized myths. And still others may settle for consensus on proximal or procedural goals that provide a stable framework within which substantive differences may coexist.

All collectivities control their members, but some distinctive control arrangements are to be found in organizations. Power is the potential for influence based on sanctioning ability, and authority is normatively regulated power. In informal groups authority tends to exist as endorsed power—power constrained by norms enforced by subordinates—but in formal organizations authority primarily exists as authorized power—power circumscribed and supported by norms enforced by officers superior to the power wielder. Most organizations attempt to regulate the contributions of participants by developing evaluation systems that link performances to organizational sanctions. Although such control systems are ubiquitous, they are often cumbersome and complex, and many are flawed. This is particularly so as the goals pursued by organizations and the tasks allocated to participants become increasingly difficult in definition and uncertain in performance. In some types of organizations, control may reside more in consensually defined—and redefined—goals than in personal or position-based control systems.

Part Four

ORGANIZATIONS AND SOCIETY

We have emphasized throughout this volume that organizations are only subsystems of larger social systems: they are connected in numerous and vital ways to encompassing societal systems. What differentiates the focus of this part from previous chapters is not a concern with these connecting links but a shift in reference. Thus far, the organization itself has served as the primary point of reference. We have explored goals, structures, technologies, and participants from the standpoint of what they can reveal about the system of which they are component parts. Now we adopt a different reference: that of the host society. We ask in these two concluding chapters what organizations can do to and for the societies that support them. We examine unintended as well as intended effects.

Chapter 13 explores some of the problems and dangers associated with the operation and growth of organizations. In particular, we focus on power and its potential misuse. Organizations generate power as a consequence of their functioning. Previous chapters have examined how power can be employed in the service of organizational goals—whether those goals be to produce certain outputs or to assure the survival of the organization. Chapter 13 investigates the side effects of the power that is generated—its unanticipated consequences for both internal participants and external publics. As might be imagined, these are issues primarily raised by the natural system perspective on the functioning of organizations.

From the rational system perspective, organizations are instruments for the attainment of goals. We have asked numerous questions about the implications of this view for the organization. However, a crucial question of concern to the larger society within which they operate is how effective and efficient organizations are in meeting their goals. Are they sufficiently adept in their functions—in achieving their respective goals—that they merit social support in spite of problems they raise? Although the question of effectiveness is most readily addressed from the rational system perspective, we shall quickly discover that additional and different questions regarding organizational effectiveness are raised by natural and open systems points of view. These queries and issues are addressed in chapter 14.

chapter 13

Organizational Pathologies

*Bureaucracy has been and is a power
instrument of the first order. . . . The
individual bureaucrat cannot squirm out of the
apparatus in which he is harnessed. . . . In the
great majority of cases, he is only a single cog
in an ever-moving mechanism which prescribes
to him an essentially fixed route of march. . . .*

*The ruled, for their part, cannot dispense with
or replace the bureaucratic apparatus of
authority once it exists. For this bureaucracy
rests upon expert training, a functional
specialization of work, and an attitude set for
habitual and virtuoso-like mastery of single,
yet methodically integrated functions. . . . This
holds for public administration as well as for
private economic management. More and more
the material fate of the masses depends upon
the steady and correct functioning of the
increasingly bureaucratic organizations of
private capitalism. The idea of eliminating
these organizations becomes more and more
utopian.*

MAX WEBER (1947 tr.)

Weber was aware of the use and the possible
misuse of power in modern organizations. Inappropriate applications can
occur both internally, when participants are exploited or stunted or in other
ways damaged by their involvement, and externally, when publics who rely on
organizations for goods and services find that organizations are unresponsive
to their needs or interests. Internal problems may appear to be an issue only
for the specific individuals involved, but a moment's reflection will convince
us that damage done to organizational participants is a social, and not simply

a personal, problem. As has been noted, individuals are only partially involved in any given organization: injury inflicted on participants in one setting may be expected to affect their performance in others. Two types of problems for individual participants are frequently cited: the problem of alienation and that of overconformity or ritualism. Both are examined in the first section of this chapter.

Turning to problems involving publics, we will first examine the issue of responsiveness. What can be done to ensure that organizations are attentive to the needs and interests of external constituencies? This is a particularly acute problem in connection with public organizations, which are expected to be primarily oriented to public interests, but is by no means restricted to them. We also examine the broader issue of corporate versus individual interests, which raises more general questions about the distribution and use of power in contemporary society.

Throughout this chapter, we endeavor to show that it is not necessary to develop new concepts or arguments to explain organizational pathologies. There is a close correspondence between many of the best and the worst features of organizations. In some cases, similar processes, with slight variations, produce both the organization's strengths and its weaknesses. In other cases, the organizations's strengths *are* its weaknesses, but viewed from a different perspective.

Problems for Participants

ALIENATION

Much time and attention has been devoted over the years to attempting to ascertain the impact of organizations on the personal characteristics of their participants. There are many claims and considerable evidence regarding these effects—and most of them are conflicting! At least since the time of Adam Smith and down to the present, observers have pointed to the debilitating consequences of organizational involvement, in particular, employment, for individual participants. These destructive processes are often summarized under the concept of alienation—a concept with enough facets and varied interpretations to serve as an adequate umbrella under which to gather a quite varied set of criticisms.

Even Marx, who more than any other theorist called attention to the importance of alienation of workers, identified several possible forms of alienation (see Marx, 1963 tr.; Faunce, 1968). A worker may be alienated from the *product* of his labor. Labor gives value to the objects it creates, but as a worker loses control over his product, it comes to exist "independently, outside himself, and alien to him, and . . . stands opposed to him as an autonomous power" (Marx, 1963 tr.: 122–23). Workers can also be alienated from the *process* of production. This occurs to the extent that

> the work is external to the worker, that it is not part of his nature; and that, consequently, he does not fulfil himself in his work but denies himself, has a feeling of misery rather than well-being, does not develop freely his mental and physical energies but is physically exhausted and mentally debased. . . . His work is not voluntary but imposed, forced labor. (Marx, 1963 tr.: 124–25)

As a consequence of the first two processes, man becomes alienated from his *fellow men.* Marx explains:

> The alien being to whom labour and the product of labour belong, to whose service labour is devoted, and to whose enjoyment the product of labour goes, can only be man himself. If the product of labour does not belong to the worker, but confronts him as an alien power, this can only be because it belongs to a man other than the worker. (Ibid., p. 130)

Enter, the capitalist. And enter the argument that it is not work that alienates, but exploitation of workers by the misuse of power.

Before turning to some evidence regarding the pervasiveness and distribution of alienation, a second influential formulation deserves mention. Like Marx, Seeman (1959; 1975) views alienation as a multifaceted concept, identifying six varieties: (1) powerlessness—the sense of little control over events; (2) meaninglessness—the sense of incomprehensibility of personal and social affairs; (3) normlessness—commitment to socially unapproved means for the achievement of goals; (4) cultural estrangement—rejection of commonly held values and standards; (5) self-estrangement—engagement in activities that are not intrinsically rewarding; and (6) social isolation—the sense of exclusion or rejection. Seeman has argued that powerlessness and self-estrangement are the two types of alienation that have most meaning in the work place; and these seem most consistent with Marx's distinctions. A great many measures including several multiple-item scales have been developed to assess one or the other of these dimensions (see Seeman, 1975), most of them treating these conditions as internal, social-psychological states. Israel (1971) has taken strong exception to this practice, insisting that alienation is more accurately and usefully viewed as an objective condition of the social structure, not a subjective attitude or disposition. Individuals may not be able to recognize that they are alienated: sentiments may not accurately reflect circumstances.

In spite of Israel's concerns, most empirical studies relating to alienation are based on data obtained from individual respondents who report their feelings or attitudes—for example, work satisfaction and dissatisfaction, levels of interest or commitment—or their behavior—for example, turnover, absenteeism, health and mental health symptoms. Most surveys conducted in this country over the past 40 years report: (1) generally high levels of worker satisfaction and morale but (2) large variation in satisfaction and symptoms across differing occupational strata and work situations.[1] These surveys also show that higher satisfaction tends to be associated with such factors as intrinsic interest of the work, level of control, level of pay and economic security, and opportunities for social interaction (see Blauner, 1960; Sheppard and Herrick, 1972; Special Task Force, 1973).

Such clear and expected results do not hold up very well in more detailed and limited investigations of the relation between job characteristics and worker attitudes. For example, Turner and Lawrence (1965) developed an index to measure such factors as job variety, autonomy, interaction, knowledge and skills required, and responsibility and applied it to 47 different factory jobs. Their expectation that employees in more challenging and complex jobs would exhibit higher satisfaction and lower absenteeism was not fully supported: these relations appeared to be mediated by worker characteristics, in particular, differences in cultural backgrounds. Similarly, Hackman and Lawler (1971) report positive but relatively modest associations of such job factors as autonomy, variety, intrinsic meaningfulness, and feedback with individual reports of overall satisfaction. Such studies have led these and other analysts to conclude that there is no simple and direct correspondence between job characteristics and individual reactions; these relations are influenced by individual values and dispositions. For example, whether or not a job that offers variety and challenge is found to be satisfying depends on whether the person in that position values variety and challenge—whether the person has a "need" for such experiences[2] (see also Hulin and Blood, 1968; Lichtman and Hunt, 1971). However, such "need-satisfaction" models—which allow individual needs to mediate between job characteristics and individual responses—have been challenged by Salancik and Pfeffer (1977) on both theoretical and empirical grounds. Using arguments that rely heavily on a more complex and loosely coupled theoretical model, they criticize:

- the assumption of one-way causality: that job characteristics create attitudes rather than allowing for the possibility that attitudes lead to the attribution of characteristics to jobs

[1]Such survey results are criticized on many grounds, some of which have already been indicated. Critics note their emphasis on subjective as compared to objective measures, their stress on attitudes rather than behaviors, the charge that questions regarding satisfaction may be meaningless to workers lacking realistic alternatives, and that measures of satisfaction reflect many "extrinsic" aspects of the job having no relation to the nature of the work itself (see Bell, 1960; Israel, 1971).

[2]Earlier formulations (for example, Maslow, 1954; Argyris, 1957) also posit individual needs but assume that they are rather invariant across participants.

• the presumption of a tight connection between an individual's attitudes and his or her behavior

• the assumption that individual needs are relatively stable over time and across situations

• the assumption that job characteristics are "realities in the environment" rather than socially constructed phenomena

Moreover, they assert that the predictions developed on the basis of the need-satisfaction model are so diffuse and varied that nearly every possible pattern of results appears consistent with them; that is, they are virtually impossible to refute.

A number of analysts have claimed that the impact of organizations on their participants extends far beyond the walls of the organization itself. Argyris (1957; 1973) summarizes several studies that indicate that workers' experience of "constraint and isolation" on the job carries over into their free time with such workers being less involved in organized leisure-time, community, or political activities. Kanter (1977b) reviews a number of studies that suggest that both men's and women's occupational experiences have important implications for their family roles. She asserts that these studies contradict the "myth of separate worlds" perpetuated by companies who do not wish to assume responsibility for the effects of their policies and practices on the "personal" lives of their employees (and also by the habits of social scientists who tend to specialize in studying organizations or families but not their interdependence). Similarly, Ouchi argues that employing organizations have a vested interest in failing to recognize their psychological casualties:

> The costs of psychological failure are not borne entirely by the firm, but rather are externalized to the society generally. That is, employees who reach the point of emotional disability, who become unsatisfactory workers, are the first to be laid off during depressions or, in extreme cases, are fired. The firm which has "used up" people emotionally does not have to face the cost of restoring them. In much the same manner that firms were able until recently to pollute the air and the water without paying the costs of using up these resources, they continue to be able to pollute our mental health with impunity. (Ouchi, 1979: 36–37)

And Kanter concludes that "a major social welfare issue of the decades to come" is likely to be focused on the question: "Can organizations more fully and responsibly take into account their inevitable interface with the personal lives of their participants?" (1977b: 89). Our own view is much closer to that of Seeman, whose survey of research on alienation leads him to conclude:

> Given the tendency to assume that work is of primary importance in defining the self and in connecting the individual with the larger society, and given the

centrality of work in the Marxian sources on alienation, it seems surprising how limited the demonstration has actually been concerning this purported generalization (from the job proper to the extra-job milieu) of alienated labor. (Seeman, 1975: 108)

That is, we do not question the importance of the issues raised, but only the quality of the evidence produced to this point.

We are most concerned, however, with one of the proposed solutions for dealing with the problem of alienation.[3] This solution, endorsed by a long and distinguished list of social analysts, is that organizations should absorb more aspects of the personalities of their participants, that they should become the primary focus of social integration, personal identity, and meaning, that they should function as the new communities, or Gemeinschaften, of modern society. From Saint-Simon (1952 tr.) and Durkheim (1949 tr.) through Barnard (1938) and Mayo (1945) to Selznick (1957) and Ouchi and Johnson (1978), organization theorists have looked to production organizations as a primary source of social integration in a social structure that is judged to be increasingly anomic and disorganized. Wolin calls attention to the underlying conservative and elitist stance that nurtures this point of view:

> The fondness for large scale organization displayed by contemporary writers largely stems from anxieties provoked by the emergence of the mass. They see organizations as mediating institutions, shaping disoriented individuals to socially useful behavior and endowing them with a desperately needed sense of values. These large entities supply the stabilizing centers, which not only integrate and structure the amorphous masses, but control them as well. (Wolin, 1960: 427)

That organizations have some impact on the personal characteristics and the mental health of their participants we do not dispute. That these effects often are detrimental to participants and, hence, to the larger society, is a hypothesis that calls for more investigation. But that organizations should be viewed as the principal centers of moral and social integration in modern society we cannot accept.

As indicated in chapter 7, we see the emergence of organizations as special-purpose systems as being closely associated with the emergence of the ideology of individualism, including the doctrine of natural rights and the value of individual freedom. The development of the rational-legal out of the patrimonial forms, to use Weber's terms, signals the emergence of norms and struc-

---

[3]A number of fairly specific attempted solutions to alienation, including job enlargement and increased participation of workers in decisions that affect them, have already been described (see chapter 4). In our opinion, there is not strong evidence to support the efficacy of these approaches, and their financial costs are often underestimated (see Strauss, 1963), but they appear to be generally beneficial to participants, and they do not pose serious dangers to the larger society.

tures that place restrictions on the hierarchy of the organization and reduces the leverage of the organization in relation to the individual. We endorse these developments and view with alarm proposals to expand the power and influence of organizations over individuals. This argument will be amplified at the end of this chapter.

OVERCONFORMITY

In his justly famous essay on "Bureaucratic Structure and Personality," Merton calls attention to a set of processes by which "the very elements which conduce toward efficiency in general produce inefficiency in specific instances" (1957: 200). He argues that structural devices established to ensure reliability and adequacy of performance—an emphasis on rules, discipline, graded career —can "also lead to an over-concern with strict adherence to regulations which induces timidity, conservatism, and technicism" (Ibid., p. 201). Merton continues:

> Adherence to the rules, originally conceived as a means, becomes transformed into an end-in-itself; there occurs the familiar process of *displacement of goals* whereby an instrumental value becomes a terminal value. (Ibid., p. 199)

Other possible sources of goal displacement are described by natural system analysts such as Selznick (1949) and by Dalton (1959) who emphasize the commitments individuals develop to their tools, working arrangements, procedures, and work groups (see chapter 4). Rational system analysts March and Simon (1958: 150–58) examine the manner in which means-ends chains designed to support rationality of decision making (see chapters 3 and 5) also foster goal displacement, which they refer to as "sub-goal formation." They point out that cognitive processes operating at the individual, the group, and the organizational levels all contribute to these developments, supplementing the cathectic processes emphasized by Merton, Selznick, and Dalton. Since goals are subdivided and factored among different individuals and groups, goal displacement is encouraged by selective perception and attention processes among individuals, the selective content of in-group communication, and the selective exposure to information occasioned by the division of labor within the larger organization. Goals assigned to individuals and groups as means are viewed as ends in themselves. Scientists in R & D units emphasize creativity without regard to feasibility; manufacturing units emphasize producibility without attention to marketability, and so on.

If we take a somewhat larger view, however, we will see that goal displacement is not confined to organizations but is quite widespread in modern societies. Indeed, we would argue that it is synonymous with differentiation of the social structure and elaboration of the cultural system. As societies and cultures develop, activities formerly regarded as means become ends in themselves: eating becomes dining; buildings and garments needed for protection from the elements take on symbolic importance and give rise to architecture and to fashion; sexual relations intended "by Nature" as a means to the survival of the species become a terminal value, elaborated in romantic love and sex as play. The myriad occupations that emerge in modern societies may be viewed as instances of means transformed into ends: scientists pursue truth for its own sake; physicians prolong life as an ultimate value; and teachers devote their lives to socialization of the young. And we have noted, time and again, that the goals of organizations can be viewed only as specialized functions or means from the perspective of the larger society.

Once we realize that goal displacement is the hallmark of any advanced civilization, it seems unfair and somewhat disingenuous to single out bureaucrats and accuse them of unique vices. They are subject to a process in which we all participate.

It appears to us that the basis for concern is not the displacement of ends by means but the continued pursuit of means that have somehow become disconnected from, or are at odds with, the ends they were designed to serve. In times of rapid change, we can easily imagine such dislocations becoming more common: ultimate goals change, but it is difficult to rapidly design and implement necessary adjustments down the chains of means-ends connections. Efforts to modify organizational structures enabling them to process information more rapidly—augmenting the hierarchy and developing lateral connections (see chapter 10)—may be interpreted as attempts to shorten and improve the consistency of these chains. Similarly, emphasizing the overriding importance of collectively valued goals as a basis for decision making and action provides another approach to counteracting the disassociation of subgoals and goals (see chapter 12).

Returning to the narrower topic of rigidity or overconformity, results from two large surveys suggest that rather than increasing rigidity, participation in organizations encourages individual flexibility and openness to new ideas. The first study, conducted by Inkeles (1969) reports the results of a cross-national survey of 1,000 men each from six developing societies. The study identified a series of interrelated attitudes labeled "modernity," which included such attitudes as openness to new experiences, assertion of increasing independence from the authority of traditional figures, abandonment of passivity and fatalism, interest in planning and punctuality, and an interest in political issues and in keeping abreast of the news. The two most important influences on individuals associated with their development of "modern" attitudes were school attendance and work in a factory. On the importance of education, Inkeles comments:

These effects of the school, I believe, reside not mainly in its formal, explicit, self-conscious pedagogic activity, but rather are inherent in the school as an *organization*.... It teaches ways of orienting oneself toward others, and of conducting oneself, which could have important bearings on the performance of one's adult roles in the structure of modern society. (Inkeles, 1969: 213)

And as for the factory experience:

Just as we view the school as communicating lessons beyond reading and arith-
metic, so we thought of the factory as training men in more than the minimal
lessons of technology and skills necessary to industrial production. We conceived
of the factory as an organization serving as a general school in attitudes, values,
and ways of behaving which are more adaptive for life in a modern society. (Ibid.)

Inkeles found organizational participation to be a liberating, consciousness-expanding experience for individuals in developing societies.

Kohn (1971) used survey data from a sample of over 3,000 men employed in a variety of civilian occupations to examine the effect of bureaucratic employment on individual attitudes. Characteristics of employment settings were measured simply in terms of the number of levels of supervision and the size of the organization; individual attitudes were assessed in terms of three dimensions: (1) emphasis placed on conformity or respectability; (2) intolerance or rigid conformity and resistance to change; and (3) intellectual rigidity. The resulting associations were not particularly strong but were consistent. Kohn found that:

Men who work in bureaucratic firms or organizations tend to value, not conformity, but self-direction. They are more open-minded, have more personally
responsible standards of morality, and are more receptive to change than are men
who work in nonbureaucratic organizations. They show greater flexibility in
dealing both with perceptual and with ideational problems. (Kohn, 1971: 465)

Controlling for educational differences reduced but did not eliminate the positive relation between organizational employment and individual flexibility. The data also suggest that such "bureaucratic" factors as greater job security, somewhat higher levels of income, and substantively more complex work contributed to these attitudinal differences.[4] Like Inkeles, Kohn emphasizes the liberalizing effects of organizational involvement on individual participants.

[4]This latter argument relating complexity of work to psychological functioning is pursued in Kohn and Schooler (1973) where it is shown that although there is a reciprocal relation between substantive complexity of work and intellectual flexibility of the performer, the job characteristics have a stronger effect on the person's psychological functioning than the reverse.

Lest we begin to feel overly sanguine at this point, we need only to confront Milgram's (1973; 1974) series of experiments on conformity. Milgram's design called for a three-person situation in which a scientist-teacher is assisted by a second person in attempting to teach a student a series of word pairs. The experiment is described as examining the effects of punishment on learning; and it is the task of the assistant to administer punishments—electrical shocks —to the student when he or she gives an incorrect answer. Intensity of the shocks administered increases systematically throughout the experiment, from a low of 15 volts to a maximum of 450 volts: the upper end of the scale on the generator is labeled "Extreme Intensity/Shock; Danger, Severe Shock"; and the final position, "XXX." In reality, the assistant is the true subject of the experiment; both the teacher and the student are actors, and no real shocks are administered. The real purpose of the study is to determine how much (apparent) pain one individual will inflict on another when ordered to do so.

The results are unsettling, to say the least. Across a wide variety of types of subjects—from Yale undergraduates to adult professionals and blue-collar workers to individuals from many different countries—most of the subjects, approximately 60 percent overall, conformed to the demands of the scientist and administered electrical shock treatments at the highest levels possible to the "student." The possibility that all these subjects were sadists was ruled out: left to their own devices with no instruction as to "appropriate" shock levels from the scientist, the great majority of subjects administered very low, apparently painless, shocks to subjects.

On examination, the experimental setting is a powerful one: many factors induce conformity. The scientist-teacher enjoys the authority of office as well as of expertise. The setting—a university laboratory—exudes propriety and legitimacy. The subject is a temporary, short-term assistant—not ostensibly the focus of the study but only a supportive or auxiliary figure. To disrupt the experiment by refusing to carry out orders is, apparently, a difficult thing to do. In authority structures, the orientation tends to be directed upward. As Milgram notes:

> the person feels responsible *to* the authority directing him but feels no responsibility *for* the content of the actions that the authority prescribes. Morality does not disappear—it acquires a radically different focus: the subordinate person feels shame or pride depending on how adequately he has performed the actions called for by authority. (Milgram, 1973: 77)

Other experimental variations suggest factors that affect the level of conformity observed. Distance from the punitive action affected conformity: assistants who were asked to force the subject's hand down on an electric plate were less likely to conform than those who simply selected the shock level and pulled a switch; and assistants who were asked only to read the word list were more likely to conform than those that were more directly involved in administering the punishment. Pertaining to this latter group, Milgram observes:

> Predictably, they excused their behavior by saying that the responsibility belonged to the man who actually pulled the switch. This may illustrate a dangerously typical arrangement in a complex society: it is easy to ignore responsibility when one is only an intermediate link in a chain of action. (Ibid.)

The terrible consequences that may be associated with "simply following orders" are graphically illustrated by the behavior of officials in Hitler's death camps. It is to stress such simple bases for these heinous crimes that Arendt (1963) subtitles her analysis of the actions of Adolf Eichmann, chief executor of Hitler's "final solution": "A Report on the Banality of Evil."

While we would not presume to entirely account for the complex problem of overconformity in organizations, one variable of apparent importance can be singled out: insecurity or uncertainty. Recall that Kohn reported that greater job security of workers was associated with higher flexibility and less resistance to change. We would argue that Milgram's experimental subjects were highly insecure, recognizing that they were amateur, temporary contributors to a professional, ongoing, scientific study. And numerous analysts (Arendt, 1951; Neumann, 1942) have emphasized that totalitarian states such as Nazi Germany are characterized by duplications of office, divisions of power between state and party, and arbitrary acts by charismatic leaders, so that the entire system creates great anxiety and insecurity among its office holders. Two case studies of organizations—Blau's (1955) study of a law enforcement agency and Kanter's (1977a) study of a large industrial corporation—lend support to this thesis. Blau reports that the least secure agents were the most resistant to change and the most susceptible to ritualistic adherence to existing procedures. And Kanter asserts that most of the pressures for conformity in business corporations can be attributed to uncertainty. Writing of managers, for example, Kanter asserts:

> It is the uncertainty quotient in managerial work, as it has come to be defined in the large modern corporation, that causes management to become so socially restricting: to develop tight inner circles excluding social strangers; to keep control in the hands of socially homogeneous peers; to stress conformity and insist upon a diffuse, unbounded loyalty; and to prefer ease of communication and thus social certainty over the strains of dealing with people who are "different." (Kanter, 1977a: 49)

Finally, an experiment by Fox and Staw (1979) reports that subjects who were told that their assignment to an office was temporary and dependent on the quality of their performance were more likely to rigidly adhere to an earlier poor decision than were subjects told that they had permanent assignments. Similarly, the more resistance a decision encountered, the more likely subjects were to reaffirm them. Fox and Staw summarize and generalize from their series of experiments:

> The results demonstrate the effect of political vulnerability upon commitment to a course of action. When an administrator is worried about keeping his job or fending off critics within an organization, he is less likely to be flexible in his decision making. Thus, the trapped administrator can be thought of as one who is most likely to increase rather than decrease his commitment to a previously chosen policy and most likely to become inflexible in his defense of such positions. (Fox and Staw, 1979: 465)

Insecurity and uncertainty appear to produce overconformity and rigidity.

UNCERTAINTY, ALIENATION, AND OVERCONFORMITY

Uncertainty again! We have asked this concept to bear a heavy burden for us throughout this volume. Uncertainty is the source of variety and of power, and it is the enemy of rationality and planning. Too much uncertainty can cause individuals to seek protection in ritualism and oversimplification of alternatives; too little uncertainty can cause individuals to wither in boredom and alienation.

Organizations and individuals are forever seeking to reduce uncertainty. Organizations attempt to buffer it out; and individuals are always programming themselves and others "out of a challenging and novel situation, and then losing interest" (Leavitt, 1964: 546). Fortunately for both, however, they never completely succeed. Uncertainty floods over the barriers bringing variety and challenge. And, as Goldner observes:

> What starts out as a search for ways to reduce problems and uncertainties in organizations leads ... to the increase of other uncertainties. Rationalization sows the seeds of increased complexity and hence of pressures for yet new forms of rationalization. (Goldner, 1970: 97–98)

How to avoid levels of uncertainty that are too high or too low and to seek out levels that are "just right" in their mix of security and stimulation—this is a central challenge confronting all organizations and all participants within them.

Problems for Publics

All organizations must provide benefits to external publics—customers, clients, citizens—as a condition for their continued existence. The contributions required from these publics vary according to the nature of the organization but may involve direct payments for products or services received, indirect support in the form of taxes, and normative support in the form of good will and legitimacy. A concern with organizational responsiveness to the demands of external publics is most often raised in connection with public organizations, since in this type of organization the public is expected to be the primary beneficiary of the organization's activities. However, problems can also develop in the relations between publics and organizations in the private sector. We will examine both situations.

Public Sector Organizations   Weber, in company with many other past and present political analysts, believed that the most serious challenge facing contemporary societies was to maintain control over the expanding state bureaucracies. Numerous observers before Weber, including Mill, Bagehot, Le Play, and Mosca, noted the growth in numbers and power of paid officials in governmental positions, but Weber's analyses provide the most complete and systematic conceptualization of this major change in governmental systems (see Albrow, 1970). Unlike some of the previous critics, Weber insisted that the primary problem associated with the growth of bureaucracy was not that of inefficiency and mismanagement. Indeed, in comparison with earlier administrative forms, Weber cogently argued that the bureaucratic structures were highly efficient and reliable (see chapters 2 and 3). But for Weber, these characteristics—these administrative virtues—also constituted their most serious threat.[5] Accompanying increased bureaucratization was the strong likelihood of growth in the power of public officials. Weber argued:

> Under normal conditions, the power position of a fully developed bureaucracy is always overpowering. The "political master" finds himself in the position of the "dilettante" who stands opposite the "expert," facing the trained official who

[5]Weber was not alone in admitting the likely efficiency of the bureaucracy but expressing reservations about the use of this instrument. Thus, in one of his celebrated essays on bureaucracy, the poet Ezra Pound responds to the claim that bureaucrats are active and attentive to their duty by noting: "the idea of activity as a merit is, when applied to bureaucrats, as deadly as the idea of activity among tuberculous bacillae" (1973: 219)

stands within the management of administration. This holds whether the "master" whom the bureaucracy serves is a "people" . . . or a parliament. . . . It holds whether the master is an aristocratic, collegiate body, legally or actually based on self-recruitment, or whether he is a popularly elected president, a hereditary and "absolute" or a "constitutional" monarch. (Weber, 1946 tr.: 232–33)

Weber's explanation for this development was quite straightforward: "More and more the specialized knowledge of the expert became the foundation for the power position of the officeholder" (1946 tr.: 235). Recall in this connection Weber's description of the transition from patrimonial to bureaucratic administrative forms (see chapter 3). As a ruler's territory increased, it would become more necessary to decentralize operations and to delegate authority to members of the administrative staff. The division of labor among the staff members becomes more fixed; specialized competence of officers increases and, at the same time, the ruler's ability to oversee each operation is reduced. Relative to the ruler, each staff member becomes more knowledgeable in each specific area of operation. The staff also becomes more aware of themselves as a distinct social group with common interests. We have, in brief, a classic instance of a shift in power-dependence relations: each subordinate is individually less powerful than the ruler; but collectively they have become more powerful and, by acting in concert, can impose conditions on the ruler's exercise of power (see chapter 12). These constraints on the ruler's power, which developed slowly and haltingly over long periods of time, include such bureaucratic "safeguards" as civil service commissions and elaborate codes of conduct. Rosenberg has described the effects of these developments in his analysis of the evolution of the Prussian state:

> The raising of standardized prerequisites for admission had a profound effect upon the bureaucracy as a social elite and as a political group. Whatever the motives and ostensible objectives of the ministerial sponsors of the reformed merit system, the new service tests turned out to be, in the hands of the bureaucratic nobility, a wonderful device for consolidating its control over personnel recruitment and for gaining greater freedom from royal molestations in this crucial area. (Rosenberg, 1958: 180)

The increasing dependence of the dilettante on the expert goes a long way toward accounting for the shift of power "down" from titular rulers to the nominal subordinates—the administrative officials.[6]

[6]Note that the same arguments were used in chapter 12 to account for the increasing shift of power in individual organizations—both governmental and nongovernmental—from the owners and general managers to the technical experts and specialist managers. This process results, as noted, in increases in the size of the dominant coalition within organizations.

In the case of democratic systems, where power is expected to reside in the hands of the governed, other factors operate to shift power "up" from the people to administrative elites. The most influential analysis of these processes is that provided by Michels (1949 tr.). Rather than focusing exclusively on state bureaucracies, Michels insisted that processes that withdraw power from the people and place it in the hands of bureaucrats can be studied equally well in organizations such as political parties that are expected to serve the interests of their rank-and-file members.[7] Michel's (1949 tr.) major work is based on a case study of the social Democratic party in pre–World War I Germany (see chapter 4). His famous aphorism, "Who says organization, says oligarchy," (Ibid., 418) summarizes his central argument that oligarchic tendencies, operating to shift power from the majority and place it in the hands of an elite minority, are built into the very structure of organizational arrangements. They are an unintended consequence of organization. He points to the division of functions which creates specialized knowledge, to the hierarchy of offices which fosters and legitimates the uneven distribution of information and decision-making privileges, and to the structure of incentives which encourages officials to remain in office but discourages rank-and-file members from involvement in the day-to-day business of the party. Michels's formulation emphasizes the internal factors giving rise to oligarchical processes; his descriptive account of the development of the Social Democratic party, however, places equal importance on the organization's relation with its environment. Throughout the period from 1890 to 1910, this party, the first of the strong working class parties, was fighting for its existence. Leaders emphasized the need to present a unified front; internal disagreement and dissent were viewed as a luxury to be foregone until the party came to power; and leaders were reluctant to engage in any activities that weakened the strength of the organization in relation to its external environment.

Michels thus poses the following dilemma: a party or a union must build a strong organization and assure its survival to achieve its objectives, yet preoccupation with such organizational problems leads to the surrender of these very objectives. "Thus, from a means, organization becomes an end" (Ibid., p. 390). Experience since Michels's time tends to confirm his thesis. Most unions, most professional associations and other types of voluntary associations, and most political parties exhibit oligarchical leadership structures, the democratic machinery established to prevent such arrangements functioning primarily as a feeble device allowing rank-and-file participants to

[7]Lipset (1960: 357) refers to such organizations as "private governments." Blau and I (Blau and Scott, 1962: 45) refer to them as "mutual benefit associations." They include such organizations as political parties, unions, and professional associations. Since they are formed to serve the interests of their members, most such organizations develop ideologies and procedures that support the participation of the majority in setting the goals of the organization.

rubber-stamp executive decisions and "elect" slates of nominees running in uncontested elections (see Barber, 1950; Editors of the Yale Law Journal, 1954; Wilson, 1973). Even the well-known study by Lipset, Trow, and Coleman (1956) of a "deviant case," a democratically run union, suggests that although such processes are not inevitable, the conditions—both internal and external—causing the drift of power from rank-and-file participants to the upper levels of the organization are sufficiently widespread to vindicate Michels's pessimistic generalization.

Lest we forget, the focus of the present discussion is on representativeness: the degree to which administrative and political bodies reflect the interests of those whom they are presumed to serve. Michels insists that the leaders of the German Social Democratic party forsook the values and interests of its membership, betraying socialist values and working class interests for bourgeois values and selfish interests. While it is true that the party's goals shifted over time, it is not obvious that this process was resisted by the members or contrary to their interests. Thus, Coser (1951) has argued that the shift to the right in the party's program may not have resulted primarily from the bureaucratic conservatism of the leaders but from the rapid improvement in the social and economic situation of the working class during this period. Gouldner (1955) endorses this general line of argument by insisting that there is as much evidence to support an "iron law of democracy" as an "iron law of oligarchy." Gouldner's law asserts that political and administrative elites in both nations and organizations cannot endure for long in the absence of some support from the governed. Gouldner also counters on logical grounds:

> Even as Michels himself saw, if oligarchical waves repeatedly wash away the bridges of democracy, this eternal recurrence can happen only because men doggedly rebuild them after each inundation. (Gouldner, 1955: 506)

Before leaving the topic of democratic processes within organizations, we wish to make one additional point. We have consciously shifted the level of analysis from the larger society and its bureaucratic apparatus to the individual organization and its administrative staff. In doing so, we agreed with Michels that processes operating at the organizational level may be applicable to the societal level and vice versa. However, we need also to be aware of Lipset's conclusion regarding the relation between the two levels:

> Institutionalized democracy within private governments is not a necessary condition for democracy in the large society, and may in fact at times weaken the democratic process of civil society. (Lipset, 1960: 395)

Specifically, Lipset notes that processes that act to incorporate members more fully in the life of their association and hence activate them in its political processes may also serve to isolate them from the larger community and make them more rigid and single-minded in their commitments. Lipset summarizes the dilemma:

> Integration of members within a trade-union, a political party, a farm organization, a professional society, may increase the chances that members of such organizations will be active in the group and have more control over its policies. But extending the functions of such organizations so as to integrate their members may threaten the larger political system because it reduces the forces making for compromise and understanding among conflicting groups. (Ibid., p. 396)

Arguments such as these support our earlier conclusions concerning the dangers of treating individual organizations as if they were the primary centers of moral and social—and political—integration.

With respect to the problem of ensuring responsiveness of governmental officials in the larger society, political analysts generally agree that formal safeguards such as constitutions and legal codes are not in themselves sufficient to curb the power of officeholders. Additional mechanisms are needed to ensure responsiveness. In an instructive historical survey of governmental institutions within the United States, Kaufman (1956; 1969) has identified several "principles" to secure their responsiveness which have come to the fore during differing periods of this nation's history. He argues that the public first put its faith in the principle of *representativeness*, placing great confidence in electoral institutions and granting broad powers to the legislatures, both state and federal. However, as ballots grew longer, voters were unable to exercise intelligent choices, and legislatures proved to be highly vulnerable to the corrupting pressures of special interests. During the second, post–Civil War period, the public endorsed the principle of *neutral competence:* a host of independent boards and commissions were created, the Civil Service Commission was created (in 1883), and the watchword became "take administration out of politics" (Kaufman, 1956: 1060). The major drawback to this approach was, and continues to be, that it led to the fragmentation of government: to the creation of "highly independent islands of decision-making." Further, because administration was protected from politics, the impact of elections on the conduct of government was minimized.

Concerned with this new source of recalcitrance, the public supported, beginning during the 1930s and 1940s, the principle of *executive leadership*. The specific mechanisms utilized during this third phase have been the introduction of the executive budget as a tool of centralized planning and control; the frequent use of administration reorganization, as executives struggled to reduce the number of independent agencies and centralize them in some meaningful pattern; and the growth of the executive staff. At first glance the latter mechanism appears to reflect simply the need for increased information processing on the part of governmental executives: the use of augmented hierarchies in political systems (see chapter 10). Such needs are involved, but they are subordinate to other requirements. The central function of the enlarged executive staffs is to increase political control over the "line" administrators—the civil servants. To do this, the executive must recruit staff members possessing two qualities, in order of importance: loyalty and specialized expertise. Expertise is required to defend the "dilettante" (executive) from the specialized knowledge of public officials; loyalty is essential to ensure that the expertise will be harnessed in the service of the executive's goals. In many ways this development may be seen as an attempt to re-politicize administration, in belated recognition of the truth that expertise may be neutral, but experts never can be.[8]

Kaufman (1969) argues that the late 1960s witnessed a return to the principle of representation, with the introduction of different mechanisms to breath new life into this old value. Electoral reforms extended the franchise to new groups of voters and, more importantly, attempted to reform the systems by which elected officials were nominated and their campaigns financially supported. And for the first time, there were attempts to allow public representatives to participate not only in the creation but in the administration of federal programs. As noted in chapter 9, a new generation of federal agencies has developed during the past two decades which stresses decentralized decision making and the inclusion of representation from the affected groups. It is characteristic of all of these programs that broad discretionary powers are delegated to the administrative units: the language of the statutes sets overall policy directions but does not provide precise legal guidelines to govern administrative action. As Lowi notes: "Broad discretion makes a politician out of a bureaucrat" (1969: pp. 300–301). And since administrators help to set policy, the public is legitimately concerned about the influences to which they are subject. "The further down the line one delegates power, the further into the administrative process one is forced to provide representation" (Ibid., p. 233).

From the earliest days of the Republic, our forefathers have been wary of the abuse of power by public servants and have taken pains to limit and divide power—among the three traditional branches of government as well as within each branch among various offices, commissions, bureaus, and agencies. Executive offices forge political alliances with congressional committees, and commissions and bureaus become linked to special interests both inside and outside of the government. Although there are many diagnoses of our current plight, the most prevalent complaints heard from contemporary students of bureau-

---

[8]It is of some interest to observe that the fullest development of this structural arrangement is to be found in totalitarian systems such as Nazi Germany or the communist regimes. The so-called parallel structures in which the state bureaucracy is duplicated (and penetrated) by a party bureaucracy is a widely recognized feature of such political systems (see Friedrich and Brzezinski, 1956).

cratic politics are (1) that public power is sufficiently fragmented that elected officials cannot ordinarily count on individual agencies to support and implement their policy initiatives and (2) that private special interests have so penetrated public agencies that officials are incapable of acting in ways supportive of the larger public interests (see Neustadt, 1960; Lowi, 1969; Allison, 1971). In sum, it is alleged that today's bureaucrats are insufficiently responsive to their political superiors and overly responsive to special interests.

This overly cozy relation between political bureaus and private interests has already been discussed in a different context. In chapter 9, considerable attention was devoted to describing bridging strategies as an important means of increasing the security of organizations in their task environments. As we noted, the increasing scale and scope of governmental activity encourages organizations of all types to view public agencies as salient features of their environments and as targets of cooptation. Government officials, for their part, are vulnerable to influences from such groups for many reasons: they must relate to these organized interests on a regular basis, they may become dependent on them for information, cooperation, political support, and even for future employment. Thus, contemporary governmental bureaus appear to have insufficient social insulation from specific sources of power in their environment (see chapter 9); they are often unresponsive to the public interest because they are overly responsive to the interests of special publics.

Private Sector Organizations   Much more briefly, we must note that recent analysts are increasingly concerned with the responsiveness of private organizations to the interests of their clients and the larger public. In an important and influential essay, *Exit, Voice, and Loyalty,* Hirschman (1970) distinguishes between two general options open to disgruntled publics wishing to express dissatisfaction with the types and quality of services received. The first, "exit," involves the withdrawal of patronage. Dissatisfied customers simply withdraw from a relation with one firm and seek out another that is expected to serve their interests more adequately. Exit is the typical economic response; it is typified in the relations between private firms and their customers and presumes the existence of alternatives. The second option, "voice," is broadly defined as "any attempt at all to change, rather than to escape from, an objectionable state of affairs" (Hirschman, 1970: 30). Voice is the typical political option—expressed through elections, petitions, complaints, protests and riots—because it is more likely to be exercised in situations in which a monopoly exists. Voice is a more costly option than exit, demanding at a minimum the investment of time and energy; in extreme cases, its exercise can entail personal risk and sacrifice.

Hirschman argues that private firms can greatly benefit from publics who take the trouble to exercise the option of voice rather than exit. He notes that the quality of services provided by firms can deteriorate when alternative suppliers are available to some, since the more discerning customers withdraw their business leaving those who are less quality-conscious—or have no alternatives—to endure substandard service. Such problems are especially characteristic of "lazy monopolies," such as subsidized railroads or public educational systems. Hirschman argues that publics would benefit from the use of mixed options: incentives need to be provided to encourage quality-conscious customers to exercise voice before resorting to exit—this is one of the major functions of "loyalty"; and public organizations should be encouraged to develop exit options, for example, the use of educational vouchers to enable students to seek out alternative suppliers of educational services.

Lindblom (1977) extends and enlarges Hirschman's comparisons of the varying controls available to publics in regulating public and private organizations. He points out that the most frequently employed voice options—elections—are relatively blunt control devices: the selection of a decision maker, especially when that person is placed in a complex political and organizational arena and subjected to varying cross-pressures on numerous issues, may provide little real control to the voter. By contrast, the exit options of buying or refusing to buy an organization's products or services can be exercised frequently and provide a direct signal to producers about what customers think of their products. On closer examination, however, it turns out that the public's control over private companies is "limited to saying yes or no on what is to be produced and in what quantities." (Lindblom, 1977: 154) On a broad range of other decisions, which Lindblom refers to as "delegated decisions," private corporations exercise broad discretion:

> The delegated decisions are all the other decisions instrumental to production: among others, on technology, organization of the work force, plant location, and executive prerogatives. Even in an idealized market system, consumer control over them ranges from weak to nonexistent. (Ibid., p. 154)

A moment's reflection will suggest that these decisions can be of profound significance for the public interests:

> The discretionary decision of a single large corporation (to move in or out) can create or destroy a town, pollute the air for an entire city, upset the balance of payments between countries, and wipe out the livelihood of thousands of employees. (Ibid., p. 155)

Some observers have been content to rely on the development of a sense of "social responsibility" among corporate executives (see Berle, 1963; Cheit, 1964). Others, such as Lindblom, insist that market (exit) incentives must be supplemented with political (voice) controls if social responsibility is to become a reality.

A final concern to be raised about the functioning of organizations in relation to publics relates to the relentlessness of their behavior. This problem, while neglected by most critics and analysts, is in our view the most serious raised by the existence of organizations. It refers not to a malfunction of the organization but to the pathological aspects of "normal" organizational activities.

Coleman's (1974) analysis is most compelling. As noted earlier (see chapter 7), Coleman distinguishes between natural persons, like you and me, and corporate actors: organizations. Organizations are not comprised of persons but of positions, and persons are not completely contained within organizations. Persons contribute to and invest in organizations specific resources over which they lose full control. (The corporate actor is empowered to make decisions concerning the use of the resources available to it, and except in the rare and debilitating case in which an individual retains veto power over the use of his or her resources, individuals must be willing to give up a measure of control over their resources as the price for collective action.) With the creation of a corporate actor, a new set of interests comes into existence.

From the perspective of the personal actor, organizations are agencies for achieving desired objectives. However, from the point of view of the corporate actor, individuals are agents hired to pursue the goals of the collective actor. Individual actors are means for attaining corporate ends. Coleman clearly spells out the implications of this view:

> It is the corporate actors, the organizations that draw their power from persons and employ that power to corporate ends, that are the primary actors in the social structure of modern society.
>
> What does this mean in practice? It means a peculiar bias in the direction that social and economic activities take. It means that among the variety of interests that men have, those interests that have been successfully collected to create corporate actors are the interests that dominate society. (Coleman, 1974: 49)

Unorganized interests of persons are neglected in a society dominated by corporate actors. Further, corporate interests differ from those of natural persons in being more narrow, more intense, more refined, and more single-minded.

> ... decisions about the employment of resources are more and more removed from the multiplicity of dampening and modifying interests of which a real person is composed—more and more the resultant of a balance of narrow intense interests of which corporate actors are composed. (Ibid., p. 29)

Individual administrators are constrained by organizational goals and the definition of their roles. They are expected to act as agents of the organization and as stewards of its resources. University trustees cannot in good conscience use the resources of their institution to relieve poverty or to build low-cost housing for members of the surrounding community. Pentagon officials are expected to build our armaments and strengthen our defenses regardless of the deleterious effects of such activities on the national economy or on the long-range prospects for survival of the human race. Organizations do not speak with one voice, as we have seen, and they are frequently loosely coupled coalitions of interests, but compared with natural persons, they are relatively specialized in their purposes and organized so as to pursue them relentlessly.

Ashby, the noted general system theorist, has pointed out that all "synthetic" organisms, including organizations, exhibit this tendency toward specialization of a sort likely to be dysfunctional for those who create them:

> there is no difficulty, in principle, in developing synthetic organisms as complex, and as intelligent as we please. But we must notice two fundamental qualifications; first, their intelligence will be an adaptation to, and a specialization toward, their particular environment, with no implication of validity for any other environment such as ours; and secondly, their intelligence will be directed toward keeping their own essential variables within limits. They will be fundamentally selfish. (Ashby, 1968: 116)

Given the expectation that organizations will take a relatively narrow band of interests and pursue them unremittingly, our reluctance to enshrine organizations as the social and moral centers of the new society may seem more intelligible. This reluctance is shared. For example, Hart and W. G. Scott express alarm at the growing acceptance of a new set of values they label "the organizational imperative" which presumes that "whatever is good for man can only be achieved through modern organization" and "therefore, all behavior must enhance the health of such modern organizations" (1975: 261). Our concerns are also shared, and best formulated, by Wolin, who spells out the implication of the view that organizations can or should become social communities absorbing their members. He argues that many forces

> have converged to produce a picture of society as a series of tight little islands, each evolving toward political self-sufficiency, each striving to absorb the individual members, each without any natural affiliations with a more comprehensive unity. A typical example of this thinking was the comment of the former Dean of the Harvard Business School. After praising the "accomplishment" whereby the factory had become "the stabilizing force around which (the workers) developed satisfying lives," he went on to point out that this had been achieved "in spite of technological changes within the plant and social chaos in the community outside." What is significant in this remark is the implicit belief that group

life cannot only be perfected in the face of a chaotic "outside," but that by steadily increasing the number of healthy groups there will no longer be any "outside" to worry about. Equally implicit, the political order is assumed to be part of this "outside," "too remote morally and spatially to possess anything of the living reality of active collaboration for individuals." Thus the contemporary vision of the social universe is one where political society, in its general sense, has disappeared. (Wolin, 1960: 431–32)

We wish to disassociate ourselves from this vision.

In our introduction to part 4, we commented that all of the pathologies of organizations to be identified relate in some manner to the problem of power. This statement applies to the current topic. Coleman (1974) points out that in a social structure containing both natural persons and corporate actors, it is possible for one natural person to lose power without a corresponding gain on the part of another person. Persons can lose power to corporate actors. Coleman argues that this loss or transfer is currently going on at a rapid rate, a situation giving rise to a widespread feeling of powerlessness among individuals. And Coleman points out that as a result of this transfer

the outcome of events is only partly determined by the interests of natural persons, giving a society that functions less than fully in the interests of the persons who make it up. (Coleman, 1974: 39)

This seems to us to represent the ultimate form of alienation. In Marx's simpler world, power stripped from one person (the worker) belonged to another (the capitalist). In today's more complex world, power lost by one person may not be gained by any similar person but absorbed by a corporate actor and employed in pursuit of its specialized purposes.

Summary

Pathologies in the operation of contemporary organizations afflict both individual participants and external publics. We emphasize those that are based on the abuse of power.

Problems affecting individual participants include alienation and overconformity. Alienation can be defined either subjectively as a sense of powerlessness and self-estrangement or objectively as a condition under which workers lose control over the products of their labor or the value created by it. Most empirical studies are based on the subjective conception and reveal that the level of alienation among workers in this country is not high but that it varies greatly by type of occupation; and that similar objective positions are experienced and reacted to differently by individuals. Although it is suspected that worker alienation will affect nonwork situations such as family life, there are few convincing studies establishing such relationships. We criticize the proposal that work organizations should function as the primary center of social and moral integration for individuals.

Organizational participants are frequently castigated for ritualism in the sense that they convert means into ends. Such transformations are, however, widespread throughout highly differentiated societies and do not become problematic unless there is a disjunction between means and ends. Studies reveal that organizational participation can be a source of flexibility and liberation as well as of timidity and over-conformity. Job insecurity and uncertainty appear to be powerful factors governing conformity. Designers of organizational positions should seek to set uncertainty levels such that a proper mix of security and stimulation is achieved.

The responsiveness of organizations to the needs of external publics is of concern for all types of organizations but especially those in which the public is designated as the prime beneficiary. The central problem associated with the growth of public organizations is the problem of maintaining their responsiveness to public interests. Responsiveness may be curtailed by the specialization and increasing expertise of administrative officials, the developing class interests of the administrative cadre, the uneven distribution of information and incentives for participation, and pressures for unity in the face of external threats. Responsiveness is sought through such mechanisms as securing representativeness, promoting neutral competence, and stressing executive leadership. It is suggested that some of the difficulties which beset public organizations are also created by their *over*-responsiveness to public interests—the interests of *special* publics.

Private sector organizations are expected to be responsive to economic signals—for example, the withdrawal of business by customers in search of better quality or lower prices. Such options are not available to customers lacking alternatives; they must attempt through political means to change organizations from which they cannot escape. It is increasingly suggested that both private and public organizations should be made susceptible to both economic and political signals.

Even when organizations perform effectively and efficiently, they may, nevertheless, cause difficulties for the larger society because of their tendency to embody and mobilize support for relatively narrow goals. Individual interests that happen to coincide with organizational domains are well served; those that do not are liable to be seriously neglected. Our interests as individuals may be alienated not only by the actions of powerful others who strip us of our rights and resources but also by the normal functioning of impersonal organizations to whom we bequeath our resources and over which we lose control.

chapter 14

Organizational Effectiveness

> *There is no such thing as "good organization"*
> *in any absolute sense. Always it is relative; and*
> *an organization that is good in one context or*
> *under one criterion may be bad under another.*

> W. ROSS ASHBY (1968)

In recent years organizational analysts have become increasingly interested in the topic of organizational effectiveness. A growing number of books and collections of papers attests to this development (see Price, 1968; Ghorpade, 1971; Goodman and Pennings, 1977; Steers, 1977). During the 1950s and early 1960s, the topic was generally neglected, in part because of the belief that considerations of effectiveness represented only an applied or practical, not a theoretical, concern. Gradually, however, analysts began to perceive that there could be as much theoretical justification in examining the consequences of varying structural arrangements as in probing their determinants. And an important boost to the topic occurred when contingency theorists began to argue that some types of structures were better suited to certain tasks or environments than were others. The question was raised: Better suited in what sense? and the answer given was often couched in terms of effectiveness. In this sense, effectiveness is argued by some theorists to be a determinant as well as a consequence of organizational structure.

The topic of organizational effectiveness is eschewed by some analysts on the ground that it necessarily deals with values and preferences that cannot be determined objectively. Such criticisms, however, apply not to the general topic but only to certain formulations of it. We will not seek to determine, for example, whether a given organization is or is not effective in some general sense. Rather, we shall attempt to learn what types of criteria of effectiveness are suggested by what constituencies and what types of indicators of effectiveness are proposed with what implications for organizational assessment. In sum, as was the case in our discussions of such value-loaded topics as decision making, goal setting, and power, we will attempt to remain descriptive and analytic in our approach rather than normative and prescriptive. (We confess that some of our comments in the previous chapter on pathologies were prescriptive.)

Three major topics are addressed in the following discussion: what are the major criteria that have been proposed to define effectiveness; what are the approaches to assessing effectiveness; and what types of explanations are given to account for differences in effectiveness?[1] As we will see, each of these topics is affected by the type of organization examined, in particular, by whether it is or is not responsive to market mechanisms.

Determining Criteria of Effectiveness

To the novice, defining and determining the effectiveness of an organization must seem a relatively straightforward affair: to inquire into effectiveness is to ask how well an organization is doing, relative to some set of standards. This is not wrong, but by this time, we experts in organizational analysis know that the pursuit of this simple question will lead us into some complex and controversial issues. There are many possible bases for generating criteria of effectiveness, and as we would expect, many different constituencies have an interest in the effectiveness of any organization and will want to propose criteria that reflect these interests.

MULTIPLE CRITERIA

Price (1968), Steers (1975), and Campbell (1977) as well as others have assembled lengthy lists of criteria that have been used by one or more analysts in measuring effectiveness. Campbell, for example, lists 30 different criteria, ranging from productivity and profits to growth, turnover, stability, and cohesion. Steers (1975) limited attention to 17 studies of organizational effectiveness in which multiple criteria of effectiveness were devised. Noting that many differing criteria of effectiveness were used in these studies, Steers points out:

> One of the most apparent conclusions emerging from a comparison of these multivariate models is the lack of consensus as to what constitutes a useful and valid set of effectiveness measures. While each model sets forth its three or four defining characteristics for success, there is surprisingly little overlap across the various approaches. (Steers, 1975: 547, 549)

In attempting to understand why so many and such varied criteria of

[1]Some of this discussion of these topics draws on my previously published papers on organizational effectiveness (see Scott, 1977*a;* Scott et al., 1978).

effectiveness have been proposed, we do not need to search very far beyond the thesis of this volume: quite diverse conceptions of organizations are held by various analysts, and associated with each of these conceptions will be a somewhat distinctive set of criteria for evaluating the effectiveness of organizations. Although several schemas for differentiating among these conceptions have been proposed, we will argue that our old friends—the rational, natural, and open systems perspectives—account for much of the variance in measures of effectiveness.

Under a rational system model, since organizations are viewed as instruments for the attainment of goals (see chapter 3), the criteria emphasized focus on the number and quality of outputs and the economies realized in transforming inputs into outputs. General criteria include measures of total output and of quality, of productivity and efficiency. More so than for the other two models, measures of effectiveness from a rational system perspective take into account the specific goals of the organization as the basis for generating effectiveness criteria. Thus, automobile companies focus on how many cars are manufactured during a given period in absolute numbers or in relation to cost measures; and employment bureaus emphasize how many clients are placed in positions, perhaps in relation to the number of persons processed.[2]

As we know, the natural system model views organizations as collectivities capable of achieving specified goals but simultaneously engaged in other activities required to maintain themselves as a social unit. Thus, natural system analysts insist on adding a set of support goals to the output goals emphasized by the rational system model. Further, these support goals are expected to dominate output goals if the two do not coincide: organizations are governed by the overriding goal of survival (see chapter 4). The criteria generated by this conception include measures of participant satisfaction and morale (indicators of whether the organization's inducements are sufficient to evoke contributions from participants adequate to ensure survival), the interpersonal skills of managers, and survival itself.

The open systems perspective views organizations as highly interdependent with their environments and as engaged in system-elaborating as well as system-maintaining activities. Information acquisition and processing is viewed as an especially critical activity since an organization's long-term well-being is dependent on its ability to detect and respond to subtle changes in its task environment (see chapter 5). Yuchtman and Seashore specify one criterion that they argue is most appropriate for assessing the effectiveness of organizations from the open systems perspective: "bargaining position, as reflected in

---

[2]Because of its focus on goals, the rational system model is virtually synonymous with the "goals model" as described by Etzioni (1960). Several critics have pointed out that because of the emphasis placed by the rational system or goals model on the specific types of goals pursued, these models do not provide an adequate basis for comparing the effectiveness of differing types of organizations (see Yuchtman and Seashore, 1967).

the ability of the organization, in either absolute or relative terms, to exploit its environment in the acquisition of scarce and valued resources" (1967: 898). Criteria such as profitability, which may be viewed as the excess of returns over expenditures, are also emphasized by open systems analysts. And a great many theorists stress the importance of adaptability and flexibility as a criterion of effectiveness. Weick (1977) emphasizes these dimensions when he insists that effective organizations are characterized by a diversity of linguistic forms, techniques for breaking out of normal cognitive and normative constraints, means of simultaneously crediting and discrediting information received, and structural units that are loosely articulated so as to maximize sensitivity to the environment and diversity of response.[3]

Analysts' diverse conceptions of organizations are not the only source of variation in effectiveness criteria. Other important bases of diversity include time perspective and level of analysis. Time considerations enter into the generation and application of effectiveness criteria in two senses. First, the criteria employed may vary depending on whether a relatively shorter or longer time frame is adopted. Steers provides an example of this distinction:

> if current production, a short-run effectiveness criterion, is maximized at the expense of research and development investments in future products, an organization may ultimately find itself with an outmoded product and threatened for its very survival, a long-run criterion. (Steers, 1975: 553)

How critical a time frame is may depend on how rapidly the environment is changing. Hannan and Freeman (1977: 116), working from an ecological perspective, point out that highly specialized organizations well adapted to their environment may outperform generalist organizations at a given point in time, but may fare much less well over a longer time period to the extent that the environment has undergone change, Second, organizations are necessarily at different stages of their life cycles, and criteria appropriate for assessing effectiveness at one stage may be less so for another. As Seashore has noted: "the meaning of growth for the health, survival, and overall effectiveness of the organization was very different at different stages of the organizational life cycle" (1962).

We have stressed the importance of level of analysis throughout this volume, and it is a critical factor in accounting for variations in effectiveness criteria. Our conclusions concerning the relative effectiveness of organizations will vary greatly depending on whether we emphasize their impact on individual participants, choose the organization itself as our frame of reference, or inquire into their contributions to societal systems broader than and external

---

[3]In his inimitable fashion, Weick summarizes his criteria as follows: "Specifically, I would suggest that the effective organization is (1) garrulous, (2) clumsy, (3) superstitious, (4) hypocritical, (5) monstrous, (6) octopoid, (7) wandering, and (8) grouchy" (1977: 193–94).

to themselves. Cummings argues for the former, social-psychological level criteria for assessing organizational effectiveness. He proposes that

> an effective organization is one in which the greatest percentage of participants perceive themselves as free to use the organization and its subsystems as instruments for their own ends. (Cummings, 1977: 60)

Most analysts take the organization itself as the appropriate level of analysis for assessing effectiveness. Yuchtman and Seashore (1967: 896) explicitly adopt this posture, suggesting that a relevant view of effectiveness answers the question: "How well is the organization doing for itself?" Still other investigators adopt a more ecological framework and propose that organizations should be evaluated in terms of their contributions to other more general systems. Parsons's (1960) approach to the study of organizations exemplifies this functionalist type of criteria.

Variations in theoretical perspectives on organizations, in time horizons and developmental stage, and in level of analysis—these factors help to account for the diversity of criteria proposed in analyzing effectiveness. Yet another source of diversity is to be found in the varying sets of participants and constituents associated with organizations.

PARTICIPANTS, CONSTITUENTS, AND CRITERIA

Whether organizations are viewed as rational, natural, or open systems, our conceptions of their goals, participants, and constituencies have become progressively more complex. We have been instructed by Simon to view even "simple" output goals as complex and incorporating multiple facets (see chapters 3 and 5), and we have learned from Etzioni and Perrow to add support or maintenance goals to output goals (see chapter 4). This more complex conception of goals is reinforced by viewing organizations as composed of collections of subgroups of participants who possess various social characteristics, are in different social locations, and exhibit divergent views and interests regarding what the organization is and what it should be doing (see chapters 5 and 12). This conception of the organization as a political system can be expanded to include outside constituencies who hold goals "for" the organization (Thompson, 1967: 127), and who attempt to impose these goals on the organization.

It is important to emphasize that when we speak of goals in relation to ascertaining the effectiveness of organizations, we are focusing on the use of goals to supply evaluation criteria. As argued in chapter 12, goals are used to evaluate organizational activities as well as to motivate and direct them. In a rational world, we would expect the criteria that are developed to direct organizational activities to be the same as those employed to evaluate them;

but as we have emphasized, events in organizations are not always as rational and tightly coupled as some theorists would have us believe. Instead, we must be prepared to observe different criteria employed by those who assign tasks and those who evaluate performance (see Dornbusch and Scott, 1975). Discrepancies are more likely to occur when the control system becomes differentiated and these functions are assigned to different actors, but they can occur when the same persons or groups perform both directing and evaluating activities. An oft-cited problem in organizations develops when vague and broad criteria are used to direct task activities but very explicit criteria are employed to evaluate them, with the consequence that evaluation criteria deflect attention and effort from the original stated objectives to a different or narrower set of goals embodied in the evaluation system. Evaluation criteria often focus on the more easily measured task attributes and ignore others less readily assessed: thus, social workers may be directed by their supervisors to provide therapeutic casework services but be evaluated primarily on the basis of the number and timeliness of their visits to clients and the correctness of calculating budgets (see Scott, 1969). Such discrepancies are likely to result in a displacement of goals, as participants come to realize what criteria are used to determine evaluations and to dispense rewards (see also Blau, 1955; Dalton, 1959; Dornbusch and Scott, 1975).

Varying goals—viewed both as directive and as evaluative criteria—will be held by different participant groups and constituencies in organizations. The managers of organizations may not speak with one voice but with many, since they may be comprised of a shifting coalition of interests. Similarly, top managers' goals for directing and evaluating activities may not coincide with or be completely reflected in the criteria used by middle-level personnel such as supervisors or technical specialists. Performers vary in the extent to which their own conceptions of their work coincide with those of their superiors, and also in their capacity to enforce their preferences. Finally, many "external" constituencies—stockholders, clients, suppliers and buyers, regulators, community leaders, and news media—have genuine interests in the functioning of an organization and may be expected to attempt to advocate and, if possible, impose their own effectiveness criteria on the organization. In general, the number of persons and groups who propose criteria for evaluating the performance of an organization will be a much larger set than the number who explicitly seek to direct its activities. A cat may look at a king, and a reporter for the home-town newspaper may scrutinize the performance of the town's leading industry.

According to this conception of organizations, we would expect little commonality in the criteria employed by the various parties who assess organizational effectiveness. This expectation is shared by Friedlander and Pickle (1968), who inpute appropriate interests to such groups as owners, employees, creditors, suppliers, customers, governmental regulators, and the host community. Their data on a sample of small business organizations show that performance assessed by these varying criteria results in a pattern of low and often negative correlation coefficients: to do well on a criterion preferred by one constituency is to do poorly on a criterion favored by another. Friedlander and Pickle conclude that "organizations find it difficult to fulfill simultaneously the variety of demands made upon them" (1968: 302-3).

Another consideration complicating the examination of effectiveness is the recent challenges to the assumption that organizations necessarily exhibit a unified or consistent set of performances. The political models just reviewed allow for divergence and conflict of interests among participants but presume their resolution through negotiation and power processes. In the end, the organization is presumed to pursue a single program. Alternative models which we have explored in earlier chapters suggest the utility of viewing some organizations as "organized anarchies" or as loosely coupled systems containing subunits that exhibit a high degree of autonomy and are capable of pursuing inconsistent objectives (see chapters 11 and 12). This conception admits of the possibility that, with respect to any specific criterion of effectiveness, an organization can be both effective and ineffective depending on what component units are being evaluated!

Given the wide variety of participant groups and constituencies that can attempt to set criteria for organizational effectiveness, what generalizations, if any, can be suggested to guide investigations in this area? We offer three predictions. First, the criteria proposed by each group will be self-interested ones. Customers will desire higher quality at lower cost, suppliers will wish to sell more dearly and wholesalers to buy more cheaply, workers will prefer higher wages and greater fringe benefits, and managers will seek higher profits and lower costs. We should not look for heroes or villains but for parties with varying interests. And all parties will evaluate the performance of the organization in terms of criteria that benefit themselves. Second, although no criteria are disinterested—each will benefit some groups more than others—all will be stated so as to appear universalistic and objective. This generalization receives support from Pfeffer and Salancik's (1974) study of the allocation of resources among university departments. They report that the stronger departments succeed in budget allocation contests not by imposing particularistic criteria on decisions but by ensuring that the universalistic criteria selected favor their own position. For example, strong departments that have larger graduate student enrollments will favor this criterion in allocating resources while departments with larger numbers of undergraduate majors will seek to impose this criterion as a distribution rule. Third, given multiple sets of actors pursuing their own interests and a situation of scarce resources, we would expect little commonality or convergence and some conflicts in the criteria employed by the various parties to assess organizational effectiveness, a prediction supported by the study conducted by Friedlander and Pickle (1968).

One final constituency remains to be considered. Researchers who attempt to assess the effectiveness of organizations are not immune to these sociopolitical processes. Which, and whose, criteria we choose to emphasize in our studies of organizations will depend on our own interests in undertaking the study. We must be willing to state clearly what criteria we propose to employ, recognizing that whatever they are and whoever espouses them, they are always normative conceptions, serving some interests more than others, and likely to be both limited and controversial.

MARKET AND NONMARKET ORGANIZATIONS

The distinction between market-based and nonmarket organizations is especially salient when the question of effectiveness is raised. When properly functioning, the market provides a mechanism for linking the interests of participants and constituencies in such a manner that participants do not prosper unless they serve the interests of their external constituencies. The effectiveness of market-controlled organizations is directly determined by their customers: if their interests are satisfied, then they will continue to supply the inputs required by the organization; if not, then they can withhold their contributions, causing the organization to suffer and perhaps ultimately to fail. Under ideal market conditions an organization's output goals and system-maintenance goals are tightly linked. However, for reasons explored in part 3, many organizations have bargained, or grown or merged their way out of competitive market situations and, increasingly, are the target of governmental regulation.[4]

Other organizations, primarily governmental agencies, operate from the outset in nonmarket environments. Thus, Downs employs as his major criterion for defining a bureau the condition that "the major portion of its output is not directly or indirectly evaluated in any markets external to the organization by means of voluntary *quid pro quo* transactions" (1967: 25). As Downs emphasizes, an important implication of this condition is that "there is no direct relationship between the services a bureau provides and the income it receives for providing them" (Ibid., p. 30). As governments have come under pressure from hard-pressed taxpayers to make every tax dollar count, new techniques have been developed in an effort to ascertain the effectiveness of governmental agencies and, more specifically, government-funded programs. The emergence of evaluation research, both as a set of developing methodologies and as a collection of new professional service organizations, may be

[4]As noted in chapter 9, although instituted as a mechanism to protect the interests of the public, regulatory agencies are often "captured" by the organizations they were empowered to control and operate in the latter's interests (see Stigler, 1971; Pfeffer and Salancik, 1978: 202–13).

viewed as a response to this demand. Evaluation research attempts to provide a basis for assessing the effectiveness and efficiency of governmental programs and thus help to inform decisions concerning what programs are to be closed, continued, or expanded. Although these efforts began with quite naive assumptions regarding techniques for assessing program and agency effectiveness, they have rapidly become more sophisticated, both technically and politically (see Suchman, 1967; Weiss, 1972).

Much of the difficulty in assessing the effectiveness of nonmarket organizations relates to the lack of clear output measures. What types of measures or indicators are used for assessing effectiveness, as well as what standards are employed, is the next topic to be considered.

Assessing Effectiveness

Our model of the evaluation process depicted in chapter 12 proposed that for an evaluation to occur criteria must be selected, including the identification of properties or dimensions and the setting of standards; work must be sampled, with decisions made concerning the types of indicators to be employed and the nature of the sample to be drawn; and sampled values must be compared with the selected standards (see Dornbusch and Scott, 1975). In our view, the same components are applicable whether the intent is to evaluate an individual performer or an entire organization. To this point, we have only discussed the problems encountered in determining the properties or dimensions of the organizational performance to be evaluated. In the current section, we discuss the setting of standards and the selection of indicators for assessing organization effectiveness and briefly comment on decisions regarding selection of the sample.

SETTING STANDARDS

The setting of standards is a central component in establishing criteria for evaluating the effectiveness of an organization. By definition, standards are normative and not descriptive statements. The problem of how standards for assessing organizations are set is an interesting one but has received relatively little attention from social scientists. Cyert and March have attempted to adapt the psychological concept of aspiration level to explain how organizations establish goals for use as evaluative standards. They argue that:

organizational goals in a particular time period are a function of (1) organizational goals of the previous time period, (2) organizational experience with respect to that goal in the previous time period, and (3) experience of comparable organizations with respect to the goal dimension in the previous time period. (Cyert and March, 1963: 123)

Thompson (1967: 84–87) proposes a somewhat more complex model in which types of assessment are viewed as a function of a combination of two factors: (1) whether the standards of desirability are relatively clearly formulated or ambiguous; and (2) whether the beliefs about cause-effect relations are relatively complete or are incomplete.[5] He argues that when standards are clear and cause-effect relations are known, then *efficiency* tests are appropriate. Such tests assess not simply whether a desired effect was produced but whether it was done so efficiently—that is, with a minimum of inputs. If standards are clear but cause-effect relations are uncertain, then *instrumental* tests are suitable. These tests ascertain only whether the desired state was achieved and do not demand conservation of resources. When standards of desirability are themselves ambiguous, then the organization must resort to *social* tests. Social tests are those validated by consensus or by authority. Their validity depends on how many or on who endorses them. Institutionalized organizations as defined by Meyer and Rowan (1977) are likely to depend on social tests for their assessment of effectiveness. Such organizations

> become sensitive to, and employ, external criteria of worth. Such criteria include, for instance, such ceremonial awards as the Nobel Prize, endorsements by important people, the standard prices of professionals and consultants, or the prestige of programs or personnel in external social circles. (Meyer and Rowan, 1977: 350)

Thompson's typology is far from definitive, but it calls attention not only to the diversity of standards employed in assessing organizations but also to factors that help to account for these differences.

Selecting Indicators

Among the most critical decisions to be made in attempting to assess organizational effectiveness is the choice of measures or indicators to be employed. Three general types of indicators have been identified: those based on outcomes, on processes, and on structures (see Donabedian, 1966; Suchman, 1967; Scott, 1977*a*). The advantages and disadvantages of each type will be reviewed.

---

[5]This second factor is a measure of knowledge of the technology utilized during the throughput process; it is similar to the dimension of predictability (see chapter 10).

Outcomes Outcome indicators focus attention on specific characteristics of materials or objects on which the organization has performed some operation. Examples of outcome indicators are changes in the knowledge or attitudes of students in educational organizations, or changes in the health status of patients in medical institutions. Outcomes are often regarded as the quintessential indicators of effectiveness, but they also may present serious problems of interpretation. Outcomes are never pure indicators of quality of performance since they reflect not only the care and accuracy with which work activities are carried out but also the current state of the technology and the characteristics of the organization's input and output environments. These matters are of little import when cause-effect knowledge is relatively complete and when organizations are able to exercise adequate controls over their input and output sectors, approaching the condition of a closed system. In such situations, represented by the manufacture of standardized equipment in competitive markets, outcomes serve as safe indices of quality and quantity of organizational performance. However, many types of organizations lack such controls over their work processes and task environments. For example, a patient's medical condition following surgery will reflect not only the quality of care rendered by the surgical staff and the hospital personnel but also the development of medical science with respect to the particular condition treated, as well as the patient's general physical condition and extent of surgical disease at the time of the operation. Such problems are too much for some analysts, who dismiss the attempt to use outcome measures to assess effectiveness under these circumstances. Thus, Mann and Yett argue:

> There are those who argue that the output of a health facility should be specified in terms of its effect on the patient. . . . We reject this definition of hospital output for the same reason that we do not regard the output of a beauty salon as beauty. (Mann and Yett, 1968: 196–97)

In our view, the use of outcome measures presents difficult, but not unsolvable, problems in assessing effectiveness of organizations such as hospitals and schools. The problem of inadequate knowledge of cause-effect relations can be handled by the use of relative rather than absolute performance standards, so that the performance of an organization is compared against others carrying on similar work. This approach presumes that the organizations assessed can —or should—participate in the same cultural system and have access to the same general knowledge pool. A particular organization possessing more relevant knowledge—for example, having better trained personnel—would be expected to perform better than one possessing less knowledge, but the use of relative standards assures that an organization is not penalized for lacking knowledge that no one has.

The problem posed by the contribution of variations among input characteristics to variations in outcomes experienced is less easily resolved. Although we can safely assume that organizations have access to the same knowledge, we cannot assume that they have access to the same client pool or supply sources. Indeed, one of the principal ways in which organizations vary is in the amount and quality of inputs they are able to garner. The pattern of inputs characterizing various types of organizations is not as simple as might appear on superficial examination. For example, as might be expected, prestigious universities recruit highly intelligent students, as indicated by scores on standard entrance examinations or past performance in academic settings, while less highly regarded institutions accept higher proportions of less qualified students. By contrast, highly regarded teaching hospitals focus primarily on the care of the very sick or on those whose problems pose the greatest challenge to medical science. In these organizations, there is an inverse relation between presumed quality of institution and patient condition. We would expect organizations to seek to take credit for acquiring inputs that enhance their outcomes—a widely used indicator of quality for universities is the characteristics of the student body they are able to attract—but to resist being held accountable for inputs that negatively affect outcomes. Thus, teaching hospitals insist that if patient outcome measures are employed as indicators of performance quality, they be standardized to take account of differences in patient mix. Statistical techniques are available that allow analysts to adjust outcome measures to take into account differences in characteristics of inputs.[6]

Outcome measures may also be affected by the characteristics of output environments. For example, indicators of outcomes relating to sales for products, or to placement or rehabilitation for prisoners or mental patients, will reflect not simply organizational performance but also market conditions or the receptivity of community groups external to the organization. As with inputs, we would expect organizations to prefer to take credit for conditions enhancing outcomes but insist that conditions having a negative effect be taken into account if outcomes are evaluated.

More generally, the decision as to how to treat input characteristics and output environments is not primarily a methodological but a theoretical issue. Do we wish to adjust for differences in student intelligence among universities in assessing student performance, or do we wish to regard student recruitment as an important aspect of a university's performance? Do we wish to adjust for market conditions in assessing a firm's retail sales, or do we wish to consider ability to build a solid market niche an important component of the firm's performance? Answers to these and similar questions depend on whether we seek to concentrate attention simply on the organization's throughput

---

[6]My colleagues and I have developed methods for adjusting patient outcome measures in order to assess the relative effectiveness of hospitals in providing surgical services. (See Scott et al., 1978; Flood et al., 1979.)

processes—its technical core activities—or desire to include in our assessment the performance of the organization's bridging units—its input and output components.

Still other issues are involved in the use of outcome measures to assess organizational effectiveness. Briefly, it is difficult to determine the appropriate timing of such measures. Some organizations insist that their full effects may not be apparent for long periods following their performance. For example, some educators claim that relevant academic outcomes can only be assessed long after the students have left school and have attempted to apply their knowledge in the "real world." And when is the appropriate time to assess a hospital's effect on a patient's health—immediately following a major therapeutic intervention such as surgery, at discharge, or following a post-hospitalization recovery period? Another problem in employing outcome indicators is the lack of relevant information. Many types of organizations have little or no data on outcomes achieved: they quickly lose contact with their "products" —whether these be human graduates or manufactured commodities. The collection of relevant outcome data can become very costly indeed if it entails tracking down such products after they are distributed throughout the environment.

Partly because of these quite formidable difficulties in assessing and interpreting outcome measures, other types of indicators of organizational effectiveness are often preferred. These measures—of processes and structures—can be more briefly described.

Processes   Process measures focus attention on the quantity or quality of activities carried on by the organization. As Suchman notes, this type of indicator

> represents an assessment of input or energy regardless of output. It is intended
> to answer the questions, "What did you do?" and "How well did you do it?"

Process measures assess effort rather than effect. Some process measures assess work quantity—for example, staying with our hospital illustration, we may ask how many laboratory tests were conducted during a given period or how many patients were seen in the emergency room. Others assess work quality—for example, hospitals might be rated by the frequency with which medication errors occur or by the proportion of healthy tissue removed from patients during surgery. Still other measures assess the extent of quality control efforts —for instance, the autopsy rate in hospitals or the proportion of X-rays reviewed by radiologists.

In some respects, process measures are more valid measures of the characteristics of organizational performance. Rather than requiring inferences from outcomes to performance characteristics, process measures directly assess performance values. On the other hand, it is important to emphasize that all process measures evaluate efforts rather than achievements; and when the focus is on quality of performance rather than quantity, they assess conformity to a given standard but do not evaluate the adequacy or correctness of the standards themselves. They are based on the assumption that it is known what activities are required to ensure effectiveness of performance. Students of medical care are currently challenging the assumption that there is a strong correlation between conformity to current standards of medical practice and improvements in patient outcomes (see Brook, 1973); as well as the assumption that higher levels of medical care usage result in improved health status (see Fuchs, 1974). More generally, social critics such as Illich (1972; 1976) claim that the substitution of process for outcome is one of the great shell games perpetrated by modern institutions against individuals. Illich argues that contemporary individuals are trained

> to confuse process and substance. Once these become blurred, a new logic is assumed: the more treatment there is, the better are the results; or, escalation leads to success. The pupil is thereby "schooled" to confuse teaching with learning, grade advancement with education, a diploma with competence, and fluency with the ability to say something new. His imagination is "schooled" to accept service in place of value. Medical treatment is mistaken for health care, social work for the improvement of community life, police protection for safety, military poise for national security, the rat race for productive work. Health, learning, dignity, independence, and creative endeavor are deigned as little more than the performance of the institutions that claim to serve these ends, and their improvement is made to depend on allocating more resources to the management of hospitals, schools, and other agencies in question. (Illich, 1972: 1)

Recognizing that Illich's broad accusations have some merit, we would, however, express two sorts of reservations. The first relates to an argument we made in chapter 13. Focusing attention on processes rather than outcomes represents a type of goal displacement. However, as noted earlier, goal displacement is a very widespread phenomenon and need not be regarded as pathological. Only when means and ends become disconnected is there cause for distress. Our second demurring relates to the case of institutionalized organizations, in which, to a large extent, process *is* substance. In these organizations, conformity to ritually defined procedures produces a successful outcome, by definition. Ceremony is substance in many contemporary organizations, including religious bodies, legal firms, and many professionally staffed organizations.

Organizations are more likely to compile data on work processes than on outcomes. Performance quality and quantity are often regularly monitored. Gathering information on work processes, however, can still be problematic. Inspections based on observation of ongoing performances are both expensive and reactive—that is, likely to influence the behavior observed. In most work situations there are numerous barriers to work visibility, and workers often resist attempts to directly observe their work in process. Many kinds of work occur under circumstances that render routine inspection impossible; and other kinds, such as those emphasizing mental activities, are by their nature difficult to observe. Because of such difficulties, organizations may rely on self-reports of activities performed; however, such data are likely to be both biased and incomplete representations of work processes (see Dornbusch and Scott, 1975: 145–62). Because of these and related difficulties in obtaining process measures, many organizations rely on structural indicators of effectiveness.

Structures Structural indicators assess the capacity of the organization for effective performance. Included within this category are all measures based on organizational features or participant characteristics presumed to have an impact on organizational effectiveness. Manufacturing organizations might be assessed by the value and age of their machine tools; hospitals are assessed by the adequacy of their facilities and equipment and by the qualifications of the medical staff as reflected in past training and certification; and schools are assessed by the qualities of their faculties, measured in terms of types of degrees acquired, and by such features as the number of volumes in their libraries. These types of measures form the basis of accreditation reviews and organizational and occupational licensure systems.

If process measures are once removed from outcomes, then structure indicators are twice remote, for these measures index not the work performed by structures but their *capacity* to perform work—not the activities carried out by organizational participants but their qualifications to perform the work. Structural indicators focus attention on organizational inputs as surrogate measures for outputs. Economists warn us that quality of outputs should not be confused with quality (or cost) of inputs, but Yuchtman and Seashore (1967) are close to embracing this position in their influential paper on organizational effectiveness. As noted above, they suggest that the effectiveness of an organization can be defined in terms of its ability to acquire scarce and valued resources—for example, expensive facilities and highly qualified personnel—making the explicit assumption that an organization's bargaining position in its input environment is "a function of all the three phases of organizational behavior—the importation of resources, their use (including allocating and processing), and their exportation in some output form that aids further input" (Yuchtman and Seashore, 1967: 898).

As was the case with measures of organizational process, a number of observers have suggested that an emphasis on structural measures may have detrimental consequences for quality of outcomes. For example, numerous observers have argued that personnel licensure requirements have become a major obstacle to innovation in work procedures and to the optimal deployment of workers (see Somers, 1969; Tancredi and Woods, 1972). Thus, we have the interesting situation in which some measures of organizational effectiveness based on the assessment of process or of structure are argued to be negatively related to some measures of effectiveness based on outcomes.

Selecting Samples

Once indicators have been selected, decisions must still be made regarding the gathering of information relevant to these measures. We leave aside here discussion of specific techniques of data gathering as well as decisions pertaining to sample size, assuring representativeness, and other technical considerations in order to emphasize the critical importance of the definition of the universe from which the sample is to be drawn. A basic decision confronting the analyst who assesses the effectiveness of any organization is whether to focus on the actual work performed by the organization or instead to ask whether the organization is attending to the appropriate work. The first option takes as given the current program of the organizations—its structures, processes, or outcomes—and seeks to ascertain their quality or effectiveness. The second option assumes a broader perspective, asking whether the organization is engaged in the right program. Never mind how good it is at what it does, is it doing the right things? Reinhardt (1973) labels the first criterion "microquality" and the second, "macroquality." Applying this distinction to a service organization, an assessment of microquality would focus on the quality of structures, processes, or outcomes actually experienced by clients who were the recipients of the organization's services. By contrast, an assessment of macroquality would seek to determine whether the appropriate services were being provided or, more critically, whether the proper clients were receiving services. The effectiveness of a medical care organization might be assessed in terms of the health status of the clients who had received services (microquality) or by the health status of the population residing within the organization's service area (macroquality).

Participants, Constituents, and Measures

Just as with evaluation criteria, we would expect differing participant and constituency groups to prefer some types of measures over others. Generally, we expect organizational managers to emphasize structural measures of effectiveness, in part because these reflect factors that are more under their control than other types of indicators. Thus, organizational administrators are likely to have considerable influence over the types of facilities provided or the standards used in hiring personnel. By contrast, we would expect performers or rank-and-file participants to emphasize process measures of effectiveness.

Skilled and semiskilled workers, who have little or no discretion in the selection of their activities, will prefer to be evaluated on the basis of their conformity to their performance programs rather than on the efficacy of these programs. And professional personnel who are granted discretion in their choice of activities, will also usually prefer to be evaluated on the basis of process measures—their conformity to "standards of good practice"—since inadequacies in the knowledge base mean that they lack full control over outcomes.

Clients who use the products or receive the services are likely to focus primarily on outcome measures of effectiveness. They will evaluate the organization's product in terms of the extent to which it has met their own needs and expectations. Did the motor run? Was something of interest or use learned? Was their pain relieved or their functioning improved? In addition, clients who receive personal services are likely to place considerable value on certain types of process measures having to do with promptness, courtesy, and sensitivity of treatment. In circumstances where outcomes are difficult to evaluate, process measures will receive more weight from clients than outcome indicators. The most extreme cases involve institutionalized organizations in which no outcomes at all can be demonstrated to occur regularly—although they are alleged to occur—so that both performers and recipients devote attention to evaluating conformity to established norms of practice.

All of the interest groups considered to this point—organizational managers, performers, and consumers—are likely to focus on microquality indicators of effectiveness. They will prefer to focus on the structures, processes, and outcomes associated with the work that the organization is actually performing. But another interest group, which represents the public at large, including some public regulatory bodies, will be more likely to emphasize measures of macroquality. Is the organization concentrating its attention and resources on the proper products or problems? Do eligible clients have access to its services? Is the community as a whole benefiting from its operation?

Our final constituency are the researchers dedicated to the objective, scientific analysis of organizational effectiveness. We would hope to find this group busily engaged in analyzing *all* types of indicators of effectiveness, exploring their interrelation, and employing criteria variously drawn from all of the interested parties. Although we have not conducted the type of systematic survey of the literature required to support such a conclusion, it appears that we analysts have emphasized the structural and process measures of effectiveness—those measures preferred by organizational managers and performers—to the neglect of outcome measures—those preferred by clients and the larger public. Both ideological and economic factors help to produce this bias in orientation. It is our belief that organizational analysts are more likely to identify with organizational managers and professional performers than with client and public interests. Indeed, most of the research on organizations is conducted by persons who train future managers while consulting for present ones. Also, most of the data available to us for analysis are collected by the organizations for their own purposes or are based on information supplied by organizational managers. Organizations, as noted above, are much less likely to collect data on outcomes than data based on their structural features and processes. If we want data on outcomes—and especially on outcomes that represent measures of macroquality—we will have to collect them ourselves, or persuade governmental agencies to collect them for us. We should not minimize the cost nor should we minimize the value of such data in correcting the bias that currently exists in indicators of organizational effectiveness.

Explaining Effectiveness

Given the multiple possible meanings and measures of effectiveness that have been proposed, our comments on explanations of effectiveness can be brief since they are mostly by way of warning. When effectiveness can be viewed as comprising such varied criteria as flexibility, low turnover, and growth, we must seek explanatory variables as varied as those they are asked to account for. Given that many of the proposed measures of effectiveness are uncorrelated or even negatively correlated, we should not expect to find general explanations that will distinguish effective from ineffective organizations. We must agree to settle for modest and limited measures of specific aspects of organizational structures, processes, and outcomes.

Since the appearance of the open systems perspective, a popular approach to explaining variations in effectiveness has involved the use of contingency models: organizations whose internal features best match the demands of their technologies or task environments are expected to be most effective (see chapter 5). The adequacy of such models depends, among other things, on the quality of our ideas about the appropriate relation (match) between task or environmental demands and organizational arrangements. We have attempted to summarize, in chapters 9 through 11, some of these evolving principles, and while we do not apologize for the state of our knowledge, we readily admit that there is much room for improvement. The principles developed are generally vague and need to be carefully adapted for application to specific settings. That this is not a straightforward task is illustrated by Perrow's recent critique of Neuhauser's attempt to apply these ideas to the organization of doctors' work in hospitals. Neuhauser (1971) embraces the widely accepted design principle that when work is complex and uncertain, attempts to control performance with the use of highly specified procedures—high formalization—will lower work quality. Perrow would certainly subscribe to this general principle but takes issue with Neuhauser's specific application of it to the hospital setting:

Tasks are complex on the medical side of the hospitals, so when dealing with doctors, specification of procedures should be low. But the specifications of what kind of procedures? Any, it seems. For example, he includes the number of tests required at admissions . . . and the number of limitations placed upon the surgery that people can perform (a general practitioner cannot do heart surgery). Using knee-jerk theorizing, he says that if there are a lot of specifications of these kinds, quality should be low. Presumably he could have included scrubbing before surgery as a specification of procedures that would lower quality when tasks are complex. (Perrow, 1972: 420)

Perrow's tone is overly caustic, but his point is well taken; and the problem illustrated is all too common in organizational analysis. We are too often in thralldom before a general principle, applying it mindlessly to situations whose complexity swamps whatever truth might have been revealed by a more thoughtful approach. Let us not be misunderstood. We need the guidance of general principles. But we also require sufficiently detailed knowledge of the organizations and their technologies and environments to be able to select valid indicators of the variables to be assessed. Surgeons do need to be able to exercise discretion in some critical areas of their work, but this requirement need not be inconsistent with the precise specification of other aspects of their performance. If we wish to explain effects, there is no substitute for a knowledge of the specific causal processes linking them with relevant inputs, technologies, and work arrangements.

Contingency models often overlook the open systems concept of equifinality: that many different causal paths can lead to the same effect. In particular, it is often presumed that an organization's ability to maximize its productivity or its profits is due to the superior design of its production structures and the resulting technical efficiency. However, we should know by this time that organizations are technical systems but not simply technical systems. As Katz and Kahn remind us:

> The textbook path to organizational survival is internal efficiency: build the better mousetrap or build the old trap less expensively. There is, however, a whole class of alternative or supplementary solutions—the political devices that maximize organizational return at some cost to other organizations or individuals. (Katz and Kahn, 1978: 249)

Pfeffer and Salancik stress the importance of these political solutions throughout their analysis of organizational functioning, concluding: "The effectiveness of an organization is a sociopolitical question" (1978: 11). Consumers and (some) regulators seek ways to link an organization's effectiveness in goal attainment to its effectiveness in resource acquisition and survival. Sometimes they succeed but often they fail: an organization's resource acquisition and survival is not always tightly linked with the quality of its services to the publics it claims to benefit.

Summary

Criteria for evaluating organizational effectiveness cannot be produced by some objective, apolitical process. They are always normative and often controversial; and they are as varied as the theoretical models used to describe organizations and the constituencies that have some interest in their functioning. Similarly, the indicators to be used in assessing organizational effectiveness must also be chosen from among several possible types and data gathered from several possible sampling frames. Measures based on outcomes, processes, and structural features of organizations are likely to produce inconsistent conclusions and are differentially favored by various constituencies. We should not seek explanations for organizational effectiveness in general, since such general criteria are not available; and we must be cautious in celebrating the truism that organizations that are better adapted to their environments are more likely to survive. Adaptation can be achieved in numerous ways, many of which contribute to the survival of the organization but fail to serve the interests of external constituencies.

References

ABEGGLEN, JAMES C. *The Japanese Factory: Aspects of Its Social Organization.* Glencoe, Ill.: Free Press, 1958.

ADAMS, J. STACEY. "Inequity in Social Exchange," in *Advances in Experimental Social Psychology,* vol. 2, pp. 267–300, ed. Leonard Berkowitz. New York: Academic Press, 1965.

AIKEN, MICHAEL, and JERALD HAGE. "Organizational Interdependence and Intraorganizational Structure," *American Sociological Review,* 33 (December 1968), 912–29.

ALBROW, MARTIN. *Bureaucracy.* New York: Praeger, 1970.

ALCHIAN, A. A., and H. DEMSETZ. "Production, Information Costs, and Economic Organization," *American Economic Review,* 62 (December 1972), 777–95.

ALDRICH, HOWARD E. "Technology and Organizational Structure: A Reexamination of the Findings of the Aston Group," *Administrative Science Quarterly,* 17 (March 1972), 26–43.

————. *Organizations and Environments.* Englewood Cliffs, N.J.: Prentice-Hall, 1979.

ALDRICH, HOWARD E., and SERGIO MINDLIN. "Uncertainty and Dependence: Two Perspectives on Environment," in *Organization and Environment,* pp. 149–70, ed. Lucien Karpit. Beverly Hills, Ca.: Sage Publications, Inc., 1978.

ALDRICH, HOWARD E., and JEFFREY PFEFFER. "Environments of Organizations," *Annual Review of Sociology,* 2 (1976), 79–105.

ALLISON, GRAHAM T. *Essence of Decision: Explaining the Cuban Missile Crisis.* Boston: Little, Brown, 1971.

AMBER, G. H., and P. S. AMBER. *Anatomy of Automation.* Englewood Cliffs, N.J.: Prentice-Hall, 1962.

ANDERSON, BO, JOSEPH BERGER, BERNARD P. COHEN, and MORRIS ZELDITCH, JR. "Status Classes in Organizations," *Administrative Science Quarterly,* 11 (September 1966), 264–83.

APTER, DAVID E. "A Comparative Method for the Study of Politics," *American Journal of Sociology,* 64 (November 1958), 221–37.

ARENDT, HANNAH. *The Origins of Totalitarianism.* New York: Harcourt, Brace, 1951.

————. *Eichmann in Jerusalem.* New York: Viking, 1963.

ARGYRIS, CHRIS. *Personality and Organization.* New York: Harper, 1957.

―――. *Interpersonal Competence and Organizational Effectiveness.* Homewood, Ill.: Richard D. Irwin, 1962.

―――. "Personality and Organization Theory Revisited," *Administrative Science Quarterly,* 18 (June 1973), 141–67.

ARROW, KENNETH J. *The Limits of Organization.* New York: W. W. Norton & Co., Inc., 1974.

ASHBY, W. ROSS. *A Design for a Brain.* New York: John Wiley, 1952.

―――. "The Effect of Experience on a Determinant Dynamic System," *Behavioral Science,* 1 (January 1956), 35–42.

―――. "Principles of Self-Organizing System," in *Modern Systems Research for the Behavioral Scientist,* pp. 108–18, ed. Walter Buckley. Chicago: Aldine, 1968.

AVERITT, RICHARD T. *The Dual Economy: The Dynamics of American Industry Structure.* New York: W. W. Norton & Co., Inc., 1968.

BACH, GEORGE LELAND. *Microeconomics.* Englewood Cliffs, N.J.: Prentice-Hall, 1977.

BAKER, ALTON W., and RALPH C. DAVIS. *Ratios of Staff to Line Employees and Stages of Differentiation of Staff Functions.* Columbus: Bureau of Business Research, Ohio State University, 1954.

BALES, ROBERT F. "Some Uniformities of Behavior in Small Social Systems," in *Readings in Social Psychology* (2nd ed.), eds. Guy E. Swanson, Theodor M. Newcomb, and Eugene L. Hartley. New York: Holt, Rinehart and Winston, 1952.

―――. "The Equilibrium Problem in Small Groups," in *Working Papers in the Theory of Action,* Talcott Parsons, Robert F. Bales, and Edward A. Shils. Glencoe, Ill.: Free Press, 1953.

BALES, ROBERT F., and PHILIP E. SLATER. "Role Differentiation in Small Decision-Making Groups," in *Family, Socialization and Interaction Process,* pp. 259–306, eds. Talcott Parsons and Robert F. Bales. New York: Free Press, 1955.

BARBER, BERNARD. "Participation and Mass Apathy in Associations," in *Studies in Leadership,* pp. 477–504, ed. Alvin W. Gouldner. New York: Harper, 1950.

BARKER, E. *The Development of Public Services in Western Europe, 1660–1930.* New York: Oxford University Press, 1944.

BARNARD, CHESTER I. *The Functions of the Executive.* Cambridge, Mass.: Harvard University Press, 1938.

―――. *Organization and Management.* Cambridge, Mass.: Harvard University Press, 1948.

BATESON, GREGORY. *Steps to an Ecology of Mind.* New York: Ballantine, 1972.

BAVELAS, ALEX. "Communication Patterns in Task-Oriented Groups," in *The Policy Sciences,* pp. 193–202, eds. Daniel Lerner and Harold D. Lasswell. Stanford, Ca.: Stanford University Press, 1951.

BECKHARD, RICHARD. "Organizational Issues in the Team Delivery of Comprehensive Health Care," *Milbank Memorial Fund Quarterly,* 50 (July 1972), Part 1, 287–316.

BEER, STAFFORD. *Cybernetics and Management.* New York: John Wiley, 1964.

BELKNAP, IVAN. *The Human Problems of a State Mental Hospital.* New York: McGraw-Hill, 1956.

BELL, DANIEL. "Work and Its Discontents: The Cult of Efficiency in America," in *The End of Ideology,* pp. 222–62, Daniel Bell. Glencoe, Ill.: Free Press, 1960.

BELL, GERALD D. "Determinants of Span of Control," *American Journal of Sociology,* 73 (July 1967), 100–109.

BEN-DAVID, JOSEPH. "Professions in the Class System of Present-Day Societies," *Current Sociology,* 12 (1963), 247–330.

BENDIX, REINHARD. *Work and Authority in Industry.* New York: John Wiley, 1956.

———. *Max Weber: An Intellectual Portrait.* Garden City, N.Y.: Doubleday, 1960.

BENDIX, REINHARD, and LLOYD H. FISHER. "The Perspectives of Elton Mayo," *Review of Economics and Statistics,* 31 (November 1949), 312–19.

BENDIX, REINHARD, and SEYMOUR MARTIN LIPSET. "Karl Marx's Theory of Social Classes," in *Class, Status and Power,* (rev. ed.) pp. 6–11, eds. Reinhard Bendix and Seymour Martin Lipset. New York: Free Press, 1966.

BENNIS, WARREN G. "Leadership Theory and Administrative Behavior," *Administrative Science Quarterly,* 4 (December 1959), 259–301.

———. *Changing Organizations.* New York: McGraw-Hill, 1966.

BENNIS, WARREN G., and PHILIP E. SLATER. *The Temporary Society.* New York: Harper & Row, Pub., 1968.

BENSON, J. KENNETH. "Organizations: A Dialectical View," *Administrative Science Quarterly,* 22 (March 1977), 1–21.

BERGER, PETER L., and THOMAS LUCKMANN. *The Social Construction of Reality.* New York: Doubleday, 1967.

BERGER, MORROE. *Bureaucracy and Society in Modern Egypt.* Princeton, N.J.: Princeton University Press, 1957.

BERLE, A. A. *The American Economic Republic.* New York: Harcourt, Brace and World, 1963.

BERTALANFFY, LUDWIG VON. "General System Theory," in *General Systems: Yearbook of the Society for the Advancement of General Systems Theory,* eds. Ludwig von Bertalanffy and Anatol Rapoport, 1 (1956), 1–10.

———. "General System Theory—A Critical Review," in *General Systems: Yearbook of the Society for General Systems Research,* eds. Ludwig von Bertalanffy and Anatol Rapoport, 7 (1962), 1–20.

BIDWELL, CHARLES E. "The School as a Formal Organization," in *Handbook of Organizations,* pp. 972–1022, ed. James G. March. Chicago: Rand McNally, 1965.

BINSTOCK, ROBERT H., and MARTIN A. LEVIN. "The Political Dilemmas of Intervention Policies," in *Handbook of Aging and the Social Sciences,* pp. 511–35, eds. Robert H. Binstock and Ethel Shanas. New York: Van Nostrand Reinhold, 1976.

BLAKE, DAVID H., and ROBERT S. WALTERS. *The Politics of Global Economic Relations.* Englewood Cliffs, N.J.: Prentice-Hall, 1976.

BLAKE, R. R., and J. S. MOUTON. *The Managerial Grid.* Houston: Gulf, 1964.

BLAKE, R. R., H. A. SHEPHARD, and J. S. MOUTON. *Intergroup Conflict in Organizations.* Ann Arbor, Mich.: Foundation for Research on Human Behavior, 1964.

BLAU, PETER M. *The Dynamics of Bureaucracy.* Chicago: University of Chicago Press, 1955. (Rev. 1963).

––––. *Bureaucracy in Modern Society.* New York: Random House, 1956.

––––. "Formal Organization: Dimensions of Analysis," *American Journal of Sociology,* 63 (July 1957), 58–69.

––––. "Structural Effects," *American Sociological Review,* 25 (April 1960), 178–93.

––––. *Exchange and Power in Social Life.* New York: John Wiley, 1964.

––––. "The Hierarchy of Authority in Organizations," *American Journal of Sociology,* 73 (January 1968), 453–67.

––––. "A Formal Theory of Differentiation in Organizations," *American Sociological Review, 35 (April 1970), 201–18.*

––––. *The Organization of Academic Work.* New York: John Wiley, 1973.

BLAU, PETER M., and OTIS DUDLEY DUNCAN. *The American Occupational Structure.* New York: John Wiley, 1967.

BLAU, PETER M., and RICHARD A. SCHOENHERR. *The Structure of Organizations.* New York: Basic Books, 1971.

BLAU, PETER M., and W. RICHARD SCOTT. *Formal Organizations.* San Francisco: Chandler, 1962.

BLAU, PETER M., WOLF V. HEYDEBRAND, and ROBERT E. STAUFFER. "The Structure of Small Bureaucracies," *American Sociological Review,* 31 (April 1966), 179–91.

BLAUNER, ROBERT. "Work Satisfaction and Industrial Trends in Modern Society," in *Labor and Trade Unionism,* pp. 339–60, eds. Walter Galenson and Seymour Martin Lipset. New York: John Wiley, 1960.

BLEDSTEIN, BURTON J. *The Culture of Professionalism.* New York: W. W. Norton & Co., Inc., 1976.

BLUESTONE, BARRY, WILLIAM M. MURPHY, and MARY STEVENSON. *Low Wages and the Working Poor.* Ann Arbor, Mich.: Institute of Labor and Industrial Relations, University of Michigan and Wayne State University, 1973.

BLUMBERG, PAUL. *Industrial Democracy: The Sociology of Participation.* New York: Schocken Books, 1968.

BOAS, MAX, and STEVE CHAIN. *Big Mac: The Unauthorized Story of McDonald's.* New York: New American Library, 1977.

BOK, DEREK C. "The Federal Government and the University," *The Public Interest,* 58 (Winter 1980), 80–101.

BOORMAN, SCOTT, and HARRISON C. WHITE. "Social Structures from Multiple Networks: II. Role Structures," *American Journal of Sociology,* 81 (May 1976), 1384–446.

BOULDING, KENNETH E. *The Organizational Revolution.* New York: Harper and Brothers, 1953.

———. "General Systems Theory—The Skeleton of Science," *Management Science,* 2 (April 1956), 197–208.

BRAVERMAN, HARRY. *Labor and Monopoly Capital: The Degradation of Work in the Twentieth Century.* New York: Monthly Review Press, 1974.

BRAYFIELD, ARTHUR H., and WALTER H. CROCKETT. "Employee Attitudes and Employee Performance," *Psychological Bulletin,* 52 (September 1955), 396–424.

BROOK, ROBERT H. *Quality of Care Assessment: A Comparison of Five Methods of Peer Review.* Washington, D.C.: Bureau of Health Services Research and Evaluation, July 1973.

BUCKLEY, WALTER. *Sociology and Modern Systems Theory.* Englewood Cliffs, N.J.: Prentice-Hall, 1967.

BURNS, TOM. "The Comparative Study of Organizations," in *Methods of Organizational Research,* pp. 113–70, ed. Victor H. Vroom. Pittsburgh: University of Pittsburgh Press, 1967.

BURNS, TOM, and GEORGE M. STALKER. *The Management of Innovation.* London: Tavistock Publications, 1961.

CAMPBELL, DONALD. "Variation and Selective Retention in Socio-Cultural Evolution," *General Systems: Yearbook of the Society for General Systems Research,* 16 (1969), 69–85.

CAMPBELL, JOHN P. "On the Nature of Organizational Effectiveness," in *New Perspectives on Organizational Effectiveness,* pp. 13–55, eds. Paul S. Goodman and Johannes M. Pennings. San Francisco: Jossey-Bass, 1977.

CAREY, ALEX. "The Hawthorne Studies: A Radical Criticism," *American Sociological Review,* 32 (June 1967), 403–16.

CARR-SAUNDERS, ALEXANDER M., and P. A. WILSON. *The Professions.* Oxford: Clarendon, 1933.

CARTER, LAUNOR, WILLIAM HAYTHORN, BEATRICE SHRIVER, and JOHN LANZETTA. "The Behavior of Leaders and Other Group Members," in *Group Dynamics,* pp. 551–60, eds. Dorwin Cartwright and Alvin Zander. Evanston, Ill.: Row, Peterson, 1953.

CARTWRIGHT, DORWIN. "Influence, Leadership, Control," in *Handbook of Organizations,* pp. 1–47, ed. James G. March. Chicago: Rand McNally, 1965.

CARZO, ROCCO, JR., and JOHN N. YANOUZAS. *Formal Organization: A Systems Approach.* Homewood, Ill.: Richard D. Irwin and Dorsey, 1967.

CHANDLER, ALFRED D., JR. *Strategy and Structure: Chapters in the History of the American Industrial Enterprise.* Cambridge, Ma.: The M.I.T. Press, 1962.

CHEIT, EARL F. "The New Place of Business: Why Managers Cultivate Social Responsibility," in *The Business Establishment,* pp. 152–92, ed. Earl F. Cheit. New York: John Wiley, 1964.

CHILD, JOHN. "Organizational Structure, Environment and Performance: The Role of Strategic Choice," *Sociology,* 6 (January 1972), 1–22.

CHILD, JOHN, and ROGER MANSFIELD. "Technology, Size and Organization Structure," *Sociology,* 6 (September 1972), 369–93.

CHRISTIE, L. S., R. S. LUCE, and J. MACY, JR. "Communication and Learning in Task-Oriented Groups," Technical Report No. 231. Cambridge: Research Laboratory of Electronics, Massachusetts Institute of Technology, 1952.

CLARK, BURTON R. *Adult Education in Transition.* Berkeley: University of California Press, 1956.

————. "Faculty Organization and Authority," in *The Study of Academic Administration,* pp. 37–51, ed. Terry F. Lunsford. Boulder, Co.: Western Interstate Commission for Higher Education, 1963.

————. "Interorganizational Patterns in Education," *Administrative Science Quarterly,* 10 (September 1965), 224–37.

CLARK, PETER. "Cultural Context as a Determinant of Organizational Rationality: A Comparison of the Tobacco Industries in Britain and France," in *Organizations Alike and Unlike,* pp. 272–86, eds. Cornelis J. Lammers and David J. Hickson. London: Routledge & Kegan Paul, 1979.

CLARK, PETER M., and JAMES Q. WILSON. "Incentive Systems: A Theory of Organizations," *Administrative Science Quarterly,* 6 (September 1961), 129–66.

CLEMMER, DONALD. *The Prison Community.* Boston: Christopher, 1940.

CLOUGH, DONALD J. *Concepts in Management Science.* Englewood Cliffs, N.J.: Prentice-Hall, 1963.

COASE, R. H. "The Nature of the Firm," *Economica N.S.,* 4 (November 1937), 386–405.

COCH, L., and J. R. P. FRENCH, JR. "Overcoming Resistance to Change," *Human Relations,* 1:4 (1948), 512–32.

COHEN, BERNARD P. "On the Construction of Sociological Explanations," *Synthese,* 24 (December 1972), 401–9.

COHEN, KALMAN J., and RICHARD M. CYERT. "Simulation of Organizational Behavior," in *Handbook of Organizations,* pp. 305–34, ed. James G. March. Chicago: Rand McNally, 1965.

COHEN, MICHAEL D., and JAMES G. MARCH. *Leadership and Ambiguity: The American College President.* New York: McGraw-Hill, 1974.

————. "Decisions, Presidents, and Status," in *Ambiguity and Choice in Organizations,* pp. 174–205, eds. James G. March and Johan P. Olsen. Bergen, Norway: Universitetsforlaget, 1976.

COHEN, MICHAEL D., JAMES G. MARCH, and JOHAN P. OLSEN. "A Garbage Can Model of Organizational Choice," *Administrative Science Quarterly,* 17 (March 1972), 1–25.

————. "People, Problems, Solutions and the Ambiguity of Relevance," in *Ambiguity and Choice in Organizations,* pp. 24–37, eds. James G. March and Johan P. Olsen. Bergen, Norway: Universitetsforlaget, 1976.

COLEMAN, JAMES S. *Power and the Structure of Society.* New York: W. W. Norton & Co., Inc., 1974.

————. "Social Structure and a Theory of Action," in *Approaches to the Study of Social Structure,* pp. 76–93, ed. Peter M. Blau. New York: Free Press, 1975.

COLLINS, BARRY E., and BERTRAM H. RAVEN. "Group Structure: Attraction, Coalitions, Communication, and Power," in *The Handbook of Social Psychology* (2nd ed.), pp. 102–204, Gardner Lindzey and Elliot Aronson. Reading, Ma.: Addison-Wesley, 1969.

COLLINS, ORVIS. "Ethnic Behavior in Industry: Sponsorship and Rejection in a New England Factory," *American Journal of Sociology,* 21 (1946), 293–98.

COLLINS, RANDALL. "Functional and Conflict Theories of Educational Stratification," *American Sociological Review,* 36 (December 1971), 1002–19.

————. *The Credential Society.* New York: Academic Press, 1979.

COMMONS, JOHN R. *Legal Foundations of Capitalism.* New York: Macmillan, 1924.

COMSTOCK, DONALD E., and W. RICHARD SCOTT. "Technology and the Structure of Subunits: Distinguishing Individual and Workgroup Effects," *Administrative Science Quarterly,* 22 (June 1977), 177–202.

COOK, T. D., and DONALD T. CAMPBELL. "The Design and Conduct of Quasi-Experiments and True Experiments in Field Settings," in *Handbook of Industrial and Organizational Psychology,* ed. M. D. Dunnette. Chicago: Rand McNally, 1976.

COSER, ROSE LAUB. "An Analysis of the Early German Socialist Movement." Unpublished M.A. thesis, Department of Sociology, Columbia University, 1951.

CROZIER, MICHEL. *The Bureaucratic Phenomenon.* Chicago: University of Chicago Press, 1964.

CUMMINGS, LARRY L. "Emergence of the Instrumental Organization," in *New Perspectives on Organizational Effectiveness,* pp. 56–62, eds. Paul S. Goodman and Johannes M. Pennings. San Francisco: Jossey-Bass, 1977.

CYERT, RICHARD M., and JAMES G. MARCH. *A Behavioral Theory of the Firm.* Englewood Cliffs, N.J.: Prentice-Hall, 1963.

DAHL, ROBERT A. *After the Revolution?* New Haven: Yale University Press, 1970.

DAHRENDORF, RALF. *Class and Class Conflict in Industrial Society.* Stanford, Ca.: Stanford University Press, 1959 tr. (First published in 1957).

DALTON, MELVILLE. "Conflicts Between Staff and Line Managerial Officers," *American Sociological Review,* 15 (June 1950), 342–51.

————. *Men Who Manage.* New York: John Wiley, 1959.

DAVIS, KINGSLEY. *Human Society.* New York: Macmillan, 1949.

DELANY, WILLIAM. "The Development and Decline of Patrimonial and Bureaucratic Administrations," *Administrative Science Quarterly,* 7 (March 1963), 458–501.

DIAMOND, SIGMUND. "From Organization to Society," *American Journal of Sociology,* 63 (March 1958), 457–75.

DILL, WILLIAM R. "Environment as an Influence on Managerial Autonomy," *Administrative Science Quarterly,* 2 (March 1958), 409–43.

DOERINGER, PETER B., and MICHAEL J. PIORE. *Internal Labor Markets and Manpower Analysis.* Lexington, Ma.: Heath, 1971.

DONABEDIAN, AVEDIS. "Evaluating the Quality of Medical Care," *Milbank Memorial Fund Quarterly,* 44 (July 1966), part 2, 166–206.

DORE, RONALD. *British Factory–Japanese Factory.* Berkeley: University of California Press, 1973.

DORNBUSCH, SANFORD M., and W. RICHARD SCOTT, with the assistance of BRUCE C. BUSCHING and JAMES D. LAING. *Evaluation and the Exercise of Authority.* San Francisco: Jossey-Bass, 1975.

DOWNS, ANTHONY. *Inside Bureaucracy.* Boston: Little, Brown, 1967.

DRUCKER, PETER. "The New Markets and the New Capitalism," *The Public Interest,* 21 (Fall 1970), 44–79.

DUBIN, ROBERT, ed. *Human Relations in Administration,* (3rd ed.). Englewood Cliffs, N.J.: Prentice-Hall, 1968.

DUNCAN, ROBERT B. "Characteristics of Organizational Environments and Perceived Environmental Uncertainty," *Administrative Science Quarterly,* 17 (September 1972), 313–27.

DURKHEIM, EMILE. *Division of Labor in Society.* Glencoe, Ill.: Free Press, 1949 tr. (First published in 1893).

DUVERGER, MAURICE. *Political Parties.* Trans. by Barbara and Robert North. New York: John Wiley, 1963. (First published in 1951).

EDITORS OF THE YALE LAW JOURNAL. "The American Medical Association: Power, Purpose, and Politics in Organized Medicine," *The Yale Law Journal,* 63 (May 1954), 938–1022.

EISENSTADT, S. N. "Bureaucracy and Bureaucratization: A Trend Report and Bibliography," *Current Sociology,* 7:2 (1958), 99–164.

ELLUL, JACQUES. *The Technological Society.* New York: Knopf, 1964 tr. (First published in 1954).

EMERY, F. E., and E. L. TRIST. "The Causal Texture of Organizational Environments," *Human Relations,* 18 (February 1965), 21–32.

EMERSON, RICHARD M. "Power-Dependence Relations," *American Sociological Review,* 27 (February 1962), 31–40.

ETZIONI, AMITAI. "Two Approaches to Organizational Analysis: A Critique and a Suggestion," *Administrative Science Quarterly,* 5 (September 1960), 257–78.

———. *A Comparative Analysis of Complex Organizations.* New York: Free Press of Glencoe, 1961. (Rev. 1975).

———. *Modern Organizations.* Englewood Cliffs, N.J.: Prentice-Hall, 1964.

———, ed. *The Semi-Professions and Their Organization.* New York: Free Press, 1969.

EVAN, WILLIAM M. "The Organization Set: Toward a Theory of Interorganizational Relations," in *Approaches to Organizational Design,* pp. 173–88, ed. James D. Thompson. Pittsburgh: University of Pittsburgh Press, 1966.

FAUNCE, WILLIAM A. *Problems of an Industrial Society.* New York: McGraw-Hill, 1968.

FAYOL, HENRI. *General and Industrial Management.* Trans. by Constance Stours. London: Pitman, 1949 tr. (First published in 1919).

FESTINGER, LEON. *A Theory of Cognitive Dissonance.* Evanston, Ill.: Row, Peterson, 1957.

FIEDLER, FRED E. "A Contingency Model of Leadership Effectiveness," in *Advances in Experimental Social Psychology,* ed. Leonard Berkowitz. New York: Academic Press, 1964.

―――. "Validation and Extension of the Contingency Model of Leadership Effectiveness: A Review of Empirical Findings," *Psychological Bulletin,* 76 (August 1971), 128–48.

FLEXNER, ABRAHAM. "Is Social Work a Profession?" *Proceedings of the National Conference of Charities and Corrections,* pp. 576–90. Chicago: Hildmann Printing Co., 1915.

FLOOD, ANN BARRY, WAYNE EWY, W. RICHARD SCOTT, WILLIAM H. FORREST, JR., and BYRON WILLIAM BROWN, JR. "The Relationship Between Intensity and Duration of Medical Services and Outcomes for Hospitalized Patients," *Medical Care,* 17 (November 1979), 1088–1102.

FOX, FREDERICK V., and BARRY M. STAW. "The Trapped Administrator: Effects of Job Insecurity and Policy Resistance Upon Commitment to a Course of Action," *Administrative Science Quarterly,* 24 (September 1979), 449–71.

FOX, RENÉE. *Experiment Perilous.* Glencoe, Ill.: Free Press, 1959.

FREEDMAN, MARCIA. *Labor Markets: Segments and Shelters.* Montclair, N.J.: Allanheld, Osmun, 1976.

FREEMAN, JOHN H. "The Unit of Analysis in Organizational Research," in *Environments and Organizations,* pp. 335–51, ed. Marshall W. Meyer. San Francisco: Jossey-Bass, 1978.

FREEMAN, JOHN H., and MICHAEL T. HANNAN. "Growth and Decline Processes in Organizations," *American Sociological Review,* 40 (April 1975), 215–28.

FREIDSON, ELIOT. *Professional Dominance: The Social Structure of Medical Care.* Chicago: Aldine, 1970a.

―――. *Profession of Medicine.* New York: Dodd, Mead, 1970b.

―――. "Professions and the Occupational Principle," in *The Professions and Their Prospects,* pp. 19–33, ed. Eliot Freidson. Beverly Hills, Ca.: Sage Publications, Inc., 1973.

―――. *Doctoring Together: A Study of Professional Social Control.* New York: Elsevier, 1975.

―――. "The Futures of Professionalisation," in *Health and the Division of Labor,* pp. 14–38, eds. Margaret Stacey et al. London: Croom Helm, 1977.

FREIDSON, ELIOT, and BUFORD RHEA. "Processes of Control in a Company of Equals," *Social Problems,* 11 (Fall 1963), 119–31.

FRIEDLANDER, FRANK and HAL PICKLE. "Components of Effectiveness in Small Organizations," *Administrative Science Quarterly,* 13 (September 1968), 289–304.

FRIEDMAN, MILTON. *Capitalism and Freedom.* Chicago: University of Chicago Press, 1962.

FRIEDRICH, CARL J., and ZBIGNIEW K. BRZEZINSKI. *Totalitarian Dictatorship and Autocracy.* Cambridge, Mass.: Harvard University Press, 1956.

FUCHS, VICTOR R. *Who Shall Live? Health, Economics, and Social Choice.* New York: Basic Books, 1974.

GALBRAITH, JAY. *Designing Complex Organizations.* Reading, Mass.: Addison-Wesley, 1973.

――――. *Organization Design.* Reading, Mass.: Addison-Wesley, 1977.

GALBRAITH, JOHN KENNETH. *American Capitalism.* Boston: Houghton Mifflin, 1952.

――――. *The New Industrial State.* Boston: Houghton Mifflin, 1967.

GAMSON, WILLIAM. *The Strategy of Protest.* Homewood, Ill.: Dorsey, 1975.

GHORPADE, JAISINGH, ed. *Assessment of Organizational Effectiveness.* Pacific Palisades, Ca.: Goodyear, 1971.

GLASSMAN, ROBERT. "Persistence and Loose Coupling in Living Systems," *Behavioral Science,* 18 (March 1973), 83–98.

GOFFMAN, ERVING. *Asylums.* Garden City, N.Y.: Doubleday, Anchor Books, 1961.

GOLDMAN, PAUL, and DONALD R. VAN HOUTEN. "Managerial Strategies and the Worker: A Marxist Analysis of Bureaucracy," *The Sociological Quarterly,* 18 (Winter 1977), 108–25.

GOLDNER, FRED H. "The Division of Labor: Process and Power," in *Power in Organizations,* pp. 97–143, ed. Mayer N. Zald. Nashville, Tenn.: Vanderbilt University Press, 1970.

GOODE, WILLIAM J. "Community Within a Community: The Professions," *American Sociological Review,* 22 (April 1957), 194–200.

GOODMAN, PAUL. *People or Personnel* and *Like a Conquered Providence.* New York: Vintage, 1968.

GOODMAN, PAUL S., and JOHANNES M. PENNINGS, eds. *New Perspectives on Organizational Effectiveness.* San Francisco: Jossey-Bass, 1977.

GOSNELL, HAROLD F. *Machine Politics: Chicago Model.* Chicago: University of Chicago Press, 1937.

GOSS, MARY E. W. "Influence and Authority Among Physicians in an Outpatient Clinic," *American Sociological Review,* 26 (February 1961), 39–50.

GOULDNER, ALVIN W. *Patterns of Industrial Bureaucracy.* Glencoe, Ill.: Free Press, 1954.

――――. "Metaphysical Pathos and the Theory of Bureaucracy," *American Political Science Review,* 49 (June 1955), 496–507.

――――. "Organizational Analysis," in *Sociology Today,* pp. 400–28, eds. Robert K. Merton, Leonard Broom, and Leonard S. Cottrell, Jr. New York: Basic Books, 1959.

GREENBLATT, MILTON, DANIEL J. LEVINSON, and RICHARD WILLIAMS, eds. *The Patient and the Mental Hospital.* Glencoe, Ill.: Free Press, 1957.

GRIMES, A. J., and S. M. KLEIN. "The Technological Imperative: The Relative Impact of Task Unit, Modal Technology, and Hierarchy on Structure," *Academy of Management Journal*, 16 (December 1973), 583–97.

GROSS, EDWARD. "Some Functional Consequences of Primary Controls in Formal Work Organizations," *American Sociological Review*, 18 (August 1953), 368–73.

———. "Universities as Organizations: A Research Approach," *American Sociological Review*, 33 (August 1968), 518–44.

GROSS, NEAL, WARD S. MASON, and ALEXANDER W. MCEACHERN. *Explorations in Role Analysis.* New York: John Wiley, 1958.

GUETZKOW, HAROLD. "Communications in Organizations," in *Handbook of Organizations*, pp. 534–73, ed. James G. March. Chicago: Rand McNally, 1965.

GUETZKOW, HAROLD, and HERBERT A. SIMON. "The Impact of Certain Communication Nets upon Organization and Performance in Task-Oriented Groups," *Management Science*, 1 (April-July 1955), 233–50.

GULICK, LUTHER, and L. URWICK, eds. *Papers on the Science of Administration.* New York: Institute of Public Administration, Columbia University, 1937.

GUSFIELD, JOSEPH R. "The Study of Social Movements," *International Encyclopedia of the Social Sciences*, vol 14, 445–52. New York: Macmillan, 1968.

HAAS, J. EUGENE, RICHARD H. HALL, and NORMAN J. JOHNSON. "Toward an Empirically Derived Taxonomy of Organizations," in *Studies on Behavior in Organizations*, pp. 157–80, ed. Raymond V. Bowers. Athens, Ga.: University of Georgia Press, 1966.

HABERSTROH, CHADWICK J. "Organization Design and Systems Analysis," in *Handbook of Organizations*, pp. 1171–211, ed. James G. March. Chicago: Rand McNally, 1965.

HACKMAN, J. RICHARD, and EDWARD E. LAWLER III. "Employee Reactions to Job Characteristics," *Journal of Applied Psychology Monograph*, 55 (June 1971), 259–86.

HAGE, JERALD. "An Axiomatic Theory of Organizations," *Administrative Science Quarterly*, 10 (December 1965), 289–320.

HAGE, JERALD, and MICHAEL AIKEN. "Routine Technology, Social Structure, and Organization Goals," *Administrative Science Quarterly*, 14 (September 1969), 366–76.

HALL, A. D., and R. E. FAGEN. "Definition of System," *General Systems: The Yearbook of the Society for the Advancement of General Systems Theory*, 1 (1956), 18–28.

HALL, RICHARD H. "The Concept of Bureaucracy: An Empirical Assessment," *American Journal of Sociology*, 69 (July 1963), 32–40.

———. "Some Organizational Considerations in the Professional-Organizational Relationship," *Administrative Science Quarterly*, 12 (December 1967), 461–78.

———. "Professionalization and Bureaucratization," *American Sociological Review*, 33 (February 1968), 92–104.

————. *Organizations: Structure and Process.* Englewood Cliffs, N.J.: Prentice-Hall, 1972. (Rev. 1977).

HALL, RICHARD H., J. EUGENE HAAS, and NORMAN J. JOHNSON. "An Examination of the Blau-Scott and Etzioni Typologies," *Administrative Science Quarterly,* 12 (June 1967*a*), 118–39.

————. "Organizational Size, Complexity, and Formalization," *American Sociological Review,* 32 (December 1967*b*), 903–12.

HALL, RICHARD H., and CHARLES R. TITTLE. "Bureaucracy and Its Correlates," *American Journal of Sociology,* 72 (November 1966), 267–72.

HANNAN, MICHAEL T., and JOHN FREEMAN. "The Population Ecology of Organizations," *American Journal of Sociology,* 82 (March 1977), 929–64.

HART, DAVID K., and WILLIAM G. SCOTT. "The Organizational Imperative," *Administration and Society,* 7 (November 1975), 259–85.

HARVEY, EDWARD. "Technology and the Structure of Organizations," *American Sociological Review,* 33 (April 1968), 247–59.

HAWLEY, AMOS. *Human Ecology.* New York: Ronald, 1950.

HEMPEL, C. "The Logic of Functional Analysis," in *Symposium on Sociological Theory,* pp. 271–307, ed. Llewellyn Gross. Evanston, Ill.: Row, Peterson, 1959.

HENDERSON, LAWRENCE J. *Pareto's General Sociology.* Cambridge, Mass.: Harvard University Press, 1935.

HERZBERG, FREDERICK. *Work and the Nature of Man.* Cleveland: World Publishing, 1966.

HEYDEBRAND, WOLF V. "Autonomy, Complexity, and Non-Bureaucratic Coordination in Professional Organizations," in *Comparative Organizations,* ed. Wolf V. Heydebrand. Englewood Cliffs, N.J.: Prentice-Hall, 1973.

HICKSON, DAVID J., C. R. HININGS, C. A. LEE, R. E. SCHNECK, and J. M. PENNINGS. "A Strategic Contingencies' Theory of Intraorganizational Power," *Administrative Science Quarterly,* 16 (June 1971), 216–29.

HICKSON, DAVID J., D. S. PUGH, and DIANA C. PHEYSEY. "Operations Technology and Organization Structure: An Empirical Reappraisal," *Administrative Science Quarterly,* 14 (September 1969), 378–97.

HILLERY, GEORGE A., JR. *Communal Organizations: A Study of Local Societies.* Chicago: University of Chicago Press, 1968.

HIND, ROBERT R., SANFORD M. DORNBUSCH, and W. RICHARD SCOTT. "A Theory of Evaluation Applied to a University Faculty," *Sociology of Education,* 47 (Winter 1974), 114–28.

HININGS, C. R., D. J. HICKSON, J. M. PENNINGS, and R. E. SCHNECK. "Structural Conditions of Intraorganizational Power," *Administrative Science Quarterly,* 19 (March 1974), 22–44.

HIRSCHMAN, ALBERT O. *Exit, Voice, and Loyalty.* Cambridge, Mass.: Harvard University Press, 1970.

HOFSTADTER, RICHARD. *Social Darwinism in American Thought, 1860–1915.* Philadelphia: University of Pennsylvania Press, 1945.

HOLDAWAY, EDWARD A., and THOMAS A. BLOWERS. "Administrative Ratios and Organizational Size: A Longitudinal Examination," *American Sociological Review,* 36 (April 1971), 278–86.

HOLLANDER, EDWIN P., and JAMES W. JULIAN. "Contemporary Trends in the Analysis of Leadership Processes," *Psychological Bulletin,* 71 (May 1969), 387–97.

HOMANS, GEORGE C. *The Human Group.* New York: Harcourt, 1950.

————. *Social Behavior: Its Elementary Forms.* New York: Harcourt, Brace and World, 1961.

HOPKINS, TERENCE K. "Bureaucratic Authority: The Convergence of Weber and Barnard," in *Complex Organizations: A Sociological Reader,* ed. Amitai Etzioni. New York: Holt, Rinehart and Winston, 1961.

HOUSE, WILLIAM C., ed. *The Impact of Information Technology on Management Operation.* Princeton, N.J.: Auerbach Publishers, 1971.

HREBINIAK, LAWRENCE G. "Job Technology, Supervision and Work Group Structure, *Administrative Science Quarterly,* 19 (September 1974), 395–410.

HUDSON, ROBERT B. "Rational Planning and Organizational Imperatives: Prospects for Area Planning in Aging," *Annals of the American Academy of Political and Social Science,* 415 (September 1974), 41–54.

HUGHES, EVERETT C. "The Knitting of Racial Groups in Industry," *American Sociological Review,* 11 (October 1946), 512–19.

————. *Men and Their Work.* Glencoe, Ill.: Free Press, 1958.

HULIN, CHARLES L., and MILTON R. BLOOD. "Job Enlargement, Individual Differences, and Worker Responses, *Psychological Bulletin,* 69 (January 1968), 41–55.

IANNI, FRANCIS A. J. *A Family Business: Kinship and Social Control in Organized Crime.* New York: Russell Sage Foundation, 1972.

ILLICH, IVAN. *Deschooling Society.* New York: Harper & Row, Pub. (Harrow Books), 1972.

————. *Medical Nemesis.* New York: Random House, 1976.

INKELES, ALEX. "Making Men Modern: On the Causes and Consequences of Individual Change in Six Developing Countries," *American Journal of Sociology,* 75 (September 1969), 208–25.

ISRAEL, JOACHIM. *Alienation: From Marx to Modern Sociology.* Boston: Allyn & Bacon, 1971.

JACOBS, DAVID. "Dependency and Vulnerability: An Exchange Approach to the Control of Organizations," *Administrative Science Quarterly,* 19 (March 1974), 45–59.

JACOBY, HENRY. *The Bureaucratization of the World.* Trans. by Eveline L. Kanes. Berkeley: University of California Press, 1973.

JOHNSON, RICHARD A., FREMONT E. KAST, and JAMES E. ROSENZWEIG. *The Theory and Management of Systems* (2nd ed.) New York: McGraw-Hill, 1967.

JURKOVICH, RAY. "A Core Typology of Organizational Environments," *Administrative Science Quarterly,* 19 (September 1974), 380–94.

KAHN, ROBERT L., D. M. WOLFE, R. P. QUINN, J. D. SNOEK, and ROBERT A. ROSENTHAL. *Organizational Stress.* New York: John Wiley, 1964.

KALLEK, SHIRLEY. "Potential Applications of Census Bureau Economic Series in Microdata Analysis," *American Economic Review,* 65 (May 1975), 257–62.

KANTER, ROSABETH MOSS. *Committment and Community: Communes and Utopias in Sociological Perspective.* Cambridge, Mass.: Harvard University Press, 1972.

————. *Men and Women of the Corporation.* New York: Basic Books, 1977a.

————. *Work and Family in the United States: A Critical Review and Agenda for Research and Policy.* New York: Russell Sage Foundation, 1977b.

KASARDA, JOHN D. "The Structural Implications of Social System Size: A Three-Level Analysis," *American Sociological Review,* 39 (February 1974), 19–28.

KATZ, DANIEL, and ROBERT L. KAHN. "Some Recent Findings in Human Relations Research in Industry," in *Readings in Social Psychology,* (2nd ed.), pp. 650–65, eds. Guy E. Swanson, Theodor M. Newcomb, and Eugene L. Hartley. New York: Holt, 1952.

————. *The Social Psychology of Organizations.* New York: John Wiley, 1966. (Rev. 1978).

KATZ, DANIEL, N. MACCOBY, G. GURIN, and L. FLOOR. *Productivity, Supervision and Morale Among Railroad Workers.* Ann Arbor, Mich.: Institute for Social Research, 1951.

KATZ, DANIEL, N. MACCOBY, and N. MORSE. *Productivity, Supervision and Morale in an Office Situation.* Ann Arbor, Mich.: Institute for Social Research, 1950.

KATZ, ELIHU, and S. N. EISENSTADT. "Some Sociological Observations on the Response of Israeli Organizations to New Immigrants," *Administrative Science Quarterly,* 5 (June 1960), 113–33.

KAUFMAN, HERBERT. "Emerging Conflicts in the Doctrines of Public Administration," *American Political Science Review,* 50 (December 1956), 1057–73.

————. "Administrative Decentralization and Political Power," *Public Administration Review,* 29 (January-February 1969), 3–15.

————. "The Natural History of Human Organizations," *Administration and Society,* 7 (August 1975), 131–49.

————. *Are Government Organizations Immortal?* Washington, D.C.: Brookings Institution, 1976.

KENDALL, PATRICIA L., and PAUL F. LAZARSFELD. "Problems of Survey Analysis," in *Continuities in Social Research: Studies in the Scope and Method of "The American Soldier,"* pp. 133–96, eds. Robert K. Merton and Paul F. Lazarsfeld. Glencoe, Ill.: Free Press, 1950.

KENNEDY, ROBERT F. *Thirteen Days: A Memoir of the Cuban Missile Crisis.* New York: W. W. Norton & Co., Inc., 1969.

KERR, CLARK, JOHN T. DUNLOP, FREDERICK HARBISON, and CHARLES A. MYERS. *Industrialism and Industrial Man. (2nd ed.):* New York: Oxford University Press, 1964.

KHANDWALLA, PRADIP N. "Mass Output Orientation of Operations Technology and Organizational Structure," *Administrative Science Quarterly,* 19 (March 1974), 74–97.

————. *The Design of Organizations.* New York: Harcourt Brace Jovanovich, 1977.

KIMBERLY, JOHN. "Organizational Size and the Structuralist Perspective: A Review, Critique and Proposal," *Administrative Science Quarterly,* 21 (December 1976), 571–97.

KING, NATHAN. "Clarification and Evaluation of the Two-Factor Theory of Job Satisfaction," *Psychological Bulletin,* 74 (July 1970), 18–31.

KOHLMEIER, LOUIS M., JR. *The Regulators: Watchdog Agencies and the Public Interest.* New York: Harper & Row, Pub., 1969.

KOHN, MELVIN L. "Bureaucratic Man: A Portrait and an Interpretation," *American Sociological Review,* 36 (June 1971), 461–74.

KOHN, MELVIN L., and CARMI SCHOOLER. "Occupational Experience and Psychological Functioning: An Assessment of Reciprocal Effects," *American Sociological Review,* 38 (February 1973), 97–118.

KORNHAUSER, WILLIAM. *Scientists in Industry: Conflict and Accommodation.* Berkeley: University of California Press, 1962.

KRAUSE, ELLIOTT A. "Functions of a Bureaucratic Ideology: 'Citizen Participation,' " *Social Problems,* 16 (Fall 1968), 129–43.

————. *Power and Illness: The Political Sociology of Health and Medical Care.* New York: Elsevier, 1977.

KRUPP, SHERMAN. *Pattern in Organization Analysis.* Philadelphia: Chilton, 1961.

KUHN, THOMAS S. *The Structure of Scientific Revolutions.* Chicago: University of Chicago Press, 1962.

LAMMERS, CORNELIS J., and DAVID J. HICKSON. "A Cross-National and Cross-Institutional Typology of Organizations," in *Organizations Alike and Unlike,* pp. 420–34, eds. Cornelis J. Lammers and David J. Hickson, London: Routledge & Kegan Paul, 1979*a*.

————. "Are Organizations Culture-Bound?" in *Organizations Alike and Unlike,* pp. 402–19, eds. Cornelis J. Lammers and David J. Hickson. London: Routledge & Kegan Paul, 1979*b*.

————, eds. *Organizations Alike and Unlike: International and Interinstitutional Studies in the Sociology of Organizations.* London: Routledge & Kegan Paul, 1979c.

LANDSBERGER, HENRY A. *Hawthorne Revisited.* Ithaca, N.Y.: Cornell University Press, 1958.

————. "Parsons' Theory of Organizations," in *Social Theories of Talcott Parsons,* pp. 214–49, ed. Max Black. Englewood Cliffs, N.J.: Prentice-Hall, 1961.

————. *Comparative Perspectives on Formal Organizations.* Boston: Little, Brown, 1970.

LAUMANN, EDWARD O., and FRANZ U. PAPPI. *Networks of Collective Action.* New York: Academic Press, 1976.

LAWRENCE, PAUL R., and JAY W. LORSCH. *Organization and Environment: Managing Differentiation and Integration.* Boston: Graduate School of Business Administration, Harvard University, 1967.

LAZARSFELD, PAUL F. "Problems in Methodology," in *Sociology Today,* pp. 39–78, eds. Robert K. Merton, Leonard Broom, and Leonard S. Cottrell, Jr. New York: Basic Books, 1959.

LAZARSFELD, PAUL F., and HERBERT MENZEL. "On the Relation Between Individual and Collective Properties," in *Complex Organizations: A Sociological Reader,* pp. 422–40, ed. Amitai Etzioni. New York: Holt, Rinehart and Winston, 1961.

LAZARSFELD, PAUL F., and WAGNER THIELENS, JR. *The Academic Mind.* Glencoe, Ill.: Free Press, 1958.

LEAVITT, HAROLD J. "Some Effects of Certain Communication Patterns on Group Performance," *Journal of Abnormal and Social Psychology,* 46 (1951), 38–50.

————. "Unhuman Organizations," in *Readings in Managerial Psychology,* pp. 542–56, eds. Harold J. Leavitt and Louis R. Pondy. Chicago: University of Chicago Press, 1964.

————. "Applied Organizational Change in Industry: Structural, Technological and Humanistic Approaches," in *Handbook of Organizations,* pp. 1144–70, ed. James G. March. Chicago: Rand McNally, 1965.

LEAVITT, HAROLD J., WILLIAM R. DILL, and HENRY B. EYRING. *The Organizational World.* New York: Harcourt Brace Jovanovich, 1973.

LEFTON, MARK, and WILLIAM R. ROSENGREN. "Organizations and Clients: Lateral and Longitudinal Dimensions," *American Sociological Review,* 31 (December 1966), 802–10.

LEVENSON, BERNARD. "Bureaucratic Succession," in *Complex Organizations: A Sociological Reader,* pp. 362–75, ed. Amitai Etzioni. New York: Holt, Rinehart and Winston, 1961.

LEVINE, SOL, and PAUL E. WHITE. "Exchange as a Conceptual Framework for the Study of Interorganizational Relationships," *Administrative Science Quarterly,* 5 (March 1961), 583–601.

LEWIN, KURT. *Resolving Social Conflicts.* New York: Harper, 1948.

LICHTMAN, CARY M., and RAYMOND G. HUNT. "Personality and Organization Theory: A Review of Some Conceptual Literature," *Psychological Bulletin,* 76 (October 1971), 271–94.

LIGHT, IVAN H. *Ethnic Enterprise in America.* Berkeley: University of California Press, 1972.

LIKERT, RENSIS. *New Patterns of Management.* New York: McGraw-Hill, 1961.

LIKERT, RENSIS, and JANE C. LIKERT. *New Ways of Managing Conflict.* New York: McGraw-Hill, 1976.

LILIENTHAL, DAVID E. *TVA: Democracy on the March.* New York: Harper and Brothers, 1944.

LINDBLOM, CHARLES E. "The 'Science' of Muddling Through," *Public Administration Review,* 19 (Spring 1959), 79–88.

———. *Politics and Markets.* New York: Basic Books, 1977.

LIPPITT, RONALD, NORMAN POLANSKY, FRITZ REDL, and SIDNEY ROSEN. "The Dynamics of Power," in *Group Dynamics,* pp. 462–82, eds. Dorwin Cartwright and Alvin Zander. Evanston, Ill.: Row, Peterson, 1953.

LIPSET, SEYMOUR MARTIN. *Political Man.* New York: Doubleday, 1960.

LIPSET, SEYMOUR MARTIN, MARTIN A. TROW, and JAMES S. COLEMAN. *Union Democracy.* Glencoe, Ill.: Free Press, 1956.

LITTERER, JOSEPH A., ed. *Organizations: Structure and Behavior.* New York: John Wiley, 1963.

LITWAK, EUGENE. "Models of Bureaucracy Which Permit Conflict," *American Journal of Sociology,* 67 (September 1961), 177–84.

———. "Technological Innovation and Theoretical Functions of Primary Groups and Bureaucratic Structures," *American Journal of Sociology,* 73 (January 1968), 468–81.

LITWAK, EUGENE, and LYDIA F. HYLTON. "Interorganizational Analysis: A Hypothesis on Coordinating Agencies," *Administrative Science Quarterly,* 6 (March 1962), 395–420.

LITWAK, EUGENE, and HENRY J. MEYER. "A Balance Theory of Coordination Between Bureaucratic Organizations and Community Primary Groups," *Administrative Science Quarterly,* 11 (June 1966), 31–58.

LOWI, THEODORE J. *The End of Liberalism.* New York: W. W. Norton & Co., Inc., 1969.

LOWIN, AARON, and JAMES R. CRAIG. "The Influence of Level of Performance on Managerial Style: An Experimental Object-Lesson in the Ambiguity of Correlational Data," *Organizational Behavior and Human Performance,* 3 (November 1968), 440–58.

MCCARTHY, JOHN D., and MAYER N. ZALD. "Resource Mobilization and Social Movements: A Partial Theory," *American Journal of Sociology,* 82 (May 1977), 1212–41.

MCCAULEY, BRIAN L., SANFORD M. DORNBUSCH, and W. RICHARD SCOTT. "Evaluation and Authority in Alternative Schools and Public Schools," Technical Report #23. Stanford, Ca.: Stanford Center for Research and Development in Teaching, 1972.

MCGREGOR, DOUGLAS. *The Human Side of Enterprise.* New York: McGraw-Hill, 1960.

MACIVER, ROBERT M. *The Web of Government.* New York: Macmillan, 1947.

McKELVEY, BILL. "Guidelines for the Empirical Classification of Organizations," *Administrative Science Quarterly,* 20 (December 1975), 509–25.

———. "Organizational Systematics: Taxonomic Lessons from Biology," *Management Science,* 24 (September 1978), 1428–40.

McLEAN, ALAN. *Mental Health and Work Organizations.* Chicago: Rand McNally, 1970.

McLUHAN, MARSHALL. *Understanding Media: The Extensions of Man.* New York: Signet, 1964.

McMILLAN, CHARLES J., DAVID J. HICKSON, CHRISTOPHER R. HININGS, and RODNEY E. SCHNECK. "The Structure of Work Organizations Across Societies," *Academy of Management Journal,* 16 (December 1973), 555–69.

MAIER, NORMAN R. F. *Principles of Human Relations.* New York: John Wiley, 1952.

MAILER, NORMAN. "The Steps of the Pentagon," *Harper's,* 236 (March 1968), 47–142.

MALINOWSKI, BRONISLAW. "The Group and the Individual in Functional Analysis," *American Journal of Sociology,* 44 (1939), 938–64.

MANN, JUDITH K., and DONALD E. YETT. "The Analysis of Hospital Costs: A Review Article," *Journal of Business,* 41 (April 1968), 191–202.

MANNHEIM, KARL. *Man and Society in an Age of Reconstruction.* Trans. by Edward Shils. New York: Harcourt Brace Jovanovich, 1950. (First published in 1935).

MANSFIELD, ROGER. "Bureaucracy and Centralization: An Examination of Organizational Structure," *Administrative Science Quarterly,* 18 (December 1973), 77–88.

MARCH, JAMES G. "The Technology of Foolishness," in *Ambiguity and Choice in Organizations,* pp. 69–81, eds. James G. March and Johan P. Olsen. Bergen, Norway: Universitetsforlaget, 1976.

———. "Bounded Rationality, Ambiguity, and the Engineering of Choice," *Bell Journal of Economics,* 9 (Autumn 1978), 587–608.

MARCH, JAMES G., and JOHAN P. OLSEN. *Ambiguity and Choice in Organizations.* Bergen, Norway: Universitetsforlaget, 1976*a*.

———. "Organizational Choice Under Ambiguity," in *Ambiguity and Choice in Organizations,* pp. 10–23, eds. James G. March and Johan P. Olsen. Bergen, Norway: Universitetsforlaget, 1976*b*.

MARCH, JAMES G., and HERBERT A. SIMON. *Organizations.* New York: John Wiley, 1958.

MARX, KARL. *Capital.* Moscow: Foreign Languages Publishing House, 1954 tr., 1st ed. (First published in 1867).

———. *Karl Marx: Early Writings.* Trans. and ed. by T. B. Bottomore. London: C. A. Watts, 1963. (First published as the Economic and Philosophical Manuscripts, 1844).

———. *Karl Marx: Selected Writings in Sociology and Social Philosophy.* Trans. by T. B. Bottomore. New York: McGraw-Hill, 1964. (First published 1844 to 1847).

———. "Economic and Philosophic Manuscripts of 1844: Selections," in *The Marx-Engels Reader,* ed. Robert C. Tucker. New York: W. W. Norton & Co., Inc., 1972.

MARX, KARL, and FREDERICK ENGELS. *Manifesto of the Communist Party.* Moscow: Foreign Languages Publishing House, 1955 tr. (First published 1848).

MARX, MORSTEIN. *The Administrative State.* Chicago: University of Chicago Press, 1957.

MASLOW, ABRAHAM. *Motivation and Personality.* New York: Harper, 1954.

MASSIE, JOSEPH L. "Management Theory," in *Handbook of Organizations,* pp. 387–422, ed. James G. March. Chicago: Rand McNally, 1965.

MAURICE, MARC. "For a Study of "The Societal Effect": Universality and Specificity in Organization Research," in *Organizations Alike and Unlike,* pp. 42–60, eds. Cornelis J. Lammers and David J. Hickson. London: Routledge & Kegan Paul, 1979.

MAYO, ELTON. *The Social Problems of an Industrial Civilization.* Boston: Graduate School of Business Administration, Harvard University, 1945.

MECHANIC, DAVID. "Sources of Power of Lower Participants in Complex Organization," *Administrative Science Quarterly,* 7 (December 1962), 349–62.

MELMAN, SEYMOUR. "The Rise of Administrative Overhead in the Manufacturing Industries of the United States, 1899–1947," *Oxford Economic Papers,* 3 (1951), 62–112.

MERTON, ROBERT K. *Social Theory and Social Structure* (2nd ed.). Glencoe, Ill.: Free Press, 1957.

MERTON, ROBERT K., AILSA P. GRAY, BARBARA HOCKEY, and HANAN C. SELVIN, eds. *Reader in Bureaucracy.* Glencoe, Ill.: Free Press, 1952.

MERTON, ROBERT K., GEORGE READER, and PATRICIA L. KENDALL, eds. *The Student Physician.* Cambridge, Ma.: Harvard University Press, 1957.

MESSINGER, SHELDON L. "Organizational Transformation: A Case Study of a Declining Social Movement," *American Sociological Review,* 20 (February 1955), 3–10.

MEYER, JOHN W. "The Effects of Education as an Institution," *American Journal of Sociology,* 83 (July 1977), 55–77.

———. "Strategies for Further Research: Varieties of Environmental Variation," in *Environments and Organizations,* pp. 352–68, ed. Marshall W. Meyer. San Francisco: Jossey-Bass, 1978.

MEYER, JOHN W., and BRIAN ROWAN. "Institutionalized Organizations: Formal Structure as Myth and Ceremony," *American Journal of Sociology,* 83 (September 1977), 340–63.

———. "The Structure of Educational Organizations," in *Environments and Organizations,* pp. 78–109, ed. Marshall W. Meyer. San Francisco: Jossey-Bass, 1978.

MEYER, JOHN W., W. RICHARD SCOTT, SALLY COLE, and JO-ANN K. INTILI. "Instructional Dissensus and Institutional Consensus in Schools," in *Environments and Organizations,* pp. 233–63, ed. Marshall W. Meyer. San Francisco: Jossey-Bass, 1978.

MEYER, JOHN W., W. RICHARD SCOTT, and TERRENCE E. DEAL. "Institutional and Technical Sources of Organizational Structure: Explaining the Structure of Educational Organizations." in *Organization and the Human Services: Cross-Disciplinary Reflections,* ed. Herman Stein. Philadelphia: Temple University Press, 1981.

MEYER, MARSHALL W. "Size and the Structure of Organizations: A Causal Analysis," *American Sociological Review,* 37 (August 1972), 434–41.

———. "Organizational Structure as Signaling," *Pacific Sociological Review,* 22 (October 1979), 481–500.

MICHELS, ROBERT. *Political Parties.* Trans. by Eden and Cedar Paul. Glencoe, Ill.: Free Press, 1949. (First published in 1915).

MILES, MATTHEW B. "On Temporary Systems," in *Innovations in Education,* pp. 437–90, ed. Matthew B. Miles. New York: Teachers College, Columbia University, 1964.

MILGRAM, STANLEY. "The Perils of Obedience," *Harper's* (December 1973), 62–66; 75–77.

———. *Obedience to Authority.* New York: Harper & Row, Pub., 1974.

MILLER, GEORGE A. "What Is Information Measurement?" *American Psychologist,* 8 (1953), 3–12.

MILLER, GEORGE A. "Professionals in Bureaucracy: Alienation Among Industrial Scientists and Engineers," *American Sociological Review,* 32 (October 1967), 755–68.

MILLER, JAMES GRIER. *Living Systems.* New York: McGraw-Hill, 1978.

MILLER, S. M. *Breaking the Credentials Barrier.* New York: Ford Foundation, 1968.

MILLS, C. WRIGHT. *The Power Elite.* New York: Oxford University Press, 1956.

MISES, LUDWIG VON. *Bureaucracy.* New Haven: Yale University Press, 1944.

MOE, EDWARD O. "Consulting with a Community System: A Case Study," *Journal of Social Issues,* 15:2 (1959), 28–35.

MOHR, LAWRENCE B. "Organizational Technology and Organizational Structures," *Administrative Science Quarterly,* 16 (December 1971), 444–59.

MONTAGNA, PAUL D. "Professionalization and Bureaucratization in Large Professional Organizations," *American Journal of Sociology,* 72 (September 1968), 138–45.

———. *Occupations and Society: Toward a Sociology of the Labor Market.* New York: John Wiley, 1977.

MOONEY, JAMES D. "The Principles of Organization," in *Papers on the Science of Administration,* pp. 89–98, eds. Luther Gulick and L. Urwick. New York: Institute of Public Administration, Columbia University, 1937.

MOONEY, JAMES D., and ALLAN C. REILEY. *The Principles of Organization.* New York: Harper, 1939.

MORSE, CHANDLER. "The Functional Imperatives," in *Social Theories of Talcott Parsons,* pp. 100–152, ed. Max Black. Englewood Cliffs, N.J.: Prentice-Hall, 1961.

MOUZELIS, NICOS P. *Organization and Bureaucracy: An Analysis of Modern Theories.* Chicago: Aldine, 1968.

MOYNIHAN, DANIEL P. *Maximum Feasible Misunderstanding.* New York: Free Press, 1970.

MUSTO, DAVID A. "Whatever Happened to 'Community Mental Health'?" *The Public Interest,* 39 (Spring 1975), 53–79.

MYERS, CHARLES A., ed. *The Impact of Computers on Management.* Cambridge, Mass.: The M.I.T. Press, 1967.

NAGEL, ERNEST. *The Structure of Science.* New York: Harcourt, Brace and World, 1961.

NATIONAL TRAINING LABORATORIES. *Explorations in Human Relations Training.* Washington, D.C.: National Training Laboratories, 1953.

NEGANDHI, ANANT R. "Convergence in Organizational Practices: An Empirical Study of Industrial Enterprises in Developing Countries," in *Organizations Alike and Unlike,* pp. 272–86, eds. Cornelis J. Lammers and David J. Hickson. London: Routledge & Kegan Paul, 1979.

NEUHAUSER, DUNCAN. *The Relationship Between Administrative Activities and Hospital Performance.* Chicago: Center for Health Administration Studies, University of Chicago, Research Series 28, 1971.

———. "The Hospital as a Matrix Organization," *Hospital Administration,* 17 (Fall 1972), 8–25.

NEUMANN, FRANZ. *Behemoth.* London: Victor Follancz, 1942.

NEUSTADT, RICHARD. *Presidential Power.* New York: John Wiley, 1960.

NUTTER, G. WARREN. "Concentration," *International Encyclopedia of the Social Sciences,* vol. 3, 218–22. New York: Crowell-Collier and Macmillan, 1968.

OBERSCHALL, ANTHONY. *Social Conflict and Social Movements.* Englewood Cliffs, N.J.: Prentice-Hall, 1973.

ODIONE, GEORGE S. *Management by Objective.* New York: Pitman, 1965.

OFFICE OF MANAGEMENT AND BUDGET. *Standard Industrial Classification Manual.* Washington, D.C.: U.S. Government Printing Office, 1972.

OLSON, MANCUR, JR. *The Logic of Collective Action.* Cambridge, Mass.: Harvard University Press, 1965.

OUCHI, WILLIAM G. "Markets, Bureaucracies and Clans." Unpublished paper, Graduate School of Management, University of California, Los Angeles, July 1979.

———. "Markets, Bureaucracies and Clans," *Administrative Science Quarterly,* 25 (March 1980), 129–41.

OUCHI, WILLIAM G., and ALFRED M. JAEGER. "Type Z Organization: Stability in the Midst of Mobility," *Academy of Management Review,* 3 (April 1978), 305–14.

OUCHI, WILLIAM G., and JERRY B. JOHNSON. "Types of Organizational Control and Their Relationship to Emotional Well-Being," *Administrative Science Quarterly,* 23 (June 1978), 293–317.

PARKINSON, C. NORTHCOTE. *Parkinson's Law and Other Studies in Administration.* Boston: Houghton Mifflin, 1957.

PARSONS, TALCOTT. "The Professions and Social Structure," *Social Forces,* 17 (May 1939), 457–67.

———. "Introduction," to *The Theory of Social and Economic Organization,* pp. 3–86, Max Weber. Glencoe, Ill.: Free Press, 1947.

———. *The Social System.* Glencoe, Ill.: Free Press, 1951.

———. "A Revised Analytical Approach to the Theory of Social Stratification," in *Class, Status and Power: A Reader in Social Stratification,* pp. 92–129, eds. Reinhard Bendix and Seymour M. Lipset, Glencoe, Ill.: Free Press, 1953.

———. *Structure and Process in Modern Societies.* Glencoe, Ill.: Free Press, 1960.

———. *Societies: Evolutionary and Comparative Perspectives.* Englewood Cliffs, N.J.: Prentice-Hall, 1966.

PARSONS, TALCOTT, ROBERT F. BALES, and EDWARD A. SHILS. *Working Papers in the Theory of Action.* Glencoe, Ill.: Free Press, 1953.

PATCHEN, MARTIN. *The Choice of Wage Comparisons.* Englewood Cliffs, N.J.: Prentice-Hall, 1961.

PELZ, DONALD C. "Influence: A Key to Effective Leadership in the First-Line Supervisor," *Personnel,* 29 (1952), 209–17.

PENNINGS, J. "Measures of Organizational Structure: A Methodological Note," *American Journal of Sociology,* 79 (November 1973), 686–704.

PERROW, CHARLES. "The Analysis of Goals in Complex Organizations," *American Sociological Review,* 26 (December 1961), 854–66.

———. "A Framework for the Comparative Analysis of Organizations," *American Sociological Review,* 32 (April 1967), 194–208.

———. *Organizational Analysis: A Sociological View.* Belmont, Ca.: Wadsworth, 1970.

———. "Review of Neuhauser, D.: *The Relationship Between Administrative Activities and Hospital Performance,"Administrative Science Quarterly,* 17 (September 1972), 419–21.

———. *Complex Organizations: A Critical Essay* (2nd ed.). Glenview, Ill.: Scott, Foresman, 1979.

PFEFFER, JEFFREY. "Size and Composition of Corporate Boards of Directors: The Organization and Its Environment," *Administrative Science Quarterly,* 17 (June 1972*a*), 218–28.

———. "Merger as a Response to Organizational Interdependence," *Administrative Science Quarterly,* 17 (September 1972*b*), 382–92.

———. "Size, Composition, and Function of Hospital Boards of Directors: A Study of Organization-Environment Linkage," *Administrative Science Quarterly,* 18 (September 1973), 349–64.

———. "Administrative Regulation and Licensing: Social Problem or Solution?" *Social Problems,* 21 (April 1974), 468–79.

———. "The Micropolitics of Organizations," in *Environments and Organizations,* pp. 29–50, ed. Marshall W. Meyer. San Francisco: Jossey-Bass, 1978.

PFEFFER, JEFFREY, and PHILLIP NOWAK. "Joint Ventures and Interorganizational Dependence," *Administrative Science Quarterly,* 21 (September 1976), 398–418.

PFEFFER, JEFFREY, and GERALD R. SALANCIK. "Organizational Decision Making as a Political Process: The Case of a University Budget," *Administrative Science Quarterly,* 19 (June 1974), 135–51.

——. *The External Control of Organizations.* New York: Harper & Row, Pub., 1978.

PIRENNE, HENRI. "Guilds," in *Encyclopedia of the Social Sciences,* vol. 7, 208–14, eds. E. B. Seligman and A. Johnson. New York: Macmillan, 1949.

PIVEN, FRANCES FOX, and RICHARD A. CLOWARD. *Regulating the Poor.* New York: Pantheon, 1971.

POLANYI, KARL. *The Great Transformation.* New York: Holt, 1944.

PONDY, LOUIS R., and IAN I. MITROFF. "Beyond Open System Models of Organization," in *Research in Organizational Behavior,* vol. 1, 3–39, ed. Barry M. Staw. Greenwich, Conn.: JAI Press, 1979.

PORTER, LYMAN W., and EDWARD E. LAWLER, III. *Managerial Attitudes and Performance.* Homewood, Ill.: Richard D. Irwin, 1968.

PORTER, LYMAN W., EDWARD E. LAWLER, and J. R. HACKMAN. *Behavior in Organizations.* New York: McGraw-Hill, 1975.

POUND, EZRA. *Selected Prose, 1909–1965,* ed. William Cookson. New York: New Directions, 1973.

PRICE, JAMES L. *Organizational Effectiveness.* Homewood, Ill.: Richard D. Irwin, 1968.

PRINGLE, J. W. S. "On the Parallel Between Learning and Evolution," *Behaviour,* 3 (1951), 174–215.

PUGH, D. S., D. J. HICKSON, C. R. HININGS, K. M. MACDONALD, C. TURNER, and T. LUPTON. "A Conceptual Scheme for Organizational Analysis," *Administrative Science Quarterly,* 8 (December 1963), 289–315.

PUGH, D. S., D. J. HICKSON, C. R. HININGS, and C. TURNER. "Dimensions of Organization Structure," *Administrative Science Quarterly,* 13 (June 1968), 65–91.

——. "The Context of Organization Structures," *Administrative Science Quarterly,* 14 (March 1969), 91–114.

PUGH, D. S., D. J. HICKSON, and C. R. HININGS. "An Empirical Taxonomy of Structures of Work Organizations," *Administrative Science Quarterly,* 14 (March 1969), 115–26.

RACKHAM, JEFFREY, and JOAN WOODWARD. "The Measurement of Technical Variables," in *Industrial Organization: Behaviour and Control,* ed. Joan Woodward. London: Oxford University Press, 1970.

RADCLIFFE-BROWN, A. R. *Structure and Function in Primitive Society.* Glencoe, Ill.: Free Press, 1952.

REES, ALBERT, and GEORGE SHULTZ. *Workers and Wages in an Urban Labor Market.* Chicago: University of Chicago Press, 1970.

REINHARDT, UWE E. "Proposed Changes in the Organization of Health-Care Delivery: An Overview and a Critique," *Milbank Memorial Fund Quarterly,* 51 (Spring 1973), 169–222.

REEVES, WILLIAM JOSEPH. *Librarians as Professionals.* Lexington, Mass.: Lexington Books, Heath, 1980.

ROBOCK, STEFAN H., and KENNETH SIMMONDS. *International Business and Multinational Enterprises.* Homewood, Ill.: Richard D. Irwin, 1973.

ROETHLISBERGER, F. J., and WILLIAM J. DICKSON. *Management and the Worker.* Cambridge, Mass.: Harvard University Press, 1939.

ROGERS, EVERETT M., and REKHA AGARWALA-ROGERS. *Communication in Organizations.* New York: Free Press, 1976.

ROSENBERG, HANS. *Bureaucracy, Aristocracy and Autocracy: The Prussian Experience 1660–1815.* Cambridge, Mass.: Harvard University Press, 1958.

ROSZAK, THEODORE. *The Making of a Counter Culture.* Garden City, New York: Doubleday, Anchor, 1969.

ROTHSCHILD-WHITT, JOYCE. "The Collectivist Organization: An Alternative to Rational Bureaucratic Models," *American Sociological Review,* 44 (August 1979), 509–27.

ROY, DONALD. "Quota Restriction and Goldbricking in a Machine Shop," *American Journal of Sociology,* 57 (March 1952), 427–42.

RUSHING, WILLIAM A. "Organizational Rules and Surveillance: Propositions in Comparative Organization Analysis," *Administrative Science Quarterly,* 10 (March 1966 *a*), 423–43.

———. "Organizational Size and Administration," *Pacific Sociological Review,* 9 (Fall 1966*b*), 100–108.

———. "Hardness of Material as an External Constraint on the Division of Labor in Manufacturing Industries," *Administrative Science Quarterly,* 13 (September 1968), 229–45.

SAINT-SIMON, HENRI COMTE DE. *Selected Writings.* Trans. by F. M. H. Markham. New York: Macmillan, 1952 tr. (First published in 1859.)

SALANCIK, GERALD R., and JEFFREY PFEFFER. "An Examination of Need-Satisfaction Models of Job Attitudes," *Administrative Science Quarterly,* 22 (September 1977), 427–56.

SATOW, ROBERTA LYNN. "Value-Rational Authority and Professional Organizations: Weber's Missing Type," *Administrative Science Quarterly,* 20 (December 1975), 526–31.

SAYLES, LEONARD R. *Behavior of Industrial Work Groups.* New York: John Wiley, 1958.

SCHOENHERR, RICHARD A., and JOSE PEREZ VILARIÑO. "Organizational Role Commitment in the Catholic Church in Spain and USA," in *Organizations Alike and Unlike,* pp. 346–72, eds. Cornelis J. Lammers and David J. Hickson. London: Routledge & Kegan Paul, 1979.

SCHOPLER, JOHN. "Social Power," in *Advances in Experimental Social Psychology,* vol. 2, 177–219, ed. Leonard Berkowitz. New York: Academic Press, 1965.

SCHRÖDINGER, ERWIN. *What Is Life?* Cambridge: Cambridge University Press, 1945.

SCHUMPETER, JOSEPH A. *Capitalism, Socialism and Democracy* (2nd ed.). New York: Harper, 1947.

SCHWAB, DONALD P., and LARRY L. CUMMINGS. "Theories of Performance and Satisfaction: A Review," *Industrial Relations,* 9 (October 1970), 408–30.

SCOTT, W. RICHARD. "Theory of Organizations," in *Handbook of Modern Sociology,* pp. 485–529, ed. Robert E. L. Faris. Chicago: Rand McNally, 1964.

———. "Field Methods in the Study of Organizations," in *Handbook of Organizations,* pp. 261–304, ed. James G. March. Chicago: Rand McNally, 1965*a.*

———. "Reactions to Supervision in a Heteronomous Professional Organization," *Administrative Science Quarterly,* 10 (June 1965*b*), 65–81.

———. "Professionals in Bureaucracies: Areas of Conflict," in *Professionalization,* pp. 265–75, eds. Howard M. Vollmer and Donald L. Mills. Englewood Cliffs, N.J.: Prentice-Hall, 1966.

———. "Professional Employees in a Bureaucratic Structure: Social Work," in *The Semi-Professions and Their Organization,* ed. Amitai Etzioni. New York: Free Press, 1969.

———. *Social Processes and Social Structures: An Introduction to Sociology.* New York: Holt, Rinehart and Winston, 1970.

———. "Professionals in Hospitals: Technology and the Organization of Work," in *Organization Research on Health Institutions,* pp. 139–58, discussion, pp. 173–89, ed. Basil S. Georgopoulos. Ann Arbor, Mich.: Institute for Social Research, University of Michigan, 1972.

———. "Organizational Structure," *Annual Review of Sociology,* 1 (1975), 1–20.

———. "Effectiveness of Organizational Effectiveness Studies," in *New Perspectives on Organizational Effectiveness,* pp. 63–95, eds. Paul S. Goodman and Johannes M. Pennings. San Francisco: Jossey-Bass, 1977*a.*

———. "Some Problems in the Study of Organization Structure," *Mid-American Review of Sociology,* 2 (Spring 1977*b*), 1–16.

———. "Theoretical Perspectives," in *Environments and Organizations,* pp. 21–28, ed. Marshall W. Meyer. San Francisco: Jossey-Bass, 1978.

SCOTT, W. RICHARD, SANFORD M. DORNBUSCH, BRUCE C. BUSCHING, and JAMES D. LAING, "Organizational Evaluation and Authority," *Administrative Science Quarterly,* 12 (June 1967), 93–117.

SCOTT, W. RICHARD, SANFORD M. DORNBUSCH, CONNIE J. EVASHWICK, LEONARD MAGNANI, and INGER SAGATUN. "Task Conceptions and Work Arrangements," Technical Report #47, Laboratory for Social Research. Stanford, Ca.: Stanford University, 1971.

SCOTT, W. RICHARD, ANN BARRY FLOOD, WAYNE EWY, and WILLIAM H. FORREST, JR. "Organizational Effectiveness and the Quality of Surgical Care in Hospitals," in *Environments and Organizations,* pp. 290–305, ed. Marshall W. Meyer. San Francisco: Jossey-Bass, 1978.

SEASHORE, STANLEY E. *Group Cohesiveness in the Industrial Work Group.* Ann Arbor, Mich.: Institute for Social Research, 1954.

———. *The Assessment of Organizational Performance.* Ann Arbor, Mich.: Survey Research Center, University of Michigan, 1962.

SEEMAN, MELVIN. "On the Meaning of Alienation," *American Sociological Review,* 24 (December 1959), 783–91.

———. "Alienation Studies," *Annual Review of Sociology,* 1 (1975), 91–123.

SELZNICK, PHILIP. "Foundations of the Theory of Organization," *American Sociological Review,* 13 (February 1948), 25–35.

———. *TVA and the Grass Roots.* Berkeley: University of California Press, 1949.

———. *Leadership in Administration.* New York: Harper & Row, Pub., 1957.

SEWELL, WILLIAM H., and ROBERT M. HAUSER. *Education, Occupation and Earnings: Achievement in the Early Career.* New York: Academic Press, 1975.

SHANNON, CLAUDE E., and WARREN WEAVER. *The Mathematical Theory of Communication.* Urbana: University of Illinois Press, 1963.

SHAW, M. E. "Some Effects of Problem Complexity upon Problem Solution Efficiency in Various Communication Nets," *Journal of Experimental Psychology,* 48 (1954), 211–17.

———. "Communication Networks," in *Advances in Experimental Social Psychology,* vol. 1, 111–47, ed. Leonard Berkowitz. New York: Academic Press, 1964.

SHEPPARD, HAROLD L., and NEAL HERRICK. *Where Have All the Robots Gone?* New York: Free Press, 1972.

SHERIF, MUZAFER, and CAROLINE W. SHERIF. *Groups in Harmony and Tension.* New York: Harper & Row, Pub., 1953.

SHILS, EDWARD E. *Political Development in the New States.* The Hague: Morton & Co., 1960.

SILVERMAN, DAVID. *The Theory of Organizations: A Sociological Framework.* New York: Basic Books, 1971.

SIMMEL, GEORG. *Conflict* and *The Web of Group Affiliation.* Glencoe, Ill.: Free Press, 1955 tr. (The first essay was first published in 1908, the second in 1922).

SIMON, HERBERT A. *Administrative Behavior* (2nd ed.). New York: Macmillan, 1957.

———. *The New Science of Management Decision.* New York: Harper, 1960.

———. "The Architecture of Complexity," *Proceedings of the American Philosophical Society,* 106 (December 1962), 467–82.

———. "On the Concept of Organizational Goal," *Administrative Science Quarterly,* 9 (June 1964), 1–22.

SIMON, HERBERT A., DONALD W. SMITHBERG, and VICTOR A. THOMPSON. *Public Administration.* New York: Knopf, 1950.

SLATER, PHILIP E. "Role Differentiation in Small Groups," *American Sociological Review,* 20 (June 1955), 300–310.

SMIGEL, ERWIN O. *The Wall Street Lawyer: Professional Organization Man?* New York: Free Press, 1964.

SMITH, ADAM. *An Inquiry into the Nature and Causes of the Wealth of Nations.* London: 1776.

SMITH, BRUCE L. R. *The Rand Corporation.* Cambridge, Mass.: Harvard University Press, 1966.

SMITH, THOMAS SPENCE, and R. DANFORTH ROSS. "Cultural Controls on the Demography of Hierarchy: A Time-Series Analysis of Warfare and the Growth of the United States Army, 1960-1968." Unpublished paper, University of Rochester, 1978.

SOMERS, ANNE R. *Hospital Regulation: The Dilemma of Public Policy.* Princeton, N.J.: Industrial Relations Section, Princeton University, 1969.

SPECIAL TASK FORCE TO THE SECRETARY OF HEALTH, EDUCATION AND WELFARE. *Work in America.* Cambridge, Mass.: The M.I.T. Press, 1973.

STANTON, ALFRED H., and MORRIS S. SCHWARTZ. *The Mental Hospital.* New York: Basic Books, 1954.

STAW, BARRY M. "Rationality and Justification in Organizational Life," in *Research in Organizational Behavior,* vol. 2, 45–80, eds. Barry M. Staw and Larry L. Cummings. Greenwich, Conn.: JAI Press, 1980.

STEERS, RICHARD M. "Problems in the Measurement of Organizational Effectiveness," *Administrative Science Quarterly,* 20 (December 1975), 546–58.

———. *Organizational Effectiveness: A Behavioral View.* Pacific Palisades, Goodyear, 1977.

STEINBRUNER, JOHN D. *The Cybernetic Theory of Decision.* Princeton, N.J.: Princeton University Press, 1974.

STEINER, GEORGE A., and WILLIAM G. RYAN. *Industrial Project Management.* New York: Crowell-Collier and Macmillan, 1968.

STERN, ROBERT N. "The Development of an Interorganizational Control Network: The Case of Intercollegiate Athletics," *Administrative Science Quarterly,* 24 (June 1979), 242–66.

STIGLER, GEORGE J. "The Theory of Economic Regulation," *Bell Journal of Economics and Management Science,* 2 (Spring 1971), 3–21.

STINCHCOMBE, ARTHUR L. "Bureaucratic and Craft Administration of Production: A Comparative Study," *Administrative Science Quarterly,* 4 (September 1959), 168–87.

———. "Social Structure and Organizations," in *Handbook of Organizations,* pp. 142–93, ed. James G. March. Chicago: Rand McNally, 1965.

———. *Creating Efficient Industrial Administrations.* New York: Academic Press, 1974.

STOGDILL, R. M., and A. E. COONS, eds. *Leader Behavior: Its Description and Measurement.* Research Monograph 88. Columbus, Ohio: Bureau of Business Research, Ohio State University, 1957.

STOLZENBERG, ROSS, M. "Bringing the Boss Back in: Employer Size, Employee Schooling, and Socioeconomic Achievement," *American Sociological Review,* 43 (December 1978), 813–28.

STONE, EUGENE. *Research Methods in Organizational Behavior.* Santa Monica, Ca.: Goodyear, 1978.

STRAUSS, GEORGE. "Some Notes on Power-Equalization," in *The Social Science of Organizations,* pp. 39–84, ed. Harold J. Leavitt. Englewood Cliffs, N.J.: Prentice-Hall, 1963.

STREET, DAVID, GEORGE T. MARTIN, JR., and LAURA KRAMER GORDON. *The Welfare Industry: Functionaries and Recipients in Public Aid.* Beverly Hills, Ca.: Sage Publications, Inc., 1979.

STREET, DAVID, ROBERT VINTER, and CHARLES PERROW. *Organization for Treatment.* New York: Free Press, 1966.

SUCHMAN, EDWARD A. *Evaluative Research.* New York: Russell Sage Foundation, 1967.

SUNDQUIST, JAMES L. *Making Federalism Work.* Washington, D.C.: Brookings Institution, 1969.

SWANSON, GUY E. "The Tasks of Sociology," *Science,* 192 (May 1976), 665–67.

———. "A Basis of Authority and Identity in Post-Industrial Society," in *Authority and Identity,* eds. Burkhart Holzner and Roland Robertson. Oxford, England: Blackwell's, 1980.

SWIDLER, ANN. *Organization Without Authority: Dilemmas of Social Control in Free Schools.* Cambridge, Mass.: Harvard University Press, 1979.

SWINTH, ROBERT L. *Organizational Systems for Management: Designing, Planning and Implementation.* Columbus, Ohio: Grid, 1974.

SYKES, A. J. M. "Economic Interests and the Hawthorne Researchers: A Comment," *Human Relations,* 18 (August 1965), 253–63.

TALBERT, JOAN, and CHRISTINE E. BOSE. "Wage-Attainment Processes: The Retail Clerk Case," *American Journal of Sociology,* 83 (September 1977), 403–24.

TANCREDI, LAURENCE R., and WOODS, J. "The Social Control of Medical Practice: Licensure Versus Output Monitoring," *Milbank Memorial Fund Quarterly,* 50 (January 1972), part 1, 99–126.

TANNENBAUM, ARNOLD S. *Control in Organizations.* New York: McGraw-Hill, 1968.

TANNENBAUM, ARNOLD S., BOGDAN KAVCIC, MENACHEM ROSNER, MINO VIANELLO, and GEORG WIESER. *Hierarchy in Organizations.* San Francisco, Ca.: Jossey-Bass, 1974.

TAUSKY, CURT. *Work Organizations: Major Theoretical Perspectives.* Itasca, Ill.: F. E. Peacock, 1970.

TAYLOR, DONALD W. "Decision Making and Problem Solving," in *Handbook of Organizations,* pp. 48–86, ed. James G. March. Chicago: Rand McNally, 1965.

TAYLOR, FREDERICK W. *The Principles of Scientific Management.* New York: Harper, 1911.

————. *Scientific Management.* New York: Harper and Brothers, 1947.

TERREBERRY, SHIRLEY. "The Evolution of Organizational Environments," *Administrative Science Quarterly,* 12 (March 1968), 590–613.

TERRIEN, FRED W., and DONALD L. MILLS. "The Effect of Changing Size upon the Internal Structure of Organizations," *American Sociological Review,* 29 (February 1955), 11–13.

THIBAUT, JOHN W., and HAROLD H. KELLEY. *The Social Psychology of Groups.* New York: John Wiley, 1959.

THOMPSON, JAMES D. *Organizations in Action.* New York: McGraw-Hill, 1967.

THOMPSON, JAMES D., and FREDERICK L. BATES. "Technology, Organization, and Administration," *Administrative Science Quarterly,* 2 (December 1957), 325–42.

THOMPSON, JAMES D., and ARTHUR TUDEN. "Strategies, Structures, and Processes of Organizational Decision," in *Comparative Studies in Administration,* pp. 195–216, eds. James D. Thompson et al. Pittsburgh: University of Pittsburgh Press, 1959.

THOMPSON, VICTOR A. *Modern Organization.* New York: Knopf, 1961.

TOFFLER, ALVIN. *Future Shock.* New York: Random House, 1970.

TOUT, T. F. *The English Civil Service in the Fourteenth Century.* Manchester, England: University Press, 1916.

TRIST, E. L., and K. W. BAMFORTH. "Social and Psychological Consequences of the Longwall Method of Coal-Getting," *Human Relations,* 4 (February 1951), 3–28.

TROW, D. B. "Autonomy and Job Satisfaction in Task-Oriented Groups," *Journal of Abnormal and Social Psychology,* 54 (1957), 204–9.

TURK, HERMAN. "Interorganizational Networks in Urban Society: Initial Perspectives and Comparative Research," *American Sociological Review,* 35 (February 1970), 1–19.

————. *Organizations in Modern Life.* San Francisco: Jossey-Bass, 1977.

TURNER, ARTHUR N., and PAUL R. LAWRENCE. *Industrial Jobs and the Worker: An Investigation of Response to Task Attributes.* Boston: Harvard University, Graduate School of Business Administration, 1965.

UDY, STANLEY H., JR. " 'Bureaucracy' and 'rationality' in Weber's Organization Theory," *American Sociological Review,* 24 (December 1959a), 791–95.

————. *Organization of Work.* New Haven: Human Relations Area Files Press, 1959b.

————. "Administrative Rationality, Social Setting, and Organizational Development," *American Journal of Sociology,* 68 (November 1962), 299–308.

————. *Work in Traditional and Modern Society.* Englewood Cliffs, N.J.: Prentice-Hall, 1970.

VAN DE VEN, ANDREW H., and ANDRE DELBECQ. "A Task Contingent Model of Work-Unit Structure," *Administrative Science Quarterly,* 19 (June 1974), 183–97.

VAN DE VEN, ANDREW H., ANDRE L. DELBECQ, and RICHARD KOENIG, JR. "Determinants of Coordination Modes Within Organizations," *American Sociological Review,* 41 (April 1976), 322–38.

VAN DORN, JACQUES. "Organizations and the Social Order: A Pluralist Approach," in *Organizations Alike and Unlike,* pp. 61–75, eds. Cornelis J. Lammers and David J. Hickson. London: Routledge & Kegan Paul, 1979.

VAUPEL, JAMES W., and JOAN P. CURHAN. *The Making of Multinational Enterprise.* Cambridge, Mass.: Harvard University Press, 1969.

VEBLEN, THORSTEIN. *The Theory of Business Enterprise.* New York: Scribner's, 1904.

VERBA, SIDNEY. *Small Groups and Political Behavior.* Princeton, N.J.: Princeton University Press, 1961.

VROOM, VICTOR H. "Industrial Social Psychology," in *The Handbook of Social Psychology* (2nd ed.), vol. 5, 196–268, eds. Gardner Lindzey and Elliot Aronson. Reading, Mass.: Addison-Wesley, 1969.

WALKER, CHARLES R., and ROBERT H. GUEST. *The Man on the Assembly Line.* Cambridge, Mass.: Harvard University Press, 1952.

WALLACE, WALTER L. "Structure and Action in the Theories of Coleman and Parsons," in *Approaches to the Study of Social Structure,* pp. 121–34, ed. Peter M. Blau. New York: Free Press, 1975.

WALTON, RICHARD E. *Interpersonal Peacemaking: Confrontations and Third Party Consultation.* Reading: Mass.: Addison-Wesley, 1969.

WALTON, RICHARD E., and JOHN M. DUTTON. "The Management of Interdepartmental Conflict: A Model and Review," *Administrative Science Quarterly,* 14 (March 1969), 73–84.

WALTON, RICHARD E., JOHN M. DUTTON, and H. GORDON FITCH. "A Study of Conflict in the Process, Structure, and Attitudes of Lateral Relationships," in *Some Theories of Organization,* (rev. ed.), 444–65, eds. Chadwick J. Haberstroh and Albert H. Rubenstein. Homewood, Ill.: Richard D. Irwin and Dorsey, 1966.

WAMSLEY, GARY L., and MAYER N. ZALD. *The Political Economy of Public Organizations.* Lexington, Mass.: Heath, 1973.

WARD, JOHN WILLIAM. "The Ideal of Individualism and the Reality of Organization," in *The Business Establishment,* pp. 37–76, ed. Earl F. Cheit. New York: John Wiley, 1964.

WARNER, W. LLOYD, and J. O. LOW. *The Social System of the Modern Factory.* New Haven, Conn.: Yale University Press, 1947.

WARREN, ROLAND L. *The Community in America.* Chicago: Rand McNally, 1963.

———. "The Interorganizational Field as a Focus for Investigation," *Administrative Science Quarterly,* 12 (December 1967), 396–419.

WARRINER, CHARLES K. "Empirical Taxonomies of Organizations: Problematics in Their Development." Paper presented at Annual Meetings of the American Sociological Association, Section on Occupations and Organizations, Boston, Mass., 29 August 1979.

WEBER, MAX. *The Protestant Ethic and the Spirit of Capitalism.* Trans. by Talcott Parsons. (First published in 1904–1905). New York: Scribner's, 1958 tr.

———. *From Max Weber: Essays in Sociology,* eds. Hans H. Gerth and C. Wright Mills. New York: Oxford University Press, 1946 tr. (First published in 1906–1924).

————. *The Theory of Social and Economic Organization,* eds. A. H. Henderson and Talcott Parsons. Glencoe, Ill.: Free Press, 1947 tr. (First published in 1924).

WEICK, KARL E. "Laboratory Experimentation with Organizations," in *Handbook of Organizations,* pp. 194–260, ed. James G. March. Chicago: Rand McNally, 1965.

————. *The Social Psychology of Organizing.* Reading, Mass.: Addison-Wesley, 1969 (2nd ed. 1979).

————. "Middle Range Theories of Social Systems," *Behavioral Science,* 19 (November 1974), 357–67.

————. "Educational Organizations as Loosely Coupled Systems," *Administrative Science Quarterly,* 21 (March 1976), 1–19.

————. "Re-Punctuating the Problem," in *New Perspectives on Organizational Effectiveness,* pp. 193–225, eds. Paul S. Goodman and Johannes M. Pennings. San Francisco: Jossey-Bass, 1977.

WEISS, CAROL H. *Evaluation Research.* Englewood Cliffs, N.J.: Prentice-Hall, 1972.

WELDON, PETER D. "An Examination of the Blau-Scott and Etzioni Typologies: A Critique," *Administrative Science Quarterly,* 17 (March 1972), 76–80.

WHEELER, STAN. "The Structure of Formally Organized Socialization Settings," in *Socialization After Childhood,* pp. 53–116, Orville G. Brim and Stan Wheeler. New York: John Wiley, 1966.

WHITE, RALPH, and RONALD LIPPITT. "Leader Behavior and Member Reaction in Three 'Social Climates,'" in *Group Dynamics,* pp. 586–611, eds. Dorwin Cartwright and Alvin Zander. Evanston, Ill.: Row, Peterson, 1953.

WHITEHEAD, ALFRED NORTH. *The Aims of Education.* New York: Macmillan, 1929.

WHYTE, MARTIN KING. "Bureaucracy and Modernization in China: the Maoist Critique," *American Sociological Review,* 38 (April 1973), 149–63.

WHYTE, WILLIAM FOOTE, ed. *Industry and Society.* New York: McGraw-Hill, 1946.

————. *Human Relations in the Restaurant Industry.* New York: McGraw-Hill, 1948.

————. "Small Groups and Large Organizations," in *Social Psychology at the Crossroads,* pp. 297–312, eds. John H. Rohrer and Muzafer Sherif. New York: Harper, 1951.

————. *Man and Organization.* Homewood, Ill.: Richard D. Irwin, 1959.

WHYTE, WILLIAM FOOTE, et al. *Money and Motivation: An Analysis of Incentives in Industry.* New York: Harper, 1955.

WHYTE, WILLIAM H., JR. *The Organization Man.* New York: Simon & Schuster, 1956.

WIELAND, GEORGE F., and ROBERT A. ULLRICH. *Organizations: Behavior, Design, and Change.* Homewood, Ill.: Richard D. Irwin, 1976.

WIENER, NORBERT. *I Am a Mathematician.* New York: Doubleday, 1956.

WILDAVSKY, AARON B. "A Methodological Critique of Duverger's *Political Parties,*" *The Journal of Politics,* 21 (1959), 303–18.

WILENSKY, HAROLD L. "The Professionalization of Everyone?" *American Journal of Sociology,* 70 (September 1964), 137–58.

WILLER, DAVID E. "Max Weber's Missing Authority Type," *Sociological Inquiry,* 37 (Spring 1967), 231–39.

WILLIAMS, LAWRENCE K., WILLIAM F. WHYTE, and CHARLES S. GREEN. "Do Cultural Differences Affect Workers' Attitudes?" *Industrial Relations,* 5 (May 1966), 105–17.

WILLIAMSON, OLIVER E. *Corporate Control and Business Behavior.* Englewood Cliffs, N.J.: Prentice-Hall, 1970.

———. *Markets and Hierarchies: Analysis and Antitrust Implications.* New York: Free Press, 1975.

WILSON, JAMES Q. *The Amateur Democrat.* Chicago: University of Chicago Press, 1962.

———. *Political Organizations.* New York: Basic Books, 1973.

———. *The Investigators: Managing FBI and Narcotics Agents.* New York: Basic Books, 1978.

WILSON, ROBERT N. "Teamwork in the Operating Room," *Human Organization,* 12 (Winter 1954), 9–14.

WOLIN, SHELDON S. *Politics and Vision: Continuity and Innovation in Western Political Thought.* Boston: Little, Brown, 1960.

WOODWARD, JOAN. *Management and Technology.* London: H. M. S. O., 1958.

———. *Industrial Organization: Theory and Practice.* New York: Oxford University Press, 1965.

———, ed. *Industrial Organization: Behaviour and Control.* London: Oxford University Press, 1970.

YUCHTMAN, EPHRAIM, and STANLEY E. SEASHORE. "A System Resource Approach to Organizational Effectiveness," *American Sociological Review,* 32 (December 1967), 891–903.

ZALD, MAYER N. "Political Economy: A Framework for Comparative Analysis," in *Power in Organizations,* pp. 221–61, ed. Mayer N. Zald. Nashville: Vanderbilt University Press, 1970.

ZALD, MAYER N., and ROBERT ASH. "Social Movement Organization: Growth, Decay and Change," *Social Forces,* 44 (March 1966), 327–34.

ZALD, MAYER N., and PATRICIA DENTON. "From Evangelism to General Service: The Transformation of the YMCA," *Administrative Science Quarterly,* 8 (September 1963), 214–34.

ZELDITCH, MORRIS, JR. "Can You Really Study an Army in the Laboratory?" in *A Sociological Reader on Complex Organizations* (2nd ed.), pp. 528–39, ed. Amitai Etzioni. New York: Holt, Rinehart and Winston, 1969.

ZUCKER, LYNNE G. "The Role of Institutionalization in Cultural Persistence," *American Sociological Review,* 42 (October 1977), 726–43.

Name Index

Abegglen, J. C., 165, 288
Adams, J. S., 159
Agarwala-Rogers, R., 217
Aiken, M., 11, 210, 225, 226, 244
Albrow, M., 72, 305
Alchian, A. A., 146
Aldrich, H. E., 51, 53, 115, 116, 162, 168, 169, 171, 172, 204, 244
Allison, G. T., 6, 311
Amber, G. H., 210
Amber, P. S., 210
Anderson, B., 184
Apter, D. E., 40
Arendt, H., 58, 303
Argyris, C., 5, 84, 89, 101, 296, 297
Arrow, K. J., 113, 144, 145, 147, 149, 152
Ashby, W. R., 103, 108, 112, 174, 314, 317
Averitt, R. T., 186

Bach, G. L., 39
Bagehot, W., 305
Baker, A. W., 236
Bales, R. F., 31, 60, 95, 96, 277
Bamforth, K. W., 209
Barber, B., 308
Barker, E., 187
Barnard, C., 9, 16, 19, 73, 101, 146, 158, 261, 281, 298
Bates, F. L., 209
Bateson, G., 117
Bavelas, A., 148, 149
Beckhard, R., 224
Bedeaux, C., 63
Beer, S., 107, 111, 112
Belknap, I., 42
Bell, D., 64, 90, 296
Bell, G. D., 223, 226, 227
Ben-David, J., 167, 168
Bendix, R., 23, 24, 40, 64, 67, 72, 89, 90, 236, 257, 282
Bennis, W. G., 25, 77, 99, 220
Benson, J. K., 230, 231, 254
Berger, J., 184

Berger, M., 165, 167
Berger, P. L., 141
Berle, A. A., 312
Bertalanffy, L., von, 102, 110
Bidwell, C. E., 223
Binstock, R. H., 195
Bismarck, Prince Otto von, 34
Blake, D. H., 251
Blake, R. R., 89, 248
Blau, P. M., 9, 10, 11, 13, 20, 24, 29, 32, 39, 41, 42, 44, 45, 46, 48, 71, 79, 82, 85, 88, 99, 128, 130, 149, 156, 172, 182, 185, 186, 193, 223, 224, 235, 237, 238, 239, 241, 242, 252, 275, 277, 279, 303, 307, 322
Blauner, R., 155, 296
Bledstein, B. J., 155
Blood, M. R., 90, 296
Blowers, T. A., 240
Bluestone, B., 186
Blumberg, P., 89
Boas, M., 177
Bok, D. C., 200, 201, 202
Boorman, S., 171
Bose, C. E., 187
Boulding, K. E., 103, 104, 105, 139, 140, 141, 143, 174
Braverman, H., 64, 77, 90, 153
Brayfield, A. H., 90
Brook, R. H., 330
Brown, B. W., 328
Brzezinski, Z. K., 310
Buckley, W., 85, 102, 103, 106, 109, 110, 118, 246
Burke, E., 101
Burns, T., 45, 218, 224
Busching, B. C., 283

Campbell, D. T., 11, 115, 117, 118
Campbell, J. P., 318
Carey, A., 90
Carr-Saunders, A. M., 155
Carter, L., 60
Cartwright, D., 88, 276

Subject Index